Unity of Faith and Reason in Action

Unity of Faith and Reason in Action

A Journey of Discovery

BY

H. B. Danesh

Juxta Publishing Limited - Hong Kong

ISBN-10 0-9698024-1-2
ISBN-13 978-0-9698024-1-9

Printed in the United States and United Kingdom by Juxta Publishing Ltd

Cover painting: Untitled, 2008, by Lorraine Pritchard. Copyright 2008 by Lorraine Pritchard. The original of this painting is in the author's art collection.

Photo of the author: Copyright 2009 by Vic Voytek

www.juxta.com

To
the long-suffering
Bahá'ís of Iran
who in the face of unceasing and appalling tyranny,
injustice, and cruelty
have displayed the utmost nobility,
courage, and loving kindness
towards their oppressors
and who continue to dedicate their all to
the service of humanity and the cause of world peace

The face of him on whom I gazed I can never forget, though I cannot describe it. Those piercing eyes seemed to read one's very soul; power and authority sat on that ample brow; while the deep lines on the forehead and face implied an age which the jet-black hair and beard flowing down in indistinguishable luxuriance almost to the waist seemed to belie. No need to ask in whose presence I stood, as I bowed myself before one who is the object of a devotion and love which kings might envy and emperors sigh for in vain. A mild dignified voice bade me be seated, and then continued:

> 'Praise be to God that thou hast attained!...Thou hast come to see a prisoner and an exile....We desire but the good of the world and the happiness of the nations; yet they deem us a stirrer up of strife and sedition worthy of bondage and banishment....That all nations should become one in faith and all men as brothers; that the bonds of affection and unity between the sons of men should be strengthened; that diversity of religion should cease and differences of race be annulled—what harm is there in this?...

> Yet so it shall be; these fruitless strifes, these ruinous wars shall pass away, and the 'Most Great Peace' shall come....Do not you in Europe need this also? Is not this that which Christ foretold?...Yet do we see your kings and rulers lavishing their treasures more freely on means for the destruction of the human race than on that which would conduce to the happiness of mankind....

> These strifes and this bloodshed and discord must cease, and all men be as one kindred and one family....Let not a man glory in this, that he loves his country; let him rather glory in this, that he loves his kind....*

—*Bahá'u'lláh*

---

*In the spring of 1890, Edward Granville Browne, Fellow of Pembroke College, Cambridge, and the eminent orientalist came to 'Akká to visit Bahá'u'lláh [Glory of God]. The above excerpts are from his account of interview with Bahá'u'lláh, whom he quotes.

Religion and science are the two wings upon which man's intelligence can soar into the heights, with which the human soul can progress. It is not possible to fly with one wing alone! Should a man try to fly with the wing of religion alone he would quickly fall into the quagmire of superstition, whilst on the other hand, with the wing of science alone he would also make no progress, but fall into the despairing slough of materialism. All religions of the present day have fallen into superstitious practices, out of harmony alike with the true principles of the teaching they represent and with the scientific discoveries of the time. Many religious leaders have grown to think that the importance of religion lies mainly in the adherence to a collection of certain dogmas and the practice of rites and ceremonies! Those whose souls they profess to cure are taught to believe likewise, and these cling tenaciously to the outward forms, confusing them with the inward truth.

Now, these forms and rituals differ in the various churches and amongst the different sects, and even contradict one another; giving rise to discord, hatred, and disunion. The outcome of all this dissension is the belief of many cultured men that religion and science are contradictory terms, that religion needs no powers of reflection, and should in no wise be regulated by science....The unfortunate effect of this is that science has drifted apart from religion....If religion were in harmony with science and they walked together, much of the hatred and bitterness now bringing misery to the human race would be at an end.

—'Abdu'l-Bahá*

---

*'Abdu'l-Bahá, the Centre of the Covenant of the Bahá'í Faith, after His release as a prisoner of the Ottomans in 1908, set out on a series of journeys which, in 1911–1913, took Him to Europe and America. The above statement is from a talk he delivered in Paris on November 12, 1913.

CONTENTS

Acknowledgments

This book is in one sense a personal memoir and thus an account of many precious relationships and friendships established over decades. Those individuals and their collective contributions to my life were many and highly consequential. My beloved and insightful parents set the tone and direction of my life. Michele, my love and life partner, and our two treasured sons, Arman and Roshan, made life truly worth living. My dear siblings, all six of them, each in his or her unique and important manner, enriched my life. And my teachers, friends, students, and patients taught me unique lessons about all aspects of living and growing and becoming. To them all, I am most profoundly indebted.

While writing this book, several individuals made direct and invaluable contributions to its focus, contents, and organization. Michele in the course of some in-depth deliberations helped me to sharpen the focus and further emphasize the significance of the events and concepts contained in the book. Arman and Roshan each assisted in the writing and production of this book, drawing from their considerable intellectual and creative pools of talent.

Christine Zerbinis, a highly valued co-worker of many years, dedicated untold hours to the review and editing of this book and offered prized suggestions for its contents. Rhett Diessner, Brian Kirsh, and Peter P. Morgan, much-admired colleagues, and Diba Madjzub, a valued friend, reviewed the entire manuscript and provided in-depth, insightful recommendations that greatly enriched the contents of the book. Many others to whom I presented different segments of the book in various conference, workshop, and classroom settings also helped to further develop my thoughts with their probing and insightful questions and comments.

My abiding gratitude to all these precious individuals for their unique contributions.

INTRODUCTION

WHAT, WHY, HOW?

We live in a time of much confusion about the role and place of religion in our world. Many have lost their faith in religion. Others have become outright hostile towards it. And still others consider religion to be irrelevant to their personal and community lives. People want to know why they should consider adopting any religion—particularly in light of the consequential role that religion has played in the past and still plays in all aspects of human life. There are misgivings about the divisive and authoritarian approaches adopted by most religions and the violence that these religions have inflicted on the masses of humanity under the guise of 'salvation', 'jihad', 'crusade', and similar notions. There are deep concerns about such concepts as being 'the chosen', 'the last', the 'saved', and the sole possessors of 'Truth' that are found in various religions and encourage each to claim superiority over others.

As well, there are many questions about God. Is God real? If so, why we do not experience the presence of God in our world and our lives? Is God merciful? If so, why is there so much misery? Is God powerful? If so, why the ascendancy of the oppressors? Is God just? If so, why the universal prevalence of injustice? Is God all-knowing? If so, why the seemingly irrational and illogical beliefs and practices of various religious communities and why so many seemingly different and irreconcilable religions?

Added to these questions is the highly significant and problematic issue of discordance between science and religion, as currently understood and practiced. The popularity of books such as *The God Delusion* by scientist Richard Dawkins and *Darwin's Dangerous Idea* and *Breaking the Spell: Religion as a Natural Phenomenon* by philosopher Daniel Dennett is due to the fact that they put into words the current confusion about the nature, role, and source of religion. Many wonder whether it is possible to have a religion that is in harmony with science and whether science could ever find itself in harmony with any religion. These are genuine perplexities, especially in an age when both religion and science are being so callously abused.

Throughout history each new Revelation has been, at varying degrees, misinterpreted, misunderstood, misapplied, and abused, almost always with the sanction and encouragement of the clergy of the established religions. The religious leaders, usually with the consent of the political leaders in their respective societies, have frequently used the uninformed mass of the believers to safeguard their positions of leadership and have hindered the progress of every new Revelation and many new scientific developments that they perceived as a threat. However, during the past two centuries humanity's relationship with religion has had some unique dimensions due to three simultaneous, interrelated, and significant developments. The most obvious of these developments is the emergence of modern science along with its dramatic and highly important impact on all aspects of human life. The second, equally important, but less appreciated development is psychosocial in nature and refers to the advent of the coming of age of humanity, now in the last phase of its turbulent adolescence. The third development, the least known and potentially most consequential, is the fact that a new revealed religion—the Bahá'í Faith—has appeared in our times. Religion has been renewed, and a new level of spiritual insight and guidance has been offered to humanity. But this new revelation is almost completely ignored by scientists and academic institutions, and either violently opposed—in the Islamic world—or almost completely ignored by other established religions around the globe. Consequently, the Bahá'í Faith remains relatively unknown in academia and among the masses of humanity, both by those who believe in religion and those who do not.

These three developments—ascendancy of science, humanity's coming of age, and the emergence of a new revealed religion—took place against the background of the irrational authoritarian domination of dictatorial leaders of the established religions and governments. Therefore, it is not surprising that a significant segment of humanity has rightly rebelled against both secular and religious institutions and their leaders. Greatly emboldened by the power of modern science, adolescent humanity rejected religion, pronounced God dead, and embarked on a frantic search for replacements for religion. On their part, many leaders of established religions, fearful of losing their authority, power, and control and unable to provide satisfactory answers to the legitimate questions raised by many of their informed followers, responded with either militancy or fanaticism. Consequently, the disappointed multitudes desperately searched for a replacement for religion. Some tried to replace religion with science. Others created pseudo-religions to fill the spiritual vacuum thus created in their personal, interpersonal, and community lives. And still others used religion as a tool for gaining power for political dominance through the instrument of fanatical beliefs and militant practices. However, regardless of how religion was rejected, replaced, or abused, one fact has remained constant: because humans are fundamentally religious beings, the search for the spiritual and the transcendent is an ever-present quest of the human mind and heart. That we are psychologically primed for religion is commonly acknowledged. However, the dominant materialistic science sees this as an accident of nature, something having gone wrong.[1,2]

In this book I attempt to demonstrate how "religion and science" and "faith and reason" in their authentic forms, are indeed distinct but complementary ways of knowing, essential for a reasoned, creative, enlightened, and meaningful life. Chapter one is dedicated to the framework through which we understand religion, science, the world, and ourselves. In chapter two, a new perspective on the concept of religion and its role in human life and civilization is presented. Together, these chapters, provide the necessary framework for the rest of the book. In chapter three, entitled, "The Bahá'í Faith: Religion Renewed," I share the beginnings of the Bahá'í Faith in general and my encounter with it in particular. Chapter four deals with the all-important issue of the purpose of human life and the place of religion in it. In chapters five and six, the two fundamental institutions of marriage and family are studied in light of new spiritual insights and current scientific research. Chapter seven focuses on the crucial issue of education. Chapters eight and nine cover topics related to the role and impact of religion on the social dimension of human life, including issues of leadership, governance, consultative decision-making, and peace-based conflict resolution. Chapter ten offers reflections on how science and religion together can indeed create a *civilization of peace*—the most ancient and elusive quest of humanity. The afterword aims to integrate this varied and expansive look at the place, impact, and essential role of religion in our lives. I have focused on these topics because I am personally familiar with them and also because I am convinced that the role of religion in each of these dimensions of our lives—personal, interpersonal, social, and global—is both indispensable and profound.

These chapters are accounts of a life journey in the realms of faith, reason, and action. As in any journey, certain parameters of orientation and understanding are revisited over time under different circumstances and in specific contexts. These, intentional repetitions serve as either reflections on the same themes in each new context or deeper understanding of their multifaceted dimensions. It is hoped that this approach will further elucidate the main concepts addressed in the book.

I will attempt to share my understanding of how the Baháʼí Faith addresses some of the fundamental and perplexing issues surrounding religion, how it demonstrates the basic unity of all religions, and how it reconciles faith with reason. I also focus on the manner in which religion in general and the Baháʼí Faith in particular shapes all human relationships and activities. My professional life as a psychiatrist and as a university professor is divided into two distinct but interrelated periods. The first period of thirty years (1963–1992) was devoted to psychiatric practice and teaching with a focus on the biological, psychological, social, as well as spiritual aspects of human individual, family, and group life. The second period of 17 years thus far (1993–2010) has been devoted to the most fundamental challenge of our time—peace. These two broad areas of experience—the well-being and development of individuals and families, and the welfare and peace of communities and nations—are interrelated and complementary. They both deal with the phenomenon of human relationships in their most intimate and personal dimensions and in their social and universal expressions.

Religion is concerned with relationships: our relationship with ourselves, other human beings, the world of nature, the world of thought, the worlds beyond this world that we can imagine but do not understand, and our relationship with the ultimate—God. Thus, I felt blessed with the gift of harmony between my professional and academic interests and pursuits, on the one hand, and my spiritual aspirations and ethical principles, on the other. They were complementary and mutually enriching and revolved around the ever-sought state of peace in all departments of life.

The decision to become a Baháʼí was the most consequential in my life. While I am fully sympathetic with many criticisms expressed by thoughtful individuals about abuse of religion and have also wondered about these issues for many years, my introduction to the Baháʼí Faith removed all my reservations. In fact, one of the reasons that I chose the Baháʼí Faith as my spiritual frame of reference and the channel for assertion of my trust, love, and faith in God and religion is because of the convincing explanations and insights that this newest revealed world religion offers with respect to these and many other puzzling issues about religion and its role in human individual and social life. And the main reason for writing this book is to share with others what I consider to be the most precious gift I have received in my life.

Finally, a note of clarification about the issue of language and gender is in order. This book is written in gender-neutral language. However, the quotations from the Bahá'í Writings, by far the majority of which are in either Arabic or Persian (Farsi), are translated using masculine pronouns to refer inclusively to both men and women. Arabic and English languages, are both gender-specific, whereas the Persian language is gender-neutral. Prior to the 1970s, gender bias-free writing was not yet an issue in the English language. Thus, the official translations of the Bahá'í Writings (Scriptures) into English were and continue to be rendered according to the norms of English language usage in the 19th and early 20th centuries. It is also important to note that although the Persian language is gender neutral, the translation of Persian texts into English have used the same approach as adopted for translation of Arabic into English, in order to maintain a coherent unity in the Bahá'í Scriptures in English.

H.B.D.
Victoria, Canada
July 2010

PART ONE

ON RELIGION

CHAPTER ONE

TOWARDS AN INTEGRATIVE UNDERSTANDING OF RELIGION

The gift of God to this enlightened age is the knowledge of the oneness of mankind and of the fundamental oneness of religion. (London, 1911)[1]

—'Abdu'l-Bahá (1844–1921)

Before God we are all equally wise—and equally foolish.[2]

—Albert Einstein (1879–1955)

That which is in conformity with science is also in conformity with religion.[3]

—Imam Ali (599–661 CE; 24 BH–40 AH)

Believing Falsehood

Human capacity for self-deception is infinite. How frequently we encounter individuals who sincerely and erroneously believe in falsehood. I remember a talk I had with a colleague in Chicago during our residency training in psychiatry. We were discussing the causes of evil deeds by intelligent and capable human beings. In the course of our discussion I asked him who he thought was the most destructive person of the 20th century. I expected him to identify someone like Hitler who sacrificed millions of people at the altar of the false ideology of racial superiority. However, because my colleague was from Germany, I thought that he might identify another individual such as Stalin who, on the basis of his paranoid and cowardly personality, sent millions of innocent people to their death. But my friend totally surprised me by unhesitatingly stating that in his opinion the most evil person of all time was Winston Churchill! He then described in detail how countless civilians had died during the latter part of the Second World War because of the bombardments of various German cities by British warplanes.

Because I knew this person and was aware that he was fundamentally a very decent, informed, intelligent, and reasonable individual, I thought to myself that there should be an explanation for his surprising point of view. Later in the course of my three decades of psychiatric work, I encountered numerous occasions in which people sincerely believed in falsehood. In fact some of the major psychiatric disorders are considered pathological primarily because they are based on delusions—believing in something that is not true. However, when we further engage with such persons and make a concerted and sincere effort to understand why a person would believe in falsehood and "the unreasonable," it becomes evident that, by far, in the majority of these cases the reason for their beliefs lies in what is variably referred to as the *frame of reference* or *mindset* or *worldview* they hold.

We human beings need a frame of reference to make sense of our world, and because of this fundamental need, we formulate for ourselves a set of explanations with which we could make sense of life in its unexpected and complex expressions. And when the reality becomes confusing or unbearable, not infrequently, the mind creates its own reality in order to make sense of the painful, unacceptable, and/or puzzling experience. Consequently, such individuals are either called "crazy" by others or are in fact suffering from serious mental disorder.

However, this phenomenon is not limited to those who are manifestly suffering from some type of psychological distress. We see the phenomenon of "believing falsehood" in the general population, among leaders of the society, in the scientific community, and within various religious, racial, ethnic, national, and ideological groups. At the core of belief in falsehood is fear of knowing the truth, in general, and truth about ourselves in particular. We each have a framework within which we like to see ourselves and be seen by others. However, knowing oneself can be a painful and disquieting experience because at the core of our being we are aware of our many shortcomings. We know that we are not always as loving and caring as we want others to perceive us to be. We are aware that we do not always function within the framework of absolute truth and honesty. We are often unsure about the full authenticity and sincerity of the decisions we make and the deeds we perform. In other words, at any given time, in the depths of our souls we know that we could be more loving, truthful, and authentic. However, many times we fail in this process, not because we do not aspire to higher levels of functioning as human beings, but rather because we are afraid to expose our shortcomings as human beings. We fear our "image" will suffer if we admit, even to ourselves, that we may be wrong. This fear of self-knowledge is so powerful and pervasive, that we tend to create veils between reality and ourselves. These veils are many, among them the veils of prejudice, superstition, historical myths, actual ignorance, unquestioned faith as well as the veil of knowledge. The problem with these veils, particularly the veils of knowledge and unquestioned faith, is that they are usually combined with considerable pride and close-mindedness.

To acquire greater self-knowledge and objectivity, we need to better understand the framework within which we perceive ourselves, others, and the objective realities we encounter. Throughout the years I have been trying to find a framework that we could use—to the extent possible— to investigate various issues and questions we encounter as objectively and freely as possible. In particular, I have been interested in seeing how we can approach issues of religion, science, and self-knowledge in a manner that is free from preconceived notions, established prejudices, and desired outcomes. In other words, how can we search for truth in an independent, logical, and fact-based manner? The framework that is offered in this chapter is the one I have developed and used with regard to the issues of science, religion, and self-knowledge and found to be both enlightening and helpful. One may well ask why do we need any framework. And the answer is that "no framework" is also a framework, a framework of search for truth with closed eyes, minds, and hearts. When our eyes are closed, our minds are made-up, and our sentiments already attached, then we will miss much, and in the darkness of our search we frequently find the truth we want to find—the subjective truth—rather than the objective Truth, which must be the ultimate purpose of scientific research, spiritual quest, and better understanding of oneself.

HOW DO WE UNDERSTAND?

The main premise of this book is that the manner in which we understand and approach science, religion, ourselves, and the world is determined and shaped by three fundamental factors: our worldview, our understanding of unity as main law of existence, and our state of development. This chapter discusses these three issues and the remaining chapters explore the impact of these factors on our approach to religion, to ourselves, to the family, and to society.

I will argue that at the core of human existence is the ever-present and unavoidable relationship between God and humanity. We are created through the generative will of God and have been endowed with the precious gift of understanding, so that we could accomplish two fundamental tasks—to know and to love. We accomplish these tasks through science and religion. Science, defined by Albert Einstein (1879–1955) as "methodical thinking directed toward finding regulative connections between our sensual experiences,"[4] helps us to understand the mysteries of the nature through implementation of the scientific method.[5] Religion is the other main source of human understanding and is defined in an interestingly similar manner by one of the most outstanding religious figures of our time—'Abdu'l-Bahá (1844–1921).[6] He defines religion as "the essential connection which proceeds from the reality of things."[7] Elsewhere, 'Abdu'l-Bahá states, "Religion and science walk hand in hand, and any religion contrary to science is not the truth." [8]

I believe that the framework offered here helps us better understand the reasons for the calamitous misunderstandings between various religions as well as between science and religion. To recapitulate: the three factors that influence and shape our understanding about all aspects of life are: the concept of *unity* as the primary law of existence;

the concept of *worldview* as the framework within which life experiences and phenomena are understood; and the concept of human individual and group *development* that determines the quality and depth of our understanding. These three concepts are briefly discussed below.

CONCEPT OF UNITY

The concept of unity has seldom been the subject of serious research and study. However, its opposite—conflict—has been and continues to be in the forefront of psychological, social, and political research and study. Current generally held views on the nature and role of conflict in human life, although varied, are fundamentally based on the notion that conflict is an aspect of human nature and, as such, it is not only inevitable, but even necessary and desirable. Galtung and Jacobsen comment that "conflict, incompatible goals, are as human as life itself; the only conflict-free humans are dead humans" and that "war and violence are like slavery, colonialism, and patriarchy; however, they come and they go."[9] Muldoon states that "[c]onflict is the spice that seasons our most intimate relationships" and "it is woven into the fundamental fabric of nature."[10] There are other popular notions that conflict is useful for identity development, social change, and creativity. These beliefs about conflict are typically based on the idea that there are basic human needs that require satisfaction, and conflict arises when these needs are either unmet or meeting them has negatively affected others in the same pursuit.[11] The belief in the primacy of the role of conflict in human life is also used for justification of the concept of the *survival of the fittest* that informs both the biological theory of evolution put forward by Charles Darwin and social Darwinism as applied to economic, political, and social practices, justifying extreme levels of wealth and poverty, cut-throat political competition, and remote and aloof social relationships.

The concept of unity, as put forward here, states that *conflict is absence of unity*. In other words, conflict is a symptom of the disease of disunity. Therefore, in order to better understand the underlying reason for the phenomenal presence of conflict in all areas of life, including conflicts regarding both science and religion, we need to study the law of unity.

UNITY: DEFINITION AND DESCRIPTION

Unity is the process of attraction, convergence, and integration of two or more diverse entities resulting in the creation of a new entity, usually at a higher level of complexity, sophistication, and specificity of function. At the human level, the operation of the law of unity is a conscious and deliberate process.[12]

Unity is the primary law of existence. Everything that exists is the outcome of the law of unity, and the proper functioning of all entities and life processes is dependent on it. No composed entity could exist or continue to exist in the absence of unity. At the physical level, the constituent components of all physical entities are held together through the power of unity. Living organisms function and thrive as long as the harmony, equilibrium, and unity of their various cells, molecules, and organs are maintained. At the human psychosocial and spiritual levels, the law of unity brings people together, creates families and communities, and develops patterns of social interaction and cultural norms and practices. The concept of unity is the opposite of the dichotomous thinking commonly found in both individuals and groups. Unity is the creative force of life. It is the power that brings opposites together and creates new types and levels of life and existence. It is within the context of unity that diversity becomes a source of harmony and richness of relationships instead of being a cause of division and discord. Also, it is within the framework of unity that the seemingly irreconcilable demands of the biological, psychological, social, moral, and spiritual forces of life are connected and integrated, creating harmonious, healthy, and happy families and communities. The driving force of unity is love, truth its sustaining foundation, justice its enduring strength, and unity in diversity its actual expression.

EXPERIENCES OF UNITY

Unity is a very difficult concept to understand and an even more difficult condition to create. All of us have had some experience of unity—inner unity, interpersonal unity, unity with nature, unity with God. During these moments we experience the awesome and joyful qualities of unity. However, because these moments usually do not constitute our main life experiences, we tend to regard them as exceptions to the rule and erroneously conclude that humans are doomed to live a life of conflict. No doubt differences have always been, and will always be, a major aspect of human life at biological, social, and ideological levels. And there is ample evidence that these differences frequently degenerate into various forms of conflict because of our limited understanding, experience, and insight into the complex web of human relationships. In the developmental framework it could not have been otherwise. Unity, in its higher and universal expressions, is only achievable during the more advanced stages of human intellectual, emotional, moral, and spiritual development. The same principles are applicable to human collective development. In the previous stages of our social development, for example, we have successively achieved ever greater levels of unity—family, clan, tribal, city-state, and nationhood. Humanity is now embarking on creating new and more inclusive levels of unity such as world unity, unity of religion, unity of science and religion, unity of women and men, unity in equality and justice, and unity of morality and ethics.

Viewed from this perspective, life is the expression of ever higher levels of unity. It is through unity that life is created and it is towards unity that life is directed. Unity, therefore, is that prerequisite condition which enables us to use our psychological powers—to know, love, and will—to create higher and more developed individual and collective lifestyles and to prevent destructive conflicts. This ongoing movement of humanity towards ever higher levels of unity involves all aspects of our individual and collective lives.

Unity and the Experience of the Self

The concept of *self* refers to the conscious and reflective personality of the individual and encapsulates the essence of being who we are. Ancient Greeks proposed a tripartite structure of self. They also divided the psyche into three parts: the *desiring part,* the *spirited part,* and the *reasoning part.*[13] Similarly, Sigmund Freud in his theory of psychoanalysis considers the self or psyche (Greek for both self and soul) to be divided into three components: id, ego, and superego. He sees a constant struggle and conflict between id and superego, with ego as a not very effective intermediary.[14] Likewise, Carl Jung identifies animus (masculine) and anima (feminine) as the two components of the human psyche. The main challenge for creating a unified and integrated self, according to Jung, is to nurture both the masculine and the feminine aspects of the individual psyche,[15] a process that I think must parallel the practice of gender equality in society. These views on human self and psyche have one thing in common: they all see the human psyche as having several potentially conflicted parts—id, ego, and superego in Freud's formulation; animus and anima in Jung's; and the *desiring part,* the *spirited part,* and the *reasoning part* in Greek philosophy. These concepts are contrary to our experience of our "self" as an integrated, unified, and evolving entity that operates according to the law of unity.

In *The Psychology of Spirituality: From Divided Self to Integrated Self,* I observed that the experience of selfhood is uniquely human. When we speak of *self,* we are talking about our awareness that we exist now, have existed in the past, and will continue to exist in the future. Our experience of self basically remains the same throughout life and gives us a sense of constancy and wholeness that includes components of our psyche in conscious and subconscious states, in sleep and wakefulness, and in isolation and togetherness. In all these conditions we experience the fundamental unity of our selfhood. In that book I point out that the unifying agent of our selfhood is the spiritual dimension of human reality. While the title, *The Psychology of Spirituality,* refers to the core issue neglected in modern psychology—*spirituality*—the subtitle identifies the process by which we can remedy the situation— *From Divided Self to Integrated Self.*[16] In our daily lives we frequently experience states in which our thoughts, feelings, and actions are in conflict with one another and with our fundamental moral/ethical principles. These states of inner disunity make our lives conflicted, our relationships burdened, and our most noble intentions misunderstood. From a psychological perspective, at the core of our being, we humans are constantly in search of inner unity and peace, a state aptly described by the Persian poet Rumi: *"…no body, no soul, I am from the soul of souls. I have chased out duality, lived the two worlds as one."*[17]

Unity has its greatest impact when our thoughts, feelings, decisions, actions, and moral principles—in brief, our worldviews—are informed by it.

CONCEPT OF WORLDVIEW

The concept of worldview, as used here, refers to the framework within which we understand the nature of reality, human nature, the purpose of life, and the laws governing human relationships. Worldviews evolve in response to the quality of education we receive, the life experiences we have, and the environmental conditions we encounter. As such, worldviews mirror the prevailing conditions of the society and at the same time act as potent agents of change. Religion is one of the most influential sources of worldview formulation at both individual and cultural levels. Worldview in turn shapes the manner in which we understand and practice religion. This circular relationship between religion and worldview can be either enlightened and progressive, or unenlightened and regressive.

The other significant source influencing the formation of worldview is science. There is no doubt that research, conducted within the parameters of the scientific method and an all-inclusive unbiased worldview, is the most valuable and surest avenue for understanding any phenomenon. Because scientific research and study of religion both take place within the parameters of the respective worldviews of those engaged in these processes, it is not surprising that the same body of information and data could be understood and explained differently and even in diametrically opposite ways.

THREE CATEGORIES OF WORLDVIEW

We all have a worldview that gives us a framework through which we understand life, choose our value systems, establish our priorities, develop our relationships, and adopt our approach to both science and religion. We cannot function outside the framework of our worldviews. From the earliest days of our lives, through our life experiences, training, and education, and through use of our unique creative capacities, we gradually develop our respective worldviews that reflect the prevailing ideas and beliefs in our environments as well as our own distinctive personal qualities. Based on the character of these internal and external forces and our unique responses to them, each worldview has certain unique characteristics. However, in the context of this huge diversity, we can identify three metacategories of worldview: Survival-Based, Identity-Based, and Unity-Based, which I believe provide a helpful framework for understanding the reasons for the amazing degree of misunderstanding that exists both within and between scientific and religious communities. Here is a brief description of the main features of these worldviews, which I have described more fully elsewhere.[18]

Survival-Based Worldview develops under conditions of weakness, ignorance, threat, violence, poverty, and injustice. In these states we generally perceive the world as dangerous and approach it with fear, anxiety, and anger. The *survival-based worldview* revolves around issues of power, domination, force, and violence. It is authoritarian and dichotomous in its orientation, dividing the world into friends and enemies, science and religion, men and women, powerful and weak, citizens and strangers, and many other such seemingly opposing realities.

As we progress further on our path of development, we begin to experience some degree of freedom and opportunity, as well as a greater degree of personal and group ability in the context of conflicted, competitive home and community environments. In this state we tend to respond to the world as though it is a jungle in which we all have to compete and either win or lose. This worldview—the *identity-based worldview*—is based on the notion of the "survival of the fittest" and is highly individualistic, competitive, and conflicted. While the survival-based worldview is a characteristic of a child-like state of mind, the identity-based worldview corresponds to that of adolescence. These two worldviews have been and continue to be the dominant points of reference around the globe and shape our understanding of both religion and science, and the manner in which their principles are put into action.

The now gradually emerging worldview that corresponds with a more evolved, universal, and all-encompassing understanding of reality and life is scientific in its approach, inclusive in its scope, integrative in its impact, and spiritual in its principles. The cardinal characteristic of this worldview—the *unity-based worldview*—is that it operates according the principal law of unity in the context of diversity, as described above. The main characteristics of these three categories of worldview are summarized below in Table 1.1.

We develop our worldviews rather passively through environmental, cultural, and experiential influences, and usually we do not change them unless our worldview is no longer able to answer the questions and challenges we face in the course of life. Worldview transformation often takes place either in the context of crises or when we encounter highly revolutionary new insights, propelling us to higher levels of consciousness. This new consciousness challenges the prevailing worldviews and opens totally new vistas of insight and understanding. Worldview transformation is difficult and even frightening because initially it is perceived as either an attack or a negation of our sense of self and identity. However, in reality, worldview transformation is an integral aspect of change and growth, which are dimensions of the healthy development of all living conscious entities, be they individuals, social institutions such as the family, or communities and societies, and

Survival-Based Worldview	Identity-Based Worldview	Unity-Based Worldview
Normal during childhood.	Normal during adolescence.	Normal during adulthood.
Corresponds to the agrarian and pre-industrial periods of societal development.	Corresponds to the gradual coming of age of both the individual and the society.	Corresponds with the phase of maturity of humanity based on the consciousness of the oneness of humanity.
Develops under conditions of powerlessness, ignorance, poverty, injustice, anarchy, physical threat, and war.	Is particularly prevalent during emergence from authoritarian and/or revolutionary conditions and rapid social change.	Is the next stage in human social development based on the principles of truth, justice, unity, and peace.
Life processes are viewed as being dangerous.	Life is viewed as an arena of the "survival of the fittest."	Life is seen as the process of truth-finding & unity-building.
Dichotomous views of human nature as either bad (weak) or good (strong). Human beings are viewed as good or evil.	Individualistic view of human nature, individualism and highly competitive group-identities (ethnicity, nationality, race, religion, etc.).	Views human nature to be potentially noble, creative, integrative, and highly responsive to the forces of both science and religion.
The main purpose of life is survival and procreation.	The main purpose of life is to "have" and to "win." Human nature is viewed as greedy and selfish.	The main purpose of human life is to create a civilization of peace—equal, just, liberal, moral, diverse, and united.
Human relationships take place mostly in the context of domination and submission— proclivity to use force and/or conformity.	Human relationships operate mostly within the parameters of extremes of competition and rivalry in an adversarial mode.	Human relationships operate primarily within the parameters of the law of unity in the context of diversity.
Conflict and violence are inevitable.	Conflict is viewed as inherent in human nature and necessary for progress.	Conflict is the absence of unity. Unity is the main source of progress.
Authoritarianism is the main mode of leadership and governance.	Adversarial Democracy is the main mode of leadership and governance.	Integrated, unity-based democracies emerging as the main modes of leadership and governance.
Manipulation of religion and science on the part of their leaders and the leaders of the society to maintain their power over the less informed masses.	Manipulation of religion and science as instruments of competition to "have" and to "win."	Integration of religion and science to create just, enlightened, and peaceful communities.
Prevalence of superstitions, prejudice, magical thinking, fear of the unknown.	Prevalence of militarism, arrogance, emphasis on differences, and indifference to the suffering of others.	Freedom from prejudice, reliance on evidence, capacity to integrate, inclusivity, and universality.
Rigidity	Relativism	Creativity (freedom in the context of inner discipline)

Table 1.1. Some of the main characteristics of the three metacategories of worldview.

ultimately, all humanity. Table 1.1 depicts the main characteristics of these three worldviews as they pertain to our discourse about religion, science, the nature and purpose of human life, and the dynamics of development of society.[19]

SCIENCE, RELIGION, AND WORLDVIEW

Throughout history, religion has been the primary source of worldview formation. However, over the course of the past two centuries, science has also emerged as a powerful framework for formulation of new worldviews. Religion and science traverse similar paths of development. Development of science has its genesis in the concept of paradigm shift described by Thomas Kuhn. In his groundbreaking book, *The Structure of Scientific Revolution,* Kuhn states that development of science has alternating 'normal' and 'revolutionary' phases. The normal phase is the process of accumulation of more knowledge within the existing paradigm. However, gradually as the prevailing paradigm (worldview) loses its capacity to explain all issues under consideration, a revolutionary phase in that scientific discipline begins by the introduction of a totally new, and usually very different, paradigm. Kuhn asks, "What are scientific revolutions, and what is their function in scientific development?" He then answers: "[S]cientific revolutions are…those non-cumulative developmental episodes in which an older paradigm is replaced in whole or in part by an incompatible new one."[20]

One of the principal teachings of the Bahá'í Faith is the concept that religion, like science, is one and that it also goes through progressive revolutionary phases of change and renewal, in a similar manner to the development of science described by Kuhn. The concept of Progressive Revelation, clearly defined and fully described in 1862 by Bahá'u'lláh in *The Book of Certitude (Kitáb-i-Íqán),*[21] has significant similarities with the concept of scientific revolution outlined a century later by Kuhn. It is within this framework that the relationship between worldview and religion assumes its significance and demonstrates the primacy of the role of worldview in both our understanding and practice of religion. This theme will be revisited frequently throughout this book.

CONCEPT OF DEVELOPMENT

The nature and dynamics of the development of human individuals and societies are of particular significance with respect to our approach to the study of religion. Human development is affected not only by the biological laws of growth but also by the cognitive, emotional, sociological, and spiritual laws that greatly affect the unique phenomenon of development of human consciousness. In the 19th and 20th centuries, much attention was focused on the biological, psychological (cognitive and emotional), and sociological aspects of the development of human individuals and societies. However, little attention was given to another indispensable aspect of human growth—spiritual development.

The main contemporary psychological theories of human development are based on research and conceptual formulations put forward by Piaget, Freud, Erikson, and proponents of the Social Learning school of thought, among others. These theories are basically concerned with the development of the individual and pay less attention to the dynamics of development of social entities such as the family, community, nation, and humanity as a whole. All these theories, at least in their modern formulations, recognize the reciprocal nature of the impact of both biological forces and environmental and experiential processes on the development of the individual. They also recognize, to a varying degree, the active role that the person plays in his or her own development. These major theories of human development point toward the importance of the process of the formulation of a mindset (worldview)—a set of assumptions, attitudes, and habits that are gradually refined over the course of time. The most influential sources of human development, in general, and development of human consciousness, in particular, are our innate biological needs, our life experiences (particularly in early childhood), the nature and extent of our education, and our belief systems, which are transmitted from the family and the community. Within the parameters of these broad agreements, three different mindsets are identified: Mechanistic, Organismic, and Contextualistic. The Mechanistic perspective sees both the individual and the world—as well as the dynamics of their respective development and change—within a mechanical and machine-like framework. The Organismic school sees the world as a living organism in a constant state of change, adaptation, and modification. Finally, the Contextualistic perspective considers all human behavior to gain its meaning, and to be comprehensible, within a specific social-historical context. The existing theories of development all operate within one or more of these formulations.[22]

AN INTEGRATIVE CONCEPT OF DEVELOPMENT

The concept of development put forward in this book is an attempt to integrate the current theories of development with insights provided by Bahá'í views on the development of religion—Progressive Revelation. This integrative framework holds that development takes place on the axis of consciousness, which evolves in response to our ever-increasing understanding about the nature of self, others, and reality, as well as the dynamics of our relationship with these three distinctive, yet interrelated entities: self, others, and objective reality. Consciousness, therefore, shapes our worldview and the manner in which we approach all aspects of our lives. The human power of understanding, which is the main agent for the development of consciousness, involves cognitive (thoughts), emotive (feelings), and experiential forms of learning and is responsive to the forces of both nature and nurture. Development of consciousness and formulation of worldview is an evolving process involving certain distinctive stages. At the individual level, these stages have their genesis in the biological, cognitive, emotional, and spiritual dimensions of human nature and roughly involve the distinctive phases of infancy, childhood, adolescence, and adulthood. Each of these stages can, in turn, be divided into more specific substages.

The development of consciousness and worldview takes place in every aspect of human understanding and behavior. Thus, over time, we develop a greater understanding of ourselves, other human beings, the world of nature, and "reality" in all its varied expressions. This new understanding, in turn, modifies our behavior towards others and ourselves, and helps us to continuously refine the nature of all our relationships and the mode of our deliberations. The direction of worldview development is towards ever higher levels of unity, beginning from a state of primary, undifferentiated conditions of unity (uniformity), to the next phase of awareness based on differentiation and identity consciousness, and to a final stage of enlightened and all-encompassing unity in the context of diversity. The two main causes of human development are science, which discovers those fundamental laws that govern all natural phenomena, and Divine Revelation, which enunciates and elucidates spiritual laws that inform us of the purpose and direction of human life. Human experience, which is also a potent force in human development, is greatly shaped by science and religion.

The ongoing movement of humanity towards more advanced levels of unity involves all aspects of our individual and collective lives, including our approach to religion and science, human relationships, modes of governance and methods of decision-making and conflict resolution. In our world today we see ever-increasing examples of this movement towards unity in all departments of human life. These developments are addressed in later chapters.

Summary

The primary law of life is unity. All that exists is an expression of the law of unity at physical, biological, psychological, social, moral, and spiritual levels. There is a direct and positive relationship between our worldview and the type of individuals we become and the kind of societies we create. The concept of worldview refers to our understanding of the nature of reality, human nature, the purpose of human life, and moral and social laws that govern our relationships. As such, "worldview" refers to our interpretation of the biological, psychological, and spiritual aspects of life and development. Optimal human development takes place within the parameters of unity-based worldviews at individual, institutional, and social levels in the light of new scientific discoveries and spiritual developments. Our understanding and approach to the law of unity, the nature of our worldview, and the state and nature of our individual and collective development, together determine our approach to and understanding of religion, its place in our lives, and its role in the contemporary world.

Chapter Two

The Nature and Purpose of Religion

The fundamental purpose animating the Faith of God and His Religion is to safeguard the interests and promote the unity of the human race, and to foster the spirit of love and fellowship amongst men. Suffer it not to become a source of dissension and discord, of hate and enmity.[1]

—Bahá'u'lláh (1817–1892)

Religion should unite all hearts and cause wars and disputes to vanish from the face of the earth, give birth to spirituality, and bring life and light to each heart. If religion becomes a cause of dislike, hatred and division, it were better to be without it, and to withdraw from such a religion would be a truly religious act.[2]

—'Abdu'l-Bahá, 1912

A world, dimmed by the steadily dying-out light of religion, heaving with the explosive forces of a blind and triumphant nationalism; scorched with the fires of pitiless persecution, whether racial or religious; deluded by the false theories and doctrines that threaten to supplant the worship of God and the sanctification of His laws; enervated by a rampant and brutal materialism; disintegrating through the corrosive influence of moral and spiritual decadence; and enmeshed in the coils of economic anarchy and strife—such is the spectacle presented to men's eyes....[3]

—Shoghi Effendi, 1938

The general theory of religion as an accidental by-product—a misfiring of something useful—is the one I wish to advocate.[4]

—Richard Dawkins, 2006

Faith is the permission religious people give one another to believe ridiculous things.[5]

—Sam Harris, 2006

Among all my patients in the second half of life...there has not been one whose problem in the last resort was not that of finding a religious outlook on life.[6]

—Carl Jung (1875–1961)

THE UNITY-BASED CONCEPT OF RELIGION

This chapter is based on a talk I delivered 17 December 2000 at the International Conference on Modern Religious Movements in Judaism, Christianity, Islam, and the Bábí and Bahá'í Faiths, held at the Hebrew University of Jerusalem. As the co-chair—along with Professor Moshe Sharon, who holds the Bahá'í Chair at the Hebrew University of Jerusalem—of the conference, I offered a few opening remarks and later delivered my main presentation. The Hebrew University is not only a renowned centre of study of the three major world religions—Judaism, Christianity, and Islam—but also the site of the first university Chair dedicated to the study of the Bahá'í Faith.[7] The decision to organize this conference was based on several issues considered of paramount importance both with respect to religion as a subject of scholarly inquiry and religion as an essential aspect of human experience. The focus on modern religions and new developments within the more ancient and established religions is related to humanity's complicated relationship with religion itself, which is the main focus of this book.

The talk uses the framework discussed in chapter one and presents the Bahá'í Faith as the example of the concept of *unity-based religion* that has thus far eluded humanity. In my presentation I touch on a wide range of issues, including the nature of religion, the dynamics of its evolution, its fundamental objectives, the reasons why religions in the past and at present have been misunderstood and abused, and how the Bahá'í Faith proposes to unite religions and to avoid those pitfalls that have burdened and weakened various religions in the course of human history. This introduction to the Bahá'í Faith provides the necessary background information for issues with regard to the role of religion in the family, education, and society that are discussed in later chapters.

THE CHALLENGE OF RELIGION

Religion is in disrepute in our times. It is variably seen as a cause of conflicts and wars, as a body of illogical and superstitious beliefs and practices, as a refuge for the weak and the unaccomplished, as a bastion of male supremacy and control of the masses, and as a relic of the past. From one perspective, all these critical views of religion are accurate. It is true that many wars have been waged and much violence is still being justified in the name of religion. It is a fact that some theological doctrines of the major religions of the world and their numerous offshoots are superstitious in nature and encumbered with concepts and practices which are contrary to the dictates of logic and facts of science. It is a reality that by far the largest segment of the world population adheres to some form of religion and that the many of followers of all religions have limited social, educational, political, and economic resources and opportunities.[8] It is also a fact that women and the generality of the faithful have always been and still are under the rule and dictates of the clergy of their respective religions and that, with a few relatively insignificant exceptions, these religious leaders are men. As such, it is both accurate and appropriate to conclude that religion, as perceived and practiced along the above parameters, is a thing of the past and should be discarded.

'Abdu'l-Bahá (1844–1921), the Centre of the Covenant[9] of the Bahá'í Faith, commenting on the significance of the age in which we live and referring to the need for renewal of religion and discarding of outmoded theologies and practices, states:

> What a wonderful century this is! It is an age of universal reformation. Laws and statutes of governments, civil and federal, are in the process of change and transformation. Sciences and arts are being moulded anew. Thoughts are metamorphosed. The foundations of human society are changing and strengthening. Today the sciences of the past are useless....Ethical precedents and principles cannot be applied to the needs of the modern world. Thoughts and theories of past ages are fruitless now. Thrones and governments are crumbling and falling. All conditions and requisites of the past unfitted and inadequate for the present time are undergoing radical reform. It is evident therefore that counterfeit and spurious religious teaching, antiquated forms of belief and ancestral imitations which are at variance with the foundation of divine reality must also pass away and be reformed. They must be abandoned and new conditions be recognized. The morals of humanity must undergo change. New remedy and solution for human problems must be adopted. Human intellects themselves must change and be subject to the universal reformation. Just as the thoughts and hypotheses of past ages are fruitless today, likewise dogmas and codes of human invention are obsolete and barren of product in religion. Nay, it is true that they are the cause of enmity and conducive to strife in the world of humanity; war and bloodshed proceed from them and the oneness of mankind finds no recognition in their observance. Therefore it is our duty in this radiant century to investigate the essentials of divine religion,

seek the realities underlying the oneness of the world of humanity, and discover the source of fellowship and agreement which will unite mankind in the heavenly bond of love.[10]

This counsel of 'Abdu'l-Bahá is just one example of numerous statements in the Writings (Scriptures) of the Bahá'í Faith that point to another side of religion—its positive qualities and accomplishments. In the following few paragraphs, I will attempt to summarize some of these points.

A dispassionate, objective review of the origins, teachings, and accomplishments of the main religions of the world reveals several outstanding facts. Every race and group of people has a religious and spiritual orientation and history. All religions address physical, psychological, social, and spiritual aspects of human nature and prescribe moral and ethical principles that govern human relationships and conduct. In this respect the degree of agreement and harmony among religions is astounding. All the universal codes of moral and ethical conduct, as put forward by the main religions of the world, are in fundamental agreement. All religions concur that life is sacred; that human life is a process of actualization of our inherent potential qualities of body, mind, and spirit; and that the main purpose of religion is to bring meaning, direction, harmony, cooperation, beauty, and civility to the life of the individual and society alike. The examples of the lives of the Founders of the major religions of the world, those transcendent figures such as Krishna (3228–3100 BCE), Moses (1527–1406 BCE), Zoroaster (circa 1200 BC), Buddha (563–483 BCE), Jesus (4 BC–AD 29), Muhammad (AD 570–632), and Bahá'u'lláh (AD 1817–1892)[11] are outstanding unique testimonies to the fundamental nobility, integrity, universality, and unity of their teachings.

An unbiased scrutiny of the religions introduced to humanity by these Founders clearly demonstrates the unity of their message, the nobility of their purpose, and the astounding measure of their accomplishments. There is no civilization that is not directly or indirectly related to one or another of the major religions of the past. There is no paucity of examples of the lives that these religious teachings have transformed. There are numerous monuments to the positive accomplishments of each and every one of these religions in the domains of civilization, culture, arts, science, and the enrichment of individual and collective lives of people.

An extremely important finding that emerges from the study of these religions from the perspective of their original teachings, the examples of the lives of their Founders, and their respective accomplishments, is their fundamental unity. Among these points of unity are the teachings that God (or a Transcendent Reality/Original Mind) has created all that exists, including humankind, and that the gift of the rational soul and its capacities of knowledge, love, and will in their varied manifestations are the distinguishing features of the human race. These religions point out that the relationship between God and humankind is an eternal covenant and an on-going process. They state that the primary purpose of human life, for each person individually and humanity collectively, is to develop along the parameters of knowledge, love, and will; and that this process is only possible when humanity lives according to these spiritual principles. It is this fundamental unity of religions, I believe, that must become the object of study by all serious students of religion.

UNITY OF RELIGION

Bahá'u'lláh first clearly and emphatically elucidated the concept of the unity of religion and the progressive nature of its revelation in His unique treatise on religion *The Book of Certitude* (*Kitáb-i-Íqán*). In this book, which was revealed in the course of two days and two nights in 1862 in Baghdad, Bahá'u'lláh explains that God's essence is unknowable and inaccessible to the human mind, and that the relationship between God and humanity is only possible through recognition of the Manifestations of God who are the Founders of the major religions, variably referred to as Prophets, Messengers of God, Son of God, or simply by their names or titles. Bahá'u'lláh explains that if we reflect on the lives and teachings of all the Prophets of God with "discriminating eyes," we will see all of them "abiding in the same tabernacle, soaring in the same heaven, seated upon the same throne, uttering the same speech, and proclaiming the same Faith."[12] From this perspective, a panorama of the unity of religion emerges that unfortunately is buried behind clouds of superstitions, misunderstandings, and prejudices afflicting almost all religions. There are several reasons for this highly consequential misunderstanding, a few of which I will address here.

A broad review of the life span of classical religions—whether from Judeo-Christian-Islamic faiths or Hindu and Buddhist traditions—shows three distinctive phases in their evolution. The first phase—the revolutionary formative phase—is when the newly appeared religion challenges the existing worldviews in its immediate environment and other regions of the world in the course of its expansion. The new religion brings with it a new cosmology dealing with issues of the nature of reality, human nature, the purpose of life, and the parameters of human relationships. It provides a new mindset and worldview, and because of its progressive, enlightened nature, it gradually or, occasionally, rapidly gathers adherents and begins to form a new, progressive, and expanding community. However, as history clearly demonstrates, the process of acceptance of a new religion has always been accompanied by understandable apprehension, deliberate indifference, or forceful antagonism, usually a combination of all three responses. These responses are understandable, because a new religion calls for re-evaluating many aspects of our individual and social life. It challenges our established identities. It calls on us to drastically alter our sense of self, others, and relationships. In brief, it introduces a new and compelling worldview and challenges the established paradigm. These demands are at the root of the resistance to every new Revelation throughout history.

The second phase in the life of a religion—the golden age—is when the new religion comes of age and produces some of its finest fruits in all areas of human endeavor. Thus, a new and unique civilization is created within the parameters of a worldview based on the teachings of this new religion. This new civilization, as history shows, usually lasts for several centuries and brings with it monumental benefits in all areas of human life. During these periods the arts and sciences advance considerably, and the lives of the people improve dramatically. However, as history also shows, the relationship of the followers of the new religion with those of the older religions is often conflicted and violent. The reasons for this fact will be discussed later, when the process and dynamics of collective development of humanity are reviewed. Eventually, the enlightened or golden age of each religion gradually, but inevitably, comes to an end.

The third phase—decline and renewal—begins when the civilization inspired and cultivated by this religion gradually outgrows the parameters of the worldview that it itself has created. It is in this phase that religion is renewed in the context of a new Revelation from God with a new and revolutionary worldview, at once similar to and different from all existing religions. This new religion brings with it principles, laws, and perspectives on material, psychological, social, moral, and spiritual aspects of life, commensurate with the needs and capacities of humanity at the time of its appearance and centuries to come. However, as the history of religion clearly demonstrates, the established religions resist the imperatives of change and renewal and often reject the new religion with vehemence and force. An inevitable outcome of this resistance to change is that the established religions become increasingly irrelevant to the needs and challenges of their respective societies, lose their spiritual power and moral authority, become burdened with irrational and superstitious doctrines, and begin to be more a source of evil than good. History clearly shows that religious leaders are the main agents of resistance to change.

The second reason for the decline and corruption of religion is also related to the role of leadership in the religious community. Religious leaders—referred to by different names in different religions—have the most crucial impact on the course of the development and nature of conduct of their respective religious communities and their members. This is so because religious leaders are in positions of absolute authority, wielding considerable power with respect to the affairs of their respective communities, and thus are highly invested in safeguarding their own positions of control and privilege. Historically, this concentration of power and authority in the hands of religious leaders has been the source both of considerable good (particularly during the first two phases of the life of their respective religions) and of considerable evil (particularly in the third phase—the phase of decline and renewal). The history of all past religions demonstrates the awful, destructive consequences of the corruption of the leadership of religion. This is also the situation in our contemporary world. Even today, at the start of the 21st century, much political and social violence; denial of equality for women; illiteracy and ignorance (of the precepts of their religion) of the faithful masses; promotion of superstitious and prejudicial belief; denial of proven scientific facts; and sanctioning of violence in the name of religion, can all be traced back to the leadership of these religions and the manner in which they interpret and explain the teachings of their respective traditions.

There is yet another fundamental reason for the disunity among religions and the loss of their spiritual potency and the relevance of their teachings to the needs of humanity in the contemporary world. Throughout history and across all cultures, the nature of religion has been generally understood within a framework of otherness, separation, distinction, and superiority with regard to other religions. The most common view of religion has been and continues to be that there are many religions and that they differ in some fundamental ways, hence the considerable disunity and competition among most religions.

The Bahá'í perspective on religion is different. It holds that religion, as the medium of the revelation of God's purpose to humanity, is one in essence and progressive in nature and that its progression parallels the collective development of the human race. In the same manner that every individual human being traverses stages of infancy, childhood, adolescence, and adulthood, likewise, all human societies collectively evolve and develop in a similar manner. At each level of development, people in a given society have their unique capacities and needs that must be met through the twin resources of scientific knowledge and spiritual insight. In the same way that science is progressive in nature, likewise, religion is progressive.

THE COMING OF AGE OF HUMANITY

Bahá'u'lláh states "in every Dispensation the light of Divine Revelation has been vouchsafed to men in direct proportion to their spiritual capacity."[13] 'Abdu'l-Bahá further elaborates this fundamental concept:

> All created things have their degree or stage of maturity. The period of maturity in the life of a tree is the time of its fruit-bearing....
> The animal attains a stage of full growth and completeness, and in the human kingdom man reaches his maturity when the light of his intelligence attains its greatest power and development....Similarly there are periods and stages in the collective life of humanity. At one time it was passing through its stage of childhood, at another its period of youth, but now it has entered its long-predicted phase of maturity, the evidences of which are apparent everywhere....That which was applicable to human needs during the early history of the race can neither meet nor satisfy the demands of this day, this period of newness and consummation. Humanity has emerged from its former state of limitation and preliminary training....The gifts and blessings of the period of youth, although timely and sufficient during the adolescence of mankind, are now incapable of meeting the requirements of its maturity.[14]

The crucial significance of the current period in history is that the world of humanity is now traversing the final stages of its collective transition from adolescence to maturity. Many of the contemporary human challenges and problems are easily understood when we approach them from this perspective. The inordinate interest in obtaining power and pleasure; the intense competition among peoples, nations, and ideological groupings of the world; the elevation of competition to the rank of a highly valued virtue and quality; the insatiable quest for independent ethnic and religious identity; the strengthening of passions of nationalism and racism; the fierce economic competition and its attendant extremes of wealth and poverty; the ongoing rivalry between scientists and religious leaders to establish themselves as the sole reservoir of insight into all human conditions; and the ever-present desire to win and to prove one's group superior to others are just a few examples of the adolescent mind-set that is present in all cultures and regions of the world. While the challenges now faced by humanity are commensurate with its collective adulthood phase, its approach to these challenges still remains at the childhood and adolescent levels.

In this time of monumental transition, many insightful observers of humanity express the view that what is most needed in our world is a willingness on the part of leaders and peoples of the world to cooperate rather than to compete; to think universally rather than in sectarian and limited ways; to accept and celebrate the rich diversity of the human race rather than to fear it and see it as a problem; and to dedicate all the resources of the world to the cause of unity and peace rather than to resign ourselves to the maintenance of some semblance of "truce" among highly suspicious and heavily armed, contending peoples, nations, and states. These latter approaches belong to another era, the ages of our collective childhood and adolescence. Now that humanity is coming of age, substantial change in our ways of thinking, relating, and acting are called for.

Shoghi Effendi (1897–1957), the Guardian of the Bahá'í Faith,[15] describes the dynamics and characteristics of the transition of humanity to adulthood in many of his works. In the *World Order of Bahá'u'lláh*, he states:

> The long ages of infancy and childhood, through which the human race had to pass, have receded into the background. Humanity is now experiencing the commotions invariably associated with the most turbulent stage of its evolution, the stage of adolescence, when the impetuosity of youth and its vehemence reach their climax, and must gradually be superseded by the calmness, the wisdom, and the maturity that characterize the stage of manhood. Then will the human race reach that stature of ripeness which will enable it to acquire all the powers and capacities upon which its ultimate development must depend.[16]

Humanity's "coming of age" is an all-encompassing phenomenon that will affect every aspect of human existence: our individual lives, the types of marriages and families we create, the nature of our political and social institutions and practices, our understanding of the relationship between science and religion, the manner in which we approach the world and its resources, the quality of our relationships with one another and with the world of nature, and above all, our understanding of and relationship with God. Shoghi Effendi, in the same book, points out that the advent of the coming of age of the entire human race will include such accomplishments as "the emergence of a world community, the consciousness of world citizenship, the founding of a world civilization and culture."[17]

Clearly, at this juncture in the history of humanity, not many people are prepared to begin to work toward realization of these objectives, noble as they are. Nevertheless, there is increasing evidence that the consciousness of the oneness of humankind is taking on a momentum of its own. Once a significant number of peoples and leaders of thought and society recognize the truth of the reality of the oneness of humankind and begin to dedicate themselves to the task of creating a civilization based on its principles, then, and only then, will the process of the coming of age of humanity gather momentum within a healthy and creative framework. The alternative route is frighteningly dangerous and destructive, as already witnessed in the 20th century with its terrible violence and wars and continuing in the 21st century with its worldwide episodes of terrorism, of mounting deaths of multitudes from hunger and disease, and of unremitting violence and war in many parts of the world.

ONENESS OF HUMANKIND AND UNITY IN DIVERSITY

The concept of the oneness of humankind, based on the principle of unity in diversity, is central to the teachings and objectives of the Bahá'í Faith. Humanity is one. Biologically, we are one species. Psychologically, we possess the same powers of the mind—cognitive, emotive, and conative (inclination to act purposefully) powers. Spiritually we are one. The essential reality of every human being—that reality which defines our humanness and endows us with the ability to employ our biological and psychological capacities on an upward rather than downward (animal-like) trajectory—is one. While united in the fundamentals of our humanness, we are all unique and different in the manner that we express our humanity. The integration of these two facts—the oneness of humanity and the uniqueness of every individual and group—form the firmest foundations for the realization of the finest fruit of humanity in its age of collective maturity—peace.

Bahá'u'lláh repeatedly emphasizes the central role that religion must play with respect to the creation of unity and peace in the world. He states that "the fundamental purpose animating the Faith of God and His Religion is to safeguard the interests and promote the unity of the human race."[18] He declares that "[t]he well-being of mankind, its peace and security are unattainable unless and until its unity is firmly established."[19] He further asserts that "[s]o powerful is the light of unity, that it can illuminate the whole earth."[20]

'Abdu'l-Bahá likewise emphasizes the significance of and the necessity for humanity becoming conscious about its fundamental oneness. "In every Dispensation," writes 'Abdu'l-Bahá, "the light of Divine Guidance has been focused upon one central theme....In this wondrous Revelation, this glorious century, the foundation of the Faith of God and the distinguishing feature of His Law is the consciousness of the Oneness of Mankind."[21] Elsewhere, 'Abdu'l-Bahá emphasizes that

> [t]he divine religions must be the cause of oneness among men, and the means of unity and love; they must promulgate universal peace, free man from every prejudice, bestow joy and gladness, exercise kindness to all men and do away with every difference and distinction."[22]

Shoghi Effendi, in describing some of the essential features of the Bahá'í concept of the oneness of humankind and the unity of humanity, states that

> the unity of the human race, as envisaged by Bahá'u'lláh, implies the establishment of a world commonwealth in which all nations, races, creeds, and classes are closely and permanently united, and in which the autonomy of its state members and the personal freedom and initiative of the individuals that compose them are definitely and completely safeguarded.[23]

From the perspective of the Bahá'í Faith, the creation of unity at all levels of society and in all departments of life is the central purpose and task of religion. Therefore, if religion is the cause of disunity, it is better to be without it. 'Abdu'l-Bahá, referring to the teachings of the Bahá'í Faith and their main objectives, states that Bahá'u'lláh "sets forth a new principle for this day in the announcement that religion must be the cause of unity, harmony, and agreement among mankind. If it be the cause of discord and hostility, if it leads to separation and creates conflict, the absence of religion would be preferable in the world."[24]

The concepts presented in this chapter about the purpose and nature of religion are revolutionary. They point out that the religion of God is one continuous and evolving reality that propels humanity both forward and upward on the path of the evolution of its consciousness. They point out that through the Will of God, the one and only evolving religion of God is renewed whenever a new measure of spiritual guidance and regeneration is called for. These perspectives on religion are elements of a new worldview commensurate with the coming of age of humanity and the emerging global society. This worldview—the unity-based worldview—is based on the fact of the oneness of humankind and the principle of unity in diversity. The previous statement by 'Abdu'l-Bahá, suggesting that if a religion did not satisfy its primary objective of creating unity and oneness of humanity, then it is better to be without it, is particularly challenging. The question that immediately arises is this: Can we live without religion, and, if so, do we have one or more examples of a peaceful, creative, and progressive civilization without the benefit of spiritual principles emanating from Divine Revelation?

THE PURPOSE AND FUNCTIONS OF RELIGION

Religion plays a fundamental role in all aspects of human life. At the individual level, religion delineates the nature of reality and our relative access to it. Religion defines who we are; provides us with a sense of identity; gives purpose and direction to our lives; creates a framework for our relationships; confers meaning to our life experiences; delineates moral and ethical principles; and helps us to meet the inner needs and anxieties that we human beings, by virtue of being conscious of our mortality, have to face under various circumstances. At the social level, religion provides the framework for creation of a peaceful society in which the respective rights and responsibilities of individuals, families, social institutions, and the government are all delineated, thus allowing for development of a free, orderly, ethical, and creative society and the flourishing of an ever-advancing civilization. It is within these individual and societal frameworks provided by religion that the human soul (psyche) faces the challenges of living; makes sense of all that happens in life; avoids total confusion and disorientation when the unexpected happens; satisfies, to the degree possible, our ever-present need to give and receive love and to be united with others; and guides us to do good and inspires us to create. Above all, religion helps the individual and societies alike to transcend the limited boundaries of survival instincts and selfish interests to become universal and all-inclusive. These three categories of functions of religion—individual, societal, and universal—correspond with the three main human needs and rights: survival, association, and transcendence, which I will describe later (chapter four). This enumeration of some of the main functions of religion shows why religion is indispensable to human life. It also clarifies the reason why, when humanity rejects religion, it immediately replaces it with some human-made, quasi-religion.

There are basically two kinds of religion: the revealed religions of the world such as Zoroastrianism, Judaism, Buddhism, Hinduism, Christianity, Islam, and the Bahá'í Faith; and the human-made ideologies that have assumed the place of religion in the lives of peoples and, in the process, have themselves become quasi-religions. Among this latter group are humanism,[25] scientism,[26] capitalism,[27] Marxism, nationalism, materialism,[28] human-created old and New Religious Movements (NRMs),[29] and a host of other ideologies that attempt to define human nature, prescribe codes of human conduct, and provide purpose and life direction for their adherents. In addition, these ideologies give the masses of their believers a tenuous and competitive sense of identity that encourages psychological states of self-centeredness, self-satisfaction, and self-righteousness.

As stated before, by far, the majority of the peoples of the world are followers of either the established revealed religions or human-made quasi-religions and ideologies. In this respect, it should be noted that even most of the revealed religions suffer from the accretion of human-created dogmas, rituals, superstitions, prejudices, and practices, which have dramatically distanced these religions from their original and pure spiritual teachings—hence, their inability to maintain their fundamental unity and their fragmentation into many sects and factions. Thus the statement by 'Abdu'l-Bahá that if religion is the cause of disunity, it is better to be without it. Here the reference is to the perversion of religion and its contamination with ideas and practices that are contrary to its original objectives and teachings.

At first glance, these comments may seem harsh. However, this is not my intent. Rather, my primary objective is to try to dissipate the fog that surrounds the issue of religion and to invite the reader to reflect on the subject of religion in an objective manner and in the spirit of search for truth, within the framework of the scientific method in its broadest, most inclusive definition. Bahá'u'lláh, in the *Book of Certitude,* invites us to look at religion in the following manner:

> …when a true seeker determines to take the step of search in the path
> leading to the knowledge of the Ancient of Days, he must, before all

else, cleanse and purify his heart, which is the seat of revelation of the inner mysteries of God, from the obscuring dust of all acquired knowledge....He must purge his breast, which is the sanctuary of the abiding love of the Beloved, of every defilement, and sanctify his soul from all that pertaineth to water and clay, from all shadowy and ephemeral attachments. He must so cleanse his heart that no remnant of either love or hate may linger therein, lest that love blindly incline him to error, or that hate repel him away from the truth.[30]

GOD AND HUMANITY

In a remarkably concise few pages, Bahá'u'lláh describes the nature of God, the process of creation, the special nature of human reality, the purpose of life, and the reason for the appearance of the Manifestation of God. He states:

> All praise to the unity of God, and all honor to Him, the sovereign Lord, the incomparable and all-glorious Ruler of the universe, Who, out of utter nothingness, hath created the reality of all things, Who, from naught, hath brought into being the most refined and subtle elements of His creation....Nothing short of His all-encompassing grace, His all-pervading mercy, could have possibly achieved it. How could it, otherwise, have been possible for sheer nothingness to have acquired by itself the worthiness and capacity to emerge from its state of non-existence into the realm of being?

> Having created the world and all that liveth and moveth therein, He...chose to confer upon man the unique distinction and capacity to know Him and to love Him—a capacity that must needs be regarded as the generating impulse and the primary purpose underlying the whole of creation....Upon the inmost reality of each and every created thing He hath shed the light of one of His names, and made it a recipient of the glory of one of His attributes. Upon the reality of man, however, He hath focused the radiance of all of His names and attributes, and made it a mirror of His own Self....

> These energies with which [God]...hath endowed the reality of man lie, however, latent within him, even as the flame is hidden within the candle and the rays of light are potentially present in the lamp.... Neither the candle nor the lamp can be lighted through their own unaided efforts, nor can it ever be possible for the mirror to free itself from its dross. It is clear and evident that until a fire is kindled the lamp will never be ignited, and unless the dross is blotted out from the face of the mirror it can never represent the image of the sun nor reflect its light and glory.

And since there can be no tie of direct intercourse to bind the one true God with His creation, and no resemblance whatever can exist between the transient and the Eternal, the contingent and the Absolute, He hath ordained that in every age and dispensation a pure and stainless Soul be made manifest in the kingdoms of earth and heaven. Unto this subtle, this mysterious and ethereal Being He hath assigned a twofold nature; the physical, pertaining to the world of matter, and the spiritual, which is born of the substance of God Himself....

Through the Teachings of this Day Star of Truth [Manifestation of God] every man will advance and develop until he attaineth the station at which he can manifest all the potential forces with which his inmost true self hath been endowed. It is for this very purpose that in every age and dispensation the Prophets of God and His chosen Ones have appeared amongst men, and have evinced such power as is born of God and such might as only the Eternal can reveal.[31]

One of the main principles affirmed in this statement and other Writings of the Bahá'í Faith is that there is a Creator—God—who has created us and who has established a lasting, inviolable relationship—the Covenant—with humanity. We have come to this life neither by accident, nor as a result of a mindless process of adaptation. Rather, human beings and all that exists are the result of the creative Will of the Creator. However, this does not mean that the process of the appearance of life on this planet was not gradual, nor does it deny the existence of an evolutionary process involving all living beings, including the human species. The Bahá'í perspective on the origins of the human species puts emphasis on both the biological and the spiritual aspects of human reality. From the biological point of view, there are many similarities between humans and animals, and both are subject to the laws of biological evolution. However, human spiritual development takes place on the axis of the human powers of the soul and its capacities to know (intellectual) and to love (emotional), which, along with the human ability to choose and to decide, together constitute the central animating forces of our humanness.

The Bahá'í writings are very clear about the process through which the knowledge of God is accomplished and love for the Divine is expressed. God, in essence, is unknowable and unapproachable. The finite human mind cannot comprehend the infinite reality of the Godhead. However, out of mercy and justice, and in fulfillment of the eternal covenant with humanity, God sends from time-to-time, according to the needs and capacities of humanity at various stages of its collective evolution, Messengers who reveal to humanity the spiritual teachings appropriate for that age. These Messengers or Manifestations of God, these unique and transcendent figures known to history as the Founders of the great religions of the world, are the intermediaries between God and humanity. Knowledge and love of them is the closest that we can possibly get to know and love God. In *The Foundations of World Unity*, 'Abdu'l-Bahá focuses on the issue of knowledge and love of God and asks:

> Is it not astonishing that although man has been created for the knowledge and love of God, for the virtues of the human world, for spirituality, heavenly illumination and life eternal, nevertheless he continues ignorant and negligent of all this? Consider how he seeks knowledge of everything except knowledge of God. For instance, his utmost desire is to penetrate the mysteries of the lowest strata of the earth. Day by day he strives to know what can be found ten meters below the surface, what he can discover within the stone, what he can learn by archaeological research in the dust. He puts forth arduous labors to fathom terrestrial mysteries but is not at all concerned about knowing the mysteries of the Kingdom, traversing the illimitable fields of the eternal world, becoming informed of the divine realities, discovering the secrets of God, attaining the knowledge of God, witnessing the splendors of the Sun of Truth and realizing the glories of everlasting life. He is unmindful and thoughtless of these. How much he is attracted to the mysteries of matter and how completely unaware he is of the mysteries of divinity! Nay, he is utterly negligent and oblivious of the secrets of divinity. How great his ignorance![32]

How astonishing, indeed! In a response to the question as to what extent can the understanding of man comprehend God, 'Abdu'l-Bahá explains that there are two kinds of knowledge: "...the knowledge of the essence of a thing and the knowledge of its qualities."[33] However, we do not have access to the knowledge of the essence of anything, let alone God. Our knowledge of things is limited to our knowledge of their qualities. All that we are able to understand are attributes of God, as expressed in the Manifestations of God.

Another reason for humanity's neglect of its own spiritual nature may be an expression of the psychological processes of humanity in its collective adolescence. During the period of youth, the physical and material aspects of life assume profound importance and absorb most of the resources of the human psyche. Therefore, it is not surprising that in this age of humanity's collective adolescence, preoccupation with materialistic explanations of human nature is widespread. Yet another reason for humanity's preoccupation with the material and neglect of its spiritual reality has its genesis in our understanding of human nature, which is the subject of chapter four.

OBEDIENCE TO SPIRITUAL LAW

Once the teachings of a new religion are presented to humanity and, consequently, the door to a greater knowledge of spiritual laws is opened through God's Manifestation, then the responsibility of people to respond to the message of God for the age in which they live becomes the centerpiece of the eternal drama of the relationship between God and humanity. It is here that human *will* begins to express itself in its most fateful manner. It is in this process that each individual human being is invited to consider the introduction of spiritual laws to his/her life and to transcend the essentially animal-like qualities that emerge from the forces and promptings of human instinctual (animal) nature.

The drama of the interface of the Will of God and the will of humanity has always been and continues to be most astounding. The history surrounding the introduction of every new religion is an instructive account of this interface. On the one hand, there are the examples of spiritually transformed personalities, the details of whose lives and deeds have moved and continue to move the hearts and souls of countless millions over many centuries and in all parts of the world. On the other hand, there is an ever-present tendency on the part of many to try to sidestep the spiritual laws promulgated by the Founders of these religions and to resist obedience to the dictates of their laws. This resistance has its roots in the self-centeredness and self-indulgence that particularly characterize human individuals and societies in their respective stages of childhood and adolescence. However, this drama has never been as intense and of such immense consequence as it is in our times. The reason for this fact is that impetuous adolescent humanity has profound difficulty in accepting discipline, order, and submission to any rule contrary to its particular understandings and desires. The rebellious nature of the adolescent age, combined with its qualities of intense physical, emotional, and intellectual powers, tend to make the adolescent individual or group unrealistic with respect to the limits of their own knowledge and capacities and also with regard to the magnitude of the challenges before them. The adolescent character tends to be arrogant and extreme. From a psychosocial perspective, this is indeed the condition of humanity at this time in history.

The central issue regarding the interface of the Will of God and the will of humanity is that of obedience to the laws of religion. Children often obey out of fear, while adolescents are more likely to disobey and break laws. Therefore, it is not surprising that the clergy has always promoted the teachings of their respective religions through the instrumentalities of reward and punishment, hope and fear, and the use of force, coercion, and even violence. Also, it is of no surprise that contemporary adolescent humanity has chosen to pronounce God an illusion, to view religion as the "opium of the people" and a "psychological deficiency," and to discard religion altogether, replacing it with human-made ideologies and doctrines. It is also not surprising that even religious people frequently approach the fundamental spiritual teachings of their religion within the framework of materialistic, authoritarian and/or indulgent worldviews. In doing so, they have made their respective religions more of a cultural and economic commodity than a repository of the universal spiritual laws of truth, unity, service, and justice. The destructive consequences of these developments have been immense, and humanity has paid and continues to pay heavy penalties for its conscious disregard of the spiritual laws that govern its life. In the same way that disregard of physical laws with respect to, for example, the environment have wreaked havoc in the ecology of the human habitat, disregard for spiritual laws likewise has resulted in conditions of violence, deceit, greed, disease, corruption, brutality, hopelessness, confusion, and sorrow that has engulfed humankind.

The Bahá'í perspectives on spiritual laws and obedience to these laws are of special interest as we reflect on the mind-set of humanity in the latter stages of its collective adolescence. 'Abdu'l-Bahá states that "[t]he laws of God are not impositions of will, or of power, or pleasure, but the resolutions of truth, reason, and justice."[34] These laws are neither arbitrary in nature, nor given to humanity for any reason other than for the exaltation of human beings and creation of a progressive, just, and peaceful civilization. As such, these laws are expressions of God's love for humanity.

In the same manner that development of our physical, emotional, and intellectual capacities requires knowledge, motivation, practice, and discipline, likewise, our spiritual capacities are subject to similar dynamics. We need to know the nature of spiritual laws, to be willing to acquire them through discipline, and persistently to put them into practice. These are not unusual requisites. No true human accomplishment is possible without observing these requirements. The main instrument for development of spiritual capacities is acquisition of virtues. Virtues are expressions of moral excellence in action and determine the nature and quality of our conduct and behavior both in private and public. A virtuous person lives and behaves without the fear of punishment or the need to be policed and overseen. Such an individual has attained true freedom and behaves in a moral manner neither for fear of punishment nor for promise of reward. This is so because spiritually oriented individuals recognize that both punishment and reward are inherent aspects of our deeds. Our every act carries with it a corresponding measure of reward or punishment.

The Bahá'í Writings provide us with a rather long list of virtues, which could be classified under three broad categories based on the main human cognitive (knowledge), affective (love) and conative (will) powers. These three powers, in their essential qualities, level of intensity, and richness and scope of expression, are unique to the human species. They are the powers of the human psyche (soul) and are the instruments through which individual human beings are able to fulfill the purpose of their creation and harvest the fruits of their existence.

In the opening sentences of the Most Holy Book (Kitáb-i-Aqdas), the book of laws, Bahá'u'lláh clearly and emphatically outlines the first duty that every person must fulfill in this life and calls upon us to use our capacities to know, love, and will for this most essential purpose, the very reason for which we have been created:

> THE FIRST DUTY prescribed by God for His servants is the recognition of Him Who is the Dayspring of His Revelation and the Fountain of His Laws, Who representeth the Godhead in both the Kingdom of His Cause and the world of creation. Whoso achieveth this duty hath attained unto all good; and whoso is deprived thereof hath gone astray, though he be the author of every righteous deed. It behoveth every one who reacheth this most sublime station, this summit of transcendent glory, to observe every ordinance of Him Who is the Desire of the world. These twin duties are inseparable. Neither is acceptable without the other. Thus hath it been decreed by Him Who is the Source of Divine inspiration.[35]

In the sentence immediately following the prescription of the above two duties, Bahá'u'lláh explains that the teachings and commandments of God for humanity are "for the maintenance of order in the world and the security of its peoples."[36] Bahá'u'lláh then emphasizes that His commandments are the "lamps" of His loving kindness and the "keys" of His mercy and invites His followers to reciprocate this love by observing His commandments. This love relationship between God and humanity is yet another evidence of the coming of age of humanity. Bahá'u'lláh invites humanity to establish a new type of relationship with God and His religion by setting the issue of obedience to the spiritual laws in the context of a love relationship. He invites, as God's regent on earth, "Observe My commandments for love of My beauty,"[37] and reminds us of the reciprocal nature of love: "Love Me, so I may love thee. If thou lovest Me not, in no wise My love can reach thee."[38] No longer is the fear of punishment and hell or the promise of reward and paradise the motivating force for people to live a spiritual life. Humanity has now reached that level of maturity to be able to use its powers of mind in a free, unencumbered manner for the purpose of developing a spiritual lifestyle and an ever-advancing civilization of peace.

When we focus our life energies on the development of the powers of our mind within the framework of spiritual laws, we become truth seeking and truthful, unifying and universal, and agents of social justice and personal service to others. We can classify all ethical and moral codes of behavior under these three broad universal categories. These ethical standards have profound ramifications for both our individual and collective existence. However, in addition to these personal moral standards, there are other spiritual principles that address interpersonal and social aspects of our lives. In fact, the Bahá'í writings are very specific about the relationship between the personal, interpersonal, and social dimensions of our conduct. There is no separation among them. In the sacred writings of the Bahá'í Faith, we find that the knowledge of God requires self-knowledge, that spiritual and scientific knowledge must be in accord, that the love of God must be expressed in love for our fellow human beings and love of living entities, and that the worship of God constitutes pursuit of arts and sciences and living a moral, ethical life in the service of humanity and for the cause of justice and unity. (For elaboration on the issue of ethics see the section, "Towards a Universal Code of Ethics" in chapter four.)

LOVE OF GOD AND FEAR OF GOD

Before ending this discussion about spiritual laws and the relationship between God and humanity, a note of explanation is in order with regard to the issue of fear of violation of these laws. In the Bahá'í Writings we come across references regarding both love of God, which was already briefly discussed, and fear of God. Fear is a natural self-protective response to threats, and threats have their genesis in the violation of laws that govern life. Thus, for example we naturally and automatically fear fire and display great care in handling it and warn our children not to play with it. This fear is normal, healthy, and rational. However, if a person develops extreme and unreasonable fear of fire, to the degree that he will not enter a house in which there is a fireplace, then we conclude that he is suffering from a phobia—in this case *arsonphobia*. Phobias are abnormal, unhealthy, and irrational types of fear. In our world today we observe an abnormal, unhealthy, and irrational fear of God or *theophobia*. Phobia of God has profoundly negative consequences. It makes us unable to appreciate and receive the love of God, which is ever present in all aspects of our life. Theophobia also makes us neglectful, prideful, and prone to violation of the fundamental spiritual laws such as truthfulness, compassion, and justice. Therefore, it is not surprising that in the contemporary highly materialistic world we observe an abundance of moral corruption, interpersonal indifference and coldness, and social inequality and injustice. We observe these conditions in all societies, in all classes of people, and among those who reject religion and those who do not. Unlike phobia of God, fear of God—and thus fear of violation of spiritual laws and having regard for them—renders the individual free. In the same way that to respect gravity and fear violating this fundamental physical law allows us to understand the law and to align ourselves with it and eventually soar in the sky without fear of falling, in the same manner when we obey spiritual laws we will find ourselves in possession of courage and freedom in all our personal, interpersonal, and social undertakings.

In the Bahá'í Writings the concept of fear of God is often used in the context of the need to respect the spiritual laws and to fear the consequences of their violation. Among the most fundamental of spiritual laws are those with regard to issues of human safety and social order, truth seeking, truthfulness, and trustworthiness; love, unity, and unity-building; and compassion, service, fairness, and justice. The following statements refer to the wisdom of and need for fear of God and its relationship to specific spiritual laws.

FEAR OF GOD AND HUMAN SECURITY AND TRANQUILITY

In formulating the principles and laws a part hath been devoted to penalties which form an effective instrument for the security and protection of men. However, dread of the penalties maketh people desist only outwardly from committing vile and contemptible deeds, while that which guardeth and restraineth man both outwardly and inwardly hath been and still is the fear of God. It is man's true protector and his spiritual guardian.[39]

The fear of God hath ever been a sure defence and a safe stronghold for all the peoples of the world. It is the chief cause of the protection of mankind, and the supreme instrument for its preservation.[40]

In truth, religion is a radiant light and an impregnable stronghold for the protection and welfare of the peoples of the world, for the fear of God impelleth man to hold fast to that which is good, and shun all evil. Should the lamp of religion be obscured, chaos and confusion will ensue, and the lights of fairness and justice, of tranquility and peace cease to shine.[41]

FEAR OF GOD AND GOOD DEEDS

Walk ye in the fear of God, and be ye of them that lead a godly life.[42]

We exhort you to fear God, to perform praiseworthy deeds and to do that which is meet and seemly and serveth to exalt your station.[43]

Fear ye God, and take heed not to outstrip the bounds of moderation, and be numbered among the extravagant.[44]

We have admonished Our loved ones to fear God, a fear which is the fountainhead of all goodly deeds and virtues.[45]

...fear God, and be not of the prideful.[46]

...lay not aside the fear of God and be not of the negligent.[47]

His Holiness Jesus Christ was an educator of humanity. His teachings were altruistic; his bestowal universal....Galen, the Greek physician and philosopher, who lived in the second century A.D., wrote a treatise upon the civilization of nations. He was not a Christian but he has borne testimony that religious beliefs exercise an extraordinary effect upon the problems of civilization. In substance he says, here are certain people among us, followers of Jesus the Nazarene who was killed in Jerusalem. These people are truly imbued with moral principles which are the envy of philosophers. They believe in God and fear Him. They have hopes in His favors, therefore they shun all unworthy deeds and actions and incline to praiseworthy ethics and morals....[48]

Fear of God and Trustworthiness and Truthfulness

Adorn your heads with the garlands of trustworthiness and fidelity, your hearts with the attire of the Fear of God, your tongues with absolute truthfulness, your bodies with the vesture of courtesy.[49]

Fear of God and Unity

Fear ye God and sow not the seeds of dissension amongst men.[50]

Fear God, and join not with the aggressor.[51]

Fear of God and Justice

Fear God, O people, and be not of them that act unjustly.[52]

The essence of wisdom is the fear of God, the dread of His scourge and punishment, and the apprehension of His justice and decree.[53]

O Rulers of America and the Presidents of the Republics therein,… Adorn ye the temple of dominion with the ornament of justice and of the fear of God,….[54]

Fear God, and be of them that judge equitably.[55]

Love of God and Fear of God

Let them strive by day and by night to establish within their children faith and certitude, the fear of God, the love of the Beloved of the worlds, and all good qualities and traits.[56]

Train these children with divine exhortations. From their childhood instill in their hearts the love of God so they may manifest in their lives the fear of God and have confidence in the bestowals of God.[57]

Other attributes of perfection are to fear God, to love God by loving His servants, to exercise mildness and forbearance and calm, to be sincere, amenable, clement and compassionate; to have resolution and courage, trustworthiness and energy, to strive and struggle, to be generous, loyal, without malice, to have zeal and a sense of honor, to be high-minded and magnanimous, and to have regard for the rights of others. Whoever is lacking in these excellent human qualities is defective.[58]

Of course we should love God—but we must fear Him in the sense of a child fearing the righteous anger and chastisement of a parent; not cringe before Him as before a tyrant, but know His Mercy exceeds His Justice![59]

SUMMARY

In this chapter I have attempted to convey my understanding of some of the Bahá'í perspectives on religion and its role in the contemporary world. I have presented these issues with frequent references to its authoritative texts. I have not attempted to prove the validity of the Bahá'í perspectives. This, I feel is an individual responsibility. To study the Bahá'í Faith, like any other serious subject matter, the seeker needs to employ the scientific method, free from preconceived notions and preferred inclinations. Spiritual matters need to be investigated personally and validated both objectively and subjectively. A person who treads the path of investigation of spiritual truth needs to approach the task by using all three fundamental human faculties of thoughts, feelings, and actions. With these points in mind and in order to bring to focus the main points presented in this chapter, I close with a summary of the principal teachings of the Bahá'í Faith by Shoghi Effendi, the Guardian of Bahá'í Faith:

> The Revelation proclaimed by Bahá'u'lláh, His followers believe, is divine in origin, all-embracing in scope, broad in its outlook, scientific in its method, humanitarian in its principles and dynamic in the influence it exerts on the hearts and minds of men. The mission of the Founder of their Faith, they conceive it to be to proclaim that religious truth is not absolute but relative, that Divine Revelation is continuous and progressive, that the Founders of all past religions, though different in the non-essential aspects of their teachings, "abide in the same Tabernacle, soar in the same heaven, are seated upon the same throne, utter the same speech and proclaim the same Faith." His Cause, they have already demonstrated, stands identified with, and revolves around, the principle of the organic unity of mankind as representing the consummation of the whole process of human evolution. This final stage in this stupendous evolution, they assert, is not only necessary but inevitable, that it is gradually approaching, and that nothing short of the celestial potency with which a divinely ordained Message can claim to be endowed can succeed in establishing it.

> The Bahá'í Faith recognizes the unity of God and of His Prophets, upholds the principle of an unfettered search after truth, condemns all forms of superstition and prejudice, teaches that the fundamental

purpose of religion is to promote concord and harmony, that it must go hand-in-hand with science, and that it constitutes the sole and ultimate basis of a peaceful, an ordered and progressive society. It inculcates the principle of equal opportunity, rights and privileges for both sexes, advocates compulsory education, abolishes extremes of poverty and wealth, exalts work performed in the spirit of service to the rank of worship, recommends the adoption of an auxiliary international language, and provides the necessary agencies for the establishment and safeguarding of a permanent and universal peace.[60]

CHAPTER THREE

THE BAHÁ'Í FAITH
RELIGION RENEWED

In the Palace of Bahjí, or Delight, just outside the Fortress of 'Akká,…there died a few months since,…Bahá'u'lláh—the "Glory of God".…Three years ago he was visited by a Cambridge scholar and gave utterance to sentiments so noble, so Christlike, that we repeat them as our closing words:

"That all nations should become one in faith and all men as brothers; that the bonds of affection and unity between the sons of men should be strengthened; that diversity of religions should cease and differences of race be annulled. What harm is there in this? Yet so it shall be. These fruitless strifes, these ruinous wars shall pass away, and the 'Most Great Peace' shall come. Do not you in Europe need this also? Let not a man glory in this, that he loves his country; let him rather glory in this, that he loves his kind."[1]

—Dr. Henry H. Jessup, D.D., World Parliament of Religion, Chicago, 1893
The first public reference to Bahá'u'lláh in the Western Hemisphere

…Bahá'u'lláh's teaching…now present us with the highest and purest form of religious teachings.[2]

—Leo Tolstoy, 1908

If ever the name of Bahá'u'lláh or 'Abdu'l-Bahá comes to your attention, do not put their writings from you. Search out their Books, and let their glorious, peace-bringing, love-creating words and lessons sink into your hearts as they have into mine. One's busy day may seem too full for religion. Or one may have a religion that satisfies. But the teachings of these gentle, wise, and kindly men are compatible with all religion, and no religion. Seek them, and be the happier.[3]

—Dowager Queen Marie of Romania, 1926

I have had on my desk, and have read several times, the three extracts from 'Abdu'l-Bahá's Message of Social Regeneration. Taken together, they form an unanswerable argument and plea for the only way that the world can be made over. If we could put into effect this program, we should indeed have a new world order.

"The morals of humanity must undergo change. New remedy and solution for human problems must be adopted. Human intellects themselves must change and be subject to the universal reformation." In these three sentences we really have it all.[4]

—Herbert Adams Gibbons, American historian, 1934

I am...of the opinion...that the Bahá'í Movement can form the best basis for international goodwill, and that Bahá'u'lláh Himself is the Creator of an eternal bond between the East and the West....The Bahá'í Teaching is a living religion, a living philosophy....in the Bahá'í Faith one sees the continued progress of religion.[5]

—Vincenc Lesný, Polish Oriental Scholar (1882–1953)

The Bahá'í Cause is one of the great moral and social forces in all the world today. I am more convinced than ever, with the increasing moral and political crises in the world, we must have greater international co-ordination. Such a movement as the Bahá'í Cause which paves the way for universal organization of peace is necessary.[6]

—President Eduard Benes of Czechoslovakia (1884–1948)

I have faith in the Bahá'í Religion because it is the essence of all religions and the basis of it is that it accepts all races on an equal basis.[7]

—Z.T. Ing, Chinese Consul in Nicaragua, 1942

Bahá'u'lláh's sublime mission was to recover the unity of mankind through God....Thus, there is no wonder that the Bahá'í Movement is bound to sweep the most enlightened strata of society in every country.[8]

—Chikao Fujisawa, Kyushu Imperial University, 1932

'Abdu'l-Bahá will surely unite the East and the West: for He treads the mystic way with practical feet.[9]

—David Starr Jordan, Former President of Stanford University (1851–1931)

The philosophy of Bahá'u'lláh deserves the best thought we can give it.... What nobler theme than the "good of the world and the happiness of the nations" can occupy our lives? The message of universal peace will surely prevail. It is useless to combine or conspire against an idea which has in its potency to create a new earth and a new heaven and to quicken human beings with a holy passion of service.[10]

—Helen Keller (1880–1968)

BIRTH OF A PEACEFUL RELIGION IN A HOSTILE LAND

The Bahá'í Faith is the most recent of the "revealed" or "classical" religions. It started in Persia (now Iran) in 1844. Nineteenth-century Persia was a fanatical, cruel, corrupt, and oppressive society. The country comprised Muslims, who were the dominant majority, and three small religious minorities—Zoroastrians (the original religion of Persia), Jews, and Christians. The condition of these religious minorities, particularly that of the Jews and Zoroastrians, was indeed lamentable. The Jewish traveler J.J. Benjamin visited Iran in the mid-19th century and recounted, among other things, the following observations on how the Persian Jews were then treated:

> The Jews were obliged to live in separate locations from Muslims in each city because they were considered to be "unclean creatures". For the same reason, they were forbidden to go out when it rained, so that they would not sully the Muslims. When a Jew entered a shop to buy anything, he was forbidden to inspect the goods and if he, inadvertently touched the goods, he was obliged to buy them at a cost determined by the shop owner. If a Muslim killed a Jew there will be no punishment unless the family of the deceased was able to bring forward two "Mussulmans" as witnesses.—The murderer then was punished by a fine of 12 tumauns [a nominal sum].[11]

The treatment of the Zoroastrians was almost identical to that of the Jews:

> The community was regarded as outcast, impure and untouchable. Various methods were used to convert them to Islam. According to a law, if any member of family converted to Islam, he/she was entitled to all inheritance. This was a materialistic incentive to proselytize the minorities. According to Edward Browne, the walls of Zoroastrian houses had to be lower than that of the Moslems. If they were riding a donkey, upon facing a Moslem had to dismount and during the rainy days they were not allowed to appear in public, because the water that had run down through their bodies and cloths could pollute the Moslems. The Zoroastrian food was considered impure and many public places refused to serve them. Harassments and persecution were the norms of daily life. At times, Zoroastrian girls were kidnapped and forcefully converted and married to Moslems and brought to town in fanfare.[12]

The Bahá'í Faith emerged in such a milieu. The central teachings of the new religion were that there is only one God, one race of humanity, and one religion of God, which is progressively renewed. The Bahá'í Faith annulled the "law of the sword," validated all religions of the past and called for an all-embracing unity: unity of religion, of science and religion, of humanity in the context of diversity, and of men and women in the context of equality. Its aim was to establish world peace. Notwithstanding these teachings, which were practiced by its followers in a remarkably faithful manner, the new religion became the target of barbaric and cruel treatment, which still continues. Since 1844, many thousands of the followers of this new religion have been killed, tens of thousands of them have been subjected to unspeakable inhuman cruelties, and innumerable families have lost their livelihood and been deprived of elementary living needs, their children denied the opportunity to attend school, and every member of their persecuted community denied all basic human rights.[13] Here is a brief account of these persecutions:

> Throughout the history of the Faith, the Bahá'ís of Iran have been persecuted. In the mid-1800s, some 20,000 followers were killed by the authorities or by mobs, who viewed the infant movement as heretical to Islam....

> In the twentieth century, periodic outbreaks of violence were directed against Bahá'ís in Iran, and the government often used Bahá'ís as a scapegoat. In 1933, for example, Bahá'í literature was banned, Bahá'í marriages were not recognized, and Bahá'ís in public service were demoted or fired. In 1955, the government oversaw the demolition of the Bahá'í national center in Tehran with pickaxes.

> Bahá'ís understand this pattern of persecution as a manifestation of the misunderstanding and fear that often occur when a new religion emerges from the matrix of a well-established orthodoxy. The pattern has been repeated through the ages; indeed, virtually all of the world's great religions have faced intense persecution in their early history.

> In 1979, with the establishment of an Islamic Republic, the persecutions took a new direction, becoming an official government policy and being pursued in a systematic way. Since that year, more than 200 Bahá'ís have been executed or killed, hundreds more have been imprisoned, and tens of thousands have been deprived of jobs, pensions, businesses, and educational opportunities. All national Bahá'í administrative structures were banned by the government, and holy places, shrines, and cemeteries were confiscated, vandalized, or destroyed.

The 350,000-member Bahá'í community comprises the largest religious minority in that country, and Bahá'ís have been oppressed solely because of religious hatred. Islamic fundamentalists in Iran and elsewhere have long viewed the Bahá'í Faith as a threat to Islam, branding Bahá'ís as heretics and apostates. The progressive position of the Faith on women's rights, independent investigation of truth, and education has particularly rankled Muslim clerics.

In June 1983, for example, the Iranian authorities arrested [and later executed] ten Bahá'í women and girls. The charge against them: teaching children's classes on the Bahá'í Faith—the equivalent of Sunday school in the West.[14]

These atrocities against the Bahá'ís of Iran are ongoing. Here are more recent examples of ongoing persecution of Bahá'ís in Iran:

GENEVA—29 January 2008 (Bahá'í World News Service)—In the wake of a US State Department call for Iran to release Bahá'í prisoners, Amnesty International has issued an "urgent action" appeal on their behalf. The three prisoners were taken into custody in Shiraz, Iran, last November and are serving a four-year sentence on charges connected entirely with their belief and practice in the Bahá'í Faith. "We urge the regime to release all individuals held without due process and a fair trial, including the three young Bahá'í teachers being held in a Ministry of Intelligence detention center in Shiraz," said Sean McCormack, a spokesman for the State Department on 23 January 2008. Amnesty International issued its appeal on 25 January. It calls for human rights activists around the world to write directly to Iranian government officials on behalf of the Bahá'í prisoners, asking why they have been detained and calling on authorities not to ill-treat or torture them. "Haleh Rouhi Jahromi, Raha Sabet Sarvestani and Sasan Taqva, all Bahá'ís (a religious minority), have been detained by the Ministry of Intelligence in Shiraz since 19 November 2007," states the appeal, which was posted on Amnesty International's Web site on 25 January 2008....[15]

Ethan Bronner, in his October 29, 2008 piece in the *New York Times* entitled, "With Raids and Arrests, Iran Signals New Effort to Suppress Bahais," reported on the continuing harassment and persecution of Bahá'ís. The article in part stated:

One day in late September, Iranian security officials fanned out across their country and raided some 500 homes and several office buildings owned or rented by members of the Bahai faith, confiscating material and arresting dozens of people. This was hardly the first time that Bahais, Iran's largest religious minority, felt the sting of attention from the Shiite Muslim government. As in the past, the United States condemned the action. But what happened Sept. 29 was remarkable because it brought to an abrupt end an elaborate act of communal self-preservation. The materials confiscated were neither political nor religious, and the people arrested were not fighters or organizers. They were lecturers in subjects like accounting and dentistry; the materials seized were textbooks and laboratory equipment. The enterprise that was shut down was a stealth university, with nearly 1,000 students, scores of volunteer faculty members, basements converted to biology and language laboratories and a network of couriers, foreign advisers and sympathizers....The Iranian government has said nothing about the operation and has not responded to requests for comment. The Bahai faith, whose adherents number 300,000 in Iran and 5 million worldwide, began a century and a half ago in Iran. Among its central principles are full equality between the sexes, universal education and the establishment of a world federal system. In July a Bahai was hanged on charges of having converted a Muslim, the first execution of a Bahai in Iran since 1992. Two other Bahais have been condemned to death.

The Bahá'í Faith in the
Context of World Religions

Interested students of religion, once they embark on study of the Bahá'í Faith, soon discover some fundamental similarities and extremely important distinctions that exist between this new religion and the established older religions. The similarities are many, particularly when the original teachings of these religions are compared. The differences are also considerable, because of two main reasons: the progressive nature of religion—described in chapter two—and the historical and contemporary misunderstanding, misapplication, and misuse of religion by many religious leaders and their followers. The leaders and scholars of various religions have viewed the Bahá'í Faith variably, ranging from interest and curiosity to indifference and hostility. In Iran, where the Bahá'í Faith emerged, and in many other Muslim societies the Bahá'í Faith is perceived with deep hostility. One of the main reasons that the Muslims so vehemently reject the Bahá'í Faith is their belief that Islam is the last revelation from God to humanity and that the Prophet Muhammad was the "Seal of the Prophets," which they interpret to mean that Muhammad is the last Messenger of God to humanity for all time. According to these views, humanity now awaits the coming of the end of the world. In this regard, it is important to note that the followers of other religions, including Buddhism, Christianity, Judaism, Hinduism, and Zoroastrianism, also hold similar beliefs.[16] In the context of these apocalyptic expectations, it is not surprising that the Bahá'í Faith is treated with extreme hostility in many Muslim societies. Furthermore, the fact that the institution of priesthood is abolished in the Bahá'í Faith places many religious leaders in an awkward position. It is extremely hard for the Muslim clergy and, for that matter the leaders of all other religions, to accept the view that a new religion has come, that their reign of ecclesiastical authority and power has ended, and that the spiritual teachings of this new religion at once affirm, further advance, and in some cases abrogate their long-held beliefs and practices. All these issues are a direct challenge to the authority of the established patterns of religious leadership.

Furthermore, the fact the Bahá'í Faith emerged in the matrix of an Islamic society has contributed to the tendency of many to consider the Bahá'í Faith as a sect of Islam, which it is not. One may compare the relationship between Islam and the Bahá'í Faith to that of Judaism and Christianity. In the same manner that Christianity emerged from a Judaic society but is a separate religion from Judaism, likewise, the Bahá'í Faith is an independent religion from Islam, even though it appeared in an Islamic milieu. The Bahá'í Faith poses another challenge to the established religions in the sense that it accepts the validity of all revealed religions, sees a fundamental unity across them, and aims to create unity among them. This approach is at variance with the long history of rivalry, suspicion, antagonism, and violence that has existed, and still exists, between and within the established religions of the past. And because of this troubled history of interreligious suspicion and hostility, the tendency for these religions is to approach the Bahá'í Faith either in the same manner—competition and antagonism, if the Bahá'í Faith is perceived to be a threat; or with indifference and a superficial attitude, as long as it remains small and unthreatening.

PERSONAL ENCOUNTER WITH THE BAHÁ'Í FAITH

It was in the context of this history of oppression, cruelty, and danger that my parents joined the Bahá'í Faith. This decision dramatically changed our family life. My mother was the only member of her very large extended family who became a Bahá'í. In doing so, she was largely rejected by them. Although her siblings and parents kept some contact with us, they were very uncomfortable. At the beginning, they even avoided eating anything at our house, as we were perceived to be "unclean." Over the years I observed my parents sail through the many storms of life with a profound degree of calmness, certitude, understanding, and kindness, and their example made all the other difficulties we faced easier to handle.

Nevertheless, my parents' decision to become Bahá'ís put me in a very conflicted context. On the one hand, my deep love and respect for them inclined me towards their choice. On the other hand, my intense and extreme youthful sentiments regarding God, religion, and life were profoundly affected by the strong influence of the prevailing sentiments of the dominant society. When I was about ten years old, we moved from the small town of Ardekan to the city of Yazd, an ancient city, known as "the second ancient and historic city in the world" and a centre of Zoroastrian culture. The city of Yazd is first mentioned in historic records dating back to circa 3,000 BC. At that time it was called Ysatis and was a part of the domain of the Medes, ancient settlers of Persia. Yazd now has an estimated population of 700,000 people. However, when I lived there, the total population was only about 70,000. Surrounded by desert, Yazd is an architecturally unique city.[17]

From the earliest days of my life, I had a complicated and paradoxical relationship with religion. Being born and reared in an extremely religious and superstitious community and continuously confronted with God-decreed promises, threats, rewards, and punishments, I was deeply aware of the powerful role that religion plays in our lives. Every aspect of life—birth and death, marriage and family, success and failure, wealth and poverty, health and illness, etc.—was understood and approached according to religion. Although the majority of people in the two communities—Ardekan and Yazd—I lived in during my childhood until mid-adolescence were Muslims, they were not homogenous societies by any means. This was particularly true about the social make-up of the city of Yazd, where there were also several significant minority groups: Bahá'ís, Jews, Zoroastrians, and a very small number of Christians, most of whom were missionaries from the West. However, these diverse faith groups, with the exception of the Bahá'ís, were almost always structured within the boundaries of homogenous (same-faith groups) neighborhoods. Occasionally, there were a few members of a given faith who lived in other communities. And in very rare cases, there were families in which the husband and wife were of a different religion. Members of each religious group, almost always married individuals from the same religion. However, the Bahá'ís were quite different. The Bahá'í Faith, with its universal and inclusive teachings, attracted individuals from all religious groups. Thus in the Bahá'í community of my small town, there were Bahá'ís who were themselves or whose parents and grandparents were of Muslim or Zoroastrian or Jewish backgrounds, and many of them intermarried. Because of this high level of diversity, Bahá'í families were scattered throughout the city and lived in any of the primarily Muslim or Jewish or Zoroastrian neighborhoods. Bahá'ís did not have an exclusive neighborhood of their own. They belonged to everywhere and nowhere.

I attended a Zoroastrian primary school and then a high school with students from all backgrounds. During those formative years, I had an insatiable love of reading. However, several factors dramatically limited my access to books. Among these were lack of access to a public library and scarce funds to buy books. The only books available in our home were the original scriptures of the Bahá'í Faith, the Old and New Testament, the Quran, the Avesta[18]—the holy book of the Zoroastrian religion—several commentaries and comparative studies dealing with a wide range of issues including Christianity, Judaism, Islam, and the Bahá'í Faith; Marxism; a few of the classics by the Greek philosophers such as Plato and Socrates; several books of poetry by outstanding Persian Poets—Hafiz,[19] Rumi,[20] Saadi,[21] among them—and a few history and adventure books, which inflamed my youthful imagination. Therefore, it is safe to say that between the ages of 11 and 14, I was primarily immersed in reading the Bahá'í literature, aside from my school studies, which were very systematic and demanding, using the rote method. Greatly inspired by these readings, highly influenced by the example and pattern of my parents' life, and adversely affected by the almost daily acts of bullying and violence by classmates for my belonging to a Bahá'í family, at the age of fourteen and a half I chose to become a Bahá'í and joined the membership of the Bahá'í Community. My two siblings—Ali and Kamal—who were respectively 18 and 36 months younger than I—were easily able to integrate in the Bahá'í community of Yazd, and my other four siblings who were much younger had their own unique and diverse experiences in the context of a rapidly changing society.

At age sixteen I entered Shiraz Medical School and after one year of study there transferred to Isfahan Medical School, where I, along with my brothers Ali and Kamal, continued our studies and were later joined by the rest of our family. Following seven years of medical school training, including one year of residency in internal medicine, I left for the United States to specialize. I have already recounted some of my experiences in medical school and as a practicing psychiatrist in my book *The Psychology of Spirituality* (1994, 1997).[22] However, that book did not touch on the issue of religious affiliation and conversion, which was also a major aspect of my intellectual, emotional, social, and spiritual inquiry. Here I will share some reflections on these subjects, which are particularly relevant to the focus of this chapter.

Questioning Religion and Religious Conversion

In 1963 I began my specialization training in psychiatry at the Illinois State Psychiatric Institute in Chicago (an affiliate of the Department of Psychiatry, University of Illinois at Chicago). Training in psychiatry is an enlightening yet sobering experience. It opens new vistas of self-discovery. It provides opportunities to refine and sensitize one's mode of relating with others. It sheds light on some of the most perplexing questions of life—its purpose, process, beginning, and end. It introduces doubt and uncertainty about one's previously held views and perspectives. In the end, psychiatry can be an excellent channel for self-knowledge or a blind alley to self-delusion. Psychology is not a precise science. It is an amalgamation of several schools of thought about human nature in all its complex expressions. Some of these schools of psychology have produced their own literature regarding the psychology of religion with heterogeneous and often contradictory conclusions. Among the issues that I carefully studied were the psychology of religion and religious conversion. In the process I learned that almost all the major schools of psychology at that time viewed religion as a psychological deficiency and handicap at best and a psychological sickness—insanity—at worst. In the 1960s in the United States, psychoanalytic concepts, particularly those of Sigmund Freud,[23] constituted a major component of most psychiatric training curricula and were often used as defining criteria for determining human psychological health and illness and for choosing the treatment method. In my training I also received some introduction to the analytical schools of Carl Jung and Alfred Adler, as well as the newly emerging disciplines of group therapy, family therapy, community psychiatry, and biological psychiatry.

During most of the 20th century, Freud's views on religion along with those of Marx and Darwin, respectively the three giants of psychology, political philosophy, and biology, provided the framework within which scholars formulated their views, researchers conducted their research, leaders chose their approach to governance, the media promoted new lifestyles, and the general population justified their actions with regard to most issues, including those about religion. So, my psychiatric residency introduced me to powerful arguments by these and some other leading minds of the 19th and 20th centuries that ridiculed religion, denied the existence of God, understood human morality within the context of instinctual drives and selfish objectives, and profaned the sacred and the divine. As an example, Freud in his *New Introductory Lessons on Psychoanalysis,* states, "Religion is an attempt to master the sensory world in which we are situated by means of the wishful world which we have developed within us as a result of biological and psychological necessities."[24] In many of his writings, Freud is much more direct, describing religion as a *neurosis* and an *illusion.*

The attitude of Marx towards religion was likewise quite negative, and in the 1960s and '70s Marxist philosophy greatly influenced the thinking of many university departments of psychology, sociology, and political science among others. In February 1844, *Deutsch-Französische Jahrbucher,* printed several statements from *Introduction to a Contribution to the Critique of Hegel's Philosophy of Right* by Karl Marx, including this probing and ambivalent comment:

> Religious suffering is, at one and the same time, the expression of real suffering and a protest against real suffering. Religion is the sigh of the oppressed creature, the heart of a heartless world, and the soul of soulless conditions. *It is the opium of the people.* The abolition of religion as the illusory happiness of the people is the demand for their real happiness. To call on them to give up their illusions about their condition is to call on them to give up a condition that requires illusions.[25] (Italics added.)

Marx sees religion as the necessary tool in a world burdened with misery and injustice and considers its abolition impossible unless the misery is ended and rule of justice is established. Although Marxism in theory aimed to end injustice and misery of the masses, in practice in the course of seven decades it proved its inability to do so in its main bastion, the USSR. And China, the other major communist country, eventually adopted a capitalistic approach to its economic woes with considerable success.

Darwin, the other giant in this trio, arguably the most outstanding and, in the long term, the most influential of them, also had some fundamental and understandable misgivings about religion, God, and immortality. Although contemporary evolution scientists are doing their utmost to depict Darwin's views on religion and science as clearly defined and absolutely clear, nevertheless, Darwin's own writings and correspondence, provide convincing evidence that he was, in fact, quite perplexed and troubled about religion. In his autobiography we come across these struggling reflections about Christianity and God:

> During these two years [1836–1839] I was led to think much about religion. Whilst on board the *Beagle* I was quite orthodox, and I remember being heartily laughed at by several of the officers (though themselves orthodox) for quoting the Bible as an unanswerable authority on some point of morality....

> By further reflecting that the clearest evidence would be requisite to make any sane man believe in the miracles by which Christianity is supported,...I gradually came to disbelieve in Christianity as a divine revelation....

> Another source of conviction in the existence of God...follows from the extreme difficulty or rather impossibility of conceiving this immense and wonderful universe, including man with his capability of looking far backwards and far into futurity, as the result of blind chance or necessity. When thus reflecting I feel compelled to look at a first cause having an intelligent mind in some degree analogous to that of man; and I deserve to be called a theist. This conclusion was strong in my mind about the time, as far I can remember, when I wrote the *Origin of Species*; and it is since that time that it has very gradually with many fluctuations become weaker. But then arises the doubt—can the mind of man, which has, as I fully believe, been developed from a mind as low as that possessed by the lowest animal, be trusted when it draws such a grand conclusions? May not these be the result of the connection between cause and effect which strikes us as a necessary one, but probably depends merely on inherited experience?....

> I cannot pretend to throw the least light on such abstruse problems. The mystery of the beginning of all things is insoluble to us; and I for one must be content to remain an Agnostic....[26]

Darwin's attitude towards science was also burdened and anguished. In a letter to Sir J.D. Hooker, dated June 17, 1868, Darwin writes:

> I am glad you were at the *Messiah*, it is the one thing the I should like to hear again, but I dare say I should find my soul too dried up to appreciate it as in old days; and then I should feel very flat, for it is a horrid bore to feel as I constantly do, that I am a withered

leaf for every subject except Science. It sometimes makes me hate Science, though God knows I ought to be thankful for such a perennial interest, which makes me forget for some hours every day my accursed stomach.[27]

During those decades—1960s to the present—the issue of religious conversion was also under careful scrutiny. The literature in the sociology and psychology of religious conversion in those decades was not reassuring. One common view held that there was something fundamentally wrong with those who were religious, in general, and those who converted to a religion, in particular. This literature spoke of the "psychopathology" of interest in religion indicating a profound degree of deficiency in these persons. The notions that religion was a *crutch*, an indicator of *character weakness,* and an *illogical and irrational* belief system were widely held and still are.[28] Other studies concluded that some types of religious (cult) conversions were processes akin to the *brainwashing* or *mind control* practices found in Stalinist purge activities and resocialization attempts in China after the communist take-over.[29] And still other research pointed to the idea that those who convert to a religion are *passive* and *impressionable* individuals, particularly youth, who fall under the spell of charismatic religious leaders who have learned their skills of brainwashing and thought control from malevolent actors such as those under Stalin and Mao.[30] Although these views have been refuted to a very significant degree by research since then, they were strongly held and generally accepted perspectives on religion and religious conversion.[31] And the misgivings and misunderstandings about religion continue to this date.

SELF-QUESTIONING

It was within this atmosphere that I began to review my decision to become a Bahá'í, barely a decade earlier. I wondered whether the naïveté, emotionalism, and idealism along with suggestibility, impressionability, and insecurity that often characterize the period of early adolescence had somehow unduly affected my judgment and whether there was some fundamental defect in me as a person or in my understanding of my religion. In this process of questioning I decided to focus on the fundamental roles that religion plays in shaping our *worldview*—our view of reality, human nature, the purpose of life, and the nature of relationships. (See chapter one.)

I wanted to know how the Bahá'í Faith had affected my understanding of reality. Had it helped to shape my view of the human nature and my thinking about the inner essence of human reality? Are we fundamentally selfish and greedy beings, as many argue we are? Are we inherently aggressive and conflicted? Are we slaves to our instinctual and biological forces? Are we fundamentally flawed and sinful? Are we bad? What are we, and why are we? These perspectives that were rampant in the psychological and sociological literature were at complete odds with the teachings of the Bahá'í Faith about the nature of human reality and the purpose of human life.

The Bahá'í Faith teaches that human reality is noble and pure; that human biological and spiritual processes are complementary and not contradictory; that the purpose of life is to nurture and facilitate the process of efflorescence of human nobility and goodness; that love is an inherent and transcendent human quality that offsets human primitive tendencies towards selfishness, greed, and cruelty; that conflict and violence are symptoms of the disease of disunity; and that wholesome and universal education—scientific and spiritual—is the most potent tool for the actualization of the enormously rich, creative, and positive human potentials.

Also, I asked myself questions about religion, in general, and the Bahá'í Faith, in particular. I wanted to reconcile, to the extent possible, the three different understandings of religion that were current at that time and are still dominant some fifty years later. These three understandings of religion are: first, the view held by the leaders and followers of various religions—large and small, old and new—that there are many different religions at odds with one another in some fundamental and irreconcilable manner; second the prevailing academic view of religion that attempts to understand religion from the perspective of the current materialistic scientific orientation that by its very nature is incapable of understanding the spiritual dimension of religion, which is in fact its essential quality; and third, the Bahá'í perspective on religion, which defines and approaches religion from a totally new and comprehensive perspective, and which is at once spiritual and scientific, ancient and modern, and personal and universal.

As I tried to more fully investigate my own understanding of religion, in general, and the Bahá'í Faith, in particular, I reached two main conclusions. First, I realized that much of criticism about religion as it is understood and practiced is legitimate and, therefore, the skepticism and hesitation about yet another religion—the Bahá'í Faith—

appearing on the scene is fully understandable. Second, I appreciated the fact that the Bahá'í Faith is somewhat difficult to understand because it is both very similar yet dissimilar to all established religions. It is similar because the Bahá'í Faith, like all other revealed religions, teaches that there is a Creator who has created us, that human reality has both physical and spiritual dimensions, that the purpose of our life is to live a life of moral and ethical conduct, that there are certain religious duties that we should observe, that there is life after death, and that ultimately there is justice and our deeds have consequences. Bahá'í Faith is dissimilar to other religions in the sense that it holds the view that there is only one religion of God, which unfolds gradually and according to the needs of humanity in its ongoing evolution and progress. It understands religion as an evolutionary and progressive process, mystical in its origins, scientific in its method, all-inclusive in its scope, integrative in its perspectives, unity-based in its teachings, and peace-creating in its objectives. The Bahá'í Faith, like Judaism, Christianity, and Islam, makes a clear distinction between "revealed religion" and "human-made belief systems, cults, and ideologies" that are also generally clustered together under the term "religion" according to certain arbitrary and superficial criteria. In this regard, academics and practitioners of religion, particularly those in the disciplines of religious studies, sociology, psychology, anthropology, evolutionary biology, cultural studies, political science, and journalism, are often guilty of careless and uniformed conclusions and generalizations. The current, generally accepted definitions of religion put forward by these academic and scientific disciplines focus on those issues that are secondary aspects of religion. They, by and large, miss the core and fundamental aspects of religion. And this misunderstanding and carelessness has had perilous consequences.

Through this process of questioning, reevaluation, and reflection, I realized that our relationship with religion is not finite and static. In other words, when I chose to tread the path of faith and adopted the Bahá'í Faith as my religious affiliation, my task was not finished, but rather at the moment of choosing, the process had only just begun. By far the majority of people with a religious affiliation have inherited it from their parents and respective communities, and they have hardly ever questioned any aspects of their religious beliefs. And those who either discard their religion or convert to a new religion usually consider their act of conversion the endpoint of their search. However, the Bahá'í Faith demands of us *independent investigation of truth* and calls on the

believers to demonstrate the validity of their faith in *deeds and not words*.
"Let deeds and not words be your adorning"[32] is the standard by which
Bahá'ís must evaluate the quality and effectiveness of their belief. These
requirements—*independent investigation* and *deeds not words*—apply to
all individuals, regardless of whether they are born into Bahá'í families
or encounter the Bahá'í Faith independently. Thus I realized that I had
just embarked on a process of search and understanding and action
that will continue throughout my life and that I would have to be ever
mindful and aware of the process of the expression of faith in all aspects
of my life. This book is a partial reflection of that process that started
more than five and a half decades ago.

In the course of my review of attitudes toward religion that I
described above, it was extremely interesting to me to note that in the
latter half of the 19th century and thereafter two parallel and seemingly
discordant developments were taking place. On the one hand, scientists
and researchers in the newly evolving disciplines of biology, psychology,
sociology, and anthropology and a significant number of philosophers
and statesmen were powerfully challenging the teachings and religious
doctrines of the time, particularly those of Christianity, Islam, and
Judaism. On the other hand, it was equally interesting to note that
these scientific developments coincided with a new Divine Revelation
that clearly and systematically addresses those questions and doubts
that have been raised by modern materialistic science.

The Bahá'í Era began May, 1844, in the city of Shiraz in the
province of Fars, Persia (now Iran), when a young merchant—The
Báb—the forerunner to Bahá'u'lláh, (the Founder of the Bahá'í Faith)
announced the advent of a new Divine Revelation—a world religion—
able to meet the spiritual and social needs of humanity in this new
age.[33] Contemporaneously, Darwin's masterpiece—*On the Origins of
Species by Means of Natural Selection, or the Preservation of Favoured
Races in the Struggle of Life"*—was published on November 22, 1859.
The Communist Manifesto [Manifest der Kommunistischen Partei] by Karl
Marx and edited by Friedrich Engels was first published on February
1848, and a few decades later, Freud's psychoanalytic perspectives were
introduced in a series of books, beginning with *Studies on Hysteria
[Studien über Hysterie]* in 1895, co-authored with Josef Breuer. During
the same decades Friedrich Nietzsche (1844–1900) declared God dead
(*Gott ist tot*).[34]

This new religion soon attracted the attention of the multitudes,
and many individuals in Persia from Islamic, Jewish, and Zoroastrian

faith groups converted to the Bahá'í Faith. Alarmed by the rapid progress of the new religion, the despotic leaders of Persia secured the agreement of the Ottoman leaders for the exile of Bahá'u'lláh to their territory. Thus, upon His release from the "Black Pit" prison of Teheran, Bahá'u'lláh, along with the members of His family and some prominent Bahá'ís, was banished from His native land, beginning forty years of exile, imprisonment, and persecution. The exiles first lived for 11 years (1853–1863) in Baghdad (now the capital of Iraq), then for four months in Constantinople (Istanbul) and five years (1863–1868) in Adrianople (now both parts of Turkey), and eventually (1868–1992) in the prison-city of 'Akká (now a part of Israel).[35]

In the spring of 1890, Edward Granville Browne, the eminent orientalist traveled to 'Akká to visit Bahá'u'lláh. In the course of this interview, Bahá'u'lláh pointed out the main objectives of this new Revelation—the Bahá'í Faith. Here is how Brown describes his meeting:

> The face of him on whom I gazed I can never forget, though I cannot describe it. Those piercing eyes seemed to read one's very soul; power and authority sat on that ample brow; while the deep lines on the forehead and face implied an age which the jet-black hair and beard flowing down in indistinguishable luxuriance almost to the waist seemed to belie. No need to ask in whose presence I stood, as I bowed myself before one who is the object of a devotion and love which kings might envy and emperors sigh for in vain.

> A mild dignified voice bade me be seated, and then continued: *"Praise be to God that thou hast attained!... Thou hast come to see a prisoner and an exile... We desire but the good of the world and the happiness of the nations; yet they deem us a stirrer up of strife and sedition worthy of bondage and banishment.... That all nations should become one in faith and all men as brothers; that the bonds of affection and unity between the sons of men should be strengthened; that diversity of religion should cease and differences of race be annulled—what harm is there in this?...*

> *Yet so it shall be; these fruitless strifes, these ruinous wars shall pass away, and the 'Most Great Peace' shall come....Do not you in Europe need this also? Is not this that which Christ foretold?... Yet do we see your kings and rulers lavishing their treasures more freely on means for the destruction of the human race than on that which would conduce to the happiness of mankind....*

These strifes and this bloodshed and discord must cease, and all men be as one kindred and one family....Let not a man glory in this, that he loves his country; let him rather glory in this, that he loves his kind...."[36]

In our world today religion does not seem to be acting either for the *"good of the world"* or the *"happiness of the nations."* However, an impartial evaluation demonstrates how these objectives are being put into practice in the highly diverse and thinly spread worldwide Bahá'í Community. In this book I draw heavily from the sacred writings of the Bahá'í Faith; the literature of psychology, sociology, and other related fields; and from my personal experience and research. While the language of science is familiar to scientists and at least somewhat familiar to the general public, the language of the Bahá'í Faith is not generally familiar to most readers. I deliberately chose to include many quotations from the Bahá'í Writings, rather than providing a summary of those ideas in more familiar, reader-friendly language. I chose this approach for two fundamental reasons. First, I am fully aware of my inability to summarize these Writings and provide the essence of their most important contents. The second reason is closely related to the first. There is no clergy in the Bahá'í Faith. This religion calls upon every individual to engage in an independent search for truth about the purpose and the process of life and the nature of human relationship with God. Therefore, the most direct approach is for the readers to study the sacred writings of the Bahá'í Faith in their original form and authorized translations and to familiarize themselves with both their contents and their manner of expression. In other words, to fully understand a given subject, we need to understand its language of expression. In the same way that we need to be familiar with the language of biology, psychology, or mathematics in order to understand their concepts and mode of reasoning, we also need to be familiar with the language of Revelation, in order to understand its contents as fully as possible.

Here is an example of the language of Revelation. In His *Book of Certitude* Bahá'u'lláh describes the necessary approach for understanding the nature of Divine Revelation and the process of preparing oneself to comprehend the dynamics of faith and divine knowledge:

...O my brother, when a true seeker determineth to take the step of search in the path leading to the knowledge of the Ancient of Days, he must, before all else, cleanse and purify his heart, which is the seat of the revelation of the inner mysteries of God, from the obscuring dust of all acquired knowledge, and the allusions of the embodiments of satanic fancy. He must purge his breast, which is the sanctuary of the abiding love of the Beloved, of every defilement, and sanctify his soul from all that pertaineth to water and clay, from all shadowy and ephemeral attachments. He must so cleanse his heart that no remnant of either love or hate may linger therein, lest that love blindly incline him to error, or that hate repel him away from the truth. Even as thou dost witness in this day how most of the people, because of such love and hate, are bereft of the immortal Face, have strayed far from the Embodiments of the divine mysteries, and, shepherdless, are roaming through the wilderness of oblivion and error. That seeker must at all times put his trust in God, must renounce the peoples of the earth, detach himself from the world of dust, and cleave unto Him Who is the Lord of Lords. He must never seek to exalt himself above any one, must wash away from the tablet of his heart every trace of pride and vainglory, must cling unto patience and resignation, observe silence, and refrain from idle talk. For the tongue is a smouldering fire, and excess of speech a deadly poison. Material fire consumeth the body, whereas the fire of the tongue devoureth both heart and soul. The force of the former lasteth but for a time, whilst the effects of the latter endure a century.[37]

SUMMARY

The encounter with the Bahá'í Faith is a multifaceted challenge. Its immediate impact is the realization that we are not dealing with religion in its familiar form. The Bahá'í perspective on religion is unlike any other view of religion. It sees religion to be one and not many, to be progressive and not static, to be rational and not superstitious, to be inclusive and not exclusive, to be freeing and not limiting, to be a source of joy and not sorrow, a cause of humility not guilt, a fountain of honor and not shame, and in harmony with science and not in opposition to it. The Bahá'í Faith provides a new prism through which we can make a sense of our life, to better understand our true noble nature, to choose for our life the goal of contributing to the process of creating a universal and ever-advancing civilization of peace, and to establish relationships based on love, justice, equality, and unity.

These qualities are at variance with the manner in which religion is understood and practiced by different faith groups and conceptualized and analyzed by scientists and academics who study religion within framework of the prevailing materialistic science. Consequently, the Bahá'í Faith since its inception in 1844 has been the target of hostile and/ or indifferent treatment on the part of various religious communities and the shockingly inadequate, inaccurate, and superficial treatment on the part of scholars of religion and researchers.

However, we are at the dawn of a new phase in humanity's relationship with both science and religion. The abuses of science and religion have now reached to the level that they no longer can be tolerated. Humanity continues to be actively interested in religion. The human heart and mind yearns for truth-based enlightenment and unity-based relationships. There is a profound spiritual hunger that could only be satisfied when it partakes of the provisions of both religion and science in their authentic and harmonious condition. This is the task as well as the challenge that beckons every searching and open-minded person who encounters the Bahá'í Faith.

PART TWO

ON LIFE

CHAPTER FOUR

THE NATURE AND PURPOSE OF HUMAN LIFE

Having created the world and all that liveth and moveth therein, He, through the direct operation of His unconstrained and sovereign Will, chose to confer upon man the unique distinction and capacity to know Him and to love Him—a capacity that must needs be regarded as the generating impulse and the primary purpose underlying the whole of creation....Upon the inmost reality of each and every created thing He hath shed the light of one of His names, and made it a recipient of the glory of one of His attributes. Upon the reality of man, however, He hath focused the radiance of all of His names and attributes, and made it a mirror of His own Self. Alone of all created things man hath been singled out for so great a favor, so enduring a bounty.[1]*

—Bahá'u'lláh

Little reflection, little admonition is necessary for us to realize the purpose of our creation. What a heavenly potentiality God has deposited within us! What a power God has given our spirits! He has endowed us with a power to penetrate the realities of things; but we must be self-abnegating, we must have pure spirits, pure intentions, and strive with heart and soul while in the human world to attain everlasting glory.[2]*

—'Abdu'l-Bahá

The Universe we observe has precisely the properties we should expect if there is, at bottom, no design, no purpose, no evil and no good, nothing but blind, pitiless, indifference...DNA neither cares nor knows. DNA just is. And we dance to its music.[3]*

—Richard Dawkins

Which Music Should We Dance to?

Those of us who live in safe environments, are financially secure, have the gift of good health, have a good and useful job, and have loving families and friends, are indeed privileged. We live at a time when large populations of the world are greatly suffering. Disease, poverty, hunger, and violence are eroding the very foundations of life in Africa. War and carnage are rampant in the Middle East, Afghanistan, and parts of Africa; and long-lasting hostilities continue in parts of Asia, Europe, and South America. Conditions of distress and discord are present in practically every corner of the globe. It is indeed a source of both wonder and shame that at the start of the 21st century, science and technology have simultaneously brought the greatest gifts and the most devastating curse to humanity. All modern technologies of war are made possible by advances in science, which, ironically, are used by adherents of various religions. Even more ironic, is that these religions, in their pure forms, are based on the fundamental principles of love, kindness, peace, and grace. These abuses of science and religion have made thoughtful people everywhere skeptical, even hostile, about both.

While one may fully agree with the principal teachings of the Bahá'í Faith regarding issues of *oneness of humanity* and *unity in diversity,* we cannot but wonder how these teachings could possibly counter the current destructive paroxysms of violence that seem to continuously erupt in different parts of the world. Generally speaking, peoples everywhere primarily look for two things: health and happiness, neither of which is possible in conditions of conflict, violence, and war that are the main causes of poverty, grief, and destruction in the world. We, legitimately, can ask the question: How would the Bahá'í Faith address these issues? What would the shape of a future Bahá'í society be? What would be the focus, character, and quality of life informed and influenced by the teachings of the Bahá'u'lláh? These important, challenging questions will be broadly addressed in the remaining chapters. In this chapter, some Bahá'í perspectives on the all-important issue of the nature and purpose of human life are presented. The main reason for this specific focus is that, in my opinion, the Bahá'í Faith provides a comprehensive and positive framework within which the insights of religion and the discoveries of modern science can be fully integrated and applied to all aspects of life, including how we understand human nature, how we approach life challenges and opportunities, and what kind of families and societies—and by that matter what kind of a world—we create.

UNEXPECTED QUESTIONS

During one of my travels to the USSR in 1991 I visited the Karl Marx Psychiatric Hospital in Leningrad (now St. Petersburg). After the tour of the facilities, we had a meeting with the hospital's director, one of his senior staff, a young psychologist, and a gentleman who was introduced as a "philosopher" and who, in fact, was the representative of the Communist Party to ensure the ideological purity of the hospital and its staff. The Party wanted to make sure that the employees of various institutions would not become contaminated with foreign concepts and ideas. In those years whenever I traveled to either the USSR or China, I encountered these philosophers. However, in my travels only a few years later this practice was eased greatly and eventually, for all practical purposes, it was abandoned.

Earlier, I had met this "philosopher" at my talk at a forum on gender equality at one of the universities in Leningrad, and when I saw him at the meeting, I realized that he had come to my talk in order to familiarize himself with my perspectives and to prepare the hospital staff on how to receive me. And the conclusions he had reached soon became evident. Karl Marx Psychiatric Hospital was located beside an ancient Russian Orthodox Church that was in a lamentable state of disrepair, as was the hospital itself.

As the director and his entourage took me and a friend—Mehrdad Baghai, who was then an undergraduate student at Princeton University—to different parts of the hospital, we passed a corridor overlooking the church. At that moment the director turned to me and said, "And our psychotic patients who believe in ghosts and religions are particularly attracted to this building next door." This comment was followed by several other direct comments attacking religion and belittling those who believed in it. At the conclusion of the tour, we went to the office of the director and had a three-hour discussion that was ended only because the workday had concluded and they had to leave for their homes. This lengthy session had three parts. The first part was an exchange of views about the latest scientific developments in the field of psychiatry, particularly with respect to research on the brain and new chemical agents and medications and their effects on various psychiatric disorders. In a sense, they were testing me to see how informed I was about the scientific developments in our field. The second part of our discussion focused on the state of the psychiatric profession in the USSR, and was not very encouraging.

As we gradually became more engaged in a meaningful discourse and began to develop a degree of mutual trust and respect, and when, finally, the philosopher left because of other commitments, we entered the third phase of our meeting. My Russian colleagues opened their hearts and talked about several issues that were particularly of concern to them. The first issue they raised was why people trust "the nonsensical and the irrational" over "the scientific and the rational." In particular, they reported that there was a charismatic person in Leningrad who claimed that he could cure many illnesses by means of certain herbal remedies as long as he administered them under a specific large and ancient tree in one of the parks in the city. They reported that this person had a large following and was making a mockery of the psychiatrists and psychologists, because many of their patients preferred this man's treatment to that offered by the mental-health professionals. We discussed these issues along the line of what was outlined in chapter one under the section "Believing Falsehood."

Another important issue that they raised was fundamental human needs. They asked my views about this issue, which was extremely sensitive in the USSR at that time and was quite risky to discuss. The fact was that even the basic survival needs of the majority of people in the USSR at that time were not being met, and this was the main cause of much psychological distress and social discontent. During my first trip to the USSR, the two cities I visited—Leningrad and Moscow— were in sad condition with regard to their civic facilities and general maintenance of the roads, buildings, and infrastructure. My impression of these cities was that they, along with their populations, were suffering from neglect in every sense of the word. Both the physical *landscape* and the spiritual *soulscape* were devoid of beauty, refinement, and vitality. Six decades of materialistic Communist rule had not only severely damaged the human habitat but also inflicted deep and debilitating psychological, social, moral, and spiritual wounds on the population as a whole. In my contacts with people and in the course of many discussions with colleagues, students, and newly declared Russian Bahá'ís, I learned, at first hand, that at this time in the former USSR people's fundamental needs for survival and safety were being met only at a very rudimentary and crude level. Long lines for obtaining meager rations of poor-quality food; living in assigned substandard, dingy, ugly, and impossible to clean residences; working in poorly paid, uncreative, and oppressive environments; and being ever watchful of the deeply feared undercover agents, together created living circumstances devoid of some of the most fundamental human needs—safety, food, shelter, good health, freedom of expression, and the opportunity to communicate without fear and oppression.

However, not until that moment when I was asked about my views about the main human needs, had I reflected on this issue in a systematic and meaningful manner. I had always believed that there was a direct relationship between human needs, human rights, and human responsibilities, and I had understood that the three were absolutely essential for the welfare of the people and development of society. Also, personally I have had many occasions in which my personal fundamental needs and rights have been rejected and violated. Nevertheless, until then, I had not gone beyond study of the generally accepted UN charter of rights and other similar declarations. My Russian colleague's question about human needs acted as a catalyst and sharply focused my attention on the importance of this issue. Our meeting had two very different atmospheres: the time spent with the philosopher and the time after he had departed. At first, the atmosphere created by our Russian hosts was marked with mistrust, anxiety, bravado, and attempts to ridicule. But when the philosopher left and the fear of being observed and judged had dissipated, then the important question of human needs was introduced.

I began by describing the most obvious category of human needs— survival needs—and proceeded to outline the other two metacategories of needs as are described below. As I did this, our Russian colleagues said that in the USSR the survival needs of the majority of the people had not yet been satisfied, that the second category of needs were interpreted and applied within the authoritarian and dictatorial mindset, and that the very existence and reality of the third category of needs were denied. Over the years, I have further refined my thinking in this regard. The following is a summary of my formulation of the nature and scope of human needs, rights, and responsibilities, which I shared with my Russian colleagues in its earlier conceptualization.

Human Needs and Human Rights

We humans have three hierarchical metacategories of needs and rights: survival, association, and spiritual. The need for survival we share with animals. *Survival Needs* include issues of food, shelter, safety, and health. The majority of people of the world spend most of their lives in securing their survival needs. The second category, *Association Needs*—need for justice, equality, freedom, democracy, cooperation, and mutual acceptance—is the outward expression of the human capacity to love. In the interpersonal domain, most people limit their relationships to their families and close friends. At the social level, the broadest scope of association that humanity has thus far achieved is in the form of nationalism and various racial, ideological, and religious associations. For most peoples of the world, the idea of *universal association* is still either non-existent or is expressed in a very limited scope, usually within the framework of the survival imperative. The widespread sentiments against nuclear armaments in the latter decades of the 20th century and the current general concerns about the environment are two outstanding examples of the expression of our sense of interconnectedness and association in the context of our personal and collective survival needs. Hence their broad appeal!

The third category of needs—*Spiritual Needs*—is subtler than the other two categories. This category refers to the fundamental human need for meaning and purpose. We humans are at the crossroad of creation. On the one hand, we belong to the material and animal world. Our survival needs are akin to those of animals. Our association needs also find their more primitive expressions among the members of other species. However, meaning and purpose are transcendent in nature and are uniquely human qualities. They are aspects of our spirituality. While we are focused on securing our need for food, shelter, health, and other survival imperatives, and as we endeavor to establish increasingly more just and harmonious living arrangements in our families and communities, we are always aware that our life must have a meaning, a purpose, and an objective beyond the limited, albeit essential, survival and association issues.

The human capacities to know and to discover, to love and to unite, and to become agents of service and justice are at the core of our spiritual reality. They cannot be satisfied through a sense of security obtained by accumulation of wealth, development of power, and imposition of our will over others. It is through cultivation and maturation of our spiritual qualities based on truth, unity, service, and justice that we realize that our survival is intimately bound up with the survival of all other human beings and all other living entities, and that authentic association and all-inclusive love are only possible when we become truly universal in our ways of thinking, feeling, and acting. Another dimension of spirituality is our realization that this life is simply the first stage in our on-going process of growth and development as conscious and self-reflecting beings aware of passage of time and dynamics of change and transformation. This development takes place in the realm of consciousness—the awareness that we exist and that our existence could not become nonexistence.

Spiritual needs simultaneously encompass and transcend all other needs. In other words, spiritual needs determine both the quality of our survival and association needs, and the manner in which we approach them. An example may help to clarify these relationships. Food is essential for survival of all living beings. However, for humans, food has more meaning than only as an item for nurturance and survival. Through food, we express our love, display our creative abilities, demonstrate our hospitality, share in joys and sorrows of others, and even sometimes delay or dramatically decrease our own food consumption in order to feed others and to become more genuinely aware of the suffering of the hungry and starving masses of humanity. These refined approaches to food are only possible when we give equal attention to all three categories of human needs. And when we do so, food becomes a medium through which we could save millions of lives; create joyous occasions of hospitality, friendship, and celebration of life; and eventually create a civilization in which no individual would be without food. It is through this process that we transform the biological act of eating into a most important social and spiritual individual and collective task, and in doing so we render our food sacred. Thus, through the process of spiritualization we transcend our biologically determined survival needs.

Here is another example. Equality—between men and women, among various races, and inclusive of all individuals in the context of a lawful society—is one of the essential rules of human relationships that has thus far eluded humanity. However, when a society begins to operate according to the principle of gender, racial, religious, and social equality, the level of safety for women, minorities, the poor, and the dispossessed will increase dramatically; the quality of relationships among all segments of society will improve considerably; and the spiritual principles of compassion, understanding, cooperation, and unity become norms rather than exceptions, as they are now.

THE PUZZLE OF HAPPINESS

Of all human quests, happiness is one of the most puzzling. Happiness can be neither successfully pursued nor its pursuit effectively ignored. This perplexing character of happiness lies in the fact that happiness is a "state of being" rather than an "object to pursue and to have." We all want to be happy, and when we reflect on our varied experiences of happiness, certain patterns become obvious. Upon reflection we discover that we are truly happy when we are in a state of unity—inner, interpersonal, and societal. We have inner unity—and therefore, inner peace and happiness—when our thoughts, feelings, and actions are in harmony with one another and are in accord with our moral and ethical principles. Interpersonal and societal unities are outward expressions of human love and oneness and, like inner peace, are also potent and plentiful sources of authentic and creative happiness. In essence, happiness is the fruit of unity. Whenever and wherever unity is created, happiness is the outcome.

Interestingly, health (like happiness) is also the outcome of a state of equilibrium, harmony, reciprocity, and cooperation—in brief, unity. The same applies to yet another eternal quest of humanity—peace. When we reflect deeply, we begin to realize that unity, as the main law of existence, is the operating principle in states of happiness, health, peace, and goodness. As such, unity is at once a physical, biological, psychological, social, moral, and spiritual state. And it is in this context that the significance of the statement of Bahá'u'lláh to Edward Granville Browne becomes even more apparent:

> We desire but the good of the world and the happiness of the nations....That all nations should become one in faith and all men as brothers; that the bonds of affection and unity between the sons of men should be strengthened; that diversity of religion should cease and differences of race be annulled—what harm is there in this?...Yet so it shall be; these fruitless strifes, these ruinous wars shall pass away, and the 'Most Great Peace' shall come....[4]

In this statement, Bahá'u'lláh clearly states that the main goal is to create conditions of goodness and happiness for all peoples and all nations. He then directly connects the "good of the world and the happiness of the nations" with the need for unity, for the end of strife and war, and for establishment of a lasting and universal peace—"The Most Great Peace." However, in this brief statement, Bahá'u'lláh delves deeper into these issues and identifies the fundamental prerequisite for world peace to be unity of religion. He states that what is necessary is that all "nations become one in faith." This statement refers to a central theme of the teachings of Bahá'u'lláh—oneness of religion. As discussed in chapter three, the Bahá'í view of religion is based on the concept that religion, like science, is one and that the teachings of religion progress within the framework of progressive revelation of spiritual guidance through appearance of Manifestations of God.

Another implication of this statement of Bahá'u'lláh is that happiness, security, peace, good relationships, and meaning in life are all conditional on spiritual transformation. Neither science nor religion alone is able to bring any of these conditions to humanity, because in isolation they are both open to abuse. In fact, a materialistically oriented humanity is prone to abuse everything. It abuses not only science but also religion, not only love relationships but also love itself, not only the world of nature but also the human world, and not only knowledge but also the truth on which it is based. Bahá'u'lláh, by specifically addressing the issue of religious strife—which is the most consequential abuse of religion—brings to our attention that the most fundamental prerequisite for meeting all human needs is *spiritual transformation*. It is through adoption of a spiritual worldview that we bring transcendent, universal, and lasting meaning and purpose to every aspect of our lives. And spirituality and unity are closely interrelated. In other words, unity is a spiritual condition with physical, biological, psychological, social, economic, political, and ethical expressions. It is rather difficult to reconcile all these varied issues in the context of daily life. For me, the relationship between the seemingly unrelated issues of health, happiness, unity, and spirituality became clearer through a tragic but profoundly meaningful personal experience.[5]

In 1969, my 28-year-old brother Kamal called from Chicago informing me that he was seriously ill. My wife, Michele, and I had moved from Chicago to Vancouver, Canada, only 10 months earlier. During this period our first son, Arman, was born, and life seemed to be proceeding as it ought to be. And then came the devastating news of Kamal's illness. He had an advanced case of stomach cancer with a dire prognosis. He was the third oldest of seven siblings. I was the eldest, and Kamal was three years younger.

In 1965 he came to Chicago, where I had been living since 1963. In the span of five years, Kamal received his undergraduate and graduate degrees with a PhD in metallurgy from the University of Illinois

(Urbana). Six months after his graduation, Kamal was dead. I came from Vancouver in November, 1969, to be with him, arrange for his operation, and do whatever I could to decrease his considerable pain and suffering. Soon after his surgery and with the information that he had only a few months left to live, he decided to return to Iran to be with our parents and siblings. However, in order to undertake such a long and arduous trip he needed a few weeks to recover somewhat from his extremely weak and emaciated state. For this purpose we arranged for all of us to stay in two adjacent suites in an apartment hotel.

The news of Kamal's illness reached his friends soon after his surgery, and a throng of young and old visitors came every day to see him. They came with sorrowful and tearful expressions, dreading seeing a much loved dying young friend. They would enter his room with much trepidation, most would stay for long periods, and many would leave with smiles on their faces and tears in their eyes. *Joy and sorrow embraced!* They all recounted how Kamal was at ease. They found him to be extremely peaceful, reconciled, loving with all his friends, and most assured about his spiritual journey.

Kamal had a brilliant mind and a deep love for God, poetry, beauty, and people. He never competed with others. Instead he pursued excellence in all his endeavors. He was shy and reflective. Above all he was a unifier. All who knew him were attracted to his qualities of humility, trustworthiness, and kindness. They were naturally attracted to him and became his friends without hesitation. When we were saying our last goodbye at the airport, he was a skeleton in a suit with a face that conveyed the seemingly paradoxical and mysterious qualities of unity and inner peace—calm yet anticipatory, sad yet content, physically sick yet spiritually vibrant, intimately near yet already otherworldly. He has remained with me in this peaceful and peace-engendering state for forty years and will be with me in the same manner, always. Whenever I reflect on Kamal's life, I am reminded of this statement of Bahá'u'lláh:

> Know then that "life" hath a twofold meaning. The first pertaineth to the appearance of man in an elemental body....This life cometh to an end with physical death...which is a God-ordained and inescapable reality. That life, however, which is mentioned in the Books of the Prophets and the Chosen Ones of God is the life of knowledge... and his certitude of attaining unto the presence of God through the Manifestations of His Cause. This is that blessed and everlasting life that perisheth not.[6]

Making Sense of the Riddles of Life and Death

Kamal's death was just one among many deaths—timely and untimely, easy and hard, welcomed and abhorred—that I have encountered, at a very intimate level, in my work as a physician, in my extended family, and among my friends. Generally speaking, physicians have a very conflicted relationship with death. Many physicians abhor and fear death and irrationally see it as a failure on their part. In my work as a psychiatrist, I noted that in medical settings the needs of many individuals, particularly children, youth, and their parents, who were facing death, were not adequately met. I therefore dedicated a significant portion of my work to assisting children and adolescents who were facing death in order to decease their fear and anguish, to help them and their family members to go through a healthy process of grief and mourning, and to try to answer some of their most direct and challenging question. Here is how one of my first encounters went:

"Are you going to die?" a five-year-old asked me.
"Yes, but I don't know when," I answered.
"My mom is dying soon," she said.

In dealing with children and adolescents facing death, I soon realized that their questions required answers that were, at once, reassuring, truthful, and meaningful. They needed answers that would help them to make sense of their impending dreadful loss and would sustain them throughout years to come and help them face the other inevitable losses that they would experience. And, when some of these children were themselves dying, they needed to make sense of their own experience both with regard to their short lives and their impending death. And, often they also needed help to deal with their suffering and pain.

Aside from the immediate needs of an individual facing death, in the course of my psychiatric practice, I had noticed that a disproportionate of my clients who came for consultation for a range of issues—depression, marital discord, interpersonal difficulties, anxiety attacks, various phobias, profound sense of despair and pessimism, undue bravado and risk-taking, and general unhappiness with life— were burdened with the psychological pains of earlier significant losses and that, at a deeper level, their presenting symptoms indicated that they had not fully grieved and resolved those losses. They needed to fully mourn their major losses in order to be able to deal with present life challenges.

Based on these observations, when I embarked on the plan to dedicate myself to helping individuals facing loss and death, I realized that many of them would need long-term access to a person readily available to them in times of change and crises. For this five-year-old and her siblings and father, I was available for five years for consultation—on and off—as they requested. This was the case for many whom I had the privilege of counseling. I was engaged in this process on an intensive schedule for the second half of my thirty-year psychiatric practice, a period that I profoundly cherish and in the course of which I learned invaluable lessons from my courageous and insightful clients. I have reported on some of these experiences in my books *The Psychology of Spirituality*[7] and *The Mysterious Case of the IWs*, a forthcoming book for children and their parents and caregivers on better understanding the mystery of death and dealing with its psychological and spiritual challenges.[8] At a more intimate personal level, the issue of my own death and how I would respond to it came from a totally different angle.

A PERILOUS REVOLUTION

When in December 1979, following a period of considerable turmoil, Ayatollah Khomeini became the Supreme Leader of the New Islamic Republic of Iran, a new era in the fortunes of Bahá'ís of Iran and the worldwide Bahá'í Community began. From the start it was evident that under the Islamic Republic the Bahá'ís of Iran—a highly diverse community with more than 300,000 members—would be gravely endangered. This fear was soon replaced by a horrific period of persecution, displacement, imprisonment, torture, indignities, murder, and a systematic program of ethnic cleansing that has lasted for thirty years and is still continuing. During this period, thousands of Bahá'ís—young and old, men and women, rich and poor, educated urbanites and nomadic tribespeople—have lost their jobs and livelihoods, their properties and businesses confiscated, their children and youth denied education, many of them arrested and tortured, more than 200 of them killed in a calculated, barbaric manner. Among these individuals were many of my best friends, classmates in medical school, teachers and mentors, and contemporaries whom I knew closely.

Less than a year after the establishment of the Islamic Republic, on August 21, 1980, my dearest friend, Dr. Heshmatu'llah Rawhani, was arrested along with another colleague and all nine members of the

National Spiritual Assembly of the Bahá'ís of Iran (see chapter eight) and was never heard of again. They are presumed dead. Among the nine was another cherished friend, the erudite and creative Hushang Mahmudi. A month later, on September 8th, three of my most cherished teachers and mentors—Azizu'llah Dhabihiyan, Fraydun Fraidani, and Nuru'llah Akhtarkhavari—along with four other Bahá'ís were executed in my home city of Yazd. On this occasion, at 7:00 am the masked executioners allowed the prisoners to write their wills, then each was tied to a tree and shot. According to the testimony of one of the executioners, the firing was "erratic and excessive." On 30 April 1981, another of my valued mentors—Yadu'llah Vahdat— along with several other Bahá'ís was, imprisoned, tortured, and killed in the city of Shiraz.[9] In his last will he called to mind the poem:

The fire of love is alive
Even when Death arrives;
It is a lamp carried from
This house to the other![10]

In December 1981 eight of the nine members of the second National Spiritual Assembly of the Bahá'ís of Iran (elected after the disappearance of the first Assembly) were arrested, tortured, and killed. Among them was Dr. Izzatu'llah Furuhi, my classmate at the Isfahan Medical School and Dr. Jinus Mahmudi, one of the most distinguished Iranian scientists, whose husband had been killed a year earlier.[11] And the list goes on.

CALL FOR JUSTICE

During this period I was living in Canada, teaching at university, practicing psychiatry, and was a member and chairman of the National Spiritual Assembly of the Bahá'ís of Canada. With such horrendous news coming out of Iran, Bahá'ís all over the world were doing their utmost to assist their coreligionists in Iran. In Canada we asked the government to raise objections to the gross violation of the human rights of the Bahá'ís in Iran. We contacted members of parliament, and we informed the media and many influential persons about these developments. We also embarked on a vast program to settle thousands of Iranian Bahá'í refugees in Canada and many other countries around the globe.[12] Among the refugees were the families of a large number of those Bahá'ís in Iran who, on account of their faith, lost their lives. Included in these was the family of a dear colleague, Dr. Faramarz

Samandari, who was executed in Tabriz on 14 July 1980 and whose family subsequently settled in the United States.[13] A few years later, Faramarz's 10-year-old son shared a tent with my son Roshan at a summer camp. After their return from the camp, I asked Roshan about his friend. I was curious to know how things were with this young child who had lost his father in such tragic circumstances. He said all went well. "Every night, after we settled down in our tent, we talked about the time his father was killed," Roshan said, "and we cried!"

HOW WOULD I HAVE RESPONDED?

These activities on the behalf of persecuted Iranian Bahá'ís were all meritorious. However, I was in a state of profound inner turmoil. A persistent and unrelenting question was ever present in the depths of my soul: How would I have responded? I was fully aware that if I had not left Iran and had instead remained there as so many of my friends, colleagues, and contemporaries did, it was quite likely that I would also have been imprisoned, subjected to torture, and given the choice to either denounce my religion or lose my life. All my friends in Iran and many others have chosen their religion over their life. But what about me? How would I have responded? How would have I mustered the courage and resolve to stay steadfast? How would I have faced death?

At the start of this self-questioning I was filled with an enormous degree of fear, mixed with guilt and relief that I was not there. It took several months to gradually reach some resolution of these powerful and contradictory emotions. First, I had to face my own mortality, a process that was for me, at once, an intellectual, emotional, and spiritual process. Intellectually, I knew that life is the sum-total of chance (where and when we are born), specific events and circumstances we encounter, and the choices we make. In other words, life is a mixture of destiny, chance, and choice. Of these, the only part we have considerable power over is the element of choice. Thus, I concluded that I made a clear and definite choice, some two decades earlier to leave Iran and never to return. As such, that I was in Canada and not Iran was my choice.

At a more experiential and emotional level, I recalled my early experiences in Iran as a Bahá'í. In particular I remembered the calamitous events of 1955–56, several months immediately before I entered medical school. Then I was in the last part of my high school studies in Yazd, when a wave of extreme anti-Bahá'í sentiment took over the whole population of Iran. During the month of Ramadan (month of fasting in the Islamic calendar), a populist preacher by the name of Falsafi, after obtaining the permission of the government authorities in Iran, started an extremely well-organized, high-profile, and insidious anti-Bahá'í program. At the end of his daily sermons, which were broadcast on the national radio station across the country, Falsafi would focus on some aspects of the teachings and history of the Bahá'í Faith, misquoting, misrepresenting, and altering the facts; and then he would begin a rigorous and malicious attack against the main figures of the Bahá'í Faith, its elected and appointed leadership, its rank-and-file membership, and its sacred historic places and administrative centers. These sermons inflamed the minds of people, encouraged mob violence, and coordinated anti-Bahá'í activities along with other clergy in various parts of the country. As a consequence Bahá'í Centers were looted and occupied, Bahá'í cemeteries were desecrated, Bahá'í women were abducted and forced to marry Muslims, and a number of individuals around the country were killed.

At that time, our family lived in a large rented house adjacent to the Yazd Bahá'í Center. The house belonged to a prominent member of the Bahá'í Faith who had been prosecuted and imprisoned on fabricated charges, but in fact solely because of being a member of the Bahá'í Faith. During the long weeks of the month of Ramadan, every day several hundred individuals would congregate in front of our home, which was the closest street to the Bahá'í Center allowed by the police for public demonstration. These individuals would chant anti-Bahá'í refrains, discuss their plans for the occupation of the center, and express their impatience through unsavory behavior. Our father who was a fearless and highly respected individual known by many for his qualities of fairness, friendliness, and joyfulness instructed me and my two younger brothers to continue our high school studies and attend classes every day. Our three sisters, who were all younger and our youngest brother were kept home for safety reasons. The daily school schedule was divided by a two-hour lunch break during which we came home. Falsafi's sermons were broadcast at noontime every day on the loudspeakers throughout the town. Everyone was compelled to listen to it. I would carefully listen to his attacks, identify the sources from which he drew his arguments against the Bahá'í Faith, and bring the original sources to school to show that he had misquoted and misrepresented the facts.

Our class had 32 students. Three of us were Bahá'ís; over half of the students were from very religious Muslim families; and the rest either were children of Zoroastrian families or less religiously minded Muslim ones, who, nevertheless, allied themselves with the more fundamentalist group. This was not surprising, because throughout the history of the Bahá'í Faith since its inception in 1844 in Persia, seldom had Iranian Muslims, regardless of their personal beliefs and views, ever publicly and unreservedly defended the Bahá'í Faith. Only recently, a small but highly distinguished and extremely courageous number of Iranians have raised their voices in the defense of the Bahá'ís. However, the majority of Iranians remain silent. They have much to answer to posterity for their silence with regard to the violation of the human rights of their fellow Bahá'í citizens.

Because Muslims consider Bahá'ís to be "unclean" and therefore "untouchable," in our classroom we three Bahá'í students had been allocated a bench at the back of the room, where we had to sit apart from the rest of the class. Also, every day, as we left our homes for school and returned from it, the throng of the ruffians who were gathered in our street in their anticipation of attack on the Bahá'í Centre, would open a corridor wide enough for me and my brothers to proceed without their being touched by us. In the course of our march through this human corridor of a few hundred meters, we would be spat upon, called unspeakable names, and threatened with a most awful outcome once they received their go-head to attack Bahá'í properties, homes, and individuals. [14]

Everyone was waiting the approach of the 19th and 21st days of Ramadan, and we all expected that the real action would then take place. These days have very important place in the history of Islam, and their importance still plays a major role in the social and political arenas of the Muslim world. A brief review of the early decades of Islam is of value to us to better understand the nature and causes of the ongoing violence between the two major sects of Islam—Shia and Sunni—and between Muslim communities and others.

THE DISEASE OF DISUNITY

In the first decades of Islam—between the death of Prophet Muhammad on CE/AD June 8, 632 and CE/AD October 10, 680—three major events shattered for all time the unity of Islam as a religious community and gave birth to the animosities and conflicts that are still powerfully present in our times. The first of these events took place immediately after the death of the Prophet, when a disagreement over leadership and succession divided the community into two groups. The majority decided to choose a leader based on the interpretation of certain events prior to the death of the Prophet and chose Abu Bakr as the first of the four "rightly guided caliphs" or "Rashidun." Those who favored this approach were the majority of the Muslim community at that time, as they are now (about 85%) and are called Sunnis [followers of the Way of Muhammad]. The Shia [supporters of Ali] believed that before his death the Prophet Muhammad had appointed Ali—his cousin and son-in-law—as his successor and the infallible Imam. So, they did not accept the leadership of Abu Bakr, and this major fissure in Islam took deep root. Then when the third caliph was assassinated, the Muslim Community finally in CE 656 appointed Ali as the fourth caliph. However, the division and conflict continued, and on the 19th of Ramadan 661 Ali was wounded with a strike of a poison-coated sword and died two days later on the 21st of Ramadan in the city of Kufa in today's Iraq. The third episode that forever divided Sunnis and Shia took place when Ali's second son, Imam Husayn (Hossein), the third Imam of the Shia, was killed—along with seventy-two of his family members and followers—and beheaded in the Battle of Karbala in CE 680 (61 AH). This event is considered the most tragic and consequential of all these conflicts. The anniversary of the martyrdom of Imam Husayn, called Ashura, is a period of mourning and is observed by the Shia community everywhere, but particularly with enormous force and vehemence in Iran.[15]

SEVEN BAHÁ'ÍS KILLED

It is in the context of this history of early Islam that the significance of the 19th of Ramadan, as the day to occupy the Bahá'í Center, and on the 21st further extend the occupations and atrocities to the homes and businesses of the people, becomes clear. Thus, we were all waiting for these dreaded days. However, on the 17th of Ramadan the chief of police in Yazd took it upon himself to order all individuals gathered in our street to disperse and threatened to deal with them mercilessly if they acted violently in the upcoming days. Also, another terrible event at that time focused the attention of the mobs elsewhere.

On July 28, 1955, we received the news that seven Bahá'ís in the village of Hurmuzak, in Yazd Province had been killed by an angry mob that hacked their victims with axes and spades. These individuals ranged in age from nineteen to eighty. The younger ones were killed while they were tending to their farm, and the older members were killed in their homes. The proximity of Hurmuzak to Yazd and the fact that we knew all the victims elicited three different reactions. The members of the Bahá'í community were grief-stricken and awaited greater violence towards them. The fanatical Muslims began a period of celebration, congratulating each other and the rest of the community; and some of the government authorities became extremely alarmed and resolved to cool the passions and bring some order to the city. The bloodshed of the innocent brought those in authority to their senses, and further destruction was averted in Yazd. However, similar atrocities continued in other parts of Iran. [16]

By the end of academic year in our school, one other bench had been put in the back of our classroom. We were now seven students sitting there. Two of the four additional students had decided to express their strong disagreement with those attacking Bahá'ís, and the other two had actually decided to study the Bahá'í Faith. Later, they joined the Bahá'í Community.

HUMAN RESPONSE TO CRISES

As I reflect on those days of crises and danger and the manner in which by far the majority of Bahá'ís responded to them, and as I again observe the courage and authenticity with which Bahá'ís of Iran are now responding to crises far more severe in intensity and much longer in duration than that which we encountered in 1955/1956, I am acutely aware of the power of the human spirit. It is axiomatic that the human spirit has the potential capacity to respond to the severest crises with calmness, courage, love, truth, and justice. And it is a fact of human history that the most fundamental human achievements have always taken place in the domains of courage, love, truth, and justice. The lives of many of the followers of major religions and those of such historic figures as Socrates, Gandhi, and Confucius are outstanding examples of the operation of the human spirit within the parameters of courage, love, truth, and justice.

Furthermore, in the course of many years that I had the privilege and opportunity to counsel and treat many individuals with regard to the manifold crises of their lives, I observed the resiliency of the human psyche and the creative powers of the human spirit. I observed with awe and wonder how people overcame calamities, how they were able to forgive, how willingly they sacrificed their own comfort and advantage for others, and how often they were fundamentally happy in the face of all their trouble.

The human spirit aspires to evolve and transcend. However, this process is conscious and deliberate. In other words, we have not only to be aware of our considerable powers but also to be fully dedicated to the task of nurturing and developing these powers, which are only possible within the framework of truth, love, and justice. It is not accidental that these three conditions—truth, love, and justice—have always been and always will be the most sought after conditions in human life.

RECONCILING WITH REALITY

In reflecting on these realities, I was gradually able to overcome my fears, find answers to my urgent questions, and decide on a practical path aimed at a rational outcome based on spiritual principles. At the core of this process was an attempt on my part to discover some convincing and meaningful answers to three questions that have been asked by human beings from the dawn of our consciousness: Who are we? Why are we? And, How should we be? In other words, what is our true nature, where do we come from, and how should we live in order to fully harvest the fruits of our tree of life? These are ever-evolving multilayered questions, and every answer we find brings new questions and adds to the mystery of life in its manifold expressions—ease and difficulty, joy and sorrow, union and separation, uncertainty and certitude, the unexpected and the foreseen, the obvious and the puzzling.

Modern materialistic science has relatively easy and downward answers based on concepts of survival, gratification, pain-avoidance, and pure chance. It explains higher levels of human consciousness within the primitive framework of biological and instinctual processes. All we need to do is to let "nature" determine the direction and quality of our life. But from the spiritual perspective, life, in general, and human life, in particular, is a process filled with threats, opportunities, and mysteries—all of which need to be faced and continually better understood and more appropriately approached. In this process we need to simultaneously draw from spiritual principles, scientific facts, and our creative capacities and be prepared to respond fully and appropriately to any circumstances that we may encounter. This is an upward process—from the biological and instinctual to ever higher levels of consciousness and understanding.

In this process of search to better understand the nature and purpose of life, I have reached certain conclusions that are subject to ongoing clarification and modification as one learns from new life experiences and arrives at new understandings. I summarized my views on these issues in a keynote address I delivered at the plenary session of "Iceland 2000: Faith in the Future," an international conference on religion and science held in Reykjavik and Pingvellir, Iceland, July 5–8, 2000. The following section is partially based on that presentation.

WHO ARE WE? WHY ARE WE?

THE ENIGMA OF HUMAN NATURE

It is impossible to understand the nature and purpose of human life if we exclude either religion or science from our domain of inquiry. Both religion and science are essential for understanding the complex nature of human reality. We cannot fully understand ourselves if either one is excluded. However, because both science and religion are vast fields of study, I limit my focus to the spiritual and psychological aspects of human nature with which I am more familiar. Spirituality is the main fruit of religion, and psychology, along with biology, sociology, and anthropology are the branches of science most relevant to the study of the nature and purpose of human life from a scientific perspective.

Many contemporary scientists view human nature as essentially material and entirely a product of the biological and evolutionary processes of life, and consider survival and reproduction, directed by the Darwinian concept of natural selection, as the main and the ultimate goals of life.[17] There is also considerable discourse about whether humans are by nature religious or not. A number of evolutionary psychologists have formulated explanations about how the "misfiring" of certain hypothetical modules in the brain has resulted in the ubiquitous presence of religion throughout history and in all parts of the world.[18] Other researchers have proposed that human beings are innately predisposed to dualism, hence the human natural proclivity to believe in the existence of a "soul" or "spirit," apart and independent from the body. Paul Bloom, professor of psychology at Yale University, states that "[t]here is considerable evidence that adults are natural dualists—we see the world as Descartes did, as containing physical things (or bodies) and social entities (or souls)."[19]

The Bahá'í concept of human nature, based on the integrated operation of the material and spiritual aspects of human reality in the context of the law of unity, resolves the dilemma of monism and dualism. As stated in chapter two, unity is the supreme law of existence. All that exists in our universe is the outcome of the operation of the law of unity, which operates in both physical and biological entities and within social, mental, and psychological processes. From a Bahá'í perspective, human life is the outcome of unity of the body and the soul (spirit), and the main product of this unity is the human mind (rational soul). This is a reciprocal relationship. The soul is the animating force of the body, and the body is the main instrument for the expression of the powers of the soul. Neither can function without the other. However, in the same manner that the body requires proper nutrition, activity, and rest, the soul is also in need of nurturance, which it receives from the spiritual teachings of religion—in their pure and authentic form—through the medium of the mind. 'Abdu'l-Bahá explains:

> There are in the world of humanity three degrees: those of the body, the soul, and spirit. The body is the physical or animal degree of man. From the bodily point of view man is a sharer of the animal kingdom. The bodies alike of men and animals are composed of elements held together by the law of attraction. Like the animal, man possesses the faculties of the senses, is subject to heat, cold, hunger, thirst, etc.; unlike the animal, man has a rational soul, the human intelligence. This intelligence of man is the intermediary between his body and his spirit. When man allows the spirit [Spiritual Teachings of Religion], through his soul [intelligence], to enlighten his understanding, then does he contain all Creation; because man, being the culmination of all that went before and thus superior to all previous evolutions, contains all the lower world within himself. Illumined by the spirit through the instrumentality of the soul, man's radiant intelligence makes him the crowning-point of Creation.[20]

Viewed from this perspective, human life is the expression of ever higher levels of unity among the biological, intellectual, and spiritual dimensions of human reality. It is through unity that life is created and safeguarded, and it is towards unity that life is directed and advanced. Unity, therefore, is the prerequisite condition that enables us to use our unique powers of the rational soul—to know, love, and will—to create higher and more developed individual and collective lifestyles. This ongoing movement of humanity towards increasingly higher levels of unity involves all aspects of our individual and collective lives and is simultaneously both a scientific and spiritual process.

THE POWER OF UNDERSTANDING
WHERE SCIENCE AND RELIGION CONVERGE

The Bahá'í Faith puts singular emphasis on the application of both spiritual and scientific principles to every aspect of human life. In the Bahá'í writings two main sources of knowledge are identified: spiritual and scientific. The former refers to the teachings of the Manifestations of God and the latter to the fruits of the human mind and creativity. The origins of science are in the human capacities of observation, imagination, analysis, and synthesis. Science uses available data from the world of nature, the past history of humanity, and the present conditions we encounter in the course of life. The concepts and ideas we develop through these processes form the body of human arts and sciences that are unique to the human species and which are clear indicators of the creative powers of the human mind. They are also essential for the creation of an ever-advancing civilization. Human arts and sciences are the products of the human mind and the results of the human powers of understanding. Bahá'u'lláh states that God has given the human species many favors and asserts:

> First and foremost among these favors, which the Almighty hath conferred upon man, is the gift of understanding. His purpose in conferring such a gift is none other except to enable His creature to know and recognize the one true God....This gift giveth man the power to discern the truth in all things, leadeth him to that which is right, and helpeth him to discover the secrets of creation.[21]

'Abdu'l-Bahá, referring to the human power of understanding and intellect, focuses specifically on science and its functions, stating that

> the outcome of this intellectual endowment is science which is especially characteristic of man. This scientific power investigates and apprehends created objects and the laws surrounding them. It is the discoverer of the hidden and mysterious secrets of the material universe and is peculiar to man alone. The most noble and praiseworthy accomplishment of man therefore is scientific knowledge and attainment.[22]

The high regard in which science and scientists are held in the Bahá'í Faith is obvious from these two statements. Science studies that which is created. Science does not create. It does not bring into being that which does not already exist. Rather, science *discovers*. It brings to light, explains, and discovers the laws of nature and through application of these insights makes new things from what already exists. Thus, technology becomes the practical fruit of science.

By contrast, religion is the outward expression of the Word of God and—in its pure, authentic, and progressive state—has the power to *create*. It is the animating and creative force of all creation. The domain of influence of religion is both the minds and hearts of people. More importantly, true religion transforms both the individual and group, not through manipulation of emotions or domination of minds or subjugation of wills, but rather through a mysterious process in which our emotions are freed, our minds are expanded, our wills are strengthened, and all these faculties are focused on lofty and spiritualized objectives for the progress of all humankind. Through this process hearts and souls are inspired, civilizations are created, and arts and sciences are put at the service of humanity and for the exaltation of life rather than its destruction and debasement, as is the case now.

'Abdu'l-Bahá, commenting on the nature of religion and the creative power of the Word of God, states:

> Religion, moreover, is not a series of beliefs, a set of customs; religion is the teachings of the Lord God, teachings which constitute the very life of humankind, which urge high thoughts upon the mind, refine the character, and lay the groundwork for man's everlasting honour. Note thou: could these fevers in the world of the mind, these fires of war and hate, of resentment and malice among the nations, this aggression of peoples against peoples, which have destroyed the tranquility of the whole world ever be made to abate, except through the living waters of the teachings of God? No, never! And this is clear: a power above and beyond the powers of nature must needs be brought to bear, to change this black darkness into light, and these hatreds and resentments, grudges and spites, these endless wrangles and wars, into fellowship and love amongst all the peoples of the earth. This power is none other than…the mighty inflow of the Word of God.[23]

Within the framework of the creative teachings of religion in its authentic, progressive form and insights gained from the investigative powers of science, we are able not only to create safe and flourishing environments for ourselves and all other living beings but also to build an ever-advancing global civilization of peace. It is in this context that human psychological and spiritual powers play their unique role.

PSYCHOLOGY AND RELIGION

The concept of worldview, as presented in chapter one, helps us better understand humanity's approach to both religion and science. Here, I will limit myself to reviewing a few issues with regard to the attitude of researchers and practitioners of psychology towards religion—attitudes that are indicative of their respective worldviews.

The past two centuries saw fundamental worldview changes, characterized by rejection of outmoded authoritarian practices and religious dogmas, and correspondent increasing reliance on "scientifically based" understanding of human nature. Among these developments was the advent of modern psychology—the discipline that studies the human psyche or soul in the context of life. Human psychological life is complex and multifaceted; consequently, different researchers and practitioners in the field have usually focused on one aspect, and occasionally a few aspects, of the psyche.

At the beginning of the 20th century, primarily through the work of Sigmund Freud (1856–1939), Carl Jung (1875–1961), Alfred Adler (1870–1937), and a few others in the psychoanalytic school, a systematic approach to the study of the human psyche and the dynamics of its development was devised.[24] The initial objective set by Freud was to study the nature and mechanisms of the human soul. However, the pull of modern materialistic science was too strong, and during Freud's own lifetime, the study of the human soul was replaced by the study of the human mind. The soul was too elusive a concept for a scientific method of study based rigidly on the modalities of measurement, statistics, and senses. A truly scientific study of the soul required a much broader and integrative scientific method. The mind, however, was easier to study.[25] Furthermore, Freud's understanding of the soul (psyche) was based on the rejection of the religious concepts and worldviews of his Austro-Hungarian and Germanic society. The following statements are representative of Freud's understanding of religion:

> Religion is comparable to a childhood neurosis. (*The Future of an Illusion*, 1927)

> Religion is an illusion and it derives its strength from the fact that it falls in with our instinctual desires. (*New Introductory Lectures on Psychoanalysis*, 1933)

> If one attempts to assign to religion its place in man's evolution, it seems not so much to be a lasting acquisition, as a parallel to the neurosis which the civilized individual must pass through on his way from childhood to maturity. (*Moses and Monotheism*, 1939)[26]

Thus, from the very beginning of modern psychology, religion was understood and researched within a highly subjective and hostile framework by one of its most influential founders.

Gradually, many researchers, influenced by the prevailing materialistic worldviews, developed ingenious experiments on various animals and some human subjects that demonstrated many similarities between humans and animals in regard to the biological processes concerned with such issues as survival, pain avoidance and pleasure-seeking behavior, and learning processes. Based on these observations, they then drew conclusions and offered explanations about all aspects of being human: our thoughts, intuitions, dreams, creative capacities, sacrificial acts of love, and moral ways of life.

Midway through the 20th century, the process of what I call the "materialization of the soul" took a giant step forward. New discoveries of mind- and mood-altering chemical substances had two very different effects. The first effect was most welcomed. New drugs were discovered that were quite effective in relieving the immense psychological suffering of large numbers of people with such conditions as schizophrenia and affective, obsessive-compulsive, and anxiety disorders. The second effect of these new developments in the field of psychopharmacology was the deepening conviction of many scientists that all human psychological conditions were due to chemical abnormalities and physical aberrations. A large number of scientists focused their considerable talents on studying the human brain, and huge sums of money were put at their disposal to discover chemical remedies for all psychological disorders. Later in the century, study of psychology within the parameters of the Darwinian theory of evolution—Evolutionary Psychology—took a major step forward. Leda Cosmides and John Tooby of the University of California, Santa Barbara, state:

> The goal of research in evolutionary psychology is to discover and understand the design of the human mind. Evolutionary psychology is an *approach* to psychology, in which knowledge and principles from evolutionary biology are put to use in research on the structure of the human mind. It is not an area of study, like vision, reasoning, or social behavior. It is a *way of thinking* about psychology that can be applied to any topic within it.[27]

Richard Dawkins provides the following summary of the views of the evolutionary psychologists on the issue of religion:

> Evolutionary psychologists suggest that, just as the eye is an organ for seeing, and the wing an evolved organ for flying, so the brain

is a collection of organs (or "modules") for dealing with a set of specialist data-processing needs. There is a module for dealing with kinship, a module for dealing for reciprocal exchanges, a module for dealing with empathy, and so on. Religion can be seen as a by-product of misfiring of several of these modules, for example the modules for forming theories of other minds, for forming coalitions, and for discriminating in favour of in-group members and against strangers....[28]

A few pages later, Dawkins adds: "The general theory of religion as an accidental by-product—a misfiring of something useful—is the one I wish to advocate."[29]

Thus, in the course of one century, the fields of psychology and psychiatry, both dedicated to the study of the human nature, with their enormous intellectual capacities, financial resources, and considerable influential positions, dealt with one of the most universal, ancient, persistent, and uniquely significant aspects of the human life—religion—either with indifference (probably the majority) or with hostility (by some of their most influential and outspoken members). In either case, a careful review of the psychological thought on religion clearly demonstrates their general ignorance and misperception of the phenomenon of religion and its irreplaceable role in human life.

Parallel with superficial and often erroneous and/or hostile understanding of religion on the part of these scientists, the established religions, burdened with their rigid and ossified perspectives and practices, found themselves incapable of responding to an awakening and scientifically oriented humanity's demands for satisfactory explanations with regard to those irrational, prejudicial, divisive, and authoritarian belief systems and practices that characterized their understanding of their respective religions. In this state of desperation, some leaders of these established religions adopted several highly destructive strategies, including fundamentalism and militarism. And now at the start of the 21st century, we are witnessing the awesome destructive consequences of the arrogance and neglectfulness of these materialistic scientists on the one hand, and blindness and close-mindedness of some religious leaders on the other.

One reason for this lamentable state, in my opinion, is the prevalence of both the survival- and identity-based worldviews that have pitted these two groups against each other and have engaged them in a highly destructive process of competition with the aim of "defeating" the other side and "winning" the war between science and religion. Had the scientists and religious scholars reflected on their respective worldviews, had they done careful research about the essence of religion, and had they bothered to investigate all the revealed religions, they would have discovered a totally new understanding and explanation of the phenomenon of religion. They probably would have come across a published letter written in early part of the 20th century by 'Abdu'l-Bahá, the Center of the Covenant of the Bahá'í Faith, to a small number of early Bahá'ís in North America. In it he states:

> [E]very era hath a spirit; the spirit of this illumined era lieth in the teachings of Bahá'u'lláh. For these lay the foundation of the oneness of the world of humanity and promulgate universal brotherhood. They are founded upon the unity of science and religion and upon investigation of truth. They uphold the principle that religion must be the cause of amity, union and harmony among men. They establish the equality of both sexes and propound economic principles which are for the happiness of individuals. They diffuse universal education, that every soul may as much as possible have a share of knowledge. They abrogate and nullify religious, racial, political, patriotic and economic prejudices and the like....[30]

And if they had further searched, they would have found this concise description of the main teachings of this newest world religion:

> The independent search after truth, unfettered by superstition or tradition; the oneness of the entire human race, the pivotal principle and fundamental doctrine of the Faith; the basic unity of all religions; the condemnation of all forms of prejudice, whether religious, racial, class or national; the harmony which must exist between religion and science; the equality of men and women, the two wings on which the bird of human kind is able to soar; the introduction of compulsory education; the adoption of a universal auxiliary language; the abolition of the extremes of wealth and poverty; the institution of a world tribunal for the adjudication of disputes between nations; the exaltation of work, performed in the spirit of service, to the rank of worship; the glorification of justice as the ruling principle in human society, and of religion as a bulwark for the protection of all peoples and nations; and the establishment of a permanent and universal peace as the supreme goal of all mankind....[31]

However, for whatever reason, the teachings of Bahá'í Faith were ignored by scientists, religious scholars, and religious leaders; and the battle among them continues unabated.

By the end of the 20th century, the process of the "materialization of the soul" had reached its apex. Modern psychology has become a legitimate child of materialistic science, and its practitioners have evolved into *technicians of the mind* and specialists on the structure and function of the brain. But the human soul demands to be nurtured not only by means of information but also by wisdom; not only by relative emotional comfort but also by love; and not only by those deeds that safeguard the biological integrity and reproductive capacities of the organism but also by deeds that are transcendent, universal, other-directed, and inherently meaningful.

The spiritually deprived soul seeks meaning everywhere and in the absence of authentic and transcendent meaning, not infrequently, falls prey to those attractive but empty, pseudo-spiritual views on life, many of which denounce all that is related to science: the scientific method, reason, and technological advancement. It is, therefore, not surprising that in the 20th century we also witnessed the appearance of a phenomenon loosely called New Age spirituality, which is a bizarre combination of the sublime and the ridiculous, the reasonable and the superstitious, the profound and the meaningless.

The 20th century was, of course, also the century of science and technology. The scientific discoveries and technological inventions of this century were greater than all that humanity had accomplished previously in these fields of human endeavor. Likewise, a profound level of abuse of both science and technology marked this century. The extent and severity of this abuse is as such, that not infrequently the appellation "the most barbaric century in human history" is used to describe the 20th century. This magnitude of violence was only possible through use of instruments of war created by some of the brightest scientific minds. It is in light of this misuse of science and technology in the service of misguided ideologies that the following statement by Einstein assumes special significance:

> Science can only be created by those who are thoroughly imbued with aspirations toward truth and understanding. This source of feeling, however, springs from the sphere of religion....Science without religion is lame, religion without science is blind. [32]

Another significant outcome of rejection of authentic religion was the creation of pseudo-religions based on various theories and ideologies, which, as the history of the 20th century shows, were usually short-lived. Shoghi Effendi, in his sobering 1941 analysis of the consequence of rejection of religion in our times, states that

> [t]his vital force is dying out, this mighty agency has been scorned, this radiant light obscured, this impregnable stronghold abandoned, this beauteous robe discarded. God Himself has indeed been dethroned from the hearts of men, and an idolatrous world passionately and

clamorously hails and worships the false gods which its own idle fancies have fatuously created, and its misguided hands so impiously exalted. The chief idols in the desecrated temple of mankind are none other than the triple gods of Nationalism, Racialism and Communism, at whose altars governments and peoples, whether democratic or totalitarian, at peace or at war, of the East or of the West, Christian or Islamic, are, in various forms and in different degrees, now worshiping. Their high priests are the politicians and the worldly-wise, the so-called sages of the age; their sacrifice, the flesh and blood of the slaughtered multitudes; their incantations outworn shibboleths and insidious and irreverent formulas; their incense, the smoke of anguish that ascends from the lacerated hearts of the bereaved, the maimed, and the homeless.

The theories and policies, so unsound, so pernicious, which deify the state and exalt the nation above mankind, which seek to subordinate the sister races of the world to one single race, which discriminate between the black and the white, and which tolerate the dominance of one privileged class over all others—these are the dark, the false, and crooked doctrines for which any man or people who believes in them, or acts upon them, must, sooner or later, incur the wrath and chastisement of God.[33]

DYNAMICS OF SPIRITUAL TRANSFORMATION

The 20th century has another distinction aside from being the century of the emergence of modern psychology and great advancements in science and technology. This century was also the culmination of more than three centuries of a systematic and accelerating process of rejection of religion as a valid reservoir of insight and wisdom, an indispensable source of purpose and meaning for life, and an essential avenue in search of truth and reality. The rejection of religion burdened by superstition, prejudice, and irrational belief systems—as it was and still often is understood and practiced—was legitimate.

However, religion, in its pure essence and enlightened application— free from the superstitions, prejudices, and irrational belief systems—is the very causal source of spiritual transformation that is the definitive aspect of being human. The human species is the embodiment of contradictions and is capable of both good and evil. This contradiction has its genesis in the unique quality of human nature. 'Abdu'l-Bahá describes human nature in the following words:

Man is in the highest degree of materiality, and at the beginning of spirituality....He has the animal side as well as the angelic side.... That is why he is the end of imperfection and the beginning of perfection. Not in any other of the species in the world of existence is there such a difference, contrast, contradiction, and opposition, as in the species of man....In the same way, knowledge is a quality of man, and so is ignorance; truthfulness is a quality of man, so is falsehood; trustworthiness and treachery, justice and injustice, are qualities of man, and so forth. Briefly, all the perfections and virtues, and all the vices, are qualities of man.[34]

This contradictory state operates in all aspects of human life and revolves around the all-important issue of human conscious capacity for transcending its negative and destructive proclivities and replacing them with their exact opposite. In the Bahá'í Writings this process is referred to as the process of spiritual transformation. Bahá'u'lláh's treatise on Progressive Revelation—the *Book of Certitude*—addresses this issue:

...is not the object of every Revelation to effect a transformation in the whole character of mankind, a transformation that shall manifest itself both outwardly and inwardly, that shall affect both its inner life and external conditions? For if the character of mankind be not changed, the futility of God's universal Manifestations would be apparent.[35]

The fundamental concept of spirituality and the essential process of spiritual transformation are central to the objectives of the Bahá'í Faith. Spirituality is a rational, conscious, dynamic, progressive, integrative, and mystical process in which human individuals and societies achieve their fullest potential in the context of unity and in response to the forces released by progressive Divine Revelation. Inarguably, a truly spiritual orientation is scientific in its approach; is based on verified truths and facts; is free from prejudice, superstition, and dogma; is in harmony with both science and religion; is the cause of unity and peace in the context of the rich diversity of humanity; is a contributor to the refinement of human character; is the source of beauty, harmony, and creativity; and is universal with respect to its moral and ethical principles. As such, any perspective that is devoid of any of these qualities cannot be considered to be truly spiritual. It is in this context that we can conclude that as long as spirituality—which is the highest expression of our humanity and the main objective of religion—is excluded from the parameters of scientific inquiry and religious practices, important insights into the nature of human change and transformation are unattainable. Human capacities to know, love, and will are the main avenues for expression of spiritual qualities and the process of spiritual transformation.

The process of spiritual transformation is a conscious, deliberate, and thoughtful process. It involves all aspects of human endeavors: scientific pursuits, artistic creativity, ethical practices, and conscious inquiries into the mystical and as yet unknown dimensions of reality. Spiritualization takes place within the parameters of new perspectives (mindsets or worldviews) about human nature and life, which in turn, are only possible when a new level of individual and collective maturation is accomplished. Spirituality is the hallmark of the transition of humanity from its collective stages of childhood and adolescence to those of adulthood and maturity. The central intellectual and spiritual concept, which makes this transition possible, is the concept of unity. Within the framework of these twin processes of the coming of age of humanity and the ever-expanding circles of unity, we can study both the nature of human life and the dynamics of human growth and development.

From Transition to Transformation

Since the Industrial Revolution, the pace of change has dramatically accelerated, especially with respect to the living conditions of people in many parts of the world. In this process, we have experienced significant change in our interpersonal relationships within families, communities, and between different nations. To understand the nature and processes of individual and social change, we have developed such areas of study and specialization as economics, political science, biology, sociology, and psychology. These diverse disciplines now form the basis upon which we study the nature and causes of change in the past, evaluate our conditions at the present, and try to predict and direct the process of change in the future. These areas of knowledge have greatly added to our self-understanding. But we are still lacking in our ability to identify all the causes and dynamics of change, particularly with respect to human behavior and attitude. This is not surprising. Human behavior is not merely a reflection of the individual's economic conditions, social circumstances, psychological processes, instinctual needs, or evolutionary imperatives. These and other explanations as to the nature, causes, and dynamics of human behavior are all to some degree accurate. However, none of them alone (or even all of them together) is sufficient to fully explain the causes of human behavior and the dynamics of change and transformation in individuals and societies.

The main reason for this failure is the exclusion of the uniquely human dimension of spirituality from most formulations about human nature. Spirituality is the most misunderstood aspect of human nature. Some equate spirituality with religiosity and others with emotionality. Some consider spirituality to be the equivalent of being superstitious and illogical, and still others consider spirituality to be the property of arts and nature alone. Others consider anything that is beyond their comprehension to be spiritual. Some equate spirituality with being moral and ethical. And there are also other perspectives on this issue. Spirituality has some of the qualities found in these various definitions. However, spirituality is a far more complex and comprehensive reality. In fact, spirituality is the core reality of being human. It refers to the human power of consciousness and our constant search for meaning and purpose. Spirituality connects the past, the present, and the future. It integrates our sense of mortality and immortality, and helps us to face death from the perspective of existence rather than annihilation. Spirituality connects us with the Source of all creation and, in the process, enables us to become creators ourselves. Spirituality makes it possible for us to be both unique and united, thus freeing us from the dichotomous mindset, which is the cause of much destruction and sorrow.

This elusive, mysterious, yet essential reality is increasingly absent from the discourse of our times. Spirituality is not the object of research and application to conditions of life in a scientifically sound and disciplined manner. Consequently, the life-giving and enlightening properties of a spiritual lifestyle are increasingly absent from our midst. Our lives have become hardened by materialism, burdened with immorality and amorality, and impoverished by the absence of opportunities for deep reflection, prayerful meditation, and momentous inspirations. Above all, humanity has lost its connection with God. And as we exclude God from our lives, we lose those God-like qualities that we all potentially possess.

No individual or society will be able to make the momentous transformation from a power- and indulgence-orientation to a justice- and unity-orientation without achieving the singularly important task of integrating scientific and spiritual principles, then applying them to all aspects of life: individual, family, and community. Without such integration we will experience a kind of change and transition that is more an indication of variation and even deterioration, rather than growth and transformation. The challenge before us has never been greater. We require the courage to abandon the conflict-based worldviews that characterize our past history and present interests. The future cannot be built on the foundations of what has already been tried and proven wanting. The peaceful civilization that many of us aspire to create requires a new consciousness. This transformation is fundamental, not simple. However, good ideas are valuable only to the degree that they are practical. Therefore, we need to have a careful look at the practicality of such a monumental change in our individual and collective lives. The process of spiritual transformation of the society and its institutions is the focus of upcoming chapters. Here we continue with other individual aspects of spiritual transformation.

PRAYER AND TRANSFORMATION

Throughout our lives, we humans are in a dilemmatic existential state. Our consciousness of our fundamental weakness in the face of the forces of disease, unexpected calamities, and certain death, combined with our tendency to perceive ourselves as strong and invincible, puts us in a difficult and conflicted state. Depending on the nature of our worldview and the values that inform our approach to life, we deal with our existential quandary in remarkably different ways. Some face life with a profound sense of insecurity—fearful, anxious, suspicious, and uncertain. Prayers offered within this mindset are usually similar to entreaties of powerless children towards the all-powerful adults. They are basically unidirectional and passive. The praying persons request and expect that their prayers would be answered without any efforts on their part. Not infrequently, this approach to praying ends up in confusion, bewilderment, and disappointment, because their prayers are often seemingly left unheard and unanswered.

Others, approach life with bravado and a sense of omnipotence and invincibility. They believe that they are totally in control of their lives and consider praying as an act of weakness and ignorance, usually both. Such individuals either do not pray, or if do, their prayers are for victory over their competitors. We find such modes of praying when people are engaged in competitive activities and in conflicts and wars. Prayers are said for the defeat of competitors and enemies, and victory of oneself and one's group. There is yet another approach to prayer, which is offered as an essential tool for spiritual transformation.

Prayer, at its most fundamental level, is love-talk, a deeply personal and meaningful connection between self and the Source of all Love—God. It is through this relationship that we greatly enhance our capacity to love and dramatically enlarge the scope of our love, so that it will include all humanity, all living beings, and all existence. 'Abdu'l-Bahá explains:

> O thou spiritual friend! Thou hast asked the wisdom of prayer. The wisdom of prayer is this: That it causeth a connection between the servant and the True One, because in that state man with all heart and soul turneth his face towards His Highness the Almighty, seeking His association and desiring His love and compassion. The greatest happiness for a lover is to converse with his beloved, and the greatest gift for a seeker is to become familiar with the object of his longing; that is why with every soul who is attracted to the Kingdom of God, his greatest hope is to find an opportunity to entreat and supplicate before his Beloved, appeal for His mercy and grace and be immersed in the ocean of His utterance, goodness and generosity....[36]

Furthermore, through prayer an occasion conducive to deep reflection, contemplation, and meditation is created. In such a state the prayer is a modality through which, by connecting ourselves to the Source of all knowledge, we search for greater self-knowledge, seek strength to resist egotism and self-worship, and look for answers to perplexing questions—personal, scientific, philosophical, etc. Here is a prayer by 'Abdu'l-Bahá that addresses these issues:

> O God, O Thou Who hast cast Thy splendor over the luminous realities of men, shedding upon them the resplendent lights of knowledge and guidance, and hast chosen them out of all created things for this supernal grace, and hast caused them to encompass all things, to understand their inmost essence, and to disclose their mysteries, bringing them forth out of darkness into the visible world!...O Lord, help Thou Thy loved ones to acquire knowledge and the sciences and arts, and to unravel the secrets that are treasured up in the inmost reality of all created beings. Make them to hear the hidden truths that are written and embedded in the heart of all that is. Make them to be ensigns of guidance amongst all creatures, and piercing rays of the mind shedding forth their light in this, the "first life."[37]

Prayer not only greatly develops and refines our capacities to know and to love but also helps us to use our power of will to make choices based on truth, love, compassion, and goodness. It helps us to become humble. It reminds us of the intoxicating dangers of the illusion of power that we humans are so drawn to, particularly during our individual and collectives ages of childhood and adolescence, when we tend to be grandiose and arrogant. Humanity, as described in chapter two, is now rapidly coming of age and approaching the stage of collective adulthood. Our prayers, therefore, must match the requirements of this fundamental period in the human journey of maturation and transformation:

> I Beseech Thee, O my God, by all transcendent glory of Thy Name, to clothe Thy loved ones in the robe of Justice and to illumine their beings with the light of trustworthiness....[38]

> O Lord, my God! Give me Thy grace to serve Thy loved ones, strengthen me in my servitude to Thee....Help me to be selfless at the heavenly entrance of Thy gate, and aid me to be detached from all things within Thy holy precincts. Lord! Give me to drink from the Chalice of Selflessness; with its robe clothe me. And in its ocean immerse me....[39]

In the Bahá'í Faith, prayer is considered as an essential spiritual discipline. Obligatory Prayers are said in privacy, at least once a day. The following is an example of an obligatory prayer:

> I bear witness, O my God, that Thou hast created me to know Thee and to worship Thee. I testify, at this moment, to my powerlessness and to Thy might, to my poverty and to Thy wealth. There is none other God but Thee, the Help in Peril, the Self-Subsisting.[40]
>
> [Short obligatory prayer, to be recited once daily at noon.]

There are two other versions of obligatory prayers of different lengths and frequency. One can chose among these prayers for recitation on a daily basis. These prayers directly address the human powers of the soul—to know, love, and will—and act as reminders and motivating forces on how we approach the precious gifts of knowledge, love, and will in conducting our lives.

Other prayers can be said both in private and in the company of others and on special occasions, and all of them focus on the fundamental requirements of a spiritual life process—love and unity, truth and truthfulness, humility and service, compassion and justice, selflessness and universality. Here are a few examples:

> O my God! O my God! Unite the hearts of Thy servants, and reveal to them Thy great purpose. May they follow Thy commandments and abide in Thy law. Help them, O God, in their endeavor, and grant them strength to serve Thee. O God! Leave them not to themselves,

but guide their steps by the light of Thy knowledge, and cheer their hearts by Thy love. Verily, Thou art their Helper and their Lord.[41]

—Bahá'u'lláh

O Lord God! Make us as waves of the sea, as flowers of the garden, united, agreed through the bounties of Thy love. O Lord! Dilate the breasts through the signs of Thy oneness, and make all mankind as stars shining from the same height of glory, as perfect fruits growing upon Thy tree of life. Verily, Thou art the Almighty, the Self-Subsistent, the Giver, the Forgiving, the Pardoner, the Omniscient, the One Creator.[42]

—'Abdu'l-Bahá

I pray God to assemble all mankind in the shadow of the standard of peace and under the tents of love....[43]

—'Abdu'l-Bahá

On 5 August 1912 in Dublin, New Hampshire, 'Abdu'l-Bahá in response to a question concerning the relations among prayers and treatment and healing gave the following explanations about the ever-present relationship between God and all creation, the manner in which most prayers are answered, and the wisdom behind the fact that not all prayers are answered:

God will answer the prayer of every servant if that prayer is urgent. His mercy is vast, illimitable. He answers the prayers of all His servants.... God will answer anyone. He answers prayers potentially....

But [when] we ask for things which the divine wisdom does not desire for us....there is no answer to our prayer. His wisdom does not sanction what we wish. We pray, "O God! Make me wealthy!" If this prayer were universally answered, human affairs would be at a standstill. There would be none left to work in the streets, none to till the soil, none to build, none to run the trains. Therefore, it is evident that it would not be well for us if all prayers were answered. The affairs of the world would be interfered with, energies crippled and progress hindered. But whatever we ask for which is in accord with divine wisdom, God will answer. Assuredly!

For instance, a very feeble patient may ask the doctor to give him food which would be positively dangerous to his life and condition. He may beg for roast meat. The doctor is kind and wise. He knows it would be dangerous to his patient so he refuses to allow it. The doctor is merciful; the patient, ignorant. Through the doctor's kindness the patient recovers; his life is saved. Yet the patient may cry out that the doctor is unkind, not good, because he refuses to answer his pleading.

God is merciful. In His mercy He answers the prayers of all His servants when according to His supreme wisdom it is necessary.[44]

As moderation is one of the hallmarks of maturity, it is also applicable to the act of praying. In the words of the Báb [see Appendix I], a Manifestation of God and the forerunner to Bahá'u'lláh,

[t]he most acceptable prayer is the one offered with the utmost spirituality and radiance; its prolongation hath not been and is not beloved by God. The most detached and the purer the prayer, the more acceptable it is in presence of God.[45]

Finally, in the Bahá'í Faith the concepts of prayer and worship are fully integrated, and all positive and productive human activities such as pursuit of science, creation of arts, and engagement in professions and jobs that are of service to others have been elevated to the rank of worship. 'Abdu'l-Bahá explains that if a person engages with all his/her power "in the acquisition of a science or in the perfection of an art, it is as if he has been worshiping God in the churches and temples."[46] When 'Abdu'l-Bahá, in the course of His historic journey to the West, was asked, "Should Prayer take the form of action?" He responded:

Yes: In the Bahá'í Cause arts, sciences and all crafts are (counted as) worship. The man who makes a piece of notepaper to the best of his ability, conscientiously, concentrating all his forces on perfecting it, is giving praise to God. Briefly, all effort and exertion put forth by man from the fullness of his heart is worship, if it is prompted by the highest motives and the will to do service to humanity. This is worship: to serve mankind and to minister to the needs of the people. Service is prayer. A physician ministering to the sick, gently, tenderly, free from prejudice and believing in the solidarity of the human race, he is giving praise.[47]

Tests and Transformation

Another issue of significance regarding transformation is the manner in which we respond to the difficulties and challenges of life. In Bahá'í parlance, these challenges are called "tests." Tests are both indicators of our state of psychological and spiritual development, and new opportunities for our further growth and maturation. In the same manner that in school we are tested to see where we are with respect to our learning and what we need to do to further advance our studies, likewise in all other aspects of our life we need to know how we are doing and how we could further enhance the quality, scope, and depth of our lives. Tests play a fundamental role in this process and come upon us from at least four different sources: mistakes, misunderstandings, misfortunes, and malevolent intent. We all make many mistakes in life that are usually due to our ignorance, lack of experience, and/or poor judgment. Both the sign of maturity and the prerequisite for further maturity is that we acknowledge our mistakes, make utmost effort to repair the damage, and learn from them. Misunderstandings, here, refer to the areas of confusion and poor communication in our interpersonal relationships that quite often result in extremely regrettable and at times destructive consequences in our families, places of work, communities, and with regard to our duties as leaders. Once again we need to approach these situations in the same manner as we do with mistakes—to learn from them and to repair the fractured relationship. Misfortunes such as disease, natural disasters, and financial upheavals that happen often unexpectedly to many people also test our mettle and provide opportunities for us to learn new, yet undiscovered, capacities in ourselves. Finally, some of us may also be subject to malevolent intent on the part of others on the basis of jealousy, greed, or sheer meanness and hostility. This latter category of tests is most difficult to deal with because we experience a profound state of injustice that arouses in us feelings of anger and self-righteousness and a desire to retaliate in kind. As such, these tests can bring out the worst in us because we may feel both violated and victimized.

Many of us experience some or all of these varied types of tests, and from what I have observed in hundreds of individuals in the course of my professional and community work and in my own personal life, there is no doubt that these experiences need to be approached with the highest degree of understanding, insight, courage, and honesty that we have within the repertoire of our manifold capacities, some developed and others still in their state of potentiality. Once we face these tests in this manner, we dramatically enhance our capacity for psychological development and spiritual transformation.

Bahá'ís believe that miseries and misfortunes of life are of two kinds: those that are direct results of our actions and those that are due to events beyond our control, such as natural disasters. In either case, tests are beneficial for the development and refinement of human character and civilization. As we employ our intellectual and creative powers to respond to the challenges and trials of life, we gradually decrease our human-caused problems and increase our capacity to foresee and ameliorate the impact of those events that are beyond our control. These life trials help us to mature psychologically, to function at higher levels of moral and ethical conduct, to tap our creative potentials, to develop arts and sciences, and to invent new technologies and models for the purpose of improving the conditions of life for all who dwell on earth. 'Abdu'l-Bahá points out that tests are inevitable and explains:

> Were it not for tests, pure gold could not be distinguished from the impure.
>
> Were it not for tests, the courageous could not be separated from the cowardly.
>
> Were it not for tests, the people of faithfulness could not be known from the disloyal.
>
> Were it not for tests, the intellectuals and the faculties of the scholars in great colleges would not develop.
>
> Were it not for tests, sparking gems could not be known from worthless pebbles.
>
> Were it not for tests, nothing would progress in the contingent world....[48]

LIFE AND DEATH

No discourse on religion is complete without a reference to the issue of death and the afterlife. In the psychological sense, awareness of the processes of life and death is intimately related to our sense of time. In infancy, at the dawn of our consciousness, life seems eternal and death unreal. However, the unpredictable course of life, the repetitive pattern of union and separation, and the painful experiences of loss and abandonment soon make us aware of the reality of death and our mortality. The materialistic perspective of life, which considers death as the end of human existence, does not equip us with the necessary powers to deal with this immense challenge—our possible non-existence. From psychological and scientific perspectives, the concept of self-annihilation is both unimaginable and irrational. Existence cannot become nonexistent. Both the human body and human soul (consciousness) are realities that we encounter in every moment of our lives, and imagining either of them becoming nonexistent is illogical. We know how our physical body will continue to exist. But, we do not know the state of our *spiritual reality*—that reality which we experience as the *self*—after we die. We have no knowledge whatsoever about our condition after death; therefore, whatever we assume it to be is at best conjecture.

In the face of this uncertainty, two basic approaches are open to us—to deny or to accept the possibility of life after death. Those who adopt a materialistic perspective that there is no life after death often choose to deny the reality of death and behave as though they will live forever. Once this psychological pattern is firmly established, the human propensities towards selflessness, other-directedness, generosity, and humility give way to their opposites. Not infrequently, the denial of death also contributes to the individual's sense of omnipotence, often expressed in irrational risk-taking or violent behavior. Such individuals live the precious and limited days of their lives focused primarily on securing their survival and getting what they can in the competitive jungle of life.[49] This is exactly how animals live out their existence.

However, death cannot be denied forever, and eventually there comes a time when we have to face death. Because death is a journey into the unknown and frequently takes place in the context of disease, pain, and weakness, many understandably fear it. It is therefore not surprising that increasingly people who do not accept the continuity of life after death seek ways to avoid facing the unpleasant and painful conditions that often accompany death. Here is a wish expressed by the prominent atheist and scientist, Richard Dawkins:

> When I am dying, I should like my life to be taken out under a general anesthetic, exactly as if it were a diseased appendix. But I shall not be allowed that privilege, because I have the ill-luck to be born a member of *Homo sapiens* rather than, for example, *Canis familiaris* or *Felis catus*.[50]

'Abdu'l-Bahá addresses the fundamental reason for the profound fear of death as felt by most people. He points out that belief that at the moment of death the human reality becomes nonexistent is the primary cause of this fear:

> The conception of annihilation is a factor in human degradation, a cause of human debasement and lowliness, a source of human fear and abjection. It has been conducive to the dispersion and weakening of human thought whereas the realization of existence and continuity has upraised man to sublimity of ideals, established the foundations of human progress and stimulated the development of heavenly virtues; therefore it behooves man to abandon thoughts of non-existence and death which are absolutely imaginary and see himself

ever living, everlasting in the divine purpose of his creation. He must turn away from ideas which degrade the human soul, so that day by day and hour by hour he may advance upward and higher to spiritual perception of the continuity of the human reality. If he dwells upon the thought of non-existence, he will become utterly incompetent; with weakened will-power his ambition for progress will be lessened and the acquisition of human virtues will cease.[51]

The Bahá'í teachings about life after death are related to our power of understanding, discussed earlier. This capacity is variably called the mind, psyche, rational soul, soul, heart, or spirit. All these terms are applicable to the same entity, the human spiritual reality. Because the soul is not material in nature and is not composed of parts, it is not subject to decomposition, and it therefore continues to exist. The central quality of the soul is the quality of awareness and consciousness. Bahá'u'lláh states that "the soul, after its separation from the body, will continue to progress," that it will "endure" eternally, that "it will manifest the signs of God and His attributes," and that its nature after death "can never be described...."[52]

'Abdu'l-Bahá likens the relationship between this world and the next life to the relationship between the world of the womb and this life. In the same manner that we had no awareness, knowledge, or understanding of this life while we were in the world of the womb, likewise, our knowledge and understanding of the existence and nature of the next life is totally lacking. In the world of the womb we lived a life while preparing for life in this world. The same is true about this life and its relationship with the next world. Here also we have the twin opportunities and tasks of living a meaningful, fruitful, and joyful life in this world and, through acquisition of spiritual qualities and virtuous deeds, to prepare ourselves for life in the spiritual world beyond. 'Abdu'l-Bahá, in response to a question from an individual about the next life, provides the following explanations:

> As to thy question regarding discoveries made by the soul after it hath put off its human form: certainly, that world is a world of perceptions and discoveries, for the interposed veil will be lifted away and the human spirit will gaze upon souls that are above, below, and on a par with itself. It is similar to the condition of a human being in the womb, where his eyes are veiled, and all things are hidden away from him. Once he is born out of the uterine world and entereth this life, he findeth it, with relation to that of the womb, to be a place of perceptions and discoveries, and he observeth all things through his outer eye. In the same way, once he hath departed this life, he will

behold, in that world whatsoever was hidden from him here: but there he will look upon and comprehend all things with his inner eye. There will he gaze on his fellows and his peers, and those in the ranks above him, and those below. As for what is meant by the equality of souls in the all-highest realm, it is this: the souls of the believers, at the time when they first become manifest in the world of the body, are equal, and each is sanctified and pure. In this world, however, they will begin to differ one from another, some achieving the highest station, some a middle one, others remaining at the lowest stage of being. Their equal status is at the beginning of their existence; the differentiation followeth their passing away.[53]

TOWARDS A UNIVERSAL CODE OF ETHICS

I have chosen to end this chapter with a brief reference to the issue of ethics. I have done so because of several interrelated reasons. First, no civilization can be established or maintained in the absence of a specific code of ethics. In fact, civilization, by definition, is an ethical state of collective human life. Second, the processes of psychological growth and spiritual transformation and the concept of unity are ethical in nature and could not take place in the absence of a code of ethics. Third, order is a necessary prerequisite for progress. In the absence of order, a destructive chaos interjects itself into human life and creates conditions that hinder the process of development of both the individual and the society. One of the main roles of morality and ethics is to prevent the reign of disorder and confusion in human life and relationships and to provide a framework within which the processes of growth and progress could be achieved in harmony with the inherent laws of life.

The issue of ethics has always been a source of controversy among various communities, religions, and philosophical schools of thought. However, in modern times this controversy has assumed a special intensity in a world rampant with religious fanaticism and scientific materialism. Both religious fanaticism and scientific materialism engender ethics of separation, exclusion, and inequality. Religious and ideological fanaticism creates *ethics of self-righteousness*; while scientific materialism gives birth to *ethics of self-centeredness*. The former is passionate and oppressive, while the latter is cold and removed. Neither could sustain a civilization of progress and peace.

A new code of ethics is called for, based on the principle of the harmony of science and religion as the two main sources of guidance and inspiration of humankind. Here is a preliminary definition:

> Ethics is a philosophical and scientific discipline concerned with the application of spiritual principles to the processes and systems of the life of humanity. Morality is the individual application of the universal ethical principles.

This definition contains several basic features that are required for the development of a comprehensive code of ethics commensurate with the needs of the emerging global civilization. According to this definition, ethics employs the scientific method and logical avenues of enquiry and draws from the spiritual reservoir of moral guidance contained in the main teachings of religion, in order to identify those universal ethical principles that distinguish right from wrong in human conduct.

As stated previously, at the core of being human lie three capacities—to know, love, and will. These capacities are subject to the laws of growth that govern life. Therefore, under healthy conditions, our capacity to know develops through modalities of research and independent search for truth. And as we discover new truths and live according to them, our lives become truth-based and truthful. Likewise, through the ongoing process of growth, change, and transformation, our ability to love becomes ever more refined and universal, and we develop ever greater ability and motivation to become unifiers and peacemakers. The same principles of development apply to our power of free will, which in its mature evolved state becomes an instrument of service in our interpersonal relationships and a force for justice in our contributions to society. The qualities of truth and truthfulness, unity creating and peace making, and service and justice are ethical in nature and are natural outcomes of our wholesome biological, psychological, and spiritual maturation.[54]

We could also study the issue of ethics from the perspective of human primary needs on a developmental scale. During the first phase of our development—infancy and childhood in individuals and the early phase of community building as a group—our primary needs revolve around issues of survival and security. Therefore, the predominant ethics during this phase of individual and group life are *ethics of survival.* During this period all human capacities are primarily employed to ensure the survival of the organism. In the second phase of development, which is characterized by an adolescent mindset, the *ethics of identity* assume primacy. Most human behavior and actions, within the framework of adolescent mindset, are aimed at establishing our uniqueness, separateness, and individuality. These two ethical constructs—survival and identity—are most prevalent in our world today. As we, individually and collectively, come of age, a new kind of ethics, the *ethics of unity*, shall govern our approach to life and to one another. The nature and purpose of human life shall then revolve around the spiritual law of unity based on the universal and selfless application of the human capacity to love.

The transition from survival- and identity-based ethics to that of unity-based ethics is only possible in the context of a spiritual life based on the foundations of religion, in its pure, authentic, and progressive expression. The uniqueness of human nature lies, not in its similarity to animal nature, but rather in those qualities that enable us to transcend the dictates of instinctual forces operative in biological life. It is through this process that the human tendency toward selfishness, greed, ambition, deceit, and aggression is transcended and replaced by the spiritual qualities of universality, generosity, pursuit of excellence, truthfulness, and love. 'Abdu'l-Bahá, in *The Secret of Divine Civilization*, his timeless treatise on the role of religion in civilization, written in 1875, states:

> Universal benefits derive from the grace of the Divine religions, for they lead their true followers to sincerity of intent, to high purpose, to purity and spotless honor, to surpassing kindness and compassion, to the keeping of their covenants when they have covenanted, to concern for the rights of others, to liberality, to justice in every aspect of life, to humanity and philanthropy, to valor and to unflagging efforts in the service of mankind. It is religion, to sum up, which produces all human virtues, and it is these virtues which are the bright candles of civilization.[55]

Clearly, these teachings of religion have direct effect not only on the life of the individual but also on the kind of the society we create. From a Bahá'í perspective, the welfare of the individual and that of the society are totally interwoven, and one cannot be accomplished without the other.

SUMMARY

In a response to an individual Bahá'í who asked 'Abdu'l-Bahá about the rules that should guide the life of a Bahá'í, a concise response was given, which in my view contains all of the points that I have attempted to include in this chapter, and more. Here are 'Abdu'l-Bahá's counsels in point form:

- Believe in God;
- Keep your eyes focused on the Divine Revelation;
- Be enamored with the love of Bahá'u'lláh (the Manifestation of God);
- Stand firm in the Covenant;
- Be always prepared to enter the "Heaven of the Universal Light";
- Be detached from the material aspects of this world;
- Be spiritual;
- Be a summoner to love;
- Be kind to all the human race;
- Love the children and share in their sorrows;
- Be of those who foster peace;
- Offer your friendship;
- Be worthy of trust;
- Be a balm to every sore, a medicine for every ill;
- Bind the souls together;
- Rest not for a moment, so that you may
- Become a sign and symbol of God's love, and a banner of His grace.[56]

CHAPTER FIVE

MARRIAGE
A FORTRESS FOR WELL-BEING

And when He desired to manifest grace and beneficence to men, and to set the world in order, He revealed observances and created laws; among them He established the law of marriage, made it as a fortress for well-being and salvation....[1]

—Bahá'u'lláh

...the importance of marriage lieth in the bringing up of a richly blessed family, so that with entire gladness they may, even as candles, illuminate the world. For the enlightenment of the world dependeth upon the existence of man. If man did not exist in this world, it would have been like a tree without fruit.[2]

—'Abdu'l-Bahá

My advice to you is to get married. If you find a good wife, you'll be happy; if not, you'll become a philosopher.[3]

—Socrates

Marriage is the golden ring in a chain, whose beginning is a glance and whose ending is eternity.[4]

—Khalil Gibran

"In the world of existence there is indeed no greater power than the power of love."[5] Love is the magnet that brings people together, creates unity, and establishes peace. And because it is impossible to show genuine unconditional love and create true unity in the absence of equality, fairness, compassion, and justice, it follows that these seemingly independent conditions are all expressions of the power of love. Love is a multidimensional reality. It has biological, psychological, social, moral, and spiritual facets, and impacts life at all levels. Research shows that love is the essential ingredient for healthy human development in all respects.[6] All human qualities best mature in an environment that is loving and encouraging, enlightened and conducive to learning, and compassionate and fair. In all cultures and throughout human history, we observe that the twin institutions of marriage and family have proven to be most suitable and capable for providing loving and nurturing environments essential for healthy human development. In this chapter I will address the elusive topic of love, in general, and marital love, in particular. I also will discuss some of the main characteristics of marriage at each of its stages of development. The chapter following reviews the institution of the family. Both chapters draw heavily from lessons learned in the course of my three decades of psychiatric practice, a significant portion of which was devoted to clinical work focusing on marriage and family. In addition, I will specifically outline some of the main Bahá'í teachings regarding the institutions of marriage and family and some issues regarding the task of parenting.

UNRAVELING THE MYSTERIES OF LOVE
AN UNENDING PROCESS

First, when I was apart from you,
this world did not exist,
nor any other.
Second, whatever I was looking for
was always you.
Third, why did I ever learn to count to three?[7]

Thus, Rumi encapsulates the mystery, the beauty, the indispensability, and the inevitability of love—divine in its essence and human in its expression, mysterious in its origins and rational in its effects, personal in its experience and universal in its impact, immediate in its power and eternal in its influence. Love can be creative or destructive, exclusive or inclusive, moral or immoral, disciplined or promiscuous, hot or cold, joyous or painful, blind or enlightened, realistic or imagined. Love has at least seven specific facets of expression: sensual, sexual, emotional, mental, moral, social, and spiritual. At various stages of life and in different modes of living, one or more of these facets of love predominate. However, the initial kernel and the potentiality for the efflorescence of all these facets of love are present throughout life. Ideally, all aspects of love could and should be helped to develop so that the person becomes a source of genuine love with all its creative powers. In its full bloom, human love has many diverse and awe-inspiring expressions. The choices and chances of life and its unexpected and turbulent processes, as well as the varieties of personal qualities, social norms, and family practices, together create a myriad of possible combinations of various facets of love. Thus we observe those who focus primarily on the sensual and sexual, or emotional and mental, or moral and ethical (social), or spiritual and universal facets of love. And we often encounter a mix of several of these facets both in their healthy and pathological expressions. We come across those whose love is possessive, jealous, oppressive, angry, conflicted, and violent. And we also encounter the kind of love that is freeing, trusting, empowering, compassionate, and unifying. The diversity and quality of expressions of love are too numerous to fully recount here, but a few musings on love can be enlightening.

Shakespeare asks, "Who ever loved that loved not at first sight?"[8] and concludes that "[t]o be wise and love, Exceeds Man's might."[9] And Einstein, invoking the laws of physics assures us that "[g]ravitation cannot be held responsible for people falling in love."[10] And Mozart, speaking of genius observes that "[n]either a lofty degree of intelligence nor imagination nor both together go to the making of genius. Love, love, love, that is the soul of genius." However, Freud warns, "One is very crazy when in love"[11] and states that "[i]t is always possible to bind together a considerable number of people in love, so long as there are other people left over to receive the manifestations of their aggression."[12] And Martin Luther King, Jr. stresses that "[m]ankind must evolve for all human conflict a method which rejects revenge, aggression, and retaliation. The foundation of such a method is love."[13] But what this method for eradication of human conflict and aggression by means of love could be and how it would look, he did not specify. And, Confucius focuses on the practical side of love, offering this wise counsel: "Choose a job you love, and you will never have to work a day in your life."[14] 'Abdu'l-Bahá takes the discourse on love to a higher and broader level. On October 24, 1912, in Paris at a public gathering, a person from India said to 'Abdu'l-Baha, "My aim in life is to transmit as far as in me lies the message of Krishna to the world," and 'Abdu'l-Bahá said:

> The Message of Krishna is the message of love. All God's prophets have brought the message of love. None has ever thought that war and hate are good. Every one agrees in saying that love and kindness are best.
>
> Love manifests its reality in deeds, not only in words—these alone are without effect. In order that love may manifest its power there must be an object, an instrument, a motive.
>
> There are many ways of expressing the love principle; there is love for the family, for the country, for the race, there is political enthusiasm, there is also the love of community of interest in service. These are all ways and means of showing the power of love....We must find a way of spreading love among the sons of humanity.
>
> Love is unlimited, boundless, infinite! Material things are limited, circumscribed, finite. You cannot adequately express infinite love by limited means.
>
> The perfect love needs an unselfish instrument, absolutely freed from fetters of every kind.
>
> The love of family is limited; the tie of blood relationship is not the strongest bond. Frequently members of the same family disagree, and even hate each other.

Patriotic love is finite; the love of one's country causing hatred of all others, is not perfect love! Compatriots also are not free from quarrels amongst themselves.

The love of race is limited; there is some union here, but that is insufficient. Love must be free from boundaries! To love our own race may mean hatred of all others, and even people of the same race often dislike each other.

Political love also is much bound up with hatred of one party for another; this love is very limited and uncertain.

The love of community of interest in service is likewise fluctuating; frequently competitions arise, which lead to jealousy, and at length hatred replaces love....

All these ties of love are imperfect. It is clear that limited material ties are insufficient to adequately express the universal love.

The great unselfish love for humanity is bounded by none of these imperfect, semi-selfish bonds; this is the one perfect love, possible to all mankind, and can only be achieved by the power of the Divine Spirit. No worldly power can accomplish the universal love."

'Abdu'l-Bahá concluded his talk with the counsel: "Love One Another."[15]

FACETS AND STAGES OF LOVE

In an attempt to unravel the mysteries of love, two charts are presented in order to better visualize the manifold expressions and stages of love. The first diagram deals with what I call *facets of love*. By this I mean that there are distinct, yet interrelated, expressions of love that can be summarized in seven categories: sensual, sexual, emotional, mental, moral, social, and spiritual (universal). The first two categories—sensual and sexual—belong to the biological; the next two—emotional and mental—to the psychological; the fifth and sixth—moral and social—to the existential (relational); and finally the seventh—universal—to the spiritual realms of life. At any given time, all these facets of love are present in varying degrees or, at least, at a potential level, within every human being. They are inherent aspects of our humanness. However, these facets of love have also a developmental quality, and each appears more fully and forcefully at different stages of our biological, psychological, social, and spiritual development, which are to a considerable extent dependent on our own efforts.

Diagram 5.1 presents the seven facets of love along with their modes of expression, primary objectives, and their signs under healthy and unhealthy conditions. The second diagram depicts the manner in which human love evolves on the axis of time and personal effort. Although these diagrams depict the facets and stages of love on a hierarchical continuum, in actual life experience, at any given time elements of all facets and stages are present. Therefore, when we designate a certain type of relationship being for example "emotional," it means that the predominant and most frequent expressions of love by this person are with regard to this aspect of love and this specific stage of its development. However, given the necessary environment and motivation, all facets of love can be nurtured and further developed.

Diagram 5.2 depicts the various facets of love on a developmental axis, beginning with the predominance of the biological—sensual and sexual—facets of love, which are soon augmented with the psychological—emotional and mental—flowering of human love. While many love relationships stop their development at this level, many others are further enriched by the development of the moral and ethical facets of love, which are usually expressed within the framework of group identities along racial, religious, national, ethnic, linguistic, and other identity demarcations. While these various expressions and levels of development of love are positive, nevertheless, they are always prone to misapplication and even malicious application with results completely contrary to the fundamental nature and purpose of love itself. Thus we observe much hatred, injustice, prejudice, conflict, and violence in the name of honor, patriotism, racial solidarity, religious beliefs, and other types of limited love. For love to be fully and constructively expressed, it must be universal. This point needs further elaboration.

Biological facets of love are instinctually based, quite autonomic in their expression, and completely self-focused in their objective. When we satisfy our hunger, feel sexually aroused, or hear a stirring melody, we normally feel a certain level of gratification, which we usually interpret as love and often seek its repetition in the course of our lives. Thus, it is not surprising that the earliest and most primal expressions of love are found in the acts of parents feeding their children, children engaging in self-erotic activities, and adults engaging in sexual activities together. There are many other expressions of biological love throughout life, but these few examples are sufficient for our purposes here.

Facets of Love	Mode of Expression	Primary Objective	Signs of Evolved Love	Signs of Arrested Love
Sensual	Through the five senses	Gratification	Joy of living	Psychosomatic Disorders
Sexual	Sexual activities	Gratification and procreation	Capacity to give and receive; to nurture life	Sexual disorders
Emotional	Emotive and expressive	To connect and to experience	Intimacy and creativity	Conflicted passions (hot love)
Mental	Reflective and reasoned	To understand and to be understood	To search and to discover	Indifference and detachment (cold love)
Moral	Mutuality and reciprocity	To be good and to do good	Understanding and compassion	Hatred and cold-heartedness
Social	Ethics-based social institutions	Community building	Practice of justice, equality and cooperation	Injustice, tyranny and prejudice
Universal	Consciousness of the oneness of humanity	To unite	Unity in diversity; peace	Division and violence

Diagram 5.1. Facets of love.

Notes:

- "Mental" in this chart refers to "intellectual" as contrasted with "emotional" states.
- "Social" in this chart refers to the process of community building and creation of conditions of structural equality, justice, respect for human rights, etc., all of which are ethical in nature.
- "Procreation" is the primary objective of sexual activity in animals and humans alike. However, at the human level the elements of choice and chance are both present.

Biological Aspects of Love		Psychological Aspects of Love		Relational Aspects of Love		Spiritual Love
Sensual Love	Sexual Love	Emotional Love	Mental Love	Moral Love	Social Love	**Universal Love**
Sensual Love	Sexual Love	Emotional Love	Mental Love	Moral Love	**Social Love**	Universal Love
Sensual Love	Sexual Love	Emotional Love	Mental Love	**Moral Love**	Social Love	Universal Love
Sensual Love	Sexual Love	Emotional Love	**Mental Love**	Moral Love	Social Love	Universal Love
Sensual Love	Sexual Love	**Emotional Love**	Mental Love	Moral Love	Social Love	Universal Love
Sensual Love	**Sexual Love**	Emotional Love	Mental Love	Moral Love	Social Love	Universal Love
Sensual Love	Sexual Love	Emotional Love	Mental Love	Moral Love	Social Love	Universal Love

Diagram 5.2. Stages of development of the seven facets of love.

As we grow and become more familiar with our emotions and more able to integrate them with our biological facets of love, both the intensity and the excitement of love increase. Here, a set of opposite emotions, all based on the dialectic of union and separation, which is at the core of interpersonal love, dominates every aspect of the love relationship. Among the most commonly experienced forms of this dialectic are closeness and aloofness, acceptance and rejection, attachment and loss, approval and disapproval, and recognition and indifference. These are powerful human existential experiences, and each side of the dialectic produces its own set of emotions. Thus, conditions conducive to union create feelings of joy, hope, certitude, and calm; while conditions based on separation cause feelings of sorrow, despondency, fear, and anger. Relationships that are fundamentally based on the bonds of biological and emotional attachment tend to be erratic, erotic, highly conflicted, quite unstable, and often prone to violence—verbal, physical, or both. This type of love is characteristic of an adolescent approach to love, is often described as a blind or romantic love, and is quite devoid of reason and reasonableness.

When mental love, with its reflective and reasoned qualities, is added to biological and emotional love, it traverses a major milestone. This is so, because within the framework of a reflective and contemplative love, the individuals involved have the opportunity to develop ever greater measures of self-knowledge and the knowledge of the other(s). And knowledge acts as light, clarifies the unclear areas of the relationship, and brings the much-needed attributes of trust, mutuality, and understanding to it. A love relationship that in addition to its biological balance and emotional intensity is also enlightened with ever greater degrees of understanding functions as a unified whole in search of truth and beauty. Once the dimension of knowledge (mental love) is added to the love process, we not only begin to know each other better but also are able to greatly expand the horizon of our love. We soon begin to taste the ecstasies of *love of knowledge,* search and discovery, communication and deliberation, information and awareness, understanding and insight, encountering mysteries and making efforts to discover the mysteries of each new mystery. *Love of knowledge* is the fountainhead of all sciences and arts, and the creative power behind all human discoveries and inventions.

Next comes the *love of the good and the beautiful.* This love is the source of human striving for kindness and compassion, charity and generosity, sacrifice and philanthropy, togetherness and unity, cooperation and mutuality, freedom from prejudice and universality—in short the *love of morality*. While moral love is a personal attribute, once its principles—to be good and do good—are translated into social actions aimed at creating conditions of social justice and equality, then our love further expands its reach and creates social conditions and institutions that are imbued with the sentiments and practices of the *ethics of love*. As we see, development of love is an ever-deepening and ever-expanding process. Love, in its true sense, knows no boundaries and, in its most developed and authentic state, expresses itself in the context of *Universal Love,* based on the consciousness of oneness of humanity and the practice of unity in diversity with the specific objective of creating all-inclusive peace.

For love to be expressed in a healthy manner in all its facets from the biological to universal, it has to draw from the infinite source of all love—the *love of the Divine*—that love which sanctifies our biological love, purifies our emotional love, enlightens our intellectual love, universalizes our moral and social love. It is through this kind of love that we move from selfish love to the all-inclusive love of all humanity, of life, of nature, and of all that exists. In this process we lose our ego in the caldron of love. Love is the spiritual expression of our feelings, thoughts, intentions, and actions. We, therefore, cannot truly love unless we have fallen in love with the Divine. This is the love that Rumi so eloquently and simply describes. In the end, all is love and all becomes love!

The task of unraveling the mysteries of love is never-ending. This task is an ongoing process that all humanity from the very beginnings has been engaged in and will continue forever its efforts to unravel the mysteries of love. Whenever mothers give birth, fathers care for daughters and sons, teachers delight in the learning of their students, poets write their poems, artists create, scientists discover, workers excel, leaders rise to the occasion, caregivers tend to the sick, the hungry are fed, the deprived are assisted, couples fall in love, families celebrate, communities unite, and lovers dread the pain of separation and anticipate the joy of reunion; as long as we live, pray, and give praise, we shall continue to unravel new mysteries of love. And in this process we shall always remember that not "[u]ntil love takes possession of the heart no other divine bounty can be revealed in it."[16]

Elements of Marital Love

Sensual + Sexual Love + Emotional Love
= **Romantic (Blind) Love**

Romantic Love + Love of Knowledge (self-knowledge and
knowledge of others)
= **Aware Love**

Aware Love + Love of Good (ethical and moral)
= **Enlightened Love**

Romantic Love + Aware Love + Enlightened Love
= **Spritualized Love**

Divine Love
= **Spiritualized Love** (romantic, aware, enlightened,
spiritualized)

The above formulae are based on the facets and stages of love described earlier. They point out that it is not enough to have profound and powerful emotional ties to an object of love to whom we are very attracted and in whose company we experience much gratification. It is not enough to have a good mixture of sensual, sexual, and emotional love with our marital partner. There are other fundamental ingredients that need to be added, the most important of which is the ingredient of self-knowledge and knowledge of our partner (mental love). In the context of all relationships—with nature, other humans, and God—we need to know ourselves and to be sure that we do not look at ourselves through the veils of make-believe, self-deception, ignorance, arrogance, fear, and selfishness. Because, if we are not in touch with our true self, if we do not know who and what we are, and if we are not courageous enough to be authentic and truthful with ourselves, then we will not be able to be so with others. In the context of marriage, husband and wife need to help each other to get to better know themselves, individually, and together as a couple. The deeper and more probing the couple's attempts are at self-knowledge and knowledge of each other, the more intimate and trusting will be their relationship. This is so because a combination of mutual attraction, gratification, and understanding is the most potent beginning for development of marital unity. This theme will be further elaborated later in this section.

Marital love relationships are complex, and we can identify three distinct but overlapping phases in the course of its development and maturation—*falling in love, self-discovery in love,* and *unity in love*—which will be discussed in the remainder of this chapter.

CHOOSING A MATE

AN ADMIXTURE OF CHANCE AND CHOICE

Choosing a mate is a combination of chance and choice, circumstance and decision that usually take place in the context of *falling in love.* Because at any given time we can only live in one physical space, to get to know well a limited number of people, establish close friendship with a smaller number of individuals, be attracted to only few persons for the possibility of marriage, and eventually marry one of them, it follows that our preference of a marital partner is a combination of chance and choice. Even in the electronic and rapid-travel age in which we live, we are still subject to limitations of time, place, and person. However, in many cultures today and throughout human history, people have had and still have limited or no choice in mate selection. But, even in these circumstances of not choosing one's mate, there is still some measure of choice in deciding how to proceed once married. In my own family we have had several examples of the combination of chances and choice, two of which I recount here because I feel they contain instructive lessons regarding issues of marriage and marital love.

Following the accidental and untimely death of his father, my father left his mountainous village of Banadak and moved to the small town of Ardekan, both located in the province of Yazd.[17] In this town he became renowned as an "honest" government tax collector. In the Persian society at that time honest tax-collection was an oxymoron. Tax collectors were known to be corrupt, cruel, and highly powerful. My father was none of these. In fact, he was known to be an honest, kind, and unassuming government representative, and because of this novelty, he was highly respected and befriended by many.

Being a stranger in the community and not having any family members to help him to find a suitable wife, he decided to employ the good services of an intermediary who would act as a quasi-family member to make the necessary contacts, negotiations, and arrangements. My father was familiar with the members of the Bahá'í Community of Ardekan and knew of a Sadr family who were reputable and trustworthy people and who had a marriage-age daughter. He, therefore, asked the intermediary to contact the Sadr family and obtain their agreement for him to marry their daughter.

At that time two Sadr families resided in Ardekan. One was the little known Bahá'í Sadr family, and the other was the extremely well-known and powerful Sadr'ul'ulama family who were also generally referred to as Sadr. The intermediary, who was a Muslim and not familiar with the Bahá'í Sadr family, approached the other family, who consulted the patriarch of the family, Sadr'ul'ulama—the Grand Sadr, meaning the leader and senior of the learned—himself about advisability of his grand-daughter marrying my father. In particular, the girl's parents were concerned about the "rumors" that my father was a Bahá'í. Reportedly, the Grand Sadr stated: "This man is honest and of the lineage of the Prophet Himself, and we do not need to worry about anything else!" Thus, the consent for marriage was given, the intermediary accordingly informed my father, and they together began the necessary wedding preparations, all of which were handled with the family of the bride through this intermediary as my father's representative.

On the wedding day, the intermediary met my father and they proceeded on foot towards the home of the bride's family where the wedding was being held. However, my father noticed that they were not going in the direction of the home of the Bahá'í Sadr, and when he inquired, to his amazement and surprise he discovered that his intermediary had approached the Muslim Sadr rather than the intended Bahá'í Sadr family. My father realized the seriousness and sensitivity of his precarious situation. He had two choices, to cancel the wedding or go ahead and get married. The former choice was fraught with considerable danger, considering the fact that the family of the bride were the most powerful and influential in the whole region and that he was, as an outsider and as a member of a persecuted religious minority, already highly disadvantaged. The second choice, getting married with a person from a family totally unknown to him was also problematic. However, neither option provided him with personal knowledge of either woman. In the highly restrictive and oppressive Persia in the mid-1930s, it was simply socially unacceptable for young men and women to meet and get acquainted prior to their marriage. In the face of this reality, my father concluded that with respect to the personality and character of his future bride, either option was quite uncertain. He, therefore, took this strange turn of events as an act of providence and proceeded to go to the house of his soon to be in-laws. As it turned out, my parents had a magnificent marriage. They had seven children, four boys and three girls. They remained happily married until my father died in a traffic accident at the age of 65.

The second example that also demonstrates the operation of chance and choice in choosing a mate is with regard to my own marriage. In this case the element of choice was far greater than that of chance. Nevertheless, as it will be seen, chance also played a role in the process.

In December, 1963, I was one of two candidates invited for a final interview for the single available training position in the psychiatric residency program in Cincinnati, Ohio. A few days earlier, I had also received an unconditional acceptance at one of my choices in Chicago. At that time I was living in Philadelphia, where I had been a resident in the Department of Physical Medicine and Rehabilitation since my arrival in the United States six months earlier. Soon after I started my training in Physical Medicine, I realized that I had chosen the wrong area of specialization for me. The field of rehabilitation is a noble and essential area of medicine. However, it requires a special temperament and interest that I found I did not possess. I was more inclined to study the dynamics of human psychological processes in the context of medical science, learn about human psychiatric disorders, understand their biological and psychological genesis, and acquire the necessary insights and skills to treat those who suffer from such conditions. I was also interested in the relevance of psychological insights to communities and large populations. It was, therefore, best for me to pursue psychiatry as my area of medical specialization.

On Thursday, December 26, 1963, I packed my meager belongings into my car and left Philadelphia for Cincinnati. My plan was to reach Cincinnati later that day, to present myself for the interview the following morning, and, if accepted, to stay there and send my thanks and regrets to the residency program in Chicago. If not accepted, I would then proceed to Chicago. I was driving according to the speed limit on the Pennsylvania Turnpike, trying to pass a car ahead of me that was going much slower. However, unexpectedly that car (whose driver police later determined had fallen asleep) veered into my lane, and to avoid a collision I turned the wheels sharply to the left, jumped the median, and landed in the opposite traffic lanes, having made a 180-degree turn. Luckily, traffic was light and the oncoming cars were able to avoid hitting me. However, the car was badly damaged, and it was obvious that I would not be able to reach Cincinnati for the interview and, therefore, after the repairs, I proceeded directly to Chicago.

During the years of my specialization training I primarily lived in the city of Chicago and participated in the activities of the Bahá'í community, which constituted a significant part of my extracurricular and public service activities. The Chicago Bahá'í community in the early 1960s, as it is today, was very diverse, with members from different races, nationalities, religious, and ethnic backgrounds. I established several lasting and meaningful friendships, among them Genevieve and Philip Bernstein. This wonderful couple truly exemplified the Bahá'í principle of unity in diversity. Gene and Phil—as they were known to friends—came from strongly religious backgrounds, Catholic and Jewish respectively. Their families became estranged from them when they married during the early post-Depression years in America. As a young couple, quite alone and with very modest means, they faced enormous challenges and hardship with great dignity and resilience. Gene and Phil had two remarkable and devoted daughters—Judith and Michele—and eventually all four of them became Bahá'ís and joined the Chicago Bahá'í Community in the late 1950s. From then on, the entire family devoted themselves to many varied activities in the spirit of service to humanity.

I came to know this fine family well and eventually married Michele, who among other things was a highly gifted ballet artist, both as a dancer and choreographer, and an outstanding mother to our two sons, Arman and Roshan. It was at this stage in my professional life that I gradually became involved in counseling individuals and couples needing help in their love relationships and marriages. Increasingly, I observed the general confusion among my colleagues and others about the phenomenon of "love," its nature and dynamics, and in its various contexts, especially marriage. In reflecting on my life's journey over more than four decades of marriage, I realize that the central theme of the entire process for me has been about learning the mysteries, dynamics, and expressions of love, in general, and marital love, in particular.

FROM FALLING IN LOVE TO UNITY IN LOVE

Increasingly in our world the element of choice is becoming more prevalent than chance in determining a marriage partner. This trend will accelerate significantly, as the recognition, acceptance, and practice of gender equality become the norm in more societies and cultures, both old and new. This choice—choosing a mate—usually occurs in the context of the operation of the forces of romantic love—attraction, gratification, and attachment. We usually fall in love when we encounter another person to whom we are strongly attracted and who is also attracted to us. This attraction may be with regard to the physical beauty of the other person, his or her particular qualities, ways of talking and thinking, standards by which that person conducts his/her life, or the manner in which he or she brings excitement and novelty and creativity to the relationship. Another component of the process of *'falling in love'* is mutual need-gratification. We humans are needy creatures. We need security and safety, comfort and ease, appreciation and approval, courage and encouragement, and intimacy and individuality; and whenever we meet a person who can satisfy at least some of these needs, we wish to be connected with that person. Seeds of love best germinate and grow in the ground where the ingredients of mutual attraction and need gratification are abundantly present.

In the course of my years of work with many couples and those who were planning to marry and those who were in the midst of falling in love, I learned of the remarkably varied ways that people experience and express their love. The basic ingredients and processes, however, remain the same. Marital love relationships usually begin with a choice or chance encounter, freely pursued or arranged by others, and then each person in the love relationship goes through certain specific stages. However, this first stage—falling in love—has tremendous emotional and physical charge, and its impact is imprinted into our memories. Unless we are able to maintain and increase its main elements of mutual attraction and gratification, there is always a danger that either of the partners will seek new romantic relationships. Increasingly common serial romantic relationships in the contemporary world contribute greatly to the breakdown of many marriages. Because of this fact we need to better understand how we can ensure that our marital love relationship does not fall prey to the desire for a new relationship, but rather proceeds to its next phase of development.

The dynamics of transition from romantic love to an enlightened and reasoned love relationship are complex and revolve around the central issue of role of knowledge in human life, in general, and role of self-knowledge, in particular. The importance of self-knowledge has been extolled by many. However, a definitive approach to it is yet to be identified. Modern psychology, particularly the analytic schools pioneered by Freud and Jung, made the issue of self-knowledge central to their objectives. However, their definition of self-knowledge was limited and dealt primarily with the interface between biological (survival, pleasure, and pain) and psychological (identity, relationships, and sense of fulfillment) aspects of human life. In general, the analytic school rejected moral and spiritual aspects of life as distinctive dimensions of being *whole humans* and considered them to be secondary to the biological and psychological dimensions. Interestingly, in recent decades human psychology practitioners have strayed far from the objective of helping their clients to achieve even this narrow and limited measure of self-knowledge. Instead, the focus of current materialistic psychiatry and psychology, particularly evolutionary psychology, is primarily on "how we can best *adapt* to the challenges of life" rather than "how can we best *understand* ourselves in the context of life-challenges." The former approach is an adaptive process in the context of self-preservation.[18] The latter approach—self-knowledge—is a transformative process, which ensures both self-preservation and self-development.

Self-knowledge is only possible when we make concerted efforts to comprehend various aspects of our personhood—biological, psychological, social, moral, and spiritual—and integrate them into a coherent, dynamic, and harmonious framework conducive to our wholesome development. And this task cannot be accomplished alone or without active involvement with society in the context of relationships. It is through relationships that we have the greatest opportunity to know and improve ourselves. Relationships act as mirrors reflecting those aspects of our being that are usually out of our conscious field of vision. And of all relationships, marital and family relationships are the clearest mirrors because they reflect the most intimate and deepest aspects of our selfhood, from biological to spiritual. For the marriage and family to function in a healthy manner, the most important requisites are those conducive to unity. And unity calls for self-sacrifice—letting go of ego—in order for us to see ourselves and each other more clearly in the mirror of the relationship.

The process of self-sacrifice or letting go of one's ego in marital and family relationships requires a mutually trusting environment, so that the couple would be able to share their thoughts, feelings, and aspirations without fear of distortion, misunderstanding, manipulation, ridicule, indifference, or rejection. These are difficult tasks to achieve in any relationship, and thus most human relationships are often incomplete, unsatisfactory, uneven, and unfulfilling. In the course of my years of work with individuals and families and the observations and research I have done on the dynamics of human relationships, in general, and marital relationships, in particular, I have reached the conclusion that the standard by which we can, with a high degree of assurance, measure the quality and authenticity of a given relationship is the degree of its capacity to create unity. To the extent that a relationship is able to create genuine unity, to that same extent it is solid, progressive, and progressing. Unity, of course, is a challenging phenomenon, and to be successful it requires openness and truthfulness, justice and fairness, kindness and compassion, and full regard for diversity and differences. Unity is not a state of calmness and placidity. Rather, unity is akin to a surging ocean with much turbulence and motion. Unity is achieved when differences are taken into account. When diversity of views, sentiments, and objectives are thoroughly considered. When the clouds of doubt and disagreement are dissipated in the heat of loving, frank, open, fair, and passionate discourse and interaction. Unity is an active and ever-evolving state.

I became aware of the fundamental role of unity in human relationships through three different channels: personal experiences, academic and clinical observations and research, and a systematic study of the extensive and intensive attention given to the issue of unity in the Bahá'í Writings. I have addressed the issue of unity in different chapters throughout this book. In the literature of the Bahá'í Faith, unity is viewed as a fundamental spiritual condition with far-reaching biological, psychological, social, and moral implications. The following statement aptly sums up the relationship between love, knowledge, and unity:

> When the lamp of search, effort, longing, fervor, love, rapture, attraction and devotion is enkindled in the heart, and the breeze of love blows forth from the direction of unity, the darkness of error, doubt and uncertainty will be dispelled and the lights of knowledge and assurance will encompass all the pillars of existence.[19]

MARRIAGE: A UNIVERSAL INSTITUTION

Marriage is a universal institution. It has always existed in some form as one of the most important building blocks of every society. However, despite this fact, quite often people's attitude towards marriage has been and continues to be ambivalent. On the one hand, several factors make marriage a very attractive milieu in which to live our lives. Among these factors are the dominant power of attraction between men and women; the natural forces of sexuality and the need to satisfy them in the context of understanding, compassion, and intimacy; the strong desire on the part of the majority of people to have children; and the security and comfort that the institution of marriage often provides.

On the other hand, we all know of marriages that are unloving and cruel, dangerous and unsafe, unfair and unhappy, distant and uninvolved, unfair and unequal, and restrictive and oppressive. Therefore, it is not suprising that in many societies marriage was and is imposed, particularly on the girls and women. Also, it is understandable that increasing numbers of individuals decide against marriage, many leave their marriages, and still others attempt to find alternatives to the historically established model of marriage as the union of women and men. In the context of this ambivalence, the institution of marriage as a religious, legal, social, economic, and emotional bond has lost much of its reliabilty, authenticity, and potency.

The Bahá'í teachings about marriage point to both the preservation and maturation of the institution of marriage. The institution of marriage is viewed to be a "divine creation," which has existed from the beginning of human life on this planet and will continue to do so in the future. 'Abdu'l-Bahá states that

> the command of marriage is eternal. It will never be changed nor altered. This is divine creation and there is not the slightest possibility that change or alteration affect this divine creation [marriage].[20]

However, this definitive statement about the permanence of the institution of marriage does not mean that it is not subject to growth, maturation, and transformation. In fact, the Bahá'í teachings strongly and clearly emphasize that our approach to marriage *has* to change. The authoritarian, oppressive, and unequal marriages of the past are definitely and strongly rejected. Bahá'í marriage must be characterized by love and unity as well as by equality of opportunities and responsibilities between husband and wife. The partners must make attempts to know each other's characters and personalities, become good and intimate friends in the context of their marriage, and help each other in their respective efforts to grow and mature. Oppression, cruelty, and violence are completely and definitely prohibited, and the husband and wife are admonished to make all their decisions and resolve all their differences through the practice of Bahá'í consultation (see chapter nine), with its aim to reach just, fair decisions based on facts and truths of the situation in the context of unity and cooperation. In these efforts, husband and wife must respect each other's views and wishes, and must regard their divergent perspectives as instruments for reaching richer, deeper decisions, while maintaining their unity as well as their individuality. In other words, in a healthy marriage there is ample room for both husband and wife to grow and develop individually and at the same time, together, nurture their marriage and attend to its needs.[21]

In a response to a question as to whether a husband or wife could prevent the spiritual development of the other, 'Abdu'l-Bahá states that in reality neither one of them can prevent the other from pursuing his or her spiritual quest "except when the husband hath a great attachment to the wife, or the wife to the husband. When either one of the two adoreth the other to the exclusion of God, then each will prevent the other from entering into the Kingdom of God."[22] This issue brings us to the concept of union as another important aspect of the idea of marriage as a divine creation.

MARRIAGE AS A UNION

'Abdu'l-Bahá provides this distinctive definition of marriage:

> Bahá'í marriage is union and cordial affection between the two parties. They must, however, exercise the utmost care and become acquainted with each other's character. This eternal bond should be made secure by a firm covenant, and the intention should be to foster harmony, fellowship and unity....[23]

Earlier, we discussed unity as the prime law of existence and an essential condition for creation, maintenance, and development of all human relationships and social institutions (chapter two). Marriage is no exception, thus its definition as a *union*. Union, like unity, is the outcome of the process of the coming together and bonding of different entities. In the case of marriage, union refers to the coming together of husband and wife in body, mind, and spirit, which results in physical, psychological, and spiritual benefits. The generative power of marital union is a shared love that goes beyond the transient physical qualities and attributes of husband and wife, and revolves around a shared transcendent point of attraction between them. 'Abdu'l-Bahá states that this mutual point of attraction and love in Bahá'í marriage should revolve around the couple's love and dedication to the ultimate object of human quest—God:

> ...the marriage of the people of Bahá must consist of both physical and spiritual relationship for both of them are intoxicated with the wine of one cup, are attracted by one Peerless Countenance, are quickened with one Life and are illumined with one Light. This is the spiritual relationship and everlasting union. Likewise in the physical world they are bound together with strong and unbreakable ties.[24]

The issue of having a shared, transcendent, noble, and universal point of attraction in the marriage is of paramount importance. It expands the horizon of the marriage and allows the couple to create a welcoming, hospitable, and open home within the parameters of their marital covenant—fidelity, truthfulness, equality, fairness, compassion, and unity. A transcendent and sublime Mutual Point of Attraction (MPA) in marriage brings the couple closer to each other, strengthens their love for one another, sustains them in difficult life circumstances, gives meaning and purpose to the sacrifices that marriage and family life inevitably entail. In brief, a noble, universal and transcendent MPA maintains and fortifies marital union. During many years of working as a family therapist with many married couples and families, I observed that the MPA played a major role in determining the capacity and willingness of the couple to withstand the many challenges of marital and family life. I noted that while some couples were well developed as individuals and as couples in the face of such divers tasks as parenting, illness, aging, and financial insecurities, others found themselves unable and/or unwilling to meet these demands. One of the determining factors in how different couples withstood the challenges of marital and family life was the nature and quality of their MPA. Those couples with limited, conflicted, temporary, or uninspiring MPAs frequently experienced crises of considerable magnitude. By contrast, those couples who shared high and noble ideas, who consciously dedicated themselves to creating a truly united family, whose scope of interest and care went far beyond the boundaries of their families and close friends had a greater ability to create balanced and healthy physical, psychological, and spiritual marital relationships, and demonstrated outstanding resilience and fortitude under difficult conditions. Based on these observations, I have identified three broad categories of marriages with distinct MPAs. For

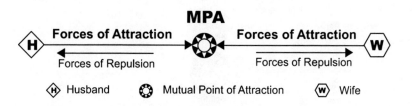

Diagram 5.3. Marriage with the husband and/or the wife as the Main Point of Attraction.

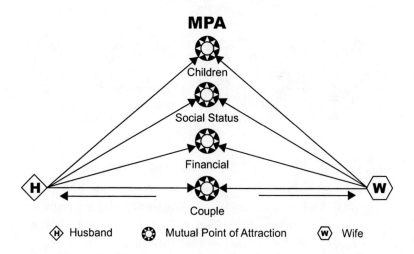

Diagram 5.4. Marriage with temporal Mutual Points of Attraction.

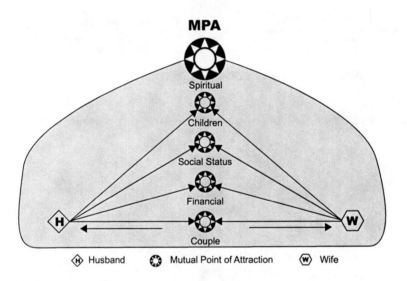

Diagram 5.5. Marriage with transcendent Mutual Point of Attraction; depicts the couple's attraction and love for a transcendent point of attraction and unity (Spiritual MPA) that, in turn, creates an uninterrupted, reciprocal, all-encompassing relationship between the couple, their children, their family and social life, all in the context of a physical, psychological, and spiritual bond of unity.

ease of reference, in the three diagrams below the dynamics of various MPAs are depicted and their significant role in shaping the functioning of the institution of the marriage is briefly outlined.

Marriages that have the husband and/or the wife as their sole or primary MPA are subject to the inevitable personal and interpersonal disappointments, misunderstandings, and unexpected developments (illness, success, failures, etc.) that occur in all marriages. In this type of marriage, the husband and wife are at once attracted to and repulsed from each other, and, depending on the frequency and intensity of these opposing sentiments, their marriage goes through stages of extreme closeness and antagonism as well as periods of less intense involvement, depending on various factors, some of which—such as illness, financial crises, unforeseen events—are beyond their control. In the face of these developments and disappointments, not infrequently, one or both partners may conclude that separation and divorce are "reasonable" and "understandable" solutions to their unsatisfactory marriage.

Marriages that are kept together primarily by joint interests and responsibilities of a temporal and time-specific nature such as parenting and financial or social considerations tend to be stable as long as these mutual areas of interest and responsibility have high priority on the respective personal agenda of the couple. However, when husband and/or wife conclude that there is no longer any important issue that connects them in their marriage, the possibility of separation and divorce increases dramatically. In the earlier phases of marriage, the couple are drawn together by forces of the novelty of their relationship, parenting responsibilities, upward financial and social progress, and other joint ventures and convictions. However, as the chances and choices of life take their toll on the couple and their marriage, the bonds that had kept them together in the earlier phases of their marriage lose their cohesive qualities, and either the wife or the husband, and not infrequently both of them, begin to feel less attached and attracted to the other. It is usually during this momentous phase that separation and divorce become a strong possibility.

Although subject to all of the various marital challenges and circumstances that do not have a spiritual perspective, marriages that are kept together through a mutual attraction to a transcendent source of love and goodness and ultimately God, tend to deal with these challenges more effectively, because of the powerful bond of unity based on their physical, psychological, social, moral, and spiritual union.

The twin issues of marriage as a *divine creation* and as a state of *union* are directly relevant to the primary purpose of marriage.

THE PURPOSE OF MARRIAGE

Whenever the topic of the purpose of marriage is approached, several distinct but interrelated reasons for marriage are offered—biological, psychological, social, and spiritual. *The biological purpose of marriage* is the propagation of the species. It is both natural and elemental in its importance. *The psychological purpose of marriage* revolves around the ever-present issue of human need to establish relationships, in general, and loving and intimate relationships, in particular. All processes of human life take place in the context of relationships—with oneself, others, nature, and ultimately God. Institutions of marriage and family provide the ideal milieu for us to establish, deepen, and refine all types of our relationships. It is in the context of the intimate and complex dynamics of marriage that we develop considerable insight about ourselves and the inner dynamics of our psyche and are forced to face our most private thoughts and deeply concealed emotions. We have no choice but to admit our shortcomings, at least to ourselves. It is in the context of marriage that we learn new ways of expressing love and also discover how inadequate, clumsy, fearful, and self-centered we may be in this regard. Likewise, it is within the intimate boundaries of marital and family relationships that we discover the extent of our ability and willingness to be compassionate, encouraging, self-sacrificing, and generous. As well, we learn of our deficiencies in these and other regards. Thus marriage functions as a mirror of our private inner self and clearly shows, in a magnified and authentic manner, a profile of our true self. This fact alone should be a sufficient reason to get married. We cannot find a better milieu than that of marriage and the family if we aim to live a life of self-knowledge, growth, and transformation.

The social benefits of marriage—community development and social order—have been known to humanity throughout history. In ancient times, as is the case in the contemporary world, it was understood that the powerful forces of physical attraction, emotional attachment, and personal sense of identity, which naturally develop between men and women in the context of intimacy, must be appropriately and effectively channeled. One important reason for the need to formalize intimate man–woman relationships in the context of marriage is to avoid the negative outcome of their failure. Failed intimate relationships are often the source of aggression and violence, extremes of jealousy and destructive competition, profound doubt about one's self-worth and lovability, and not infrequently, the cause of depression and self-destructive behavior. Thus, in traditional societies, social and religious laws governing the institution of the marriage have been quite restrictive and usually administered in authoritarian and punitive manners. The logic offered for these practices is usually summarized in the dictum that this is for the good of the couple and the society. However, as the history of marriage clearly demonstrates, in these types of marriages neither the individuals nor the society benefit; rather, they all, but particularly girls and women, suffer. As will be seen in the chapter on the family, new types of marital and family structure and relationships are needed in order to safeguard and promote the welfare of both individuals and the society.

The spiritual aspect of marriage includes the process of our becoming the source of service, love, justice, and unity for all humanity. Spirituality not only adds an extremely significant dimension to marriage itself but also renders all its other dimensions sacred and dramatically elevates their significance, scope, and impact. Life begins with the essential unity of matter and spirit at conception, then proceeds to encompass other points of unity, among the most important being united with another person in the bond of marriage and together creating a family and bringing forth children into this world. 'Abdu'l-Bahá points to the fundamental spiritual and social benefits of marriage:

> ...the importance of marriage lieth in the bringing up of a richly blessed family, so that with entire gladness they may, even as candles, illuminate the world. For the enlightenment of the world dependeth upon the existence of man. If man did not exist in this world, it would have been like a tree without fruit. My hope is that you both may become even as one tree, and may, through the outpourings of the cloud of loving-kindness, acquire freshness and charm, and may blossom and yield fruit, so that your line may eternally endure.[25]

However, as we delve deeper into the teachings of the Bahá'í Faith, it becomes evident that these lofty objectives could not be accomplished unless certain fundamental prerequisites for their success are present in the marriage and the family. Among these prerequisites is the extremely important and urgent issue of gender equality.

THE CHALLENGE OF EQUALITY

Equality between women and men is the cornerstone of the teachings of the Bahá'í Faith in all departments of human social life, but especially with regard to marriage and family. To create a marriage of equals and a family in which boys and girls and women and men are accorded equal rights and opportunities is among the principal teachings of the

Bahá'í Faith. This matter is considered to be of crucial importance, not only with respect to the happiness and well-being of the members of the human family and the strengthening of the foundations of human society but also as a major factor in the establishment of world prosperity and peace. 'Abdu'l-Bahá states that

> [t]he world of humanity has two wings—one is women and the other men. Not until both wings are equally developed can the bird fly. Should one wing remain weak, flight is impossible. Not until the world of women becomes equal to the world of men in the acquisition of virtues and perfections, can success and prosperity be attained as they ought to be.[26]

And again:

> When all mankind shall receive the same opportunity of education and the equality of men and women be realized, the foundations of war will be utterly destroyed.[27]

For members of the Bahá'í community, these views on gender equality do not constitute merely a set of progressive ideas. They are articles of faith and belief. They are the statements of truth and reality. They are unavoidable and essential blueprints for life. As such, they must become incorporated in the very process of life and be given priority over such issues as those deeply ingrained cultural norms and strongly held economic views that men should be accorded priority over women regarding their education and their position in society. In fact, the opposite is true in the Bahá'í Faith. Both parents and the institutions of the society are given the responsibility to provide equal opportunities and encouragement for education to all children, whether boys or girls. However, if under certain unusual circumstances the finances and opportunities are not available for the education of all children, then the girls must be given priority over the boys. One fundamental reason for this is the remarkably influential role that women play in the education of every new generation. Another equally important factor is that women historically have been and continue to be deprived of equal opportunities with men, and justice demands that they be given priority for their education, so that they would be able to assume equal positions of leadership and authority in the administration of the affairs of the society.

DEVELOPMENTAL STAGES OF MARRIAGE

Marriage is an evolving social entity, and we can identify three distinct but interrelated phases in the course of its normal evolution. These phases are hierarchical and cumulative at the same time. Each phase is followed by a more complex and insightful next phase, while at the same time safeguarding the main elements of the previous phase in a more refined and mature state. We gain greater levels of maturity in the course of each stage of our marriage in light of new insights from both life experiences and enlightened questioning. Each of these three stages is essential for development of marriage and cannot be eliminated without seriously affecting its healthy and wholesome growth.

Within this rather rigid framework, however, there are considerable variations in the rate, character, and emphasis of each stage of development in different marriages. While all marriages in the full course of their development traverse the same phases of growth, no two marriages are identical. Developmental stages do not force arbitrary norms on the institution of marriage and are akin to the individual stages of development from infancy and childhood through adolescence to adulthood and maturity. The diversity of marital experiences is due to the unique qualities of marriage partners and the highly varied life circumstances of each marriage that together shape the creative and distinctive development of each marriage within the universal pattern of growth of all marriages.

These issues are also crucially important for resolving marital problems that quite often occur. Resolution of marital problems requires both general and specific approaches. The general approach concerns the quality of development of the marriage and its transition from one stage to another. Within this general framework the progress and problems of every marriage are different because of the unique biological, psychological, educational, economic, and spiritual conditions of the husband and wife.

Developmental stages of marriage correspond with the phases of development of love on the axis of its biological, psychological, relational, and ethical particulars, which were described earlier in this chapter. The following three phases of marriage take into consideration the dynamics of development of love and power in marriage, the nature of marital communication, the partners' primary shared objectives of the marriage, and the degree in which a given marriage is able to provide its members the opportunity for individual growth in the context of marital unity and its healthy, full development.

Primary Union Phase

The Primary Union Phase of marriage corresponds with the process of falling in love—the romantic phase—of the relationship. Marriage relationships in this phase are rather incoherent and confused, and are marked by a mixture of hopes and despairs, expectations and disappointments, assumptions and revelations, desires and frustrations, needs and demands, and joys and sorrows. Romantic love is a blind love. In other words, each partner in the relationship sees in the other person *what he/she wants to see*. Thus, romantic love blinds us to the real qualities of the other. In the context of modern styles of marriage a strong binding force, usually in the form of romantic love with its considerable degree of mutual attraction and mutual need gratification, unites the newlywed couple. At times, these types of unions can be quite unstable. In more traditional marriages, the forces that keep the couple together are more of religious, social, legal, and economic nature. However, this type of marital union is often more imposed and less free. During this phase, the couple's parents, families, and close circle of friends, as well as the social, religious, and economic institutions of the society can play a significant role, either by strengthening or weakening the foundations of the marriage.

Parallel with these external forces, the new couple is faced with some fundamental and more personal private tasks that need to be addressed. The newlyweds need to learn how to move from personal to interpersonal modes of functioning, how to share in the joys and sorrows of life, how to be intimate with regard to their most private and intimate issues, how to enjoy sex and give sexual enjoyment, and how to relinquish individual preferences in favor of joint preferences. Above all, the couple needs to learn how to use power in the context of their growing love. These are daunting tasks, and most people are unprepared for them, making this phase of marriage very vulnerable. In this early phase of marriage, the novelty of these activities combined with the couple's inexperience, lack of clarity of their expectations, intensity of their emotions, confusion of their thoughts, and their uncertainty about themselves and each other, cause them to function in a rather primitive and elementary manner. During this period, the couple is subject to extremes and contrasting states of hope and despair, calm and anger, courage and fear, certitude and anxiety, and action and inaction. They cooperate in some respects and compete in others and are efficient in some tasks and hopeless in others. The overall picture is that of a poorly coordinated, highly confused, yet extremely powerful union of two individuals. This union, of necessity, must become more coherent, objective, and differentiated in order to be able to respond adequately to the manifold demands and opportunities of the evolving institution of marriage.

The duration of the primary union phase varies, depending on the unique characteristics of each marriage. Some couples have a fulfilling and exciting romantic relationship that gradually metamorphoses into an enlightened, creative, fulfilling, and intimate love relationship as the marriage traverses the other two phases. Other couples tend to remain in the first phase for a relatively short time before moving on to the next phase. This is particularly true for those couples who were intimately involved before they decided to get married. Still other couples tend to remain at the same level of marital development and follow a circular rather than evolving pattern. These couples tend to repeat the same mistakes and become enmeshed in the same conflicts. They live boring, monotonous, and uncreative lives fearing change and differences. Although such marriages may appear solid, they are, in fact, quite vulnerable in the face of the manifold challenges that every marriage must inevitably encounter.

From a psychological perspective, the first phase of marriage corresponds with the childhood stage of individual development. It is a phase characterized by a profound degree of self-absorption, magical thinking, make-believe, symbiotic attachment, and primary attention to self-preservation and self-gratification. All these processes are to be expected because the newly formed marriage is still in the process of establishing its clear identity and character. Therefore, it is not surprising that many couples in this phase tend to somewhat regress in their interaction with each other. Often, couples in this phase use "baby-talk," have private signals, and engage in "child-like" activities together. Eventually, every marriage enters its next phase of development—the individuation or differentiation phase.

DIFFERENTIATION PHASE

The second phase of marriage is probably its most turbulent and even frightening phase. This phase begins with one or both partners trying to free themselves to a certain extent from the confining—and not infrequently suffocating—conditions of the first phase. The couple begins to have a certain degree of nostalgia about their premarital personal freedom, and at the same time, each starts to focus more on their own individual needs and tasks than they did in the first phase. As husband and/or wife begins to be somewhat more independent, the state of symbiotic oneness and total immersion that had characterized their relationship thus far comes under pressure. The couple no longer feel as close as they did before and begin to see each other's faults, which had been either overlooked or reinterpreted in the previous phase. They gradually realize that the other person is not as perfect or as pleasing as they had previously been perceived to be. As they get to know the realities of their marital life, some of their hopes, aspirations, and expectations shatter; some of their plans fail; and some of their initial impressions of each other—both positive and negative—prove to be wrong.

Concomitant with these revelations, the husband and wife begin to yearn for a greater degree of autonomy, freedom, and individual progress. Some even begin to perceive their marriage to be a confining and limiting structure. These thoughts, feelings, and impressions usually remain uncommunicated and gradually erode the ease, certitude, intimacy, and comfort that had characterized the marriage thus far. Those marriages in which the husband and wife agree and make it a practice to share most of changes they experience fare the best, and their marriage tends to be more stable and positive. However, because this transition from the highly idealized romantic phase to the chaotic and conflicted phase of individuation is fraught with fear—fear that these changes mean that they no longer love each other as strongly as before—the couple tend to avoid looking at the process in an objective and systematic manner. In fact in many instances, the husband and wife begin to communicate less, feel more distant from each other, and at times even begin distrusting each other. The marriage in this phase is an arena of both *love*, which had characterized their marriage thus far, and *power*, which had been put in abeyance during the romantic phase. However, in this phase, power struggle and competition, which are the characteristics of the second phase—adolescent age—of the marriage, come to the forefront. It is in this context that all three entities involved—husband, wife, and the marriage—are in a state of both inner and interpersonal conflict.

Quite often, in the individuation phase much of the attention of the husband and wife is diverted from each other to self. Consequently, one or both of them may develop feelings of rejection along with its inevitable accompaniments—anger, fear, anxiety, sadness, and under extreme conditions suspicion and jealousy. All these feelings and thoughts are conducive to tension and conflict in the marriage. Under these circumstances, husband and wife separately seek places of refuge. When there are children in the marriage, many parents busy themselves almost exclusively with the care of the children. Others focus on relating with their own families and friends. If both of them are working, the couple may find solace in having intimate discussions with colleagues and friends. Others may focus intensely on their jobs and professional interests rather than their spouse. These developments, in their extreme expressions, are ominous because they weaken the bonds of love and create breeding grounds for further dissatisfaction, conflict, and resentment.

During this phase, there is a danger that one or both partners may see this process of quest for independence and individuation on their or their spouse's part to be the harbinger of separation and the break-up of the marriage. Most couples do not realize that these processes are integral parts of the healthy growth of every marriage and every couple. An awareness and understanding of these developmental processes is necessary so that the couple would not misinterpret them as an indication that either their marital love has come to an end or that their marriage is not conducive to their own personal development and growth. In fact, in most situations this is not the case. In reality, the very process of dealing with the challenges of the second phase is highly beneficial in three regards: causing their love relationship to mature, enhancing their efforts at personal development, and strengthening their marriage as an evolving institution.

ENLIGHTENED UNION PHASE

As the marriage enters its third phase of development, a qualitatively new stage begins. The uncertainties of the first phase regarding one's lovability and the turmoil of the second phase regarding one's identity give way to conditions of certainty in love, greater measures of self-knowledge and knowledge of the other, and mutual acceptance and respect. All these developments revolve around the main quality of the third phase—unity. The transition to the third phase requires that husband and wife help each other to establish the direction and nature of their respective process of personal development and together make every effort to safeguard the sanctity of their marriage and ensure its healthy development. In such a marriage, the couple who have already experienced the excitement and romance of one-directional and competitive love in its earlier stages, discover the unique and freeing joys of mature love in the context of honesty, trust, and mutuality in their individual and shared aspirations and life plans.

One of the main indicators of maturity in marriage is the ability to live a moderate and creative life, free from excesses of the first two phases of marriage within a clear and well-conceived vision of the primary purpose of life. This refers to the issue of Mutual Point of Attraction (MPA) discussed earlier in this chapter. In the enlightened union phase, the marriage should have acquired the capacity to fulfill its most crucial functions: providing security and safety for all its members in a just and compassionate manner; creating loving, caring, encouraging, and affirming relationships between husband and wife and parents and children; and having established itself as a fortress of well-being for all its members and for many others that come in contact with it. In brief, a healthy and evolved marriage is both united and unifying. Such a marriage increases the joy of life through sharing, and decreases the sorrows of life through mutual support and assistance. In such marriages moments of happiness last longer and episodes of grief become more tolerable.

One of the main functions of a healthy marriage, in all its phases is its ability to create the most appropriate environment for the growth and development of all the members of the family. During the first two phases of marriage the couple are not fully prepared to meet the manifold and complex needs of their children. In these two phases, both the institution of the marriage and the couple are in the midst of their respective earlier stages of development and maturation. Therefore, every marriage benefits greatly from the wisdom, experience, and relative objectivity that other adults, particularly the parents of the couple, can bring to the new marriage. It is here that the wisdom of the Bahá'í requirement for prior parental consent for the marriage of their children, regardless of their age, becomes evident. The fundamental purpose of the consent is to ensure the unity of all involved—husband and wife and their respective parents. Shoghi Effendi explains:

> Bahá'u'lláh has clearly stated the consent of all living parents is required for a Bahá'í marriage. This applies whether the parents are

Bahá'ís or non-Bahá'ís divorced for years or not. This great law He has laid down to strengthen the social fabric, to knit closer the ties of the home, to place a certain gratitude and respect in the hearts of children for those who have given them life and sent their souls out on the eternal journey toward their Creator.[28]

In the context of such a unity, a small community of support is immediately created, which then can be further expanded by the inclusion of other members of the extended family and also by the members of the community at large. This unified community of support is then available to the new couple and parents, if they wish to tap its considerable wealth of experience and good will. In the context of contemporary fractured families and communities, the idea of such unified extended families and communities may be perceived as unrealistic. However, this fact should be approached not as a *fait accompli,* but rather as a challenge for every marriage and family to learn the ways of unity in the context of diversity and apply them to their relationships.

Many couples have difficulty with such issues as equality of rights and responsibilities in marriage, particularly with respect to childrearing. Equality should not be mistaken with sameness. No two individuals have the same talents, abilities, capacities, or temperaments. Every person is unique. However, this uniqueness becomes even more evident in the context of marriage and the respective qualities of the husband and wife. There are certain tasks that clearly only one of the two can perform, and there are other functions that each of them have greater interest and ability to perform. In the first phase of marriage these differences are overlooked. The couple tend to see each other through the prism of *sameness.* In the second phase of marriage these differences become the cause of tension and conflict because they perceive each other in the context of competition and *otherness.* In the third phase, the husband and wife consider their diversity of capacities, tasks, and interests as the sources of richness of their union. They see each other through the prism of *unity,* and in doing so they are able to relate to one another with fairness, tenderness, and true cooperation.

Having reviewed the three phases of marriage development, it should be emphasized that in the context of a healthy and evolving marriage at any given time there exists—to a lesser or greater degree— the qualities of all three phases. There is considerable flexibility in the manner in which each marriage traverses these stages. Some have a prolonged romantic phase; many have an unduly extended phase of differentiation; and many marriages break apart in this phase. And a good number of marriages also arrive at the third phase. However, many marriages are in danger of falling into a state of lifeless monotony and resignation. Vigilance and dedication is required to ensure that every marriage is helped to grow in every respect—biological, emotional, mental, relational, moral, and spiritual.

SUMMARY

Love is the magnet that brings us together. The primary function of love is to unite, and the main outcome of unity is to create—life at the biological plane; relationships in the interpersonal realm; equality, justice, and peace at the social level; new artistic and scientific development in emotional and intellectual spheres; and new heights of universal moral and ethical awareness in the spiritual domain. As such, love and unity are indispensable to human life. The most intimate, complete, productive, and intense domain of expression of interpersonal love and unity takes place in the context of the twin institutions of marriage and family. This chapter was devoted to the study of the institution of marriage. The next chapter will focus on the institution of the family.

CHAPTER SIX

FAMILY
THE WORKSHOP OF CIVILIZATION

The fruits that best befit the tree of human life are trustworthiness and godliness, truthfulness and sincerity; but greater than all, after recognition of the unity of God…is regard for the rights that are due to one's parents.[1]

—Bahá'u'lláh

And among the teachings of Bahá'u'lláh is the promotion of education. Every child must be instructed in sciences as much as is necessary. If the parents are able to provide the expenses of this education, it is all right, otherwise the community must provide the means for the teaching of that child.[2]

—'Abdu'l-Bahá

Also a father and mother endure the greatest troubles and hardships for their children; and often when the children have reached the age of maturity, the parents pass on to the other world. Rarely does it happen that a father and mother in this world see the reward of the care and trouble they have undergone for their children. Therefore children, in return for this care and trouble, must show forth charity and beneficence, and must implore pardon and forgiveness for their parents.[3]

—'Abdu'l-Bahá

To put the world right in order, we must first put the nation in order; to put the nation in order, we must first put the family in order; to put the family in order, we must first cultivate our personal life; we must first set our hearts right.[4]

—Confucius

In the Bahá'í community, top priority is given to promotion of the welfare of the family, as well as creation and maintenance of unity in both the nuclear and the extended families. In fact, as stated before, those who decide to marry, regardless of their age, need to secure the consent of their living parents. The purpose is to ensure that the couple and their respective families are in unity with regard to this momentous decision. The task of creating harmonious, joyous, progressive, and enlightened families is one of the main challenges of our times and is a mandate that has consequential impact on the nature and direction of civilization. The family, with its biological, psychological, social, legal, moral, and spiritual dimensions, determines the nature and quality of the health and education of every new generation, contributes considerably to the welfare and stability of society, and ensures a more systematic and less chaotic progression in these times of monumental global change. In the following essay on the Unity-Based Family, I attempt to present a psycho-social-spiritual formulation of the institution of the family. The essay is based on my keynote presentation at "The World Congress on the Family: Restore Family Life and Sustain World Peace," organized by the Service and Research Foundation of Asia on Family and Culture (SERFAC), January 2–6, 2006, Chennai, India. In the essay I review the reasons why the family, in the past and at present, has not fully met its main mandate and what needs to be done to create new types of families commensurate with the needs of humanity as it comes of age.

THE FAMILY IN A GLOBAL SOCIETY

I am most honored to address this distinguished audience on such a fundamental topic and in such a remarkable country. India is the cradle of one of the most influential civilizations, home to rich and profound spiritual traditions, and a major force in the family of nations and affairs of the world of humanity. India is also the home of Mahatma Gandhi, one of the most distinguished peacemakers in history.[5] For these and other reasons it is befitting that a world congress with focus on the family and world peace should take place here. We all owe much gratitude to Dr. Catherine Bernard, director of the Service and Research Foundation of Asia on Family and Culture (SERFAC), for making this congress possible and for her valuable contributions on behalf of world peace and family life. I thank her for the opportunity to participate in this significant event. The theme of my presentation is the unity-based family and the advent of a civilization of peace.

Our academic and professional interests and insights have their roots in our background and education, areas of research and expertise, life experiences and observations, and personal beliefs and commitments. All these factors have contributed to my intense interest in issues related to the family and peace. I was born into and reared as a member of a religious minority—the Bahá'í Faith—in Iran, an authoritarian, fanatical, and oppressive society. I received my training as a psychiatrist in a highly individualistic and competitive society characterized by unbridled freedom—the United States of America. I have lived on three continents—Asia, North America, and Europe—and traveled to some 60 countries around the globe. Together, these experiences and opportunities have given me some insights into various aspects of multifaceted expressions of human group life, both in its micro-institutions such as marriage and family and its macro-organizations such as religious groups, ethnic communities, and national and international entities.

My professional life as a psychiatrist and as a university professor and president is divided into two distinct but interrelated periods. The first period of thirty years (1963–1993), was devoted to psychiatric practice and teaching with a focus on marriage and family, violence and its prevention, death and dying, and the psychology of spirituality. The second period of 17 years thus far (1994–2010), has been devoted to education for peace, leadership for peace, and peaceful conflict resolution. In 1994, when I moved to Switzerland to assist in the formation and direction of a private university (Landegg International

University),[6] I began an experimental program, which eventually evolved into several unique and interrelated programs: Education for Peace (EFP).[7] Leadership for Peace (LFP),[8] Youth Peacebuilders Network (YPN),[9] and Conflict-Free Conflict Resolution (CFCR)[10] implemented in several countries in Africa, Europe, and North America. (See chapter nine.)

These two broad areas of experience—the well-being and development of individuals and families, and the welfare and peace of communities and nations—are interrelated and complementary. Both deal with the phenomenon of human relationships in their most intimate and personal dimension, particularly in the context of marriage and family, and in their social and universal expressions in respect to issues of unity-based leadership and world peace.

In my presentation I will draw from the scientific research data, my professional observations and experiences, and my personal insights and conclusions based on an eventful and richly diverse life process. After a general review of the institution of the family, I will briefly discuss issues related to the family and its role in society in general, and with respect to peace in particular.

THE FAMILY IN REVIEW

Whenever I think of the family, I am reminded of the statement of Epictetus (c.55–c.135 CE), the Greek exponent of Stoicism: "What concerns me,'" he said, "is not the way things are, but rather the way people think things are."[11] This statement is especially relevant to the family, because people's idea of the family is usually idealistic and romantic, while in practice the family is often a place of conflict, misery, and abuse. This dichotomy between how many families are and how we want them to be is at the core of the current heated debate about the nature, relevance, and even definition of the family. In May 1994, on the occasion of the United Nations Year of the Family, I had the honor of organizing a symposium on the theme "Creating Violence-Free Families" at UNICEF House in New York City. In my opening address, I noted that the institution of the family was then, as it is now, under attack and experiencing considerable change with respect to several crucial issues.[12] Four years later, I delivered a keynote address— "The Future of the Family and the Family of the Future"—at the 1998 Beijing International Conference on Family, Social Security, and Social Welfare (3–6 April), co-sponsored by the Institute of Sociology of the

Chinese Academy of Social Sciences and the Jinglun Family Centre (Beijing) with the participation of Landegg Academy (later incorporated as Landegg International University), Switzerland. This occasion in India provides me yet another opportunity to elaborate my thoughts on the issue of the family. This essay on the family is based on these three presentations and additional research. It has also been somewhat modified to meet the main focus of this book.

Family, Society, and Civilization

Family, society, and civilization are totally interrelated, and the welfare and development of each is dependent upon the other two entities in this triangle of life and growth. The relationship between the family and society is organic in nature, with a direct impact on the welfare and progress of civilization. In fact, no civilization is possible without sound, healthy families functioning within the framework of a progressive society. The importance of both the family and society lies in several unique aspects of the human species, such as its prolonged childhood dependency, multidimensional socialization processes, and profound level of consciousness of self and others. These significant human characteristics not only form the biological, emotional, and social foundations for creation of both the family and society but also provide the necessary impetus for the continuity and interrelatedness of these two pillars of all civilizations.

The twin processes of education and socialization, combined with the human element of choice, together create a complex condition that impacts the biological, psychological, moral, and spiritual aspects of our lives. For these conditions to evolve in an optimal manner, we need healthy families and societies. A truly civilized and progressive society requires that its building blocks—the families—be in a healthy state— equal, united, educated, and productive. Such healthy families, in turn, are the best environments for development of every new generation of children and youth as other-directed, trustworthy, creative, unselfish, and unifying members of their communities.

This creative cycle is now being torn asunder by the destructive processes that are prevalent in contemporary families and societies. In our rapidly changing world, families are disintegrating at an alarming rate. And when the family disintegrates, children suffer the most. Many become self-centered, untrusting, and destructive; and as adults they, in turn, contribute to further disintegration of their society. And when society disintegrates, it becomes harsh, conflicted and violent, indifferent to the well-being of its individual members, and dangerous to the welfare of both the individuals and the collective. This vicious cycle of destruction accelerates the rate of disintegration of both the family and society.

FAMILY TODAY

In our world today, the institution of the family is facing major crises. No longer is the notion that the family is essential for the welfare of the individual and society universally and unhesitatingly accepted. There are many valid concerns raised about the role of the family, both in the past and at the present. In some quarters the very validity and usefulness of the family itself is being questioned.

The main concerns about the family revolve around the place of girls and women in the family and the manner in which they are unjustly and unequally treated by boys and men. A related concern is that these abusive practices frequently have been and still are justified in the context of cultural norms, religious beliefs, and unfounded theories and assumptions. Another extremely important issue is with regard to the role of the family in parenting and rearing of the next generations of children. As societies become more prosperous and as an increasing number of mothers join the work force, many children are being reared by individuals other than their parents and in institutions outside their homes. This is of great concern, because both the quality and quantity of parenting that these children receive is definitely different—often inferior—from what the children ideally receive from their parents. Psychological and psychiatric disciplines already have certain insights about the impact of inadequate parenting. However, in the course of the next few decades when several new generations of children enter the adult community, we will know better about the influence of current approaches to parenting of children. Yet another area of concern is the fact that much violence and prejudice against non-family members are justified in the name of family solidarity and "blood" relationship. All these and some other concerns have raised legitimate questions about the family and its role in the contemporary society. It is in this context that we need to address three questions:

1. Should the family as it exists now be abolished?
2. Can we live without the institution of the family?
3. Is there a viable alternative to the family?

Should the Family Be Abolished?

Many answer the question of whether the family should be abolished in the affirmative and identify at least three reasons why the family, as we have known and practiced it throughout history and in all cultures, should be abolished. Among these reasons are:

1. The institution of the family in the past, and to a very large degree still at the present, has been a source of control, dominance, abuse, and violence against its weaker members, namely, women and girls, the physically or psychologically disadvantaged, and not infrequently, children and the elderly.

2. The institution of the family has often sanctioned, defended, and promoted the conditions of inequality between men and women, giving men greater degrees of freedom and privilege.

3. The institution of the family has encouraged and promoted childrearing practices that have resulted in fundamental deficiencies in the character development of both boys and girls.[14]

Family and Power

The arguments for abolishing the family as the basic nucleus of society are primarily based on the central issue of power and its role in family relationships and activities. Historically, the majority of families in all societies and cultures of the world have been bastions of what I call "male power," characterized by dominance, control, and oppression of women by men. Male power has been, and still is, exercised with respect to all aspects of the life of the female members of the family: their educational rights and privileges, their sexual wishes and preferences, their social opportunities and status, their economic well-being and independence, their personal freedoms and responsibilities, and their spiritual aspirations and activities. Furthermore, the abuse of power by the institution of the family itself has also contributed to deep-rooted prejudices and hostilities by one family or clan against another.

To better understand the dynamics of power-based marriages and families, we need to more fully comprehend the challenge of equality between women and men. This is of singular importance because some of the main crises of contemporary marriages and families are related to the issue of gender inequality and the inability or unwillingness of the majority of men and some women to relate to one another on an equal basis.

CHARACTERISTICS OF EQUALITY

Equality is a sign of maturity, and maturity is the process of an ever-increasing ability to integrate and unite rather than to differentiate and separate. Individualism is the hallmark of the adolescent phase of growth. It is a condition of self-absorption and self-worship. It does not include others except for one's own benefit. Equality, conversely, is a state of unity and integration. It is a relationship characterized by willingness and ability to be cooperative, generous, and other-directed. In the contemporary world, when humanity is traversing its most problematic phase of collective adolescence, the quest for equality between women and men often deteriorates into a virulent and destructive power-struggle. The very instrument by which men have always achieved their self-centered interests is now being sought by women in order to correct the injustices of the past and the present, hence, the potentially destructive power-struggle present in many modern marriages and families. This is not surprising because power-struggle is the most common outcome of the power-based human relationships during this crucial phase of our collective coming of age. As 'Abdu'l-Bahá states:

> The world in the past has been ruled by force, and man has dominated over woman by reason of his more forceful and aggressive qualities both of body and mind. But the balance is already shifting; force is losing its dominance, and mental alertness, intuition, and the spiritual qualities of love and service, in which woman is strong, are gaining ascendancy. Hence the new age will be an age less masculine and more permeated with the feminine ideals, or, to speak more exactly, will be an age in which the masculine and feminine elements of civilization will be more evenly balanced.[13]

A brief review of some of the main characteristics of marriage helps us to distinguish between adolescent and adult approaches to the issue of power and to better understand the dynamics of power-oriented families.

Marriage as a Living Social Entity

Marriage is a living social entity that comes into being as a result of the conscious, deliberate union of a woman and a man. As such, marriage is not only a legal, religious, and social institution but also a living, growing entity subject to the laws and requirements of all living social organisms. In other words, marriage is not simply the sum total of the hopes and powers of the two individuals who bring it into being. Rather, the institution of marriage has its own dynamics and powers that transcend those of the individuals who create it. The biological counterpart of marriage is the union of the sperm and the ovum. The fertilized ovum (zygote) has powers and potentialities that are quite distinct and superior to those of either the sperm or ovum separately. Likewise, the union of a man and a woman in the conscious act of marriage creates a social organism that is distinct and apart from either the husband or the wife. Under healthy conditions, the powers of marriage are the outcome of the amalgamation, coordination, and integration of the powers of the husband and wife. This kind of power is creative and cooperative in nature. An analogy may help to elucidate this very important yet poorly understood phenomenon.

If we liken marriage to a bird with its own powers and capacities, the husband and wife are like the bird's wings, which make it possible for the bird to fly. However, the flight of the bird is dependent on the equality and harmony between the powers of both its wings. Likewise, without such equality, harmony, and coordination, the institution of marriage will not be able to reach its potential heights of accomplishment.[15] Throughout history and in all cultures, this lack of equality between women and men has been the most important contributor to the miseries of married life. In the same manner that the dominance of men over women has brought such violence and sadness to the lives of countless millions of women, the current prevalence of power-struggle in marriage will result in new forms of misery in marriage and family life. Marriages that are characterized by either power-domination or power-struggle not only make life miserable for husbands and wives but also for their children. Consequently, the entire family and society suffer.

To summarize, the answer is yes to the question of whether the family *as it exists today* should be abolished. The power-based, conflict-prone marriages and families of the past and present are no longer either acceptable or functional as humanity inevitably enters its long-awaited phase of collective maturity and begins its era of harmonious and cooperative relationships. However, if we abolish the family as we have known and practiced it, then more questions arise.

CAN WE LIVE WITHOUT THE FAMILY?

To answer the question of whether we can live without the family, we must focus on one of the main functions of the family to see if we could entrust the responsibilities it entails to another institution. The family has always been and continues to be the most suitable milieu in which the next generations of children can grow and form their views about themselves, the world, and the purpose and meaning of life. In other words, the family is the workshop of civilization, and as such it shapes the type of the world we wish to create.

CHILDREN AND PARENTING

Whenever and wherever there are children, there automatically comes into being a "family." The very presence of children puts the adults and the environment surrounding children into the role of a family. However, when the family is not based on solid ground and committed sentiments, it will not be able to parent adequately. Children by nature need protection, nurturing, care, guidance, and encouragement, which are the main properties of parental love. Children also need adult role models to emulate in order to adequately prepare themselves to become contributing adults in society. To the degree that these fundamental needs of children are met, to that same degree children grow up to be protective, nurturing, caring, enlightened, and encouraging adults and capable, healthy parents. In other words, children reared in healthy, loving families usually grow up to be healthy, loving adults and parents. The opposite is also true. To the degree that a family fails to meet the fundamental needs of children, to that same degree society will be burdened with the consequences of neglect and abuse, and will greatly suffer from the resulting conditions of apathy and violence. The parenting qualities enumerated above are aspects of love, that universal force which creates and maintains life through the power of unity. Children reared by loving parents, in turn, as adults have the capacity to create marriages and families characterized by unity, equality, and creativity. These are among the essential characteristics of the "unity-based family," which is the focus of this chapter.

As we contemplate the condition of the children of the world, one fact becomes clearly obvious: our children are not being adequately and properly parented. In the war-ravaged regions of the world, children are the most tragic victims. In poverty-stricken areas, children suffer the most. Where adequate hygiene and medical care are lacking, children die in the greatest numbers. In affluent societies, children are relegated to the tertiary level of priority after the economic/professional and personal interests/pursuits of their parents. Wherever people face racism and prejudice, children are the most innocent and helpless victims. There is hardly any place in the world where we can say with confidence that the majority of children are being reared under adequately healthy, caring, and loving conditions conducive to their wholesome development, even at a medium level. This is so because the institution of the family has become enfeebled and is often unable to meet the requirements and demands of change in the contemporary world. Neither the oppressive and authoritarian traditional families, nor the chaotic conflicted modern families engaged in their internal power-struggle is suitable to the needs of this new phase in the evolution of humanity. A new type of family and a new approach to the all-important task of rearing our children is needed.

To summarize: the answer to the question, *Can we live without the family?* is both yes and no. The family as the workshop of civilization is an indispensable part of civilized life. As such, we cannot be without it. However, the kind of family that the world now needs is not the kind of family we generally find in our world. A dramatically different type of family is needed, the nature of which is yet to be fully delineated. This brings us to the third question: Is there an alternative to the family?

IS THERE AN ALTERNATIVE TO THE FAMILY?

The question of an alternative to the family needs to be broadened to cover two main issues: alternatives to the family and alternative types of families. While the former calls for the abolition of the family or some of its most important functions, the latter searches for new prototypes of the family. Both these approaches have been tried. My objective here is not to catalog those approaches and review their merits (or demerits, as the case may be). Rather, here I will briefly focus on some of the most important functions of the family and then will put forward the concept of the Unity-Based Family (UBF), which I consider to be the next inevitable step in the evolution of the institution of the family and the only way in which we could create violence-free and peaceful, progressive, and happy families. Let us first briefly review the outcome of attempts to find alternatives to childrearing, which has traditionally been the main function of the family.

ALTERNATIVE MODES OF PARENTING

In the 20th century alone, we have had many notable experiences in relegating a major portion of the task of childrearing to other agencies and individuals in many different parts of the world. The state-administered childcare agencies in the former USSR and Eastern European countries, the phenomenal rise of public and private childcare facilities in North America and Europe, and the increasing expansion of this practice in different forms to other parts of the world are noteworthy examples of attempts to find alternatives to many parenting tasks formerly assumed by parents and other family members. Research data on the impact of daycare experience on children is mixed. There is evidence that good daycares with well-trained staff, appropriate caregiver-children ratio, and adequate financial resources are good, particularly for children from poor families and who have parents with limited parenting capacity and/or opportunity. However, such daycares are not readily available, and many children are placed in less than ideal daycares. There is also some evidence that good daycare gives children a beneficial experience, especially after age two.[16] Other studies report that the amount of time spent in daycare before four-and-a-half tends to correspond with a tendency in these children to be disobedient, have difficulty getting along with others, and to be aggressive and more prone to violence.[17]

However, there is ample evidence that the condition of children in the world, whether cared for by their families or by others in daycares and similar facilities, is quite mixed. The 2007 report of UNICEF on the condition of world children is sobering. Here are a few statistics contained in that document:

- Nearly one-third of children under five in developing countries are stunted (in terms of their physical development).
- There are 93 million children of primary-school age out of school.
- In developing countries children from the poorest households are least likely to attend primary school.
- Boys are more likely to be in primary schools than girls.

- Girls are more likely to be out of school than boys.
- Before they reached their fifth birthday, 9.7 million children died in 2006.
- Each year about 4 million newborns perish in the first 28 days of life.
- There are 158 million children (5–14) engaged in labor (2006).
- Of children aged 2–14, 86% experienced violent methods of discipline (data from 29 countries in 2005–2006).
- Physical punishment is widespread even where it is not socially approved (2005–2006).
- In 2006, 39 million people around the world were refugees or internally displaced (IDP). More than 40% of refugees and IDPs were children.[18]

A dispassionate review of the condition of the world's children compels us to conclude that no agency, whether governmental, religious, professional, or otherwise, is capable of adequately replacing a united, educated, and financially reasonably provided family with respect to the all-important task of parenting. Regardless of how well trained and well intentioned surrogate parents may be, they will not be able to replace the primal state of unity and affinity that naturally exists between parents and their children. It is within the context of the family that biological, psychological, cultural, and spiritual bonds find their fullest expression. Children who spend a significant portion of their waking hours during their infancy and early childhood away from their parents face certain unique challenges. These children to some degree experience a significant sense of loss, abandonment, and rejection by being separated from both of their parents (or a very close and constant caregiver, such as a grandparent) for long periods of their waking hours on a regular basis. Nor are these surrogate parents able to ameliorate the fear, anger, and anxiety that these inadequately parented children feel. From a psychological perspective it is not surprising if some of these children develop feelings of rejection and a sense of being unloved. I believe that the anger, fury, and rejection that many children in North America, Western Europe, Africa, Russia, Japan, more recently China, and many other countries are displaying toward their own parents, schools, and communities as well as outsiders, have their roots in feelings of being rejected and considered of secondary importance in the lives of their parents.

Children who in the first few years of their lives spend a significant portion of their waking hours on a regular basis with many other children and a few heavily burdened adults are at risk of developing what I call "clique mentality." These children, by virtue of having little one-to-one, meaningful, and loving relationship with their parents, grow up to be unduly attached to their peers and suspicious of adults. They tend to function in groups and gangs, are highly prone to manipulation by charismatic group leaders, are easily seduced to imitate and act as they are told, are extremely self-centered and self-doubting, and in their efforts at survival and gratification do not hesitate to commit irrational or destructive acts. These children make excellent soldiers or gang members and are willing to carry out acts of violence at the behest of their surrogate parents. These children have little respect for authority. In fact, they tend to view all authority with suspicion and hostility, in the same manner that they perceive their parents to be rejecting and untrustworthy. This is so because most parents, who in fact love their children dearly, nevertheless do not express their love through appropriate parenting attitudes and activities. There is a basic discrepancy between what these parents say and wish to do, and what they actually do.

These issues and considerations, taken together, provide the answer to the third question, and the simple answer is that there is no satisfactory substitute for the family and that a new, dramatically different type of family is needed.

DEFINITIONS AND FUNCTIONS OF THE FAMILY

DEFINITIONS OF THE FAMILY

Defining the family is neither an easy task nor a purely scientific endeavor. The family has been variably defined according to cultural, religious, legal, biological, social, historical, ethnic, and economic parameters. Consequently, there is little or no agreement about how exactly to define the family or outline its functions. Consider this definition by a prestigious Canadian organization the Vanier Institute of the Family, which defines family as

> any combination of two or more persons who are bound together over time by ties of mutual consent, birth and/or adoption or placement and who, together, assume responsibilities for variant combinations of some of the following:

- Physical maintenance and care of group members
- Addition of new members through procreation or adoption
- Socialization of children
- Social control of members
- Production, consumption, distribution of goods and services, and
- Affective nurturance—love[19]

This definition excludes many marriages and families that are formed for reasons other than the "ties of mutual consent." Here is another definition by the American Academy of Family Physicians, which is as vague and non-specific as possible:

The family is a group of individuals with a continuing legal, genetic and/or emotional relationship.[20]

The following three views of the family and the nature of family relationships by the U.S. Supreme Court are of special interest because they point to the challenges regarding the legal definition of the family:

1. a traditional "nuclear family" of two parents and their children, and where the parents are presumed to be acting in the best interests of their children....;

2. an extended-kin model of family made up of a community of parents, siblings, grandparents and other relatives which should be recognized as a primary family, even if the blood-ties are not as strong as a nuclear family; and

3. an individualist model where family members are fairly autonomous and that individuality should be respected.[21]

The conventional definition of the family in the Chinese culture, where the family has a primary position, puts a great emphasis on the role of males. The traditional Chinese family, or *jiā* 家, is both patrilineal (descent is determined through men) and patriarchal (the most senior male has institutionalized authority in the family).[22] Contrast this definition with the view shared by the prominent feminist, Gloria Steinem: "Families mean support and an audience to men. To women, they just mean more work."[23] These definitions of family clearly demonstrate the dilemma faced by family scholars, policy-makers, and practitioners as they attempt to place the family in its proper position in the rapidly changing modern world. It is in this context that the following reflections on both the definition and functions of the family are offered.

MAIN FUNCTIONS OF THE FAMILY

The family is the world in microcosm. It includes members from all segments of human society—men and women, young and old, the powerful and powerless, the learned and learner, and the rich and poor. Consequently, the family's health and strength have a direct positive relationship with the health and strength of both the individual and society. The family is also the most suitable arena for the expression of the human quest and capacity for truth and truthfulness, love and unity, and service and justice. As such, the family offers the context in which our fundamental humanness is expressed by providing the requisite conditions for our psychological, social, moral, and spiritual development. Furthermore, the family is the workshop of civilization. It is within the framework of the family that each new generation is helped to formulate and exercise its worldview—its view of reality, human nature, the purpose of life, and human relationships. It is in the context of the family that the next generation becomes knowledgeable about the ways of life. The family also provides for the children powerful models of decision-making, conflict resolution, personal growth and institutional (the institution of the family) development, intellectual enlightenment, and spiritual transformation. In brief, the family transmits the concepts and habits of the civilization of which it is a part.

These three characteristics—family as the world in microcosm, as the arena for individual and social development, and as the workshop of civilization—together constitute the fundamental requisites for the creation, sustenance, and development of society. To the degree that the institution of the family is healthy and evolving, to that same degree the health and progress of society is strengthened. History demonstrates that those societies that place maximum importance on the family are considerably stronger and more stable than those in which the foundations of the family are weakened. In this regard, it is important to note that the main criterion for the assessment of the health and strength of both the family and society is the depth, extent, and quality of their unity in the context of diversity. A disunited family and society are both dysfunctional and unhealthy. 'Abdu'l-Bahá describes the relationship between the welfare of the family and the well-being of the nation and all humanity:

> A family is a nation in miniature. Simply enlarge the circle of the household, and you have the nation. Enlarge the circle of nations and you have all humanity. The conditions surrounding the

family surround the nation. The happenings in the family are the happenings in the life of the nation. Would it add to the progress and advancement of a family if dissensions should arise among its members...? Nay, this would be the cause of the effacement of progress and advancement. So it is in the great family of nations, for nations are but an aggregate of families.[24]

Throughout history and in all societies, the institution of the family has been entrusted with three fundamental tasks: (1) to establish a locus of love in society to offset the harsh realities of life, (2) to bring forth and nurture children and transfer to them the collective wisdom and experience of the culture, and (3) to create a sound, flexible building block for the organic development of society and civilization. Without these fundamental functions, human civilization neither advances nor bears its life-sustaining fruits. These functions of the family correspond to fundamental tripartite human needs—survival, association, and transcendence—respectively referring to the biological, psychosocial, and spiritual aspects of human life. Adequate, ongoing satisfaction of these needs requires a safe and secure environment; an established and enforced pattern for equal, free, and just relationships; and an unhindered opportunity for each person to pursue his/her highest intellectual, artistic, and spiritual aspirations and to live a meaningful and peaceful life. The family has the potential to be an institution best equipped to meet these manifold human needs and rights.

TYPES OF FAMILY

A review of the history of the family and its companion institution—marriage—in various cultures reveals that although these institutions are ideally connected with "love," in practice many of them have been and still are based on "power." In my work with many families from various cultural backgrounds, I have identified three distinctive types of family: power-based, identity-based, and unity-based families. Here, I will briefly outline the main characteristics of these family types. But, at the outset it should be stated that in actuality most families, to a varying degree, possess some characteristics of all three types. Human life is a multidimensional, creative, and evolving process and, as such, cannot be classified according to rigid criteria. However, these classifications serve a valuable purpose by offering the guiding principles and providing a roadmap for the ongoing development, enrichment, and refinement of the unique institution of the family. Before we discuss the types of the family, it is helpful to briefly consider the role of the main human powers of knowledge, love, and will in the context of the family.

FAMILY AND THE MAIN HUMAN CAPACITIES

Earlier, the main human capacities—to know, love, and will—were discussed. These capacities are universal in their presence and transcend gender, race, and cultural boundaries and play unique, yet interrelated, roles in the family. Through the capacity to know, the husband and wife have the ability and responsibility to acquire self-knowledge and thorough knowledge of each other. They need to learn about and distinguish between those issues that contribute to their respective meaningful, wholesome development and those issues that may cause damage to their personal conditions and interpersonal relationships. Likewise, love is a fundamental force in family life. It is through love that the tree of human relationships is nurtured and the necessary conditions are created for it to bear its fairest fruits of tenderness, kindness, respect, encouragement, and happiness, in brief, unity. Members of the family need to learn not only to give love in a healthy and mature manner but also to receive love in an equally healthy manner. The art of loving, contrary to popular notions, is not easily acquired. It requires insight into the nature and dynamics of love, as well as effort to become a truly loving person and experience the exquisite joy of reciprocal love—to love and to be loved. Finally, it is by the power of our will that the ability to love and the insights gained in our efforts to know ourselves and others are put into practice.

Human will is one of the cardinal distinguishing features of being human, and all human behavior is, in one way or another, influenced by the manner in which the individual learns to use his or her power of will. Such universally observed conditions as power-seeking and power-struggle have their genesis in the workings of the human will. It is therefore not surprising that children reared in authoritarian and/or indulgent families tend to display various forms of behavior reflecting the nature of uses and abuses of will in their respective families.[25]

This brief review of the functions of the human powers of knowledge, love, and will demonstrates that all families in all cultures are subject to certain universal principles and laws. However, this constancy in the fundamental functions of the institution of the family does not imply that all families are the same, nor will they be the same in the future. In fact, the opposite is true. Among the most outstanding qualities of being human are our phenomenal powers of creativity and our interest in introducing novelty and diversity into all aspects of our personal and collective endeavors. It is this diversity that brings richness and beauty to our lives and allows us to be distinct yet one, separate yet united, independent yet interdependent.

THE POWER-BASED FAMILY

Throughout history, the institution of the family in many societies has been structured within the framework of a power-based authoritarian worldview—unequal, unjust, oppressive, and often violent. Authoritarianism is based on the principle of the supremacy of power and is dichotomous in its approach to all issues, including human relationships. As such, authoritarianism is antithetical to unity. It demands uniformity, prevents freedom, promotes inequality, and rules by means of fear and violence. The seeming unity of the traditional authoritarian family is, in fact, forced uniformity. In the authoritarian family, love is secondary to power and is given conditionally. The authoritarian person demands conformity in exchange for love. The main forces that sustain the power-based authoritarian family are, on the one hand, social, religious, economic, and cultural constraints and, on the other hand, the unifying presence of children, who by their very existence become magnets for love, care, and cohesion.

In modern times and particularly in the past several decades, the institution of the authoritarian family has rightly come under serious sustained attack and its validity convincingly challenged. In many societies women are finding courage and opportunity either to reject entering potentially authoritarian relationships or to leave such existing relationships. This pattern is now observed in both modern and traditional societies.

In the *power-based family* (PBF), or *authoritarian family*, access to knowledge is unequal. Historically, in most cultures men have had relatively more access to sources of knowledge and information, while girls and women have been systematically denied such access. In power-based families the education of boys and men takes precedence over the education of girls and women, who are assigned those roles and responsibilities that seemingly do not require formal education and refinement of one's mind. While, in fact, women's traditional responsibilities, particularly those with respect to childrearing, call for much more education and proper training than do many technical jobs considered to be proper for men. A well-trained mind is essential for the healthy development of the individual and the society, and denial of that training to anyone, particularly women, is a manifest injustice and an indication of our shortsightedness and basic ignorance of the prerequisites for creating a peaceful, prosperous, just, and happy world.

Another expression of the unhealthy use of the human capacity to know in the power-based family is in respect to the issues of truthfulness and trust. The ultimate fruit of the human capacity to know is search for scientific and spiritual truth, on the one hand, and truthfulness and trustworthiness in the context of human relationships, on the other. Because the power-based family, by its very nature, suffers to a varying degree from disorders of knowledge, it is not surprising that such families are inundated with a lack of truthfulness and trust in their interpersonal relationships.

Power-based families also suffer from disorders of love in their midst. The prevalence of power in these families makes the expression of love conditional upon one's willingness to conform and be blindly obedient. The more powerful person(s) in the family demand obedience and submission from the other members of the family and, in return, give some measure of care and compassion to them. Usually, in such families, it is the husband who expects conformity from his wife and children. However, not infrequently, both parents use their positions of power to demand unquestioned obedience and blind conformity from their children.[26]

The Price of Conformity and the Challenge of Freedom

Conformity is fundamentally different from the legitimate expectations of parents that their children be well behaved, polite, and considerate. To wish for such behavior from our children and to make necessary efforts to rear them to be good and do good are signs of our love for our children. In fact, if we do not do our best to rear our children in this manner, then we have failed to truly express our love towards them. Love, by its very nature and in its healthy expression, is a force for growth, inner discipline, universality, and enlightenment. It is the very antithesis of indulgence, promiscuity, self-centeredness, and bigotry. These latter conditions are aspects of authoritarian (power-based) parenting, an important dimension of which is indulgence in the context of conformity.

Parents who demand unquestioned conformity from their children are basically interested in controlling them. They wish to mold their children in their own image. Consequently, they discourage curiosity, originality, and creativity. They are afraid of that which is different and unique. Within the dichotomous framework of the authoritarian approach to life, the seeds of prejudice, suspicion, exclusivity, and rebellion are sown in the minds and hearts of children. These children are made to feel safe within the rigid boundaries of conformity and, in the process, become fearful of all that is different and unique. Diversity becomes a threat, and uniformity takes precedence. Alternatively, some of these children become angry, rebellious, and violent. These families see the world in the context of separation and divisions, and they do not hesitate to reject those who are different. Another unhealthy expression of love in power-based families is that while one parent is demanding and authoritarian, the other parent usually compensates by becoming indulgent and overprotective. The outcome of this combination of power and indulgence is the creation of a state of self-centeredness, which, by its very definition, is the opposite of being able to love. Power-based families tend to be conditional, ambivalent, disuniting, and conducive to creating undue dependency and self-centeredness.

In addition to the unhealthy development and expression of the human capacities to know and love, power-based families also have difficulties with the manner in which their members express their will.

Most human behavior is the expression of our capacity to choose and make decisions. Therefore, it is essential that parents and educators pay special attention to the healthy development of the "will" in children. When the human capacity to will is developed in a healthy manner, the qualities of fairness and service become its natural expressions. Poorly parented children, however, by virtue of their primal sense of aloneness and their considerable fear, anxiety, and resentment, feel very vulnerable and do everything to survive and feel safe. These characteristic conditions of authoritarian families render their children very prone to being self-centered, demanding of attention, and destructive or even violent in the face of disappointment and denial of gratification.

Power-based families are not equipped to help their children develop their faculty of will in a healthy manner. This is especially true in our world today. In the past, human societies were much more homogeneous, and the geographical distance separating different societies was considerable. People's place in society, their expected life processes, and their occupations and roles were largely predetermined. There was a rigid structure and an expectation of conformity that made life much simpler, albeit less fulfilling. People exchanged personal freedom for social security. However, in our world today, the opposite has occurred. The price of unfettered personal freedom has become the ruin of social order. These two extremes are expressions of our limited understanding and unwise use of the human will.

True freedom is not freedom to do whatever we want, whenever we want, and wherever we want, regardless of how it impacts others, as long as we are not manifestly harming others. We are truly free when we have developed that degree of inner discipline and transcendence whereby we use our capacities to know, love, and will in the service of others and for the purpose of creating conditions of equality, justice, and unity. These qualities are inadmissible in the worldview of power-based families and societies, and are usually dismissed as being unrealistic and utopian in nature. However, the fact remains that the world will not be able to advance on the path of progress and true civilization if we continue to insist on functioning within the authoritarian framework.

THE IDENTITY-BASED FAMILY

Concomitant with the accelerating rate of rejection of the authoritarian family structure, a new type of family—*the identity-based, individualistic* *family*—has emerged. The identity-based family (IBF) has its main focus on the individual members of the family, particularly the "husband and wife" and "parents and their children" as separate and often competing entities. In these families, love is approached in a competitive context and as an instrument for reassurance and validation of oneself and gratification of one's own desires. Consequently, in these types of families, the main sustaining ingredient of the family—its unity—is relegated to a secondary or even tertiary level of importance. Identity-based, individualistic families approach issues of equality, justice, and love within an abrasive, adversarial, and conflicted orientation. Here, the wishes, interests, and comfort of the individual members take precedence over the welfare of the family as a whole. These families are highly unstable and vulnerable, readily succumb to separation and divorce as a solution to the inevitable challenges of family life.

In my earlier classification of family types, I described the indulgence-based family. Indulgence is also one of the cardinal characteristics of the *identity-based family*.[27] In the 20th century, particularly since the end of the Second World War, in North America and Western Europe, and, more recently, in many other parts of the world, the identity-based family (IBF), with its undue focus on personal pleasure and gratification, has become pervasive. In these families, knowledge and expertise are pursued primarily for the purpose of personal gain. In indulgence-oriented families, love is viewed to be the same as gratification, and the powers of the human will are expressed in promiscuous and anarchic ways. Children in these families grow up to be unduly self-centered, intolerant, undisciplined, and individualistic. They avoid pain at all costs. They demand from their parents and society instant gratification of their desires, and when these demands are not met, they often resort to violence and even crime. These individuals are highly prone to developing addictions and tend to relate to others from the position of *expectations* rather than *responsibilities*. In part, these types of families and societies emerged as a reaction to the damaging authoritarian practices of the past but also because of at least three other major interrelated developments: the enormous rise of individualism in society as a whole, a tremendous increase in the material wealth of peoples and societies, and a dramatic change in the standards of moral and ethical principles.

An interesting and potentially very alarming related development in recent decades is the presence of *both* power and indulgence in many families. This unfortunate amalgamation has resulted in a further confusion in family relationships and parenting practices. Not infrequently, we observe families that are extremely permissive and undisciplined in their childrearing practices while the children are still young and relatively manageable. However, the same families become very rejecting and authoritarian towards the same children when they become older and begin to behave in ways that are either unacceptable or discomforting, often both, to their parents. These families then reject their children and call upon society—school, welfare, law-enforcement, etc.—to care for and control them. These children, feeling rejected, angry, and confused, then turn their wrath against the society and all who belong to it, including adults, other children, and the physical environment. It is under these conditions that seemingly random, illogical, purposeless, and vicious acts of violence take place, and it is through consideration of the nature of identity-based and/or power-based families that we can glimpse their underlying dynamics. These two types of the family—power-based and identity-based—clearly are unsatisfactory and not conducive to the well-being and optimal development of their individual members. A new type of family, commensurate with the challenges and opportunities of a rapidly changing humanity in the context of expanding consciousness of the principles of equality, justice, and unity, is called for.

THE UNITY-BASED FAMILY

Humanity is now in the final stages of its collective adolescence. As we mature, we normally will gradually leave behind the mindset based either on power-domination and oppression or power-struggle and extreme individualism. The transition and progression from one stage of development to another is an unavoidable aspect of life. However, this transition can be either consciously and conscientiously pursued or actively opposed and avoided. In the former case, the process of transition from one stage to another assumes a transformative and creative quality. However, when we resist the natural dynamics of human growth and progress, the outcome is stagnation and destructive tendencies. One of the main reasons that the institutions of marriage and family are now experiencing considerable problems is because the dynamics of the inevitable transition to new types of families—the unity-based families—are not yet fully understood. The most important dimension of this transition is development of a new worldview based on the consciousness of the oneness of humanity, which attains its highest expression in the all-important state of unity in diversity. It is impossible for humanity to advance further on its path of growth unless we establish a life of unity—intrapersonal, interpersonal, international, and global.

As we enter the next stage in our collective evolution, we will gradually move away from the mindsets of control and domination and/or power-struggle and indulgence, and will begin to see the world from the perspective of unity. Parallel with this process, we will also begin to move away from power-based and identity-based families to unity-based families. To better understand the characteristics of unity-based families, we will follow the same framework as we adopted for the study of the other types of families along the parameters of the main human capacities of knowledge, love, and will.

Characteristics of Unity-Based Families

In unity-based families, acquisition of knowledge is not only a right but also a responsibility of all members of the family. However, because of the inequality that now exists between men and women with respect to their education, girls and women must be given equal (and, if necessary, priority) access to education until an equitable and equal condition is attained. For far too long humanity has been deprived of women's unique contributions at an optimal level toward the development of civilization. The very quality of our world will change for the better when women are more involved, on an equal basis with men, in the administration of all human affairs—political, academic, religious, economic, etc.—and are given the opportunity to make their unique contributions to the life of the family and society under equal, just, and enlightened conditions. That is why education of women must top the agenda of all nations, governments, and social agencies of the world. The unity-based family creates conditions of equality and mutuality, and greatly helps to remove the unpardonable prevalence of the lack of truthfulness and trust in male–female relationships. These conditions, in turn, help to create much deeper conditions of intimacy and sharing, which are often absent in many marital and family interactions.

The expression of love in unity-based families—unlike those found in power-based and identity-based families—is other-directed, growth-inducing, unifying, and marked by tenderness and openness. In such families the pain of growth, which is an unavoidable aspect of true love, will not be countered by the use of the short-term, basically injurious potions of instant gratification and indulgence. Also, in the context of unity-based families the qualities of universality, creativity, curiosity, and search for truth will be actively encouraged. In these families love is unifying and all-encompassing, and children are helped to love themselves, others, and life without experiencing the "love-ambivalence" so frequently found in power-based and indulgence-based families and societies. In the unhealthy conditions of power-based and identity-based families, individuals are made to feel that they cannot simultaneously love themselves and others, their families and all other families, their countries and the whole of humanity, their co-religionists and all other peoples regardless of their belief systems. The list goes on. In its pure, mature form, love has no limits, knows no boundaries, makes no exclusions, and does not allow for violence and destructiveness. Above all, a mature and healthy love creates unity. Thus in the unity-based family a creative cycle exists: unity creates love, and love creates unity, which in turn results in more love and unity.

Finally, the development of the human will and its expressions is quite different in unity-based families. In these families the power-based and indulgence-based practices of competition, control, and excessive individualism and independence give way to those of cooperation, equality, universality, and interdependence. This transformation is due to the fact that the finest fruits of a mature will are those of service at the individual level and justice at the social level. Service and justice go hand in hand. In a unity-based family, all members endeavor to their utmost to serve one another, while at the same time, the family as an institution makes certain that equality and justice will be its modus operandi. Thus, individuals need not engage in disuniting acts of seeking personal justice that often deteriorate into conflict, revenge, and violence.

This comparison of the characteristics and dynamics of power-based and identity-based families with unity-based families clearly demonstrates the wide gaps that exist among them. Indeed, the differences among the three types of family are so immense that the immediate response of many family specialists and policy-makers is to consider such a transformation as unrealistic and utopian in nature. Consequently, they propose that we focus on more "realistic" and "practical" issues such as modes of communication, skills of self-assertion, acquisition of problem-solving and conflict resolution capacities, and a host of other competencies. These skills and strategies are important, but they fail to address the root causes of marital and familial problems.

Issues of inequality and injustice in the family quite often have their counterparts in society. Inequality and injustice are fully interrelated and mutually reinforcing. Two good examples of the interdependence of the family and society are the issues of the civil rights and women's movements in the United States. We cannot find two nobler causes, espoused by a finer group of individuals, and supported by a stronger or wealthier society, than these two movements that gained considerable momentum in the 1960s and '70s. There has been and still there are significant obstacles to achieving true equality and justice with regard to both these issues. However, four decades later, we now have considerable tangible evidence of progress in the relationship between women and men and among members of the different races. And as society further evolves along these lines, the conditions of marriages, families, and children in general, and those in the inner cities in particular will improve. With the advent of the mass media and the widespread discourse on these issues in the society, we should expect the emergence of a new generation of young women and men of various racial backgrounds who will relate to one another with true equality, understanding, unity, and unhesitant interpersonal communication and integration. It is in this context that unity-based families, constructed on the foundations of gender equality, will become more common and will create the most appropriate environments for raising truly healthy, peaceful, and accomplished children and youth.

In brief, the *unity-based family* is only possible in the context of gender equality both in interpersonal relationships and social norms/ structures. Because of the inseparable nature of unity and equality (yet to be fully realized), the unity-based family has always been and still is less common than the other two family types. In the unity-based family, power is a collective commodity shared and exercised by all family members according to their respective abilities, responsibilities, and needs. Likewise, expression of love in the unity-based family is inseparable from the issue of equality, particularly with respect to concerns about power and authority. The finest fruit of love is unity, and true unity is not possible without equality. The unity-based family functions according to the principles of gender equality; cooperative and consultative relationships; and equal consideration for the rights, interests, and responsibilities of each member of the family, as well as the welfare of the institution as an organic social entity. These families neither sanction the abuse of power and the unequal distribution of freedom, opportunity, and resources that characterize the authoritarian families; nor endorse the power-struggle and excessive competition, self-interest, self-indulgence, and individualism that are the hallmarks of identity-based families. The unity-based family promotes harmonious and complementary relationships within the family, and ensures the welfare and happiness of all its individual members, while, simultaneously contributing to the peace and progress of the family as the building block of society. The concept of the unity-based family will become clearer as we review some of the main critical challenges facing the family in every part of the world. However, before we proceed, I wish to refer to a remarkable discourse that refers to some of the main characteristics of the unity-based family. The discourse took place at the Church of the Ascension in New York City. The occasion was a talk by 'Abdu'l-Bahá on June 2, 1912. The talk was followed by a lengthy question and answer period.

Question: What is the attitude of your belief toward the family?

Answer: According to the teachings of Bahá'u'lláh the family, being a human unit, must be educated according to the rules of sanctity. All the virtues must be taught the family. The integrity of the family bond must be constantly considered, and the rights of the individual members must not be transgressed. The rights of the son, the father, the mother—none of them must be transgressed, none of them must be arbitrary. Just as the son has certain obligations to his father, the father, likewise, has certain obligations to his son. The mother, the sister and other members of the household have their certain prerogatives. All these rights and prerogatives must be conserved, yet the unity of the family must be sustained. The injury of one shall be considered the injury of all; the comfort of each, the comfort of all; the honor of one, the honor of all.[28]

In this brief response, 'Abdu'l-Bahá, nearly a century ago, clearly refers to the all-important issues of human rights and gender equality, which in the ensuing decades became the objects of serious attention in many countries globally. 'Abdu'l-Bahá further placed the subjects of human rights and gender equality in the context of unity and the principle of the oneness of humanity. These latter issues are not yet in the mainstream of contemporary thought, but now humanity, gradually and reluctantly, is beginning to consider them.

Contemporary Family Crises

In our world today, traditional authoritarian and modern individualistic families together comprise the majority of families and account for the most common family-related disorders such as gender inequality, deficient parenting, inadequate education of children, insufficient guidance of youth, repetitive episodes of conflict, and the destructive consequences of both family violence and family breakdown on all members of the family. These conditions have had an understandable but rather ominous outcome. The interest in marriage and in having children has dramatically decreased in many societies, particularly in economically and technologically more advanced countries. In many of these countries, an increasing number of individuals tend to choose cohabitation over marriage. Anne Marie Ambert, in her review and analysis of the research on cohabitation, has reached some sobering conclusions. Her review shows that more than 50% of cohabitation relationships dissolve within five years and that couples who have cohabitated before their marriage separate more often than others.[29] In fact, Wu has found that simply being married to a spouse who has previously cohabited raises the risk of divorce in that marriage.[30]

Along with the decline of interest in marriage, there has been a significant increase in the rate of divorce in many countries. A recent review of research on the causes of divorce identifies four main reasons: secularization and lessening of the power of religion, liberalization of divorce laws, individualism, and "lower threshold of tolerance" when the marriage does not meet the couple's expectations for personal fulfillment.[31] The first two of these reasons—secularization and liberalization—directly refer to the authoritarian nature of many religious traditions and social laws and their influence in creating power-based authoritarian marriages and families, which are now being increasingly rejected. The other two reasons—individualism and low tolerance—clearly point to the emergence of identity-based individualistic marriages and families in modern times.

Parallel with the dramatic decline of interest in marriage and having children, which has taken place in the context of "sexual revolution," first in the West and now in many other countries, there has been a considerable increase in the number of alternative approaches to the institutions of marriage and family. The classical models of marriage and family—a man and woman entering into a legally and culturally sanctioned union with the intention of establishing a family and having children—are now being reevaluated and new alternatives being considered. Among these alternative approaches are cohabitation, single-parent families, same-sex marriages, and communal living. After a few decades of rather widespread experimentation with some of these alternatives, their inadequacies and negative consequences are gradually becoming evident, and researchers point to some alarming developments with long-term profound social consequences.[32] The following quotation is one such example:

> The evidence *at this point* does not indicate that young women gain as much from cohabitation as from marriage, unless their partner is committed to marry them if they so want. The "sexual revolution" should not be taken as synonymous with "women's liberation" and women's best interest. While there is some good in the **sexual revolution**, it has not completely eliminated the double standard. It still has benefited males more than females in the sense that *it has made more women available to men sexually—and cohabitation has been one avenue through which this has occurred.* (All emphases in the original text.)[33]

These findings are, in my opinion, symptoms not causes of contemporary family crises. I believe that the crises of the contemporary family have their genesis in the core family issues of love, equality, and education. Here, I will briefly describe each of these crises.

FAMILY AND THE CRISIS OF LOVE

The first and foremost crisis of the contemporary family is with respect to the issue of love—love between husband and wife, between parents and children, among siblings, and within the family and the community. Marital love usually is a faint shadow of its romantic version—that irresistible quest of the human heart that brings people together and binds them in a firm bond of commitment, mutual affection, and reliance. Neither the power-based authoritarian family nor the pleasure-based individualistic family is conducive to either maintenance of romantic love or its development and expression as mature, unity-creating love. In the authoritarian family, love is at best conditional and at worst violent. In the individualistic family, love is self-centered or competitive, usually both. Love in both these types of families is likely to be selfish, greedy, jealous, conditional, and stifled. A harmonious marital love—inclusive, generous, liberating, empowering, and evolving—is most present in the context of a unity-based marriage—equal, just, united, and faithful.

This type of family has not been common in the past and even today is, unfortunately, rather rare. We need to learn the ways of mature unity-based marital love and to teach them to our children both by word and example.

The other crisis of love in contemporary families is with respect to the children who often receive either inadequate or misguided love from their parents. Love is an essential force for healthy development of individuals and societies. When children receive either "power-based conditional" or "indulgence-based competitive" love, or both, they often grow-up to be self-centered, unfocused, resentful, angry, and even at times violent adults. These outcomes are observed in such families regardless of whether they are wealthy or poor, highly educated or not, and in the West or East, North or South. It is instructive to note that in the 20th century, concomitant with humanity's monumental accomplishments in the fields of science, technology, and economics, the institution of the family in many parts of the world was seriously weakened. Consequently, new generations of children and youth, reared in overburdened and conflicted families, felt inadequately loved and, in turn, their capacity to love was dramatically lessened. It is also noteworthy that the 20th century became one of the most violent centuries in human history. These conditions, in my view, are interconnected and have their roots in three grievous conditions that are directly related to the absence of love and its replacement with power in human relationships at all levels. Here I am referring to the evils of colonialism, slavery, and intractable violence as well as their offspring—poverty, disease, and social/cultural dislocation.

In our contemporary world, we can identify three groups of families adversely affected by these major examples of injustice and inhumanity perpetrated by human beings against other human beings. *The first group comprises impoverished families anywhere in the world.* In these families, the primary concern of the parents and their children is basic survival. These parents do not have enough time to be with their children to guide and educate them. In the context of their sorely vexed and anxiety-ridden lives, these parents lack the required calm and certitude necessary to instill in their children adequate levels of assurance and courage to meet their considerable life challenges and limited opportunities. Therefore, children of these poverty-stricken masses—most of whom live in societies that have suffered from one or more of the above conditions of colonialism, slavery, and violence—are highly prone to grow up to become victims of a love-starved life with its negative and destructive consequences.

The second group comprises those families that suffered the ruins of war. The 20th century had two World Wars and many regional wars. And now, in the 21st century, issues of terrorism and widespread interethnic hostilities are being added to these wars. Such violence injures the souls as well as the bodies of individuals and shatters the fabric of the society and the bonds of human relationships. Every aspect of human life is damaged, and the society as a whole is wounded. We have not yet developed an effective approach to healing the wounds of conflict, violence, and war. Consequently, there are many wounded individuals who are not fully able to give love unconditionally and without reserve because they are so preoccupied with the pain of their own psychic wounds. These conditions apply to both the victims and perpetrators of violence, the former suffering primarily from the physical and psychosocial trauma of violence, while the latter being afflicted with the grave psychosocial and moral/spiritual consequences of committing violence. A *culture of healing* needs to be developed, involving both these groups. Rehabilitation and strengthening of the institution of the family is at the core of this process.[34]

The third group refers to the identity-based families, particularly in the West, where individualism has established deep roots and the interests of the individual are accorded greater favor than those of the collective. In this context, both the family and society are seen as places in which the wishes and desires of individuals are given outright priority. In these environments both the support of the family and the education of children are secondary to the self-centered individualism that exists most prominently in North America and Western Europe, and which is now rapidly appearing in other parts of the world as societies become influenced with prevailing Western attitudes and norms. This is a serious cultural dislocation and merits careful, sustained attention on the part of the leadership of all societies.

FAMILY AND THE CRISIS OF EDUCATION

The second crisis in the modern family, which is related to the first crisis of deficient love, concerns the inadequate or misguided education of children and youth. The family is the locus of lifelong education, particularly during the formative years of childhood and adolescence. Children's first educators are their mothers and fathers. If the education that we give our children is not conducive to their growth and development in a truly meaningful and healthy manner, then these children will inevitably suffer. The contemporary crisis of education does not only mean the intellectual education of children. There is also a crisis in the emotional, social, moral, and spiritual education of children. One common aspect of this crisis concerns the issue of peace education, the lack of which causes much misery in human society. Even worse, we tend to educate our children within the framework of conflict.

In the family, the majority of the world's children receive religious and ethnic indoctrination and education, usually in the context of in-group and out-group, us and them, citizens and foreigners, civilized and barbaric, good and bad, and saved and damned. In schools, the history taught our children is often the history of conflict. The geography learned is usually the geography of conflict. The literature studied is literature infused with conflict. The biology or economics or political science our children learn is frequently taught within the framework of conflict. In short, we give our children a conflict-based education. The conditions of the world will not improve unless we adopt a peace-based curriculum of instruction for all children. This aspect of education is gravely overlooked at home, in school, in communities, and in the media, which has emerged as one of the most influential sources of education for our children and youth. Families need guidance and assistance on how to rear their children as peaceful and peace-creating individuals, and this task needs to be shared by the parents and schools; governments and policymakers; social, academic, and religious institutions; as well as the media and the family experts. I will discuss these issues more fully in the coming chapters on education and peace.

Family and the Crisis of Gender Equality

The third important crisis with respect to the family is the issue of gender equality. Inequality between women and men is one of the most frequent complaints of women who seek marriage and family counseling or who appeal to the courts with regard to their marital problems. It is an empirical verity that most women, in families and societies throughout the world, are dealt with unjustly and are not given equal opportunities with men in respect to many aspects of their lives. In almost every society women are secondary to men in the education they receive, in the economic benefits they draw, and in their opportunities to assume leadership in their respective societies. Not until women become equal with men in all arenas of life and assume equal levels of leadership, authority, and power in the governance of society will we be able to create families that are united and societies that are peaceful. In the absence of family unity and social peace, the care and education of children and youth will continue to suffer greatly, and the vicious cycle of violence, poverty, disease, and renewed violence will be repeated endlessly. For these reasons alone, the issue of gender equality should top the agendas of all societies, and because of women's profound impact on the welfare and upbringing of every new generation of humanity, their education should be given priority.

Equality is an essential link in the chain of fundamental requisites—unity, justice, equality, and freedom—for personal and social welfare and progress. The final and ultimate link in this chain is peace in all aspects of our lives: inner, interpersonal, and intergroup. Peace, however, will be only possible if its main prerequisite—unity—is present. However, unity is accomplished only when there is justice, and the main prerequisite for justice is equality, and equal relationships are hallmarks of maturity born out of personal responsibility in the context of freedom. We are hard pressed to find, anywhere, significant examples of the integrated presence of these interdependent fundamental requisites for human well-being and development, either in families or societies. Usually, one or more of these requisites are missing.

These interdependent requisites have the quality of a hologram—each part contains the whole. In other words, in order to achieve all of these conditions, we need to begin with at least one of them. Thus, for example, when we attempt to create equality in a family, the other four conditions—justice, unity, freedom, and peace—also begin to happen because it is impossible to have any one of these conditions without the presence of the other requisites. The establishment of these conditions of human well-being and progress is developmental in nature. The more evolved an individual, institution, or society is, the more capable it is of establishing equality, justice, unity, and peace in the context of responsibility and freedom. Maturity, here, refers to the development of human consciousness with its biological, psychological, social, moral, and spiritual expressions. The diagram below, adapted from the *Education for Peace Curriculum Manual,* depicts the integrated nature of the qualities and requisites of a marriage of equality.

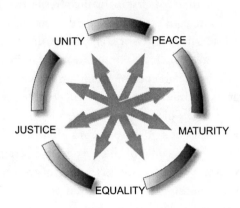

Diagram 6.1. Requisites of a marriage of equality.

Of these conditions, unity is most accessible in terms of its quality and outward expression in human relationships. In other words, it is much easier to know when unity rather than equality, justice, maturity, or peace is present. These other four conditions are more subjective and vague than unity. With respect to the family, the focus on unity automatically results in the introduction of principles of equality, justice, and maturity in family relationships, simply because it is impossible to have a united family in the absence of equality, justice, and mature responsible discharge of our responsibilities as spouses, parents, and children. Family peace is the natural outcome of these conditions.

It is in this context that, as a new model of marriage and family, the concept of the *unity-based family,* based on the foundations of gender equality, assumes its significance and urgency. For far too long women have been denied their fundamental rights as equals with men, and for this neglect humanity has lamentably deprived itself of the far-reaching benefits that women can contribute to the organization, administration, and progress of human society. The primary task before those of us who are concerned with issues of marriage and family as policy makers, professional experts, social reformers, and community leaders is to ensure that the principle of equality between women and men is fully understood, universally promoted, and systematically implemented at all levels and within all institutions of the society—family, school, workplace, government, and religion.

CREATING UNITY-BASED FAMILIES

This brief review of the functions, types, and crises of the family demonstrates that in order for the family to fully discharge its functions and meet the challenges it faces in a rapidly changing global world, the institution of the family itself needs to evolve and adapt in a manner commensurate with these realities. The greatest challenge before humanity today is to create a global civilization of peace—united in its principles, diverse in its practices, prosperous and benevolent, scientifically informed and ethically enlightened. The building block of this peace-based civilization is the unity-based family capable of ensuring the operation of the principles of equality, justice, personal development and family cohesion, free from the coercive authoritarian and conflicted individualistic models of marriage and family.[35]

Creation of the unity-based family is a daunting task because it requires a basic transformation from the prevalent dichotomous, conflict-based worldviews to unity-based worldviews, which, as described in chapter one, is difficult and challenging. The unity-based family is an entirely new type of family. The families of the past were primarily power-based and authoritarian. The families of the present are mainly either power-based or identity-based, often both. The imperatives of social change and human development, however, indicate that the families of the future will operate according to the law of unity, rejecting both the authoritarian and adversarial practices common in many families, replacing them with far more equal, harmonious, and just family relationships. However, the process of the formation of unity-based families is not automatic. It requires a conscious, deliberate, and enlightened approach involving individuals, the institution of the family, and the community. The monumental change from power-based and conflict-based types of families to those of unity-based families is, in essence, a transformative process, which was addressed in chapter three.

ARE UNITY-BASED FAMILIES ATTAINABLE?

The answer to whether unity-based families and societies are attainable is affirmative, provided that we tread the path of new ideas with practical plans and programs. We first must ask ourselves: What do we mean by "practical"? By "practical" do we mean a set of instructions as found in "how to" and self-help packages abundantly available in the marketplace of ideas? Does "practical" refer to techniques that could be applied by anyone who learns the skills required for their implementation? Or does "practical" involve acquisition of necessary insights and experiences, in conditions of earnest search for truth and profound personal transformation that will, in turn, allow us to look at ourselves and our world from totally new perspectives, free from prejudices and preconceived notions, and open to novel ideas and approaches? It is this last version of practicality to which I refer. Within this framework, I suggest that the proposed transition to unity-based families and societies is indeed practical, even inevitable. There are several reasons for this assertion.

1. *Developmental Imperatives:* The transition from power-orientation and self-centered indulgence to unity-orientation and authentic growth is not simply an idea emerging out of nowhere. The establishment of unity is the unavoidable outcome of the transition of humanity from its collective ages of infancy, childhood, and adolescence to that of adulthood. In other words, whether we like it or not, we are driven towards unity. Consider the environmental, economic, medical, and political conditions of our world. Are they not all demanding we deal with these issues from the perspective of unity? Can any nation or group of nations really isolate themselves from the rest of the world and prohibit the intrusion of ozone depletion, the Human Immunodeficiency Virus (HIV), or the effects of international trade into their territories? Is it any longer possible to keep the masses of humanity in any part of the world uninformed about the realities of the rest of the world, even in the face of the stiffest regulations? Can we afford to remain indifferent and silent about the abuse of the legitimate rights of any individual or group anywhere in the world? Is it possible to continue, unchallenged, the inexcusable practice of gender inequality still present in many families, places of work, and the domains of leadership and governance? The answer to these and similar questions is a resounding no, because of the fundamental fact that the age of unity has arrived, and the truth of the statement that "the earth is but one country and mankind its citizens"[36] is becoming increasing recognized. The primary task before all of us now is to focus our efforts on creating ever-larger circles of unity, while at the same time preserving our precious diversity.

2. *Scientific and Technological Advances:* The rapid development of the means of transmission of ideas and information, combined with the increasing ease of movement of peoples to all parts of the world and the spread of powerful multinational companies has created a de facto international community. These developments are not accidental by-products of science and technology. Rather, they are direct results of the human innate striving to know and to integrate. The forces behind human scientific discoveries and technological inventions are the powers of the human soul—to know, to love, and to will. Everything that is created by human beings is accomplished through these powers that we all possess. These powers are the basis of our fundamental oneness, and scientific discoveries and advances are the tools we human beings create to bring us together, so that we can get to know each other and to love and serve one another. How ironic that, in our inner core, we both yearn for and fear unity!

3. *Political Experiences and Lessons:* In the 20th century alone, we have gathered considerable political experience and insight that could help us facilitate the inevitable transition to the next phase of our collective development. We now have clear, indisputable proof that we cannot create unity through force and imposition. The failed costly experiments in the former USSR and Eastern European countries are sufficient examples of the truth of this statement. Likewise, we are now rapidly beginning to realize that capitalism also will not be able to usher in the era of international unity and cooperation. This is so because capitalism, as is practiced today, with its excessive emphasis on competition, profit, and individualism, is a very potent expression of the adolescent stage of development and has amply demonstrated that it is incapable of creating conditions of justice and fairness. Rather, it has created extremes of selfishness, moral bankruptcy, and extremes of wealth and poverty at such dangerous levels that the system threatens to implode and become self-destructive. The signs of this destructive process are now evident in almost all capitalistic societies.

In the face of these realities, world leaders are increasingly attracted to the principles of international cooperation and mutual assistance. There can no longer be any doubt in the minds of thoughtful individuals that we are all interdependent. However, this realization alone is insufficient to create the state of "unity in diversity," which is the characteristic of the next phase in our evolution. We clearly are in need of new perspectives about the manner in which we can organize our world. In this respect it should be said that ultimately the most important agent of social change will be today's children, if they were to be reared and educated within the mindset of unity. A new generation of leaders who see *the earth as one country and mankind as its citizens* will transform the world in a dramatic and positive manner. It is here that unity-based families assume their significance and play a crucial role in the betterment of our world.

4. *Spiritual Receptivity:* Finally, there is another development that makes the transformation described above practical. Here, I am referring to the remarkable spiritual awakening occurring in our world today. After decades of open and rebellious rejection of spirituality in favor of materialistic ideologies, scientific theories, political reforms, humanistic pursuits, issue-oriented movements, new-age spiritualism, and fundamentalist revivals, once again, peoples of the world are turning towards spirituality. This long period of deprivation has resulted in a deeply felt hunger for spirituality and is at the heart of the current frenzied search for anything that resembles, however remotely, that long lost and yearned for spiritual state that humanity has experienced from time to time in its history.

What makes our age different from bygone ages is that scientifically oriented humanity cannot, and should not, accept those concepts that are illogical, archaic, and out of touch with the realities and needs of humanity at this time. The confusing state surrounding the issues of spirituality, morality, and values, however, should not deter us from searching for authentic spirituality and its application to our lives at individual, family, and societal levels. Of all the practical steps that we need to take to bring about this transformation from oppression, conflict, and self-centeredness to equality, justice, and unity, the issue of spirituality is of the greatest importance yet presents the greatest challenge because it is through spiritual principles that we define our humanness and our uniqueness. And because spirituality is based on religion—in its pure, universal, and progressive state—it is necessary that we revisit our view of religion and our attitudes towards it. There are, however, deep-rooted attachments to the perspectives of the past, and their reappraisal and change require either a very high degree of self-confidence and trust or a very desperate state of hopelessness and misery. It is to be hoped that the former will be the motivating cause in our search for spirituality.

THREE QUESTIONS

Finally, in light of the unity paradigm, let us now consider three categories of questions. *First,* what is the state of the family in our respective communities? Are the majority of the families disunited and conflicted? Are they peaceful, and if so, is it an imposed family peace emerging from conformity and an authoritarian mandate? *Second,* what is the impact of the contemporary family (traditional or modern) on the welfare of children and society in our respective communities? Are there children in our respective societies who are neglected, violated, and deprived of their basic needs and rights for love, safety, food, shelter, medical care, peaceful home life, and enlightened education? And *third,* if the answers to the above two types of questions are unsatisfactory, what kind of new education should be offered to the families to alter the conditions of the family and their impact on both children and the society? The answers may vary in detail, but they probably will all have certain common features with respect to the tripartite issues of love, equality, and parenting that are among the main functions of the institution of the family, discussed earlier.

CONCLUSIONS AND RECOMMENDATIONS

As humanity approaches its age of collective maturity and as human societies become increasingly interdependent and integrated, the institution of the family needs to follow a similar path of maturation so as to befittingly meet the opportunities and challenges of the modern world. Here, I have argued that the unity-based family is the most suitable type of family to provide a firm foundation for the creation of an enlightened, democratic, and progressive civilization of peace. A family can be considered as unity-based, if it is able to do the following:

- To create a stronghold for the well-being, health, safety, and optimal development of all its members;
- To properly and adequately educate children so that they develop their respective *unique identities* within the parameters of a *universal identity* and are prepared and willing to conduct all their relationships within the framework of the principle of the oneness of humanity and the uniqueness and equality of all its members;
- To contribute to the development of society in the context of an ever-advancing civilization of peace; and
- To accomplish all these objectives within the parameters of love, encouragement, and unity without recourse to any form of violence.

Some may view these functions as too general and impractical, and others as too ambitious and unrealistic. However, in my considered view these objectives are both specific and realistic, and reflect the gradual, but definite, emergence of the unity-based worldview, which is the hallmark of the age of maturity of both individuals and societies. In fact, both the unity-based worldview and unity-based family are the only options before us for creating a civilization of peace.

The following recommendations are a restatement of those I made at the aforementioned conference held in New York on the occasion of the United Nations Year of the Family. They are as relevant now as they were then.

THREE RECOMMENDATIONS

The following actions and conditions are required to effect change and to create unity-based families.

Promote Unity

The reality of the oneness of humanity and its inevitable outcome—unity in diversity—must constitute the core element of the current international and interpersonal dialogue. Its facts and principles need to be included in the educational curricula, the study of the history of humanity, the agenda of world governments, the teachings of world religions, the scientific research on human origins and nature, the reporting of world events by the media, the development of new technologies, and above all, in the education of children and their parents/guardians and teachers. Acceptance of the fact of the oneness of humanity and the decision to establish unity in diversity demands a fundamental change in our mindset. This change is of a deep psychological, social, and spiritual nature, and calls for willingness on the part of the leaders of the world in all departments of human life— political, religious, academic, economic, social—to put aside their attachment and reliance on power, force, and conflict and instead learn to harvest the fruits of unity.

Give Priority to the Family

As a preparation for the advent of political unity and peace, it is essential that the reality of the oneness of humanity be universally taught and demonstrated in action. The family is the best, most effective institution to teach the concept of the oneness of humanity and to improve our capacities to live a life of unity and to become unifiers in all dimensions of our lives. The reasons for this fact are several: the family is the building block of the society, the world in microcosm, and the workshop of civilization through its role as the primary educator of each new generation. Therefore, all segments of the societies in the world need to prioritize the development of the family by educating its members on how to create unity-based families. In particular, parents and their children need to learn how to resolve conflicts and make decisions without resorting to the destructive practices of power and force on the one hand, and indulgence and permissiveness on the other. This is a very fine line to tread, and most parents do not know how to approach these issues in a healthy manner. With the development of new methods and mediums of education and training at our disposal, there is no legitimate reason for not reaching parents and their children through television, radio, the Internet, and other means, providing them with insights and techniques on how to create unity-based and violence-free families.

Give Priority to Equality

Giving priority to equality is neither an unreasonable nor impractical suggestion. However, it is challenging, as it goes against certain cultural and religious beliefs and practices. There is a tendency to view culture and religion as constant realities to which everything else must conform, while, in fact, all life is subject to the immutable laws of change and of decay and renewal. Cultures and religions are not exempt from these universal laws. At the core of contemporary crises is the reality that while change has overtaken all aspects of our lives, our attitudes and values (which derive from our cultures and religions) have either not changed or else have changed into a state of pragmatism with no overarching universal principles. In the same manner that science, through research, constantly expands the depth and expanse of its understanding, likewise, religion must be renewed so that it could meet the spiritual needs of the rapidly evolving modern global culture. (See chapter two.)

When women and girls are given a better education and an equal position in all aspects of the life of society, only then we will have healthier marriages, more united families, better educated and trained children, more cohesive and peaceful communities, stronger economies, and more peaceful, less violent societies.

CHAPTER SEVEN

EDUCATION
THE MOST CONSEQUENTIAL RESPONSIBILITY

If the learned and worldly-wise men of this age were to allow mankind to inhale the fragrance of fellowship and love, every understanding heart would apprehend the meaning of true liberty, and discover the secret of undisturbed peace and absolute composure.[1]

—Bahá'u'lláh

...mothers are the first educators of mankind; if they be imperfect, alas for the condition and future of the race.[2]

—'Abdu'l-Bahá

Education is not preparation for life; education is life itself.[3]
—John Dewey (1859–1952)

Learning without thought is labor lost; thought without learning is perilous.[4]

—Confucius

Men are born ignorant, not stupid; they are made stupid by education.[5]
—Bertrand Russell (1872–1970)

Wars, religious, racial or political, have arisen from human ignorance, misunderstanding and lack of education.[6]

—'Abdu'l-Bahá

EDUCATION

BRINGING TO MATURITY THE FRUIT OF KNOWLEDGE

This is a brilliant century. Eyes are now open to the beauty of the oneness of humanity, of love and of brotherhood. The darkness of suppression will disappear and the light of unity will shine. We cannot bring love and unity to pass merely by talking of it. Knowledge is not enough. Wealth, science, education are good, we know: but we must also work and study to bring to maturity the fruit of knowledge.[7]

—'Abdu'l-Bahá

My parents had limited formal education. My mother was reared in a well-established, influential Muslim family in Ardekan, a small city in the province of Yazd. However, unlike almost all other girls and women in her social milieu who were illiterate, she was tutored at home and received elementary education in reading, writing, and arithmetic. Later, when she became a Bahá'í, she embarked on the systematic process of self-education as an adult that nurtured her acutely sharp and inquisitive mind, a process that is still remarkably active in her nineties. My father was born into a family of religiously learned in the mountainous village of Banadak, also in the province of Yazd. He did not have an opportunity to study beyond high school because of the untimely accidental death of his father. Following this event, my father, who was about 18 years of age, left Banadak and eventually found a government job in Ardekan. My father was extremely fond of learning and, like my mother, was always a ready and eager student, an avid reader, and a dedicated promoter of education. My parents ensured that all seven of their children received the highest level of education in their chosen fields of medicine, engineering, economics, literature, and library sciences, at Iranian, European, and North American universities. They also provided for the high school and university education of two of my father's younger brothers and two sons of another brother. I remember that during my childhood and adolescence we often had at least one and sometimes two or more members of the extended family who lived with us in order to continue their education.

My father—Jaafar—was a very generous, happy, and good-natured person. He had a searching mind, a loving heart, and an open house. At the end of April 1976, my father was walking on a sidewalk returning from a joyous Bahá'í celebration[8] when he was struck by an out-of-control car driven by a novice teenaged driver. The sudden untimely death of my father had a profound impact on all the family. When such an event occurs, we suddenly become aware of the inevitability and unpredictability of death. We realize that we better be prepared for the unexpected in life, in general, and unexpected and untimely death, in particular. This is not an easy task. The human psychological tendency is either to deny the ever-present reality of death or to distance oneself from it. These maneuvers are not only ineffective but also counterproductive. Trying to insulate oneself from death—an impossible undertaking—robs us of whatever life we have left. It creates in us a constant state of apprehension, anxiety, fear, and uncertainty, combined with the feeling that time is running out and, therefore, we must increase our pace. The excessively agitated and fast-moving lifestyle of the modern world is an expression of this anxiety based on the denial of death. The ease with which we accept death in our world—death through wars, poverty, disease, violence, etc.—is another manifestation of the impact of denial of the reality of death and the resultant diminished value for life.

Facing the reality of death and our mortality is a truly educative experience. By doing so, we learn to value life and conceive plans to live our limited days on earth meaningfully. Likewise, we need to educate our children about issues of life and death and prepare them for the exciting, rewarding, but unpredictable path of existence. The death of my father afforded us the opportunity to discuss these issues at home openly as appropriate. I recall that a year later after the death of my father, my sons—who were then five and eight—and I were returning from a memorial gathering honoring a community member. It was shortly after sunset, and the country road we were traveling on was dark, overcast, and spooky in the cold November of Ottawa. The children began speaking about what kind of funeral and memorial service they would organize for me when I die. They also decided that my grave should be covered with marble and after some discussion agreed that it should be pink marble!

In this chapter I will focus on issues of parenting, self-education, and formal education and will share my own personal efforts in this regard, as a parent, as a university teacher, and as a peace educator, and as a student of Bahá'í teachings. The section immediately below is partially based on the text of a keynote presentation I prepared for the World Congress, "Giving Children a Voice: The Transforming Role of The Family in a Global Society," held in New Delhi, India, 3–8 January

2009. The title of my talk was, "All Children Are Our Children: Why the Neglect?"

PARENTING FOR A BETTER WORLD

Usually, when the topic of parenting is discussed, we naturally think of our own children and our responsibility to them as parents. This is, of course, a normal and essential aspect of parenting. However, considering the realities of our world and the fact that the welfare of our children is inseparable from that of all other children, we need to expand our notion of parenthood beyond the limited boundaries of home and family.

We live in a world in which "around 51 million births go unregistered every year"; "approximately 158 million children aged 5–14 are engaged in child labour"; "an estimated 1.2 million children are trafficked every year"; "at any given time over 300,000 child soldiers, some as young as eight, are exploited in armed conflicts"; "more than one million children worldwide are detained by law enforcement officials"; approximately two million children are "exploited through prostitution and pornography"; tens of millions of girls below age 18 are forced into marriage; and a similar number of young women and girls are subjected to genital mutilation.[9] We collective adults have created a world of conflict, corruption, violence, prejudice, poverty, and injustice that makes our children its direct victims, gives them appalling role models, and leaves them a terrible world as their inheritance.

Children survive and thrive in the context of relationships within their families, communities, and societies. Each of these entities has specific, but interrelated, responsibilities for providing healthy environments for the wholesome development of children with regard to their physical, emotional, intellectual, social, and spiritual needs. Neglect of any of these areas of need greatly affects the life of the child and the nature of his or her relationships with self, others, and the world. It is in the context of relationships that children are educated and learn about themselves and the world, and about life and its joys and sorrows. Thus, the quality of our children's lives is the yardstick by which we can measure the quality of our parenting practices and the nature of our relationship with children. This close association between the nature of our relationship with children and the condition of their lives poses several questions:

1. Who is responsible for the care of children? Parents only? Parents and the government? All of us?
2. What is the most significant predictor of children's future? Their economic conditions? Safety of their environments? The type of parenting and education they receive?
3. Why do we tolerate such cruelty and neglect of children? Is it: Because we do not care? Because they are not our children? Because these children deserve it?

Let us consider each of these questions separately. *Who is responsible for the care of our children?* Clearly, parents have the primary responsibility for all aspects of the lives of their children. However, because the lives of parents are greatly affected by the nature of communities in which they live and by the types of governance that they experience, it follows that society also has specific responsibilities for the care of children. Among these are the responsibilities to create violence-free, peaceful schools; to provide reasonable health and medical care; to address the needs of the poor and the less-privileged members of the society; and to ensure the protection of human rights of all members of society with specific attention to the rights of children and youth.

The second question—*What is the most significant predictor of children's future?*—encompasses many factors, including the issues of poverty, safety, quality of parenting, and type of education that children receive. There is ample evidence that these and other related factors dramatically affect children's lives. The common factor in all these situations is the quality of relationships and education that children experience. Good relationships build resilient, optimistic, motivated, and unifying personalities; and good education nurtures and develops intellectual capacities and creative potentials. Children thus trained are often able to remove themselves from the adverse environments into which they are born.

The third question—*Why do we tolerate such cruelty and neglect of children?*—is the most challenging. There are many reasons for this terrible fact. Some parents and leaders unfortunately do not care about the condition of the world's children. Others primarily care about their own children. And still others, one hopes a very small number, blame underprivileged children for their own miseries. These are troubling assertions, and we can dismiss them as too pessimistic and even inaccurate. But the fact remains that millions of children live in the most appalling circumstances. Many are hungry, sick, and neglected. Many die of preventable diseases. Many have no shelter, are deprived of the most basic care, and live truly miserable lives.

We and other privileged members of the world community must face these realities and must ask why so many children suffer so greatly. And we need to ask ourselves, "What are our individual and collective responsibilities towards our children and towards the world's neglected children?" and "What can we do to ensure that all children are adequately parented and cared for?" To answer these questions adequately, we need to have an integrated approach to the education of children and their parents and caregivers, with a focus on the psychological, social, and spiritual needs of children. In a world where children die by the thousands every day, are used as soldiers, are trained to be suicide bombers, and commit suicide at an ever younger age, the problems we are facing are profound and deep-rooted. There is both financial poverty and poverty of spirit. There is hunger for food and hunger for righteousness and compassion. There is physical disease and the disease of the soul. As parents, we need to address all these issues for our children; and as members of an interconnected world, we need to be similarly concerned about the welfare of all children.

Distinguished educator, John Dewey (1859–1952) observes that *"Education is not preparation for life; education is life itself."*[10] This statement implies that we never stop learning, and with regard to the manner in which the adults of the world are caring for the children of the world, there is clearly much for us to learn. Therefore, the focus on education here has two objectives. The first objective is for us as adults, parents, caregivers, policy-makers, leaders, health professionals, and scholars to reflect on the kind of education that is conducive to healthy education and development of all children. This process will have both learning and transformative outcomes. Ultimately, we need to transform adults' approach to children in order to transform the condition of the world's children. The second objective is for us to rear and educate all children in such a way that those who are now in danger of falling victim to neglect and abuse will be protected, and in such a way that all children would be helped to grow to become the type of adults who are able and willing to take care of the coming generations of children with greater sensitivity and insight than is now the case.

I will primarily focus on three areas of parenting—educating for self-knowledge, educating our family (see the unity-based family in chapter six), and educating for peace—which I believe are the most important requisites for improving the condition of children everywhere. Educational needs of children are directly related to the cardinal responsibilities of the family, community, and society. This shared responsibility is due to the fact that in the final analysis all children are our children. Humanity is one, and nowhere is our fundamental oneness more convincingly felt than in the manner we as individuals and groups respond to children and the ease and trust with which children accept appropriate parenting from adults.

EDUCATING FOR SELF-KNOWLEDGE

ACHIEVING TRUE FREEDOM

For Baháʼí parents, education is an obligatory responsibility. For them education of children is, at once, a significant factor in deciding how many children to have; how, as mothers and fathers, to share childrearing responsibilities; and what priorities to adopt for children's healthy—physical, psychological, and spiritual—development. They are mindful of the teachings of their religion that a fundamental purpose of marriage is to bring children into this world and to educate them in a manner such that they grow-up to be healthy and well developed in every respect—well-educated individuals in arts and sciences who are willing and able to contribute to the advance of human civilization, to be agents of unity and promoters of the oneness of humanity, and to be morally responsible and spiritually enlightened.[11] Regarding education, ʻAbduʼl-Bahá explains:

> Education is of three kinds: material, human and spiritual. Material education is concerned with the progress and development of the body, through gaining its sustenance, its material comfort and ease. This education is common to animals and man.
>
> Human education signifies civilization and progress—that is to say, government, administration, charitable works, trades, arts and handicrafts, sciences, great inventions and discoveries and elaborate institutions, which are the activities essential to man as distinguished from the animal.
>
> Divine education is that of the Kingdom of God: it consists in acquiring divine perfections, and this is true education; for in this state man becomes the focus of divine blessings, the manifestation of the words, "Let Us make man in Our image, and after Our likeness." This is the goal of the world of humanity.[12]

Parents need to help their children develop an understanding of themselves as possessing enormous intellectual, emotional, and spiritual potentialities that can be conducive to their "glory, honour and greatness."[13] The secret here lies in the human capacity for self-knowledge, which is only possible in the context of proper and comprehensive education. Bahá'u'lláh states that "man should know his own self and recognize that which leadeth unto loftiness or lowliness, glory or abasement, wealth or poverty."[14]

Self-knowledge has at least three dimensions: physical, psychological, and spiritual. In our world today we are most knowledgeable about the physical dimension of ourselves. Modern science has made enormous strides in this regard, to the extent that now many scientists believe that we humans are fundamentally physical/biological beings and that the psychological and spiritual dimensions of our humanness originate in our physical reality. Materialistically oriented scientists consider human psychological faculties—thinking, feeling, and choosing—and spiritual capacities—search for meaning, moral and ethical proclivities, capacity to transcend, ability to love unconditionally, remarkable creative capacities, ever-increasing awareness of the mysteries of existence, and receptivity and experience of the Divine—to be products of the body.

From a spiritual perspective, the human individual is an integrated unity of "body and soul" and "material and spiritual," and self-knowledge requires an understanding of both aspects of being human—physical and spiritual—that operate in a state of unity and total integration in life. Education, therefore, needs to introduce children to the dynamics and qualities of the law of unity that is operative at all levels of existence and life. Unity is at once a scientific and spiritual state, and understanding unity is essential for life-knowledge, in general, and self-knowledge, in particular. The task of starting children on the path of self-knowledge—a process that has a beginning but no end—requires that the parents, the school, and the community together be mindful of its requirements. In this task, the insights gained from both science and religion are essential and must be offered to children in a manner such that as they grow-up and continue on the path of their maturation, they will grow to be physically healthy, psychologically mature, socially unifying, economically productive, and spiritually enlightened.

The process of self-knowledge has three cumulative components: self-discovery, self-development, and self-sacrifice. We begin with self-discovery, a process that is most pronounced during the first three or four decades of life as we learn more about ourselves, others, and life in its manifold dimensions. The process of self-discovery is soon augmented with the efforts we make at self-development, learning more, having new experiences, and realizing that the more we know, the less we know. We constantly discover new dimensions of ourselves. We meet someone, fall in love, and suddenly become aware of totally new dimensions of ourselves. We become parents and discover yet another reservoir of love, thoughts, feelings, and capacities that we did not know we possessed. We, or someone else we know, become seriously ill, and we discover our enormous ability to handle the most painful and harrowing circumstances. We embark on scientific research and in the process discover new insights that dramatically alter our understanding of ourselves and everything else.

As the processes of self-discovery and self-development progress, we begin to acquire a greater measure of awareness of others. We become more sensitive to the joys and sorrows of people, even those not known to us personally. We gradually discover that we are connected with everyone and that our "self" is not that separate from all other "selves." And as we continue on this journey of unity, we begin to be less self-centered and more concerned about others. And as we pray in the depth of our souls for the opportunity to be able to do a worthy deed in this short life, we suddenly encounter unexpected areas of service to humanity and begin to become forgetful of self and ever mindful of others. And it is at this stage that third component of self-knowledge—self-sacrifice—takes ascendancy in our thoughts, sentiments, and deeds. And we begin to see the "earth as one country and mankind its citizens."[15] In October 1911, while commenting on the progress of England, 'Abdu'l-Bahá counseled his audience:

> Forget self and work for the whole race. Remember always that one is working for the world, not for a town or even for a country; because, as all are brethren, so every country is, as it were, one's own.[16]

From this brief discourse it is clear that the three components of self-knowledge—self-discovery, self-development, and self-sacrifice—take place in the day-to-day arena of life and in the context of full participation in the affairs of this world. The following statement by Bahá'u'lláh addresses some of these issues, including the role and purpose of education, the place of wealth in human life, and the role and status of educators in the progress of society and their relationship with the process of maturation of the human individual:

> Having attained the stage of fulfillment and reached his maturity, man standeth in need of wealth, and such wealth as he acquireth

through crafts or professions is commendable and praiseworthy in the estimation of men of wisdom, and especially in the eyes of servants who dedicate themselves to the education of the world and to the edification of its peoples. They are, in truth, cup-bearers of the life-giving water of knowledge and guides unto the ideal way. They direct the peoples of the world to the straight path and acquaint them with that which is conducive to human upliftment and exaltation. The straight path is the one which guideth man to the dayspring of perception and to the dawning-place of true understanding and leadeth him to that which will redound to glory, honour and greatness.[17]

Such an approach to parenting and education calls for a fundamental rethinking of the current practices for the training and instruction of children at home, in the school, and within the community. At the core of this rethinking is the issue of spiritual education necessary for transcending selfishness, which is one of the fundamental challenges of the materialistic worldview. At the biological level we are, by necessity, selfish. Like all other living entities, humans are biologically programmed for self-preservation, pain-avoidance, and pleasure seeking. The powerful pull of these proclivities inclines human beings to be mainly concerned with their own safety and satisfaction. However, when this proclivity takes place in the context of exclusion or conditional inclusion of others, then human relationships suffer profoundly. Relationships are essential for a healthy and productive life, and in the context of selfishness they are weakened and often disrupted.

Education, with its focus on the biological, intellectual, emotional, social, moral, and spiritual aspects of human development, plays a fundamental role in helping us to be increasingly less selfish and more other-oriented and universal in our relationships. It is in this context that unalloyed love takes root and brings forth fruits of mercy, compassion, equality, justice, unity, and peace—all of which are necessary for attaining true freedom. Bahá'í prayers for children repeatedly focus the attention of both adults and children on the ultimate object of education—to create unity, to be a cause of peace, and to serve humanity:

O God! Protect these children, graciously assist them to be educated and enable them to render service to the world of humanity....[18]

O my Lord! O my Lord!...I am a child of tender years. Nourish me from the breast of Thy mercy, train me in the bosom of thy love, educate me in the school of Thy guidance and develop me under the shadow of Thy bounty...confer upon me the disposition and nature of the righteous; make me a cause of bounty to the human world....[19]

O Lord! Make this youth radiant....Bestow upon him knowledge, grant him added strength at the break of every morn and guard him within the shelter of Thy protection so that he may be freed from error, may devote himself to the service of Thy Cause, may guide the wayward, lead the hapless, free the captives and awaken the heedless....[20]

Not only in the text of prayers and spiritual supplication but also in the context of public pronouncements and treatises, the Bahá'í Faith emphasizes the importance of education and promotes a modern and enlightened approach to it. In 1875, 'Abdu'l-Bahá (1844–1921), while an exile from his land of birth (Persia) and a prisoner of the Ottoman Government, in 'Akká (now a part of Israel) wrote his unique treatise *The Secret of Divine Civilization.* The book is addressed to the rulers and the people of Persia, but it is relevant to many societies, even today some 135 years later. Among the issues that the book covers is education. Here is a brief excerpt:

The primary, the most urgent requirement is the promotion of education. It is inconceivable that any nation should achieve prosperity and success unless this paramount, this fundamental concern is carried forward. The principal reason for the decline and fall of peoples is ignorance. Today the mass of the people are uninformed even as to ordinary affairs, how much less do they grasp the core of the important problems and complex needs of the time.

It is therefore urgent that beneficial articles and books be written, clearly and definitely establishing what the present-day requirements of the people are, and what will conduce to the happiness and advancement of society. These should be published and spread throughout the nation, so that at least the leaders among the people should become, to some degree, awakened, and arise to exert themselves along those lines which will lead to their abiding honor. The publication of high thoughts is the dynamic power in the arteries of life; it is the very soul of the world. Thoughts are a boundless sea, and the effects and varying conditions of existence are as the separate forms and individual limits of the waves; not until the sea boils up will the waves rise and scatter their pearls of knowledge on the shore of life.[21]

In response to these and other such emphatic counsels, Bahá'ís place great emphasis on education, in general, and educating for peace, in particular. As stated before, the three pillars of education I have identified are *education for self-knowledge,* which was just described; *educating the family,* which was described in chapter six; and *educating for peace,* which is discussed more specifically later in this chapter.

ON TEACHING AND HEALING

Among the most consequential choices that we make in life is our choice of profession and occupation. Through this choice we determine the kind of education we pursue, the lifestyle we adopt, the level of involvement with others we desire, and the ultimate life-accomplishment to which we aspire. As children and youth, we usually make this choice either because of an influential role model or in response to powerful life experiences. Role models—parents, teachers, heroes, others—enkindle our imagination, strengthen our resolve, and, in some instances, provide us with definitive guidance on how to proceed. Likewise, life experiences—ranging from unusual calamities such as loss of a loved one, a serious illness, or an earthquake, to living an overprotected, indulged, and carefree life—influence our choice of vocation. In addition to life experiences and role models, there is a third major influence—our worldview—in most choices that we make. Our worldviews strongly influence our vocational/professional choices. And, as we have discussed on many occasions in this book, religion has the most profound impact on the nature and focus of our worldview and, therefore, our choices of occupation and profession.

Founders of the revealed religions are both Divine Physicians and Divine Educators. With their innate knowledge, they diagnose the ills of humanity and prescribe the necessary remedies, and, simultaneously, they provide those insights, clarifications, and teachings that help humanity to progress to its next level of development and maturation. Here are a few statements from the Bahá'í Writings referring to the role of Manifestations as Divine Physicians and Divine Educators:

> The Prophets of God should be regarded as physicians whose task is to foster the well-being of the world and its peoples, that, through the spirit of oneness, they may heal the sickness of a divided humanity.[22]

> The All-Knowing Physician hath His finger on the pulse of mankind. He perceiveth the disease, and prescribeth, in His unerring wisdom, the remedy. Every age hath its own problem, and every soul its particular aspiration. The remedy the world needeth in its present-day afflictions can never be the same as that which a subsequent age may

require. Be anxiously concerned with the needs of the age ye live in, and center your deliberations on its exigencies and requirements.[23]

The prophets of God are the first educators. They bestow universal education upon man and cause him to rise from lowest levels of savagery to the highest pinnacles of spiritual development. The philosophers too are educators along lines of intellectual training. At most they have only been able to educate themselves and a limited number about them, to improve their own morals and, so to speak, civilize themselves; but they have been incapable of universal education. They have failed to cause an advancement for any given nation from savagery to civilization.[24]

The quintessence of our subject was this: What is the mission of the Prophet, and what is the object of a divine law? In answer we stated: There is no doubt that the purpose of a divine law is the education of the human race, the training of humanity.... The essential requirement and qualification of Prophethood is the training and guidance of the people. Therefore, we shall first consider the efficacy of the teachings of those who have been followed and accepted as the Prophets of God. The question that must be answered is: Have They taught mankind? Have They proved Themselves efficient Educators?[25]

In retrospect, I realize that the two choices I have made—medicine and education—were definitely influenced by my familiarity with the high regard with which the Writings of the Bahá'í Faith value arts and sciences, in general, and medicine and education, in particular. My first choice—medicine with a psychiatric specialization with a focus on issues of the family, violence, and thanatology (helping individuals facing death)—prepared the path for my second profession as a peace educator. Although I never had formal training as a teacher, nevertheless, many years of teaching medical students and other health professionals provided me with the opportunity to learn about some of the basic principles of pedagogy.

My interest in education has been multidimensional. Aside from my own education, the first and foremost education priority for my wife and me has been our dedication to the wholesome and excellent education of our children, and now grandchildren. We made conscious, deliberate, and sustained effort to ensure that they received highest levels of formal education in their selected fields of study, while at the same time receiving a systematic training with regard to their moral and spiritual education and cultivation of love for and experience of the arts, in this case training in dance with their mother—a classical ballet performer, choreographer, and teacher. My more formal activities as an educator have included creating and implementing the Education for Peace Program (see later in this chapter), helping to establish the Bahá'í International Health Agency, being one of the original founders and promoters of the Association for Bahá'í Studies, and contributing to the efforts to establish Landegg International University. Here, I will briefly refer to the issues of self-education and parenting, as well as the efforts to establish the Association for Bahá'í Studies and Landegg International University.

ATTEMPTS AT SELF-EDUCATION

When, around age fourteen, I decided to become a Bahá'í, I immediately realized that in addition to my formal education in high school and later at university, I needed to plan for myself a systematic program of self-education about those matters that were not being taught in the schools. Foremost among the issues that I wanted to learn about were the teachings of the Bahá'í Faith and their relevance to the human condition. I also wanted to know how these teachings could be understood within the parameters of science and how spiritual and scientific principles could be applied in an integrated manner to all aspects of everyday life. Fortunately, in this regard all that was needed was motivation and perseverance, because the Bahá'í Community in Iran at that time offered excellent opportunities for anyone who was interested in this approach to self-education.

During high school, my main teachers/mentors were three remarkable individuals in the city of Yazd. First among them was Fadil Yazdi,[26] a prominent Islamic scholar and religious leader. After choosing to join the Bahá'í Community, he was immediately ostracized by the Muslim majority; attempts were made on his life, forcing him to leave his hometown; and he lost his position as a religious leader along with all his material possessions and his regular income. He then became a teacher within the Bahá'í Community. Among his many teaching activities, he would annually accept a few students who were prepared to withstand his traditional and somewhat authoritarian pedagogical approach and in turn receive a wealth of information, knowledge, understanding and insight about spiritual principles and their application to various aspects of life. I decided to become his student, and for two years I went for a systematic study of the teachings of Bahá'í Faith in a class that was held six days a week 12:30–1:30 pm during the two-hour lunch recess from school. I was the only student, and Mr. Yazdi was elderly, lived alone, and needed help for the preparation of his meals. I was in charge of his simple lunch (nan, yogurt, and cucumber when it was in season), which I would purchase from the market. Then, for approximately an hour while conducting the lesson, he would slowly eat his meager lunch. This schedule was practically unchanged over the two years, and in the course of these lessons, slowly and methodically I was introduced to some of the main teachings of the Bahá'í Faith, including the concepts of oneness of God, unity of religion, and oneness of humanity. I also learned about the wisdom and purpose of prayer and other spiritual disciplines such as truth-seeking, moral conduct, and self-discipline. These classes ended when I left for Shiraz to attend medical school.

Parallel to these daily classes, I attended two other classes held once a week, one directed by Azizu'llah Dhabihiyan and the other by Fraydun Fraidani, both outstanding high-school teachers who volunteered their time and expertise for the education of the youth in the community. The contents and focus of these classes were similar to the one offered by Mr. Yazdi. These two distinguished teachers continued their educational services for many decades until, after the Islamic Revolution in Iran, they were arrested, imprisoned, tortured, and put to death for the "crime" of educating Bahá'í youth. (See the section "A Perilous Revolution" in chapter four.)

During the first six years of medical school, I continued this systematic process of self-education, and for five of these six years, I and a few other individuals attended daily classes with one of the most outstanding Bahá'í scholars of our era—Abdul-Hamid Ishraq-Khavari—who with his depth and breadth of knowledge and wisdom guided us on the path of continuing search for new understandings and insights at all times and in all conditions.[27] It was during these years that I began to see the complete interdependence of science and religion. As I progressed in my medical studies and gained more experience, I became aware of the essential role of spirituality in establishing higher levels of trust and collaboration between the patients and physicians, giving patients hope, strengthening their defense mechanisms, and helping them and their families to deal with life's adversities in a more realistic and positive manner. There were other benefits, which were more intangible and which are now being gradually better understood by health professionals. These experiences paved the way for my choice of psychiatry and my later work on spiritual aspects of human psychological health and illness that I have recounted in the *Psychology of Spirituality* and a few academic papers.

My primary objective in writing this brief statement on self-education is to pay homage to the memory of these outstanding teachers to whom I owe so much and also to many others from whom I have learned in the course of my life. As a wise person observed, "A good teacher is like a candle: it consumes itself to light the way for others."[28] My teachers were indeed most bright candles to the very end.

THE ASSOCIATION FOR BAHÁ'Í STUDIES
FROM INFORMAL EDUCATION TO FORMAL SCHOLARSHIP

In 1974, the National Spiritual Assembly of the Bahá'ís of Canada established the Canadian Association for Studies on the Bahá'í Faith (CASBF), which after a few years was expanded, operating ever since as the Association for Bahá'í Studies-North America. Since its inception in Canada, more than twenty similar associations have sprung up around the globe, some of them very active and vibrant, others less so, with some in a state of dormancy. The primary purpose of the Association is to create a forum for academics, scholars, and other interested individuals with three specific objectives: (1) to engage in systematic study and research on the Bahá'í Faith, (2) to study the relevance of these teachings to the manifold challenges and opportunities faced by humanity in this era, and (3) to study the dynamics of the rise and development of a new revealed religion at this time in history. These objectives derive from the "Bahá'í principle that regards the unfettered investigation of truth as not only an individual right but also a duty. An attempt to relate the message of Bahá'u'lláh to the fruits of a scrupulously scientific approach to phenomena in any given field of research lies at the core of Bahá'í intellectual life."[29]

I was involved in the creation and early development of this enterprise and for 18 years (1974–1992) served the Association at different times as its general-secretary, chairperson, and a member of both its Executive Committee and the Editorial Board of the *Journal of Bahá'í Studies*. My objective here is not to enumerate my experiences with the Association for Bahá'í Studies, a truly rich experience that merits its own independent chronicle. But rather, the purpose here is to share some personal reflections on the topic of *Bahá'í scholarship,* with its primary objective of integrating scientific and spiritual principles into a wholesome and unified approach to both science and religion.

REFLECTIONS ON BAHÁ'Í SCHOLARSHIP

The first annual conference of the Association for Bahá'í Studies of Japan was held in Tokyo in 1992. At that conference I was invited to share some thoughts on the issue of Bahá'í scholarship. The unedited text of this talk was published in the proceedings of the conference and was later reprinted in the *Bahá'í Scholarship: A Compilation and Essays* published by the Association for Bahá'í Studies of Australia. The following remarks on Bahá'í scholarship are based on this talk, and they reflect yet another aspect of my interest in education-related issues.

Bahá'u'lláh counsels us to independently investigate the truth, to avoid imitation, to see with our own eyes and not through the eyes of others, and to know of our own knowledge and not through the knowledge of our neighbor.[30] We are advised to free ourselves from all prejudices, to apply the scientific method to the study and application of spiritual matters, to study arts and sciences and consider such activities as acts of worship, to have high regard for the learned in our midst, and to endeavor to bring harmony to science and religion. There are many similar admonitions in the teachings of the Bahá'í Faith, and all of them point to a central issue—humanity is coming of age. And as an aspect of this maturation process, we need to revisit our preconceptions about science and religion and how they relate.

As another aspect of humanity's coming of age, Bahá'u'lláh abolishes the institution of priesthood and declares that in this dispensation no individual has spiritual control or authority over another. From the spiritual perspective, we all have the responsibility and the necessary capacities—within the unique circumstances of each individual— to nurture and develop our latent spiritual faculties and patterns of behavior. To do so effectively, our individual initiatives need to be augmented, encouraged, and enriched through our upbringing when we are children and by sharing our experiences and learning from each other as adults. Associations for Bahá'í Studies are ideal forums for helping individuals and communities of people on their path of independent investigation of spiritual principles and their application to all aspects of life.

Abolishment of the institution of priesthood and transfer of some of its more important functions—to study the sacred texts, reflect on their meanings, shape one's life accordingly, and assist others to do likewise—

to the rank-and-file members of the community created a unique and remarkably modern religious community. Gone, is the strong grip of a small number of individuals with spiritual authority over the large body of believers. Gone, is the horrific emotional and moral manipulation of the masses by a few with the claim of almost absolute moral authority. Gone, is the practice of forgiving the sins of human beings by other human beings. Gone, is the call for jihad and holy war in the name of God and religion. Gone, is the threat of hell and damnation for those who do not submit. Gone, is the claim by a few that they are the ones who understand the teachings of religion and that they are the channels between people and the Founders of their religion and, therefore, God. In the Bahá'í Faith, as we will see later (chapter ten), authority is invested in the democratically elected institutions of the Bahá'í Faith, and power to act is vested in individuals in their continuing journey of progress, maturation, change, and transformation.

Abolishment of the institution of priesthood also brings about a new understanding of the concept of scholarship with respect to the nature of religion. In *Some Answered Questions* 'Abdu'l-Bahá states that "religion is the essential connection which proceeds from the realities of things," and that the "Manifestations of God are aware of the reality of the mysteries of beings. Therefore, They establish laws which are suitable and adapted to the state of the world of man."[31] He, further states that the "essential foundations of the divine religions are unity and love."[32] From these and many similar statements in the Writings of the Bahá'í Faith, we begin to realize that at the core of understanding religion lies the need to understand those essential relationships that exist between us and God, other human beings, all living entities, and the universe as we can access it. And at the core of these relationships is the ever-present law of unity in its manifold expressions in all levels of existence. The challenge of scholarship, using the scientific method, searching for the essential relationships in all departments of life, and learning how to integrate spiritual and scientific insights into a wholesome approach to life, is the challenge of Bahá'í scholarship.

Both science and religion focus on the relationships that proceed from the realities of things, but from two different perspectives—material and spiritual. For example, concerning human beings, there are sciences that deal with the dynamics and nature of relationships between the heart, the lungs, the brain, and all other organs of the body. Various scientific disciplines such as physiology, anatomy, biochemistry, and genetics all study those laws that govern the specific functions of these organs and entities, separately and in the context of their interrelationship. However, we can also study other aspects of the human being—the manner in which we conduct research, formulate our thoughts, communicate, make decisions, choose specific lines of action, express love, search for new insights, and create music and other arts. These are all spiritual conditions of human reality that are expressed through the instrumentality of the human body. It is though this process that our capacities of knowledge (cognitive), love (emotive), and will (choice-making) are expressed in the arena of life and relationships. Such disciplines as psychology, sociology, and ethics are most suited for the scientific study of these aspects of human reality. One important feature of Bahá'í scholarship, I believe, is with regard to its ability to avoid dichotomous thinking—religion versus science, spirituality versus materialism—that currently shapes the attitude of many towards religion and science. Dichotomous thinking results in rejection of science by some, rejection of religion by others, and an unsatisfactory parallelism—science and religion are both valid but incompatible—by still others. Bahá'í scholarship aims at creating an integrated and unified approach to study of both scientific and spiritual aspects of life.

In the past two centuries, science has made truly remarkable progress, while established religions have not similarly evolved. They have not created the necessary unity and harmony amongst themselves and have remained at odds with each other. The strength of scientific approach is that once a certain new level of understanding is achieved through research and observation, other scientists welcome the new insights and try to build on them. Not so with religious leaders. In fact, they do the opposite. They reject the concept of renewal of religion without engaging in serious inquiry and without offering reasoned arguments for their rejection. A unique aspect of Bahá'í scholarship is that it unequivocally requires application of the scientific method and reasoned arguments for study of both material and spiritual phenomena. In doing so, the two main objectives of Bahá'í scholarship—*to spiritualize science* and *to bring rationality to religion*—assume prominence.

Bahá'í scholarship can be approached from two avenues of observation and research: conceptual and applied. The worldwide Bahá'í community has been engaged in the applied approach for more than 150 years. During this period the Bahá'ís have done a number of things, the results of which now merit study in a systematic manner. For example, for more than 150 years Bahá'ís have been engaged in building a highly diverse yet profoundly united worldwide community. We have to conduct research on the nature and dynamics of this community. How does it work? How has it created its unique qualities and characteristics? What are the distinguishing characteristics of this community? What are the main reasons for its success thus far, and what are the areas that need more attention and care? Is the *sense of community* present equally both at the micro- and macro-levels, in cities and villages, in the East and the West, in the North and South, in the worldwide Bahá'í community? What lessons can we learn from the operation of this community? What are the main reasons for the high level of unity of this greatly diverse community of people?

This community is not a normal gathering of people in our world today. These people are from different countries, strata of society, language groups, education levels, races, and religious and atheistic backgrounds. They come from China and North America, from Japan and Korea, from India and Pakistan, from Iran and Israel, from Africa and Europe, from the northernmost settlements of humanity to the densest jungles of the equator, and from the ancient aboriginal populations of the world and the current dominant races of humanity. However, in the context of this enormous diversity, somehow we love each other, take delight in our relationships, and are totally connected with one another. We act as though we have known each other forever, even if most of us have never before met. This conference is a good example. This is the first time that many of us are together. Many of us even do not know each other's names. I am leaving here after a few days for Hong Kong to meet another group of Bahá'ís and their friends, most of whom I have never met, and yet it will be as though we have always known each other. From there I go to Mainland China. I will meet individuals who have become Bahá'ís only within the past several months, and I can relate to them and communicate with them as though we have known each other for many years. And we do not even speak each other's languages. Now, as Bahá'ís we know that the main force that creates such a profound unity and prevents schisms that have so grievously afflicted all other religions is the institution of the Bahá'í Covenant. For us this is a central spiritual principle and an article of faith. However, this is not sufficient. We need to systematically study, as an aspect of Bahá'í scholarship, the role of the Covenant in creating the worldwide unified and diverse Bahá'í Community and to share our findings with everyone, in the hope that they may be of benefit to others. (See chapters eight and ten.)

Another example of applied scholarship is with respect to the issue of pioneering. Since the early decades of the Bahá'í Faith, Bahá'í pioneers have left their home countries and many settled in dramatically different societies. These individuals are not missionaries, as we find in Christianity. Bahá'í pioneers do not have any religious rank or authority or vocation. They are ordinary individuals who settle in other communities, seek employment, and live their lives in their adopted homelands. And through the example of their lives and the opportunities for communication and friendship with the inhabitants of their new community, they share with them the Bahá'í teachings and history as appropriate. Our experience thus far has been that a good number of people subsequently become interested in the Bahá'í Faith, recognize the relevance of its teachings to their individual and community lives, and a significant number of them become Bahá'ís. We need to study this phenomenon in a systematic manner. What are the ramifications of this movement of people going to other countries to establish diverse and united faith-based communities founded on the principle of the consciousness of the oneness of humanity? Bahá'ís have done something very courageous. They have proclaimed themselves as the citizens of the whole world. They have proclaimed that the world belongs to them and that they belong to the world, that we are all brothers and sisters and members of one community of humanity. Bahá'ís see the earth "as but one country and mankind as its citizens."[33] Now this massive movement of many thousands of people over the course of a century needs to be systematically studied.

Yet another area of applied scholarship is with regard to the nature of Bahá'í Administration. The first unofficial Bahá'í consultative body was formed in Teheran, Iran, about 1878. Some two decades later the first elected Bahá'í Spiritual Assembly was formed in 1899 in the same city. In the same year the first elected Bahá'í consultative body was formed in Chicago and one year later in New York.[34] Since then, thousands of Spiritual Assemblies have been elected in Bahá'í communities around the globe in villages, towns, and cities; upon mountains, in the desert, and in jungles; among tribal peoples and among peoples who for centuries have lived under the rule of authoritarian leaders and rigid traditions. (See chapter ten.) This is a remarkable process of true democracy in action. As soon as the Spiritual Assembly is formed, a thousand, two thousand, five thousand years of traditional authoritarian domination breaks down, and the seeds of a new approach to the administration of human affairs are sown. These Assemblies are composed of both men and women, in communities where women have forever been subjugated to men. And these elected individuals are encouraged to consult with one another to reach decisions as equals in the context of moderation, mutuality, and unity. These are remarkable developments and merit systematic, thorough research. In a world that is desperately and not very effectively trying to introduce certain ideas and practices of democracy to various populations, the Bahá'í model and its experience of democracy stands out as a truly remarkable accomplishment, which I believe is not fully appreciated even by Bahá'ís themselves, let alone by others. I am of the opinion that the main reason for this situation is the absence of systematic research and scholarly study of this and other facets of the Bahá'í Community in action.

And then, there is the other dimension of Bahá'í scholarship—theoretical and conceptual as well as research in the history and sacred writings of the Bahá'í Faith. This aspect of scholarship has received somewhat more attention, because it is quite familiar to those who work in the field of religious studies as is approached in many universities. The task of collection, collation, annotation, translation, and publication of the voluminous sacred writings of the central figures of the Bahá'í Faith is monumental and offers an extremely rich area of study and research. The same is true about study of the history of the Bahá'í Faith and the nature and dynamics of the appearance and evolution of a new revealed religion in the modern world. This is a truly unique development and merits unbiased, objective, and thorough research employing appropriate modalities for study of such an extraordinary development.

Another area of research that is both theoretical and applied is with respect to the central objective of the Bahá'í Faith—creating an ever-advancing civilization of peace. Humanity has always yearned for peace. Although the history of humanity is filled with accounts of conflict, violence, and war, people everywhere have always been in search of peace. But this ever-present quest has not been fulfilled. To this day, humanity has not been able to find a way to accomplish this cherished goal. Now, the question is why. Why, in the course of its long history and despite of its ever-strong quest for peace, has humanity not been able to establish a lasting, all-inclusive, free, and just peace? Why? As we study the Bahá'í Writings, we discover that peace is viewed as a social and political as well a psychological, moral, and spiritual state. We need to study the phenomenon of peace in its totality. However, to do so, we need to develop a theoretical framework that explains what peace is and why peace has not been accomplished in the past. We need to identify the main characteristics of a truly universal, progressive, and just peace; determine what is the relationship between inner peace, interpersonal peace, intergroup peace, and global peace; recognize what the prerequisites of peace are and how they could be accomplished through peaceful means. Peace cannot be pursued. Rather, peace is the outcome of the state of unity, which is itself dependent on the presence of justice and equality in the context of diversity. As we study these *essential relationships that originate from the realities of human existence and life,* we will gradually find convincing and effective answers to the mystery of peace. (See chapter seven.)

Another subject closely related to the issue of peace that requires new understanding is with regard to the issue of power and its related conditions of force and control. Probably one of the most consequential changes that will occur as a result of the introduction of the Bahá'í spiritual and social teachings into the affairs of humanity is a dramatic alteration in the way we understand and use power. Historically, the world of humanity has been administered through use of force. When a society is administered through force, certain behaviors and modes of relationship develop. First, the more powerful individuals seek ever more power, primarily because power increases feelings of insecurity in those who possess it and induces them to seek even more power. Thus a vicious cycle is created, and the accumulation of power by the powerful reaches dangerous levels, eventually becoming both other-destructive and self-destructive.

Second, power divides people. Power-oriented persons see the world through a dichotomous lens—them and us, friends and enemies, men and women, science and religion, our religion and other religions, good people and bad people, foreigners and citizens, and, of course, the powerful and the weak. The list goes on. Power-oriented persons separate each thing from everything else. The whole world is seen as an arena of conflict, of intense competition, of power-struggle, and of winning and losing. The world is perceived as a jungle, where the survival of the fittest is the norm and everyone must fight for his or her rights. Power-oriented individuals are authoritarian and dictatorial. They have closed minds, closed hearts, and closed homes. They are afraid of new ideas; they shun all feelings except anger; and they are suspicious of everyone. They are not hospitable. Power-oriented individuals, institutions, communities, and societies demand conformity and blind obedience, and rely on rejection, disenfranchisement, and punishment as the main tools for order in human affairs. Power-orientation has been the main mode of administration of human affairs throughout history and remains the predominant mode.

The Baháʾí Faith categorically rejects the authoritarian approach to power through the instrumentality of force. Such an approach is characteristic of the earlier stages of human development. We are living at a monumental time in history when humanity comes of age and, as a result, all previous approaches to the use of power must be transformed. The predominant past and present approaches to the use of power in human relationships—authoritarian and adversarial modes of use of force—are ineffective and inappropriate in an intellectually, emotionally, and spiritually more mature society. In the 20th and, thus far, in the 21st century we have observed how the use of force has, in ʿAbduʾl-Baháʾs words caused "turmoil" and "the ruin of the social order." He explains this process in the context of the dynamics of human maturation both in personal and social realms:

> Man reacheth perfection through good deeds, voluntarily performed, not through good deeds the doing of which was forced upon him. And sharing is a personally chosen righteous act: that is, the rich should extend assistance to the poor, they should expend their substance for the poor, but of their own free will, and not because the poor have gained this end by force. For the harvest of force is turmoil and the ruin of the social order. On the other hand voluntary sharing, the freely-chosen expending of one's substance, leadeth to society's comfort and peace. It lighteth up the world; it bestoweth honour upon humankind....[35]

Elsewhere, ʿAbduʾl-Bahá commenting on the "peace" agreement following the First World War explains that "peace" created by force is not permanent:

> At present it is certain that temporary peace is established but it is not lasting. All governments and nations have become tired of war, of the difficulties of travel, of huge expenditures, of the loss of life, of the affliction of women, of the great number of orphans, and they are driven by force to peace. But this peace is not permanent, it is temporary....[36]

As we delve deeper into the writings of the Baháʾí Faith, it becomes evident that the necessity for change of our attitude and approach to the issues of power and force is addressed at its most essential and profound level of expression—our relationship with God—and, therefore, all our relationships. Baháʾuʾlláh has proclaimed that the era of powerlessness has come. In the Short Obligatory Prayer every day Baháʾís say: "I bear witness, O My God, that Thou has created me to know Thee and to worship Thee. I testify, at this moment, to my powerlessness and Thy might...."[37] This is a truly astonishing statement. At a time when all humanity is preoccupied with power and every group is trying to make itself more powerful in relation to others, Bahá'u'lláh, the Mouthpiece of God for our age, calls upon us to remind ourselves, every day of our lives, that we are indeed powerless. Individuals interested in the scholarly study of the Bahá'í Faith need to reflect on the issue of powerlessness. What does it mean to be powerless in a world so deeply preoccupied with power in all its expressions—physical, psychological, social, political, economic, military, and religious? What are the signs of mature powerlessness in human conduct, in social interactions, in leadership and governance? Can human societies be ruled in any other way than through power?

We human beings, individually and collectively, start our lives from the position of powerlessness. Children are powerless. New nations are usually weak and powerless. Humanity in its early phase of evolution on this planet was powerless. We knew very little. We had very limited capacities to deal with challenges, threats, and afflictions of life. Powerlessness is the characteristic of the earlier stages of development. It is a *primary powerlessness* with which we are born. However, as we develop and go through the stages of childhood and adolescence, we gradually acquire more power—physical, mental, emotional, and in terms of will and determination—and feel increasingly more powerful. Humanity, now in its final stages of its collective adolescence, feels more powerful than it ever has felt. But the adolescent mindset combines power with bravado, arrogance, competition, otherness, separation, and miscalculation; and the outcome is a dangerous mix. And this is the condition of the world today.

As humanity inevitably moves—willingly, more probably, defiantly—to the next phase of its development, we will realize that we can no longer relate to one another from the position of power and force. One of the main characteristics of maturation and adulthood is that our attitude towards power alters. We begin to realize that at the core of our existence we are powerless in the face of illness, calamities, aging, and death. We also begin to realize that our true power lies not in force but in love. Generally speaking, in childhood we are the recipients of love, and we show our love by accepting the love that is offered to us by others. Thus, love is received from the powerful. Adolescent love is predominantly self-centered and is shown in a variety of ways on the continuum by selfish self-absorption on the one end and self-centered self-denial on the other. In adolescence, love and power are inseparable and are expressed in the context of power-struggle and excessive competition. With maturation comes the ability to fall in love in its more developed states, meaning that we replace power with love. Thus, in the context of mature love we feel "powerless" and proceed through life by the *force of love* rather than *force born of power*. This is the condition of *enlightened powerlessness* as compared to our earlier state of *primary (primitive) powerlessness*. In authoritarian and adversarial worldviews, power is considered essential for one's survival, security, and happiness. However, in the more mature states of development it is love that ensures the survival, safety, and happiness not merely for a few but for all because the noblest fruit of love is unity. And unity is the most potent source of mature and constructive power. We need to study the nature and dynamics of transition from power-orientation to unity-orientation, which I think is one of the most important aspects of the coming of age of humanity and the hallmark of the civilization of peace that is to come.

Bahá'u'lláh admonishes us to be "anxiously concerned with the needs of the age ye live in, and center your deliberations on its exigencies and requirements."[38] This age is a remarkable age, and we need to reflect on the urgent items that are on the agenda of humanity and the main needs of a sorely vexed and confused world. What are the characteristics of this moment in history? The fundamental characteristic of our times, as I understand, is that we are at the dawn of the rise of a new consciousness—that humanity is one, that human nature is capable of transformation, and that true freedom lies in acquisition of spiritual virtues and practices. In our lifetime we have seen the rise and fall of communism, the paroxysms of capitalism, and the vicious futility of conflict-based ideologies. We are beginning to observe that even the well-established societies, both new and old, are being weakened from within. The hidden, but ever present, termite of materialism is eating away at the very foundation of many societies, particularly in the North among economically more prosperous and technologically more modern countries. At the same time, the economically less prosperous and technologically less modern counties are burdened with the chronic afflictions of poverty, illness, prejudice, fundamentalism, and poor or absent education, conditions that are damning many populations of the world to a truly devastating life, mainly, but not exclusively in the South. We see these developments at both macro and micro levels. In my own psychiatric practice I have seen that marriages are breaking-up, families crumbling, and human relationships being strained at accelerating rates. There are homeless and destitute people in our midst whom we ignore. There are increasing levels of violence everywhere, and no solution seems to be at hand. The moral standards of society are crumbling; leaders are no longer able to lead; environmental degradation is reaching the point of no return; and a host of new and old diseases are playing havoc with the lives of millions at a time when medical sciences have reached their highest ever level of understanding and capacity. These and many other similar crises were all systematically outlined and brilliantly analyzed by Shoghi Effendi in his many books, letters, and messages to the Bahá'í world. It behooves us to systematically study such masterpieces as *The World Order of Bahá'u'lláh, The Advent of Divine Justice, The Promised Day is Come, God Passes By,* and other of his writings and to formulate a cohesive body of literature outlining the relevance of the teachings of the Bahá'í Faith to the conditions of humanity.

I wish to end this lengthy and sundry reflection on Bahá'í scholarship with this statement of the Universal House of Justice:

> Just as there is a fundamental difference between divine Revelation itself and the understanding that believers have of it, so also there is a basic distinction between scientific fact and reasoning on the one hand and the conclusions or theories of scientists on the other. There is, and can be, no conflict between true religion and true science: true religion is revealed by God, while it is through true science that the mind of man "discovers the realities of things and becomes cognizant of their peculiarities and effects, and of the qualities and properties of beings" and "comprehendeth the abstract by the aid of the concrete". However, whenever a statement is made through the lens of human understanding it is thereby limited, for human understanding is limited; and where there is limitation there is the possibility of error; and where there is error, conflicts can arise. For example, at the present time many people are convinced that it is unscientific to believe in God, but, as human enlightenment progresses, the scientists and philosophers of the future will not be, in the words of 'Abdu'l-Bahá, "deniers of the Prophets, ignorant of spiritual susceptibilities, deprived of the heavenly bounties and without belief in the supernatural".[39]

Almost 20 years after the establishment of the Association for Bahá'í Studies, in 1993 I had an opportunity to expand my interest in education by moving to Switzerland and assisting in the development of Landegg Academy—a Bahá'í-inspired institution of higher learning—which was at that time in a dire financial situation, but which also had the potential of becoming a university with certain unique features. The history of Landegg merits a separate account. However, in order to complete this chapter on education, here I include an edited version of the inaugural address presented on 30 September 1997 on the occasion of the inauguration of the Faculty of Graduate Studies of Landegg Academy. This talk, along with a brief additional explanation, provides a glimpse of the efforts that were made by a few of us to establish a Bahá'í-inspired university.

THE UNIVERSITY OF THE FUTURE

FOSTERING AN INTEGRATIVE PARADIGM OF KNOWLEDGE

It is with great pleasure and honor that I welcome you to Landegg Academy on the occasion of the formal inauguration of its Faculty of Graduate Studies, which takes place concomitant with the second international symposium, "Converging Realities: On Integrating the Scientific and the Spiritual." In 1996 when we began our deliberations on the establishment of this university, we were acutely aware of the fact that around the world many truly outstanding universities, which have stood the test of time and have contributed to the development of human knowledge and the progress of human civilization in an exemplary manner, already exist. At the same time, it is an accepted view in the academic world today that universities are now facing some fundamental crises, not only in respect to their financial needs and challenges but also with regard to their curricula and their main objectives and mandates. Therefore, we began our consultation on establishing our graduate and, subsequently, undergraduate faculties with several questions in mind.

What is the main purpose of universities? Are universities created solely for the development of knowledge and expertise in arts, humanities, and sciences? Do universities have primarily the responsibility to train capable administrators, experts, and technicians for the ever-changing world of commerce, business, and government? Should universities address the moral and ethical crises of the contemporary world, or should they maintain their cherished neutrality in this regard? And if they choose to remain neutral, is this an achievable objective or a self-deluding rationalization? Are current scientific and rational approaches sufficient for a full understanding of all aspects of the universe that surrounds us and the universe that lies within each and every one of us? And if these approaches are not sufficient, should universities develop new paradigms of learning? Or should they avoid these aspects of human existential experience and attempt to explain them all within the limiting confines of the existing models and perspectives on knowledge, science, and the scientific method?

Universities and Human Nature

We posed these and other similar questions because we perceived major crises on the horizon in respect to both the role of universities today and the nature of their enterprise in the future. The concept of a university is based on the fundamentals of human nature and the processes of evolution and progress of human civilization. The capacities to know, to understand, and to discover in a conscious and self-questioning manner are uniquely human in nature, and the abilities to learn and to be nurtured as enlightened, civilized, and transcendent beings are the hallmarks of being human. It is, therefore, not surprising that in all cultures and societies, and from the very dawn of consciousness on this planet, human beings have always been engaged in learning. Through the capacity for knowing we have observed life and existence in their rich expressions. Through the use of our power of understanding we have discovered some of those essential relationships that emerge from the realities of all things. We have been able to increasingly add to our storehouse of experience and knowledge the necessary insights for both meeting our essential needs and enhancing our true development.

Certain basic needs reflect the main aspects of a complex human nature. Cardinal among these needs are those that deal with the issues of survival, association, and transcendence. Of these needs, survival is the most immediate; association, the most compelling; and transcendence, the most essential. Therefore, it is of no surprise that much of human knowledge is focused primarily on the issue of survival and that modern science gives primacy to this issue in its explanations of various human activities and behavior. Also, it is understandable that much of the biological, psychological, and social preoccupation of human beings is limited to concerns for their individual or specific group survival. The fact that this focus has now reached unhealthy proportions, as expressed in the extreme self-centered individualism of the West and the collective coercion of many other societies around the world, merits serious attention on the part of all thoughtful and concerned individuals and societies. It is in this respect that the current orientation of universities needs to be addressed. In fact, many universities, in their mode of operation and in the content of their curriculum, are the proponents of specific worldviews. Some universities promote the doctrines of unlimited individualism; others teach the philosophies of collectivism; while at the same time both groups uphold their traditional claim of neutrality.

The issue of survival, however, is only one of the three cardinal human needs. The other two are the need for association, with its focus on challenges of equality, justice and freedom, and the need for transcendence, that unique dimension of humanness—spirituality. Universities address the second of these three concerns in a rather limited and, in my opinion, inadequate manner. In essence, the major contemporary schools of thought that provide the framework for the curriculum of various universities view most, if not all, human relationship needs within the context of survival needs—instinctual in nature and self-focused in scope—and association needs with their focus on competition in the arena of the survival of the fittest. They do not investigate the main source of all human associations—love. They do not study the dynamics of human love in all its grandeur, depth, and creativity, nor do they consider the powerful and creative force of unity as a worthy subject of scientific inquiry and experimentation. Even in their emphasis on such lofty issues as equality, justice, and freedom, they emphasize those divisions and conflicts that make their realization difficult. They do not usually address the role of unity, cooperation, and universality that are essential for creating truly equal, just, and free conditions.

Finally, the human need for spirituality and transcendence receives little, if any, attention from universities. This need, which is the distinctive aspect of human nature, is too far removed from the domain of materialistic science to be a serious and accessible subject of study and true understanding of its manifold qualities and rich processes. (For more details on human needs and rights, see chapter four.)

UNIVERSITIES AND RELIGION

Most modern universities, particularly in the West, were initially created by different religions. Their main objective was to train religious leaders and to find ways and means in which religious teachings could best be disseminated among the faithful. Authoritarian leaders who held the reins of government in their mighty grasps and who welcomed an educational system that trained obedient and fearful subjects also usually supported these universities. Gradually, other areas of study were introduced into the curriculum of universities. Medicine, history, law, mathematics, literature, and philosophy were among topics studied, all within the over-all framework of religious teachings and beliefs and dominant cultural norms and practices.

In the 18th century, the Enlightenment began the process of a new phase in the Western approach to knowledge. The emphasis on reason and freedom of inquiry and thought gradually eroded the role of religion in modern universities. A frenzied enthusiasm for freedom from the confines of religious orthodoxy and political oppression was evident among philosophes and scientists. In a relatively short period of time, a materialistic perspective of reality, along with a similarly oriented scientific methodology, dominated all facets of the curricula of many universities. The consequences of these developments were indeed very dramatic. Religion, one of the two main sources of human knowledge that had throughout earlier stages of the development of human societies controlled the opportunities for education and learning, was now placed in a secondary and defensive position. In fact, the modern era witnessed a dramatic advance in science, concomitant with a profound retreat on the part of religion. For all practical purposes, study of the phenomenon of human spirituality and its universal principles was eventually banished from universities.

As modern universities became the strongholds of materialistic science, considerable antagonism was aimed at all issues that were directly or indirectly related to religion. However, because human beings are fundamentally spiritual in nature and require a moral and ethical frame of reference for their varied and complex life activities, several new materialistic frames of reference were adopted by modern scientists and scholars, and were included in the curricula of universities. Since the mid-nineteenth century, three of these schools, based on theories put forward by Darwin, Marx, and later Freud, have had a powerful impact on all aspects of the life of humanity and have provided a set of new ethical codes based on their respective views of evolution, society, and human nature. The central theme of these theories is that the main goal of life is survival and that survival takes place in the context of an ongoing state of competition—in nature between various living creatures, in society between various individuals and interest groups, and within the individual between the forces of pleasure and life, on the one hand, and aggression and death on the other. As such, therefore, according to these theories, all human standards of behavior and ethical considerations are self-centered and aimed at survival and pleasure. Even when group interest is taken into consideration, the over-riding ethical standard is that of survival. It is understandable, therefore, that a spirit of fierce competition pervades the academic world and that most universities are the arena of individualism and self-assertion.

Universities are caldrons of new ideas, and ideas have enormous power. They shape our perspectives about ourselves, each other, and life. As such, universities have enormous immediate and long-range influence on society and are among the most crucial institutions of any civilization. The impact of universities on human societies in this century has been considerable and will continue to increase as these societies become more knowledge-based and more interdependent. Therefore, we need to evaluate the underlying causes of the existing crises in academia and to consider some of the main reasons why the promises of the Enlightenment in the West have been so clearly unfulfilled.

In the latter decades of the eighteenth century, as Peter Gay notes, the Enlightenment was at the height of its influence and the "American Experiment" included all its major themes: "The dialectic movement away from Christianity to modernity; the pessimistic though wholly secular appraisal of human nature coupled with an optimistic confidence in institutional arrangements; the pragmatic reading of history as an aid to political sociology; the humane philosophy underlying their plea for the proposed constitution...."[40] The "American Experiment" with its "declared openness to experiment undeterred by its respect for the past, its disdain for authority, and its reliance on autonomous reason, good sense, and experience, all for the sake of freedom and happiness" was the singular hope of the Enlightenment.[41]

But the "Experiment" did not go at all well. "Even America, the hope of civilized men everywhere in the eighteenth century," Gay observes, "has given to the most benevolent well-wishers grounds for grave anxiety....The world has not turned out the way the philosophes wished and half expected that it would. Old fanaticisms have been more intractable, irrational forces more inventive....Problems of race, of class, of nationalism, of boredom and despair in the midst of plenty have emerged....We have known horrors, may know horrors that the men of Enlightenment did not see in their nightmares....It remains as true today as it was in the eighteenth century: the world needs more light than it has...."[42] Indeed, the world needs more light, a new kind of enlightenment, that would not blame all the present problems on "human irrationality, self-centeredness, stupidity."[43]

In reviewing the panorama of new perspectives on human nature and society that humanity was exposed to in the nineteenth century, we come across Bahá'í thought with its remarkably new and unexplored perspectives that shed illumination on these puzzling issues. These perspectives consider both scientific and spiritual principles in their explanation of reality, human life, and the purpose of human existence. They are inclusive in nature and reject the ubiquitous dichotomous mindset that is present in all areas of contemporary human life and thought. They also provide practical suggestions for the implementation of their far-reaching concepts. Here, I will refer only to one of these concepts: the concept of the collective growth of humanity.

This concept holds that humanity is, in reality, one whole living social organism subject to the laws of growth, as is every living organism. This organism—humanity—traverses similar successive stages of development just as every individual human being goes through stages of childhood, adolescence, adulthood, and maturity. Furthermore, close observation demonstrates that in the eighteenth and nineteenth centuries Europe was traversing the advanced stages of its collective adolescence. As such, the Enlightenment was a reflection of the adolescent stage of that segment of humanity with its corresponding mindset. The quest for personal freedom and happiness, the disdain for authority, and the rejection of religion and its moral and ethical teachings are all characteristic expressions of this adolescent mindset. They are, at once, noble, naive, idealistic, and contradictory. Therefore, it should come as no surprise that the claims of the Enlightenment thinkers have not been nor could have been fulfilled. What humanity needed then, and needs even more acutely today, was not to learn how to remain at the level of adolescence indefinitely, but rather to learn how to gradually enter its age of collective adulthood. The fascination of humanity today with an adolescent worldview and culture is but a reflection of an unhealthy prolongation of this fascinating and challenging stage of our individual and collective growth. (See chapter one.) As a psychiatrist, I observe with much concern the follies and extremes of our collective adolescence.

INTEGRATIVE PARADIGM OF KNOWLEDGE

After considering these and many other pertinent issues, at Landegg we decided that our curriculum would introduce a new paradigm of knowledge in all of its work. We call this new paradigm an *integrative paradigm of knowledge*. The adjective *integrative* is very apt here. It refers to the process of bringing together various concepts, perspectives, and expressions of reality to create unity—that most fundamental law of existence and life. As we reflect on the nature of life, we realize that life is unity, and unity is life. This creative law—unity—forms the framework within which all human endeavors produce their highest and noblest results. Permit me to elaborate further on this concept of unity.

All that exists is the outcome of unity between matter and information. Thus, we observe the phenomenal presence of order, purpose, and law in the structure of the atom and galaxies and the entire material world. With the advent of life resulting from the unity of matter and higher levels of information and awareness, the degree of complexity, richness, and purposefulness of life becomes dazzling. The fundamental difference between inorganic and organic entities is that nebulous, universally observed, and insufficiently understood reality, variably referred to as the mind, consciousness, psyche, or, in the languages of philosophy and religion, spirit and soul. They all refer to the same reality. The unity of the physical and the metaphysical assumes an even more astonishing quality in humans where consciousness reaches its zenith of expression and where the spiritual and the material assume their highest integration known to us. Death occurs when this unity ceases.

The central task of the *integrative paradigm of knowledge* is the integration of those spiritual and scientific principles that govern all aspects of human life. Spiritual and physical principles refer to those laws that govern existence and life in their manifold expressions. Science is dedicated to understanding and unraveling the laws that govern the physical universe, while religion explains those spiritual laws that govern the realm of consciousness and choice. Issues of ethics and morality automatically emerge when there is choice to be made, and, therefore, all spiritual principles are moral in character and all human endeavors are subject to them. Violation of the laws of existence, be they physical or spiritual, results in predictable and usually catastrophic consequences. Conversely, an integrated, unified approach to these laws creates new, often unexpected, and richer levels of life and advancement. Science has helped us to appreciate and obey the laws that operate in the physical realm of life. The same must apply to spiritual laws. It is essential to realize that spiritual laws "are not impositions of will, or power, or pleasure, but resolutions of truth, reason, and justice."[44] With these considerations in mind, Landegg Academy decided to offer all of its academic courses within the general framework of "Applied Spirituality." At the core of the concept of Applied Spirituality is the identification of the universal spiritual principles present in the religious, cultural, and philosophical heritage of humanity and the manner in which they apply to life. These principles constitute the creative and humane qualities of all civilizations. They give meaning and purpose to all human endeavors, and they are moral and ethical in their very nature. In contrast to modern materialistic science, which is predominantly analytical and descriptive, the concept of Applied Spirituality employs both analysis and synthesis in its search for answers. At best, science is amoral and neutral. It neither offers meaning nor provides direction for the choices we make. However, human life calls for meaning and direction, and these are obtained when spiritual principles, in their pure and universal essence, are integrated in all our intellectual and scientific pursuits. Applied Spirituality is the discipline concerned with these issues and processes. It makes it possible to develop an *integrative paradigm of knowledge*.

PERILS OF DICHOTOMOUS THINKING

Another important aspect of the integrative paradigm of knowledge is its rejection of the dichotomous view of life and reality, and the adoption of an integrative or unitive perspective based on the principal law of unity. Dichotomous thinking is the primary worldview of our collective stages of childhood and adolescence. It has its roots in the psychological uncertainties, physical inequalities, knowledge deficiencies, and natural proclivities of our experience of the world and of ourselves during those earlier stages of our development. The integrative mindset is the hallmark of a human approach to reality in its more mature and advanced stages. Instead of emphasizing the differences existing between peoples, ideas, and experiences, it focuses on the underlying universal principles that unite them, while at the same time, acknowledges and celebrates their uniqueness. This concept of coexistence of unity and uniqueness— unity in diversity—forms the framework within which we encourage our students and faculty to approach their respective tasks. They are urged to abandon the currently powerful competitive milieux present at universities, as well as in society, and to begin to develop models of cooperative academic studies and research in the context of pursuit of excellence. In fact, many scientists and scholars are now engaged in very successful cooperative projects within and between various universities and research organizations. This is a very constructive process and must be supported unhesitatingly. However, the scope of these collaborations is limited. They are not universal. Expressed differently, these cooperative projects take place within an overall competitive and dichotomous framework. Consequently, their beneficial and creative outcome falls short of their maximum potential.

The integrative approach is all-inclusive and is based on the twin truths of the oneness of truth and the oneness of humanity. It utilizes both scientific and spiritual principles with respect to all human pursuits and categorically rejects all prejudices, superstitions, and destructive practices. It is scientific in its method and considers sciences and arts to be noble spiritual human activities. The integrative mindset rejects force as the primary tool for achieving personal and group objectives, and considers unity to be the greatest source of power both for individuals and for all humanity. It encompasses the principles of the equality of women and men, the nobility of human nature, and the purposefulness of human life.

In contrast, the dichotomous mindset causes separation, segregation, and conflict. It separates people along racial, sexual, religious, ethnic, geographic and ideological lines. The dichotomous mindset is a self-centered, selfish mindset. Many conflicts afflicting humanity today have their roots in this mindset of disunity and separation. This is an important issue for the universities of the future. We need, to the extent possible, to create a conflict-free atmosphere of collaboration and harmony in our classrooms and in the relationships between our faculty and students. We need to develop new models for the administration of human affairs, for the use of science and technology, and for creative solutions to human problems at all levels and for all people.

These goals require not only new conceptual perspectives but also new practical approaches to the manner in which we communicate, share our thoughts and views, make decisions, and resolve conflicts. For this purpose we have adopted the practice of consultation as the main tool of learning and research at Landegg Academy. Consultation and education have similar objectives. The purpose of education is to nurture the human cognitive, affective, and conative—knowledge, love, and will—faculties. It is through education that we learn to use our knowledge to pursue truth and enlightenment, our love to create unity and celebrate diversity, and our powers of will to serve humanity through justice and peace. The purpose of consultation, likewise, is to assist participants to use their unique capacities of knowledge, love, and will to search for truth, create unity, and make decisions characterized by justice and service. In some fundamental respects, education and consultation have the same objectives.

This presentation does not allow for full description of the principles and the art of consultation. (See chapter nine and appendix three on consultation.) Suffice it to say that consultation requires an integrative mindset to be effective, and its very practice assists those involved to further develop their ability to approach academic and scientific work within the parameters of the integrative paradigm of knowledge.

NOTES ON CURRICULUM

The curriculum of the Graduate Faculty of Landegg Academy is formulated within the parameters of the integrative paradigm of knowledge, which includes courses in the humanities and sciences as well as courses on spiritual principles. These latter courses draw from the extremely rich spiritual heritage of humanity and require an in-depth reflection on matters that resonate with existential questions about life and its meaning and purpose. It should however be emphasized that this curriculum is not merely a collection of a number of courses from various disciplines of science, humanities, religious studies, and philosophy. Rather, the curriculum is designed within the frameworks of the unitive mindset and the integrative paradigm of knowledge described above.

Conscious, deliberate pursuit of knowledge is a uniquely human concern. As conscious and aware beings, we constantly search for answers to the existential questions about who we are, why we are, and how we are. All human sciences and arts ultimately deal with these issues, either in conceptual frameworks that shed some light on these issues or as practical knowledge that contributes to human efforts for survival and to improving various aspects of our lives. These questions are all-encompassing in their scope, and the answers to them are to be found in all areas of human knowledge: the arts, sciences, philosophy and ethics, as well as religious thought and teachings. Any separation between them and the exclusion of any of them from the framework that constitutes our view of reality results in confusion, error, and destruction.

Reality is one. It is, at once, scientific and spiritual in nature. It is both subjective and objective in character because the very concept of reality and search for it is a uniquely human pursuit. In our deepest subjective states we human beings search for reality and then construct methodologies to help us find answers from a more objective angle. Subjectivity and objectivity are the two inseparable aspects of our consciousness. Likewise, scientific pursuits, artistic creativity, and spiritual quest are all aspects of the same unitary processes of human consciousness. This integrative and unitive perspective provides the framework for all the programs of Landegg Academy, and opens a new vista of knowledge appropriate to the age of maturity of humanity characterized by unity and peace.

It is a truism that all knowledge has practical dimensions and that all practical issues have ethical considerations. And these ethical issues, like knowledge itself, are at once universal and particular. They are universal in principles and particular in application. We encourage our students and faculty not only to apply these principles to their individual academic and personal pursuits but also, together with the staff of the university, to create a community that reflects all these characteristics in its manifold dimensions. In other words, the theoretical and the practical are combined, and the outcome of research becomes the basis for new approaches to life, which, in turn, become the objects of further search.

These are some of the main aspects of the *integrative paradigm of knowledge* and the concept of *Applied Spirituality* that form the framework and orientation of Landegg Academy's work towards creating a university for the future. After all, we human beings are the architects and engineers of our own individual and collective future. The future is all of us, together.

Universities and their classrooms and laboratories must be settings of consultative interactions, truth-seeking endeavors, and creative undertakings. They need to focus on the requirements for the full, healthy development of all human capacities—intellectual, emotional, and spiritual. In such environments, competition will be replaced by cooperation and individual and group pursuit of excellence. Everyone will have the opportunity to achieve their highest potential, while at the same time, these individual achievements will contribute to the progress of the whole and be put at the service of all humanity. The fundamental laws of uniqueness and unity that govern all existence find their experiential and purposeful expression first in the classroom and laboratory, then within the campus community, and finally in the context of the larger society. Knowledge, thus transformed into insight, will eventually become the wisdom required for a constructive and harmonious approach to life.

ACADEMIC FREEDOM

Another subject of consultation at Landegg Academy has been the all-important issue of academic freedom. No other issue engenders as much passion as does the topic of academic freedom, considered by many to be one of the most sacred rights for all members of the academic community under all conditions. However, despite the extensive discourse on the issue of academic freedom, there seems to be little agreement about what this freedom is and how it could best be achieved. Concepts of freedom, in general, and academic freedom, in particular, are both relatively new and have their roots particularly in the developments in the nineteenth and twentieth centuries.

Freedom and power are totally interrelated. For human beings to be free, we need power to choose and to act; and to have power, we require freedom to express ourselves and to create. Human power is either physical or metaphysical in nature. Examples of physical power are bodily strength and possession of tools of strength such as weapons and armies. Metaphysical power refers to the power of ideas, of knowledge, of unity, and of moral strength. Human history is suffused with examples of both the benefits and dangers of physical power. History is also a clear witness to the enormous impact of the metaphysical powers in shaping human life and destiny. An example helps to make this point clearer.

There is very wide acceptance in academic and societal circles that human beings are competitive by nature and that society should be so organized as to allow for the free and unhampered expression of this natural quality. The freedom to compete, however, renders the competing individuals burdened, isolated, and suspicious. It saps the energy of those involved and ultimately takes away their illusory freedom. The opposite is true about cooperation because it has the power to ease the burden of isolation and to increase the degree of harmony and trust between those involved. Ultimately, true freedom lies in our ability to do good, to be creative, and to unite. A truly free civilization evolves when its citizens possess universal moral and ethical qualities that motivate them to engage in constructive and meaningful endeavors and to create together a vibrant, healthy, creative, and cooperative social organism. Herein lie true power and true freedom. When freedom is not channeled through universal moral and ethical principles such as truth, unity, justice, and service, it becomes destructive and consequently transforms into its very opposite—chaos, anarchy, and oppression. Because freedom and unity are totally interrelated, one is not possible without the other. The welfare of the individual is dependent on the welfare of all and vice versa.

I am focusing on the issue of freedom because it is so vital to universities and their academic life. Jerome Ravetz, in his book, *Scientific Knowledge and its Social Problems* published in 1971, observed that since the Second World War, science has become heavily involved in the military-industrial complex and, in the process, has itself become "industrialized." The consequences of this kind of industrialization of science are foreboding. Ultimately, science becomes an instrument of power and force, losing its much-valued freedom. Ravetz then called for a "critical science" that will serve people, instead of being at odds with them.[45]

Almost ten years later, Shigeru Nakayama of Tokyo University raised similar concerns and suggested that industrialized science be replaced by what he called "service science." He identified two existing forms of science: academic science assessed and promoted by scientists and universities, and industrialized science sponsored and promoted by industry and government, and suggested a third kind of science, *service science,* to replace them. Service science will be assessed and sponsored by the general public and promoted by citizens.[46]

A closely related issue is the ethics of science. Robert Bellah, in his paper, "The Ethical Aims of Social Inquiry," reviews some of the main perspectives on the ethical issues pertaining to social sciences from the time of Aristotle to the present era and clearly demonstrates that all social sciences have ethical dimensions. He concludes that to "disjoin social inquiry from ethical concerns would impoverish it cognitively. Without a reference point in traditions of ethical reflection, the very categories of social thought would be empty."[47]

Another issue of concern with regard to academic freedom is with respect to the manner in which it is currently practiced in contemporary academic settings. It is no exaggeration to state that introduction of spiritual principles into discourse about almost all topics studied at the universities today is usually met with skepticism at best and outright derision and hostility at worst. This is particularly so, if those spiritual principles are expressly drawn from a specific religion. It seems that the principle of academic freedom in many universities does not apply to expression and study of spiritual principles.

These observations and recommendations indicate that a review of the long cherished views on academic freedom and scientific ethical neutrality is urgently needed. It is in this regard that Landegg Academy wants to use an integrative paradigm of knowledge that combines the best of current perspectives on academic and scientific endeavors, formulated within the parameters of the harmony of science and religion and the principle of the oneness of humanity. Such an integrative paradigm avoids the dichotomous and competitive approaches to both science and religion, and uses the practice of consultation to ensure a truly free and comprehensive development of knowledge and its use for creating a universal, ever-advancing civilization of peace.

An integrative paradigm of knowledge, in general, and of science, in particular, calls for a new perspective on scholarship. This new scholarship needs to ensure the unfettered freedom of the individual in his or her search for truth within a unitive paradigm that takes into account all sources of knowledge, both spiritual and scientific, and that uses knowledge for the exaltation of the human station, the refinement of human character, and the unity of humankind. In the same manner that materialistic science uses the powerful tool of the scientific method for understanding the physical aspects of life, integrative science should also use the scientific method for study of all details regarding the application of spiritual principles to life and their consequent impact on the progress of civilization. Ultimately, to the degree that the current atmosphere of criticism, competition, suspicion, arrogance, and conservative tendencies prevailing in the academic world are replaced with mutual encouragement, cooperation, trust, humility, and open-mindedness, to that same degree, science, religion, and humanity will benefit. To the extent that we neglect to do this, we will all suffer.

Stages of Institutional Development

The validity and relevance of ideas are dependent on their effectiveness and the creative outcome once they are applied. The *integrative* phenomenon denotes a unity of diverse entities, a continuous change towards higher levels of organization and complexity, and a purposeful progression towards meaning and result. In other words, the *integrative* phenomenon is the essential characteristic of a living organism. A university is a living social organism. It is the outcome of the integration of varied thoughts, talents, requirements, and activities on the part of a community of people, separate individuals in their uniqueness of talents and capacities but integrated in their unity and harmony of purpose. As such, universities, like all other social organisms, are subject to the laws of growth, and they traverse similar stages in the course of their evolution. This also applies to Landegg Academy. Here, I wish to share with you some observations about the nature of the organizational growth of our institution.

Living organisms and social organizations traverse several distinct stages in their process of evolution. These stages reflect the unique characteristics, needs, and functions of the organism at each phase of its maturation. The main determining factor in the development of social organizations is not their size, age, or even their resources, but rather the nature of consciousness that permeates the organization. In other words, it is the mindset, the worldview, the conscious orientation, and the quality of the awareness of the organization and its members that determines both the stage of its development and its character. However, because often not all employees of an organization fully grasp or agree with the main objectives of its vision and method of operation, it is therefore not surprising that the rate of turnover of staff in the first two stages of the evolution of an organization is usually very high.

We can identify three distinct stages in the development of any institution and societal entity. These stages are *primary union, differentiation,* and *enlightened union.* The primary phase is characterized by considerable enthusiasm, excitement, untested expectations, and willing sacrifices. It ensures the survival of the institution in its most elementary state. This phase is also characterized by uniformity. In this phase, those involved in the institution relate to one another not based on their knowledge of each other, not by the unity of their vision, not even by the unity of their objectives and aspirations. Rather, the organism comes into existence in response to the inherent human need to relate to others. This relationship, in its earlier stage is rather insecure and unstable, and the tendency is for those involved to follow the path of uniformity in order to maintain their emerging unity. Uniformity, however, can be only maintained in the context of authoritarian mindsets and practices that call for blind and thoughtless obedience. A prolonged and unexamined state of uniformity is not conducive to the healthy growth of the institution, and, eventually, either the institution implodes from within after a period of apathy and disillusionment, or else it is propelled to its next stage of development—differentiation and individuation. Landegg Academy had a short, intensely creative and demanding first phase. At the time of this inauguration, Landegg is already entering the second and most challenging and difficult phase of its evolution—the phase of *differentiation.* The differentiation phase is the period of separation, departmentalization, diversification, and complexity. Most organizations do not adequately meet the challenges of this phase. Consequently disunity, competition, and self-interest become the modus operandi of many organizations and social institutions. It is under these conditions that many social organisms fail and many others waste enormous reservoirs of talent and wealth trying to offset the negative effects of disunity. Landegg is now displaying the typical characteristics of the differentiation phase of its developments, which in my opinion is the greatest challenge before us for some time to come. Eventually, if Landegg is to succeed, it needs to arrive at its phase of enlightened union in a not very distant future.

The main characteristic of the enlightened union phase is unity and its underlying force—love—which operates at various degrees of intensity and in manifold ways of expression between people. It is through the process of unity that the institution of marriage comes into being, that families are formed, that societies are created, that nations exist, and that ultimately a global society—a new world order—will come into being. Also, it is through the power of love for knowledge and creativity that universities are established.

To avoid the pitfalls of growth, the institution needs to create a situation in which the sources of power and authority are separated from one another and made to function in harmony. This is best achieved by the introduction of the practice of consultation into the mode of operation of the organization, and the integration of consultative opportunities with those administrative practices that empower the individual members of the organization to make decisions and implement them. (See chapter nine.) The twin processes of consultation and clear administrative lines of authority and responsibility safeguard the organization from becoming authoritarian and hierarchical, and ensure that it will operate efficiently and creatively. Such an arrangement makes it possible for each member of the organization to have the benefits of consultation, supervision, and individual initiative simultaneously. We have introduced this system in our Academy. Every position has its terms of reference, one or more committees/task forces for consultation associated with it, a designated line of administrative authority to ensure overall integrity of the functions of the institution, and considerable autonomy along with correspondent responsibility to initiate and implement various tasks. Our experience, thus far, shows that while this arrangement is conducive to the development of a united and cooperative, creative, and purposeful institution, it is also very difficult to put into practice. It is through the successful completion of this phase that a given institution will enter the most productive phase of its development—*the enlightened union phase*—characterized by wisdom based on knowledge and experience, unity in diversity, humility, and the ability to integrate the personal good with the welfare of the whole.

OUR GREATEST CHALLENGE

Every new stage in the development of living systems such as universities is at once based on past accomplishments, present requirements, and future expectations. At Landegg we are fully aware of the magnificent past accomplishments of many other institutions of higher learning. Humanity owes much to them, and the progress of science and technology would not have been possible without them. Much is to be learned from their experiences and insights. However, we also feel that the requirements of this remarkable time of transition are as such that a dramatic change in both the vision and curriculum of universities is required. Already, many universities have acknowledged the need for this change, and various attempts are being made to revise both the vision and curriculum at some universities. However, these revisions are basically quantitative in nature. They are still based on the parameters of a materialistic perspective on reality. At Landegg both the vision and the curriculum are based on the integration of the scientific and the spiritual. We consider this integration to be essential for establishing a progressive and universal civilization of peace, which we perceive to be the only direction that possibly humanity could possibly take if we are to fulfill our true humanity and meet our noble destiny.

I will end my remarks with two statements, one dealing with the practical issues and the other with the vision of this institution. At the practical level, Landegg faces, in addition to its natural growth processes, three fundamental challenges. Financially, Landegg is on very unstable foundations, a situation that may doom it to extinction unless a solution is found. The second challenge is with respect to the availability of a sufficient number of individuals who are willing to be among the founding members of this institution as its students and teachers. A much larger body of paying students and contributing teachers and supporters than those we have now is needed to ensure the viability of this institution. This remains to be seen. And, finally, the third and most crucial challenge before those of us who now serve at this institution is our ability to safeguard our unity of vision and action as we enter this most turbulent phase of the growth of our institution. With these cautionary notes, I wish to conclude my remarks by sharing the vision of Landegg as a future university:

> The greatest challenge before humanity today is to create a civilization that is peaceful and just, united and diverse, prosperous and benevolent, technologically advanced and environmentally healthy, intellectually rich and ethically sound. The primary objective of the curriculum of Landegg International University is to assist its students and faculty to make fundamental contributions to the creation of such a civilization. All of Landegg's programs are thus formulated on the principles of the nobility of human nature, the unity of humankind, and the harmony of scientific and spiritual principles. The university is continually developing and evaluating its curriculum in order to anticipate the needs of humanity in the emerging world order and to prepare its students to meet those needs with insight, dedication, and expertise.

FOLLOW-UP

Landegg Academy started with considerable enthusiasm and dedication on the part of a relatively large number of individuals, most of whom served the institution *pro bono* and contributed their considerable wealth of knowledge and expertise to the academy. However, from the very beginning, the budding university faced several major challenges, among them a hefty debt and no financial backing. It relied almost exclusively on the income it could collect from tuition and other revenue-earning activities such as renting its facilities. The other challenge was the fact that the institution was totally new, was not yet accredited by an accreditation agency, and understandably drew applicants who were primarily interested in the vision, curriculum, and the promise of the new university. These applicants were from all over the globe, and around 90% asked for a non-existent scholarship, usually asking for costs of travel and living expenses in addition to the required tuition. The small group of students who were able to pay their expenses primarily came from the United States of America, Canada, the Middle East, Japan, and a few from China, India, and Europe. The graduate MA programs attracted mature individuals who placed a premium on the novel and challenging learning opportunities that the new institution was offering them. However, their number was small, and we needed more students to be financially viable. It was therefore decided to start an undergraduate program, which attracted some additional students, young, enthusiastic, idealistic, and in need of much more attention, mentorship, and guidance. Thus the income from the increased number of students was nullified by the need to hire a larger number of staff. Nevertheless, the institution was able to be self-supporting in the first few years, not repaying its debt, but also not adding to it. This was possible through generous support of a few individuals. This precarious arrangement collapsed soon after the severe terrorism crises of 11 September 2001 in the United States. Suddenly, the applications from North America that constituted more than 60% of all self-supporting students dwindled to about 20% of previous numbers. We suddenly faced a major financial crisis and were not able to overcome it. Two years later, the bank took over the properties of Landegg, and the university closed. In the course of its short life, the institution had 25 BA and 75 MA graduates, most of whom continued their advanced studies in other universities in different parts of the world and who continue to be inspired by their transforming experience while studying at this unique but short-lived institution of learning. Some of them may, in the future, attempt to revive the flame of Landegg into a new and more secure torch.

Several programs were initiated at Landegg, which have continued to evolve after the closure of the university. The most noteworthy of these programs are those dealing with the issue of peace.

EDUCATING FOR PEACE
FROM CONFORMITY AND CONFLICT TO UNITY IN DIVERSITY

One of the main pillars of an integrated, wholesome education for all children is the vital and indispensable task of rearing every new generation of children and youth according to the universal principles and practices of peace:

- that humanity is one;
- that the oneness of humanity is expressed in diversity;
- that the twin crucial challenges before humanity always are to safeguard our oneness and to nurture our diversity; and
- that the true expression of our humanness is to achieve these two tasks according to the principle of unity in diversity, without recourse to violence.

When a society begins to educate every new generation of its children and youth in their homes, schools, and communities, according to the principles of peace, then such a society, in a span of two to three decades, will begin to experience a most dramatic positive transformation in all areas of its individual and collective life, including the welfare of its children.

Among the most consequential neglect of children is with respect to the type of education they receive. There is a crisis in the intellectual, emotional, social, moral, and spiritual education of children. One common aspect of this crisis concerns the issue of peace education, the lack of which causes much misery in all societies. As noted in chapter six in the section "Family and the Crisis of Education," we do not just fail to offer systematic peace education to our children and youth; on the contrary, we tend to educate them within the framework of conflict. As long as such practices continue, peace and tranquility will elude humanity. The conditions of the world will not improve unless we adopt a peace-based curriculum of instruction for all children and youth and, by that matter for all parents, teachers, and community and political leaders. This aspect of education is gravely overlooked at home, in schools, in communities, and in the media, which has emerged as one of the most influential sources of education of our children and youth. Families and schools need guidance and assistance on how to rear their children and students as peaceful and peace-creating individuals, and this task needs to be shared not only by the parents and educators, but also by governments and policy-makers; social, academic, and religious institutions; as well as by the media and health, judiciary, and other related professions.

REQUISITES OF PEACE

The fundamental requisites of peace are quite similar to those for creating unity-based families that were discussed in chapter six. These requisites are equality, justice, and unity, qualities that are hallmarks of maturity born out of personal responsibility in the context of unity-based worldviews. The diagram below is another version of the one presented in chapter six and demonstrates the dynamic and reciprocal relationship between issues of equality, justice, unity, and peace, which children and youth need to learn throughout their formative years, so that as adults they are able to consciously and deliberately incorporate them in all aspects of their lives.

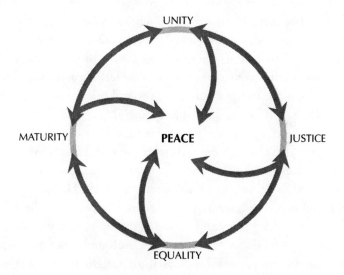

Diagram 7.1. Requisites of peace (from *Education for Peace Curriculum Manual*).[48]

The primary task before parents, educators, policymakers, government institutions and others concerned with the welfare of children is to ensure that the principles of peace and the practice of unity in diversity are fully understood, universally promoted, and systematically implemented at all levels and within all institutions of the society—family, school, workplace, government, and religion. This discourse on parenting and education demonstrates the enormous task before all of us as parents, citizens, and leaders of our increasingly integrated world. On my part, I developed the Education for Peace Program, which is briefly discussed below.

In Search of Peace

My journey to peace began in my early adolescence, when I became a Bahá'í—a severely persecuted religious minority in the midst of a hostile Muslim majority. However, as I endeavored to live my life according to its principles of oneness of humanity and unity, I regularly and forcefully experienced the hatred and hostility of my classmates, teachers, school administrators, and those whom I hardly knew. Thus my adolescent and early adulthood years were marked by many episodes of being pursued by mobs, beaten and abused, and reviled and ridiculed. This outward state of discord was balanced by an inner state of assurance that was imparted primarily by my very courageous and authentic parents. They explained that these seemingly irreconcilable differences between the two groups were not expressions of the true nature of these religions, but rather indications of a deeply rooted state of misunderstanding. They pointed out that in essence all of us are seeking assurance that our personal approach to life was based on sound principles, perspectives, and practices. But in our limited understanding and in the absence of insight and wisdom, we do not see this fundamental oneness and the shared quest that characterizes our respective paths. Instead we become focused on superficial differences that have no true significance.

Later, when I entered medical school at age 17, I began to have an unexpected and truly meaningful experience of peace. In the medical field, where disease, pain, and suffering are the currency of exchange between patients and caregivers, often a profound bond of closeness, empathy, and compassion connects those caught in this maelstrom of life. And in the process, a deeply felt sense of peace—both inner and interpersonal—permeates the relationship. This is one of the most precious rewards of my many years of medical school training and 30 years of the practice of medicine as a psychiatrist.

In the course of three decades of psychiatric practice and working with many individuals, families, and groups, I gradually, but definitely, became aware that when people seek help from a therapist, they are usually in search of peace—inner peace, peace with a marital partner; peace in the family, the workplace, and one's immediate community; and, ultimately, peace with life. And because most of us are so unfamiliar with the nature of peace and even fewer of us have had the good fortune of living truly peaceful lives, it is therefore not surprising that our attempts at helping those people who seek peace are clumsy and rudimentary in nature. The prevalence of the so-called therapeutic modalities ranging from biofeedback to talk-feedback, calming medications to deep-breath meditation, listening and good communication to self-focus and self-gratification, are just a few examples of a range of approaches, all aimed at decreasing the level of tension and conflict and gaining a certain degree of calm and hoped for peace.

With the realization that ultimately, it is peace, or at least absence of tension and suffering, that most people are searching for, I broadened the scope of my work and at Landegg I started a pilot project—Education for Peace—with the goal of developing a comprehensive program of peace-based education founded on the latest developments in the field of peace education and the related disciplines of psychology, sociology, ethics, religion, political science, and law. During the same period (1994–2003), Roshan Danesh and I offered a new conceptualization of issues pertaining to conflict and peace. We proposed that *unity* not *conflict* is the primary law of life and existence; that *unity building* is the most effective approach to both prevention and resolution of all conflicts; and that *unity in diversity* is the most assured path to *peace*. Based on this conceptual framework we developed the concept of unity-based conflict resolution, also called Conflict-Free Conflict Resolution (CFCR). As well, in collaboration with a few of my former students and colleagues, I developed a comprehensive Education for Peace (EFP) Program, based on the principle of worldview transformation from conflict-based to unity-based perspectives, which has been administered in scores of schools with tens of thousands of students in a few countries.[49] The following review of the EFP Program is, in essence, a continuation of the segment on "Educating for Peace" earlier in this chapter.

Education for Peace
Towards a Civilization of Peace

In September 1999, a three-day workshop on Conflict-Free Conflict Resolution (CFCR) was held in Sarajevo, Bosnia and Herzegovina. CFCR is based on the concept of unity as the primary law of life and the main operating principle in human relationships. CFCR defines conflict as the absence of unity and conflict resolution as the process of creating unity.[50]

Some fifty individuals, including journalists, BiH government employees, staff of the international community agencies, and other interested citizens, participated in the workshop. These individuals proportionally represented the three main ethnic populations of BiH—Bosniaks (Muslim), Croats (Catholic), and Serbs (Orthodox Christian)—as well as different strata of the society. In 1999, the scars of the 1992–95 civil war were still quite fresh on the landscape of the country, in the social conditions of the society, and, internally, in the ravaged psyches of the citizens. From the moment of arriving at the dilapidated Sarajevo airport and driving to the town, one would encounter ruined and bullet-riddled buildings beside numerous small and large new makeshift and older established cemeteries housing tens of thousands of victims of the war. On meeting people, one was immediately aware of the fatigue of violence displayed by a population drained of hope, joy, and vitality and filled with fear, anger, and suspicion. The very friendly, hospitable, and educated citizens of this unique and beautiful city were exerting their utmost to recover from the carnage of war and normalize their highly abnormal life circumstances.

The workshop took place in the context of a society wherein over the course of a few tragic years, 700,000 of its 4,427,000 citizens were killed, went missing, were displaced, or died of unknown causes. In addition, a significant number of Bosnians became refugees in many different countries.[51] Among the victims of the war were thousands of boys and men who were summarily executed in genocidal atrocities and an untold number of girls and women who were raped, violated, and abused in horrendous ways, not infrequently by those who were neighbors, friends, and relatives belonging to another ethnic group. And these atrocities took place in a society in which, in recent decades, interethnic marriages were common and people's religious or ethnic identity was seldom a source of tension and disharmony.

The workshop began in an atmosphere of tension and polite distance, and some participants asked that they be lodged in a different hotel separated from members of other ethnic populations—"their former enemies." However, by the end of the first full day of the CFCR workshop, a clearly positive change had occurred, and a process of genuine, positive communication had started. In fact, the transformation among the BiH participants was as such that on the second day of the workshop an invitation was extended to the author by the Minister of Education of Bosnia and Herzegovina to bring the Education for Peace (EFP) Program, which has many similarities with CFCR, to BiH schools as a pilot project.

THE EDUCATION FOR PEACE PROGRAM IN ACTION

The Education for Peace (EFP) Project in BiH began in May 2000 as a community development program of Landegg International University and its affiliate, the International Education for Peace Institute (EFP-International), both located in Switzerland. EFP-International, registered both in Canada and Switzerland, is an independent, not-for-profit, research, training, and service institution without any religious, political, or ethnic affiliation. The EFP-BiH Project started after receiving a formal invitation from the BiH Foreign Ministry and Ministries of Education in both BiH Entities—Bosnia and Herzegovina Federation (BiHF) and Republika Srpska (RS)—with a one-year grant from the Government of Luxembourg. The initial objective of the EFP Project in BiH was to contribute to the goal of creating a culture of peace in a few sample BiH schools by addressing what is perhaps the most critical long-term task facing this country: the training of present and future generations of children and youth to become peacemakers. In its pilot phase (May 2000–June 2002) the project operated in six schools. Located in three different cities—Banja Luka, Sarajevo, and Travnik—representing the three main ethnic groups, including an equal number of primary and secondary schools, serving populations ranging from the elite and materially advantaged to a majority of internally displaced persons, these six schools together comprised much of the diversity of Bosnia and Herzegovina society. The project sought to contribute to the advancement of a culture of peace in Bosnia and Herzegovina by focusing on three main areas:

- Fostering interethnic understanding;

- Training in the knowledge and skills of peaceful conflict resolution and creating violence-free environments (families, schools, communities); and
- Assisting in trauma relief and recovery through creation of a culture of healing within and among the participating schools.

The EFP Program directly involves the entire school communities—teachers, administrators, support staff, students, and parents/guardians—and indirectly engages the wider society, chiefly through holding local, regional, and national peace events as well as coverage by the media.

Vision of Education for Peace

The greatest challenges before humanity at the start of the 21st century are conflict, violence, terrorism, and war, along with their terrible consequences of poverty, hunger, disease, despair, environmental destruction, and poor leadership. These challenges are felt at all levels of human life—the family, school, community, society, and world. While considerable resources have always been and continue to be spent to offset the costly ravages of conflict, violence, and war as well as to pay for the high price of military defense and security measures, there are relatively few programs dedicated to a systematic, sustained plan of action to educate children and youth in the principles of peace. Consequently, every new generation repeats the mistakes of former generations, and conflict and violence become permanent facets of human societies. Paradoxically, our greatest opportunity at this time in history is the fact that we have sufficient resources and insights to create a civilization of peace. Education is the most essential tool for achieving this historic undertaking.

Conceptual Framework

Programs

Peace and education are inseparable aspects of civilization. No civilization is truly progressive without education, and no education system is truly civilizing unless it is based on the universal principles of peace. However, our homes, schools, and communities have become increasingly conflicted and violent. We, therefore, inadvertently promote a culture of conflict and violence, and consequently, our children do not learn the ways of peace. To adequately respond to these monumental challenges and opportunities, we need to lay the foundations of a sustainable and universal civilization of peace by better understanding the nature and dynamics of peace at all levels of human experience—intrapersonal, interpersonal, intergroup, international, and global. For this purpose at least three synergistic and essential tasks must be pursued locally, nationally, and globally:

- **Peace-Based Education:** To educate every new generation of the world's children and youth—with the help of their parents/guardians and teachers—to become peacemakers;
- **Peace-Based Governance:** To create forums for the leaders of the world at local, regional, national, international, and global levels to study and implement the principles of peace-based governance and leadership in their respective communities and institutions; and
- **Peace-Based Conflict Resolution:** To offer training opportunities in the principles and skills of peaceful conflict prevention and conflict resolution for citizens and leaders at local, regional, national, international, and global levels.

The programs of the International Education for Peace Institute and its sister entities are designed to specifically address these three fundamental requisites of a civilization of peace.

CURRICULUM

The EFP Integrative Curriculum is based on three premises: (1) *unity*, not conflict, is the main force in human relationships; (2) *worldview* is the main framework within which all human individual and group behavior takes shape; and (3) *peace* is the main outcome of a unity-based worldview. In the EFP Curriculum, the concept of worldview is defined as the framework within which we understand the nature of reality, human nature, the purpose of life and laws governing human relationships. The concept also includes issues of personal and group identity and narrative.

The EFP curriculum calls for a fundamental reform of children's instruction according to the principles of peace rather than conflict, as is currently the case in most schools in many parts of the world. As such, peace is not a separate subject of study, but rather it is the framework within which all subjects—from history to mathematics, biology to physics, geography to literature, political science to economics, and physical fitness to language—are studied. This approach requires special training of teachers and reconsideration of the textbooks, which are usually written from the perspective of conflict.

Because of this fundamental pedagogical requirement, in the course of the past decade of the implementation of EFP Programs, we have learned that they are most effective when the entire school community— all students, all teachers, all administrators, all support staff, and to the extent possible all parents/guardians—are included. Peace is, by its very nature, all-inclusive, and as such peace-based education is most effective when no member of the community is excluded. Another essential component of the EFP Curriculum is that it uses all modalities of learning—intellectual, emotional, and experiential—and engages the students in critical thinking, artistic creativity, and social activity. Students are assisted to share with their teachers, parents/guardians, and other students their new learning and experience of peace through the modality of regular *Peace Events* in their schools, communities, and throughout the country. These multifarious elements of the curriculum are outlined in the eleven-volume Education for Peace Integrative Curriculum.[52]

Context

As stated above, the EFP Program was introduced in three primary and three secondary schools in Bosnia and Herzegovina in May 2000, five years after a most calamitous interethnic war in the country. During the EFP pilot phase (2000–2002), and to some degree even now (2010), questions remain about the long-term future of Bosnia and Herzegovina. Extreme nationalism, interethnic tensions, and simmering discontent and suspicion were very high at the start of the 21st millennium. The economic situation was desperate; corruption was widespread; and the relative extremes of wealth and poverty, resulting from unscrupulous economic practices during the war years, added to the people's discontent and mistrust. Feelings of maltreatment and injustice were particularly high among the citizens, and the state institutions were too weak and ineffectual to address these manifold challenges.

Added to these daily life challenges were the unattended scars of the war on children and adults alike, a condition that was being increasingly expressed in severe psychological and medical disorders such as depression, addiction, delinquency, suicide, aggression, apathy, and a host of other symptoms all indicative of a state of "resigned uncertainty" with regard to their past, present, and future. No effective healing process from the traumatic experiences of the war and the ongoing unabated conflict was evident, and the social environment was not conducive to recovery from these violence-induced conditions.[53] In this context, understandably, there was much skepticism about the EFP Program and its ability to achieve its main objectives: to create, within and between the participating school communities, a *culture of peace*, a *culture of healing*, and a *culture of excellence*.

Outcome

The Education for Peace (EFP) pilot project was successful, and subsequently we were invited by the BiH Government, all Ministries of Education in that country, and the main International Community Representative entities in BiH to introduce the program to as many schools as possible. In response, we were able to secure the necessary grants from the development agencies of the governments of Canada, Japan, and Switzerland, as well as from a Rotary International chapter in Switzerland, to introduce the EFP Program into an additional 106 schools with approximately 80,000 students and tens of thousands of parents/guardians, and to train all 5,000 teachers and staff of these schools in the principles of Education for Peace. This task was accomplished over a period of four years (2003–2007). During this period, based on the lessons learned from this massive experience, the research that was conducted, and after review of the current literature on peace education, a comprehensive and integrated EFP curriculum was developed. The curriculum comprises eleven volumes, four of which have been already published, and the remaining volumes will be available in the course of the next few years. Currently, plans are underway to integrate the EFP Programs in the BiH school curricula, involving all 2,200+ primary and secondary schools in BiH with a total of some 1.5 million students, 110,000 teachers, and as many parents/guardians as possible (2008–2012).

The criteria by which the EFP Program is evaluated are to determine to what extent it has accomplished its three main objectives—to create a *culture of peace* (violence-free and cooperative relationships in the context of rule of law and democratic practices), a *culture of healing* (from the adverse effects of conflict, violence, and war), and a *culture of excellence* (academic behavioral, and relational) in the institutions and environments (family, school, community agencies, etc.) in which the program is introduced. The evaluation and research findings on the conceptual framework, methodology, and impact of the EFP Program have been already reported and need not be reproduced here.[54] However, I have provided a few excerpts from feedback by teachers and students participating in the EFP Program to demonstrate the nature of the impact of EFP on its participants. A teacher of a secondary school stated, "As a result of participating in the EFP project, my way of teaching has changed, my relationship with students has changed, and my relationship with my family has changed...all for the better." Another teacher observed, "This project has changed our vision and worldview. I feel that the vision of every teacher and student in this school has been in some way changed through this project." A high school student summed up the most cogent objectives of the EFP Program in this manner: "In this project we learned many new things: new approaches to resolving conflicts, how to create our own lives, and how to make our own decisions. But the most important thing that we learned is to be at peace with ourselves and teach other people to be peaceful. Our society doesn't have many projects like this." And a primary school student offered this observation: "Before this project things were imposed in our classes, but with EFP we do it because we love it."[55]

It is in the context of these positive results that the wise counsel of Mahatma Gandhi is confirmed in action at a large scale and at a sustained level:

> If we are to teach real peace in this world, and if we are to carry on a
> real war against war, we shall have to begin with the children.[56]

SUMMARY

This chapter on education covered a wide range of issues—informal and formal education, parenting, self-education, peace-based education, the future of universities, and some reflections on Bahá'í scholarship. The thread that connects all these varied approaches to education is the fact, that in the final analysis, true education is a lifelong, multifaceted, and integrated endeavor. Learning is an integral and unending aspect of human experience in the context of our intellectual, creative, and experiential endeavors and has the unique quality that comes with the realization that "the more we learn, the less we know." As such, learning and education are a journey through the realms of *the mysterious and the unknown on the wings of faith and reason.* Science and religion, together, open new vistas of discovery and learning to us that are essential for the betterment of human life and attainment of humanity's most noble objective in this life. Here is how 'Abdu'l-Bahá explained this process during his talk at Columbia University in New York on April 19, 1912:

> As material and physical sciences are taught here and are constantly unfolding in wider vistas of attainment, I am hopeful that spiritual development may also follow and keep pace with these outer advantages. As material knowledge is illuminating those within the walls of this great temple of learning, so also may the light of the spirit, the inner and divine light of the real philosophy glorify this institution. The most important principle of divine philosophy is the oneness of the world of humanity, the unity of mankind, the bond conjoining East and West, the tie of love which blends human hearts.[57]

PART THREE

ON SOCIETY

Chapter Eight

We are One
Emerging Consciousness
of the Oneness of Humanity

The utterance of God is a lamp, whose light is these words: Ye are the fruits of one tree, and the leaves of one branch. Deal ye one with another with the utmost love and harmony, with friendliness and fellowship.[1]

—Bahá'u'lláh (1817–1892)

…the happiness of mankind lieth in the unity and the harmony of the human race, and that spiritual and material developments are conditioned upon love and amity among all men.[2]

—'Abdu'l-Bahá (1844–1921)

The world is beautiful, but has a disease called man.[3]

—Friedrich Nietzsche (1844–1900)

Humankind has understood history as a series of battles because, to this day, it regards conflict as the central facet of life.[4]

—Anton Pavlovich Chekhov (1860–1904)

I am at peace with God. My conflict is with Man.[5]

—Charlie Chaplin (1889–1977)

Evolution is the law of policies: Darwin said it, Socrates endorsed it, Cuvier proved it and established it for all time in his paper on "The Survival of the Fittest." These are illustrious names, this is a mighty doctrine: nothing can ever remove it from its firm base, nothing dissolve it, but evolution.[6]

—Mark Twain (1835–1910)

This Age of Oneness

At the time of writing this part of the book, I was closely following the proceedings of the General Assembly of the United Nations. Many of the world's leaders were gathered in New York to consult on how to deal with some of the fundamental urgent challenges faced by humanity. Among the challenges that were on the agenda were poverty, disease, intergroup and interethnic conflict; violence in its manifold expressions; several regional wars; inequality between women and men; abuse of children in various forms all over the globe; deep-rooted prejudices based on race, religion, gender, class, and material possessions; and environmental degradation. I think we should also add issues of poor leadership and corruption to the list.

Ultimately, the responsibility to address these issues lies with the *possessors of power and authority*—the leaders of society—and the manner in which they make and implement decisions. We can identify at least seven distinct categories of leaders: political, religious, scientific, academic, professional, business, civic, and media. Each of these domains of power and authority has profound impact on the conditions of society and fortunes of the people. However, it seems that world leaders are either unable or unwilling to use their respective powers and domains of authority to significantly improve world conditions. It is apparent that nothing short of a profound transformation in world leaders' modes of operation can possibly respond adequately to the worldwide crises of misunderstanding, mistrust, mismanagement, and profound confusion and hopelessness of the masses of humanity. A fundamental urgent transformation in the worldview and mindset of leaders in all segments of human society is needed. This is a vitally important task, and its implementation lies at the core of the current challenges faced by humanity and its leaders.

These challenges have their genesis in the violation of the primary law of existence and life—unity—and in the disregard of the undeniable fact of the oneness of humankind. Humanity is one in the context of its diversity, and unity is the process of promotion and protection of this oneness and diversity. As we discussed in chapter one, all human thought, sentiment, and action, as well as the moral standards that justify them, are shaped by the nature of our worldview. Three metacategories of worldview: authoritarian (survival-based), adversarial (identity-based), and integrative (unity-based) were identified. Of these three, the first two—authoritarian and adversarial—are conflict-based and the most prevalent in our world today. The unity-based worldview, based on the principle of oneness of humanity and practice of unity in diversity, is yet to be universally accepted and practiced.

Leaders and citizens alike are subject to the inescapable impact of their respective worldviews. Therefore, the only way in which a truly positive change can be enacted is through transformation of our worldviews from conflict orientation to its opposite—unity orientation. This transformation occurs basically under two conditions: severe, intractable crises or new, radical insights, but usually a combination of the two. Whenever we as individuals and communities of people face a host of serious consequential crises and are unable to deal with them despite our best intentions, insights, and efforts, we find ourselves at a crossroads, one path leading to the seemingly familiar past and the other inviting us to an unknown new future. Focus on the past is often perceived as the easier of the two options because we tend to idealize the past and feel secure with the familiar modes of thinking, feeling, and action—worldviews. However, return to the past is a perilous journey that almost always ends in confusion and disappointment. This backward journey demands suspension of logic and reason, is willfully blind to the previously experienced pitfalls, and requires use of force—usually violent force—against the onward current of life and change. The "past" needs to be approached as a signpost for deciding the direction of the future rather than as a sanctuary to return to in times of difficulty.

The journey towards the future has its own particular challenges. It is an unknown journey and as such is fear-inducing. "Future" is more than an expedition on the continuum of time, place, and person. Future is also a journey to the realms of new ideas, insights, approaches, and experiences. It is an ever-advancing process of progress, modernization, change, and transformation. As such, the deliberate journey towards a better future requires vision, courage, and sacrifice. *Vision* is the process of seeing that which is beyond the immediate and ordinary, and projecting fundamental future developments and transformations. True vision is at once a spiritual, scientific, and practical phenomenon. The greatest visionaries in human history are the Manifestations or Messengers of God whose vision embrace centuries and ages beyond our limited, usually self-centered imagination and whose teachings transform every aspect of life of humanity—spiritual and material, scientific and artistic, personal and social, moral and ethical.

To envision the future, we need insight, courage, and sacrifice. Insight is the outcome of the process of the integration of science and religion in the context of application. Courage refers to being brave enough to think and imagine beyond the safe stagnated frameworks of prevailing perspectives and to take leaps of faith on the wings of imagination into new realms of understanding and action. To do so, we must be prepared to sacrifice, personally, economically, and socially. We must be willing to become pioneers rather than followers in the search for new knowledge, and we must be aware that as pioneers we would be perceived as "abnormal individuals and communities of people" in the context of prevailing unhealthy and conflicted norms and practices.[7]

It is in this context that I feel the current efforts of world leaders are not commensurate with the challenges they face, and consequently their efforts, however sincere and thoughtful, will not produce the desired results. That is why, despite concerted joint efforts of a large number of countries and international organizations over many decades, poverty, disease, injustice, inequality, conflict, and violence are still on the rise, both in their prevalence and severity. These problems will continue as long as the political, economic, scientific, religious, and information (media) powers are concentrated in the hands of those individuals who are, by and large, more concerned about themselves and their privileges than about exercising their noble and sacred duties as the leaders in their respective areas of activity. Thus we observe many political leaders concerned about their own positions of power and control; economic tycoons focused on accumulating wealth beyond the needs of mortal humans; scientists preoccupied with safeguarding the validity of their narrowly formulated theories; religious leaders jealously protecting their respective domains of authority over the poorly informed masses; civic leaders struggling with manifold challenges with little resources and direction; and journalists thriving in hotbeds of conflict, scandal, corruption, and violence. This type of conflict-based leadership is incapable of meeting current global challenges. What the world now most needs is unity-based leadership in all the diverse departments and aspects of life.

THE COVENANT

In the course of about one and half centuries, the Bahá'í Faith has succeeded in creating a highly united and diverse global community in the midst of a deeply divided and xenophobic world (see chapter ten). This is a singular accomplishment that merits careful study. The potential lessons learned from such an experiment might prove to be highly timely and fully applicable to the challenges of our world. This accomplishment also raises several legitimate questions. How one can be sure that the leadership in the Bahá'í Community would not eventually succumb to the same temptations of abuse of power and authority as are prevalent in other communities? What is unique about the teachings of Bahá'u'lláh that can create such an all-inclusive unity and true democracy in the context of freedom and diversity? What is the power that safeguards the enormous diversity of the Bahá'í Community in the context of its profound unity, while at the same time maintaining its moral integrity and spiritual authority? These questions touch on some fundamental aspects of Bahá'í Community life, including its approach to issues of power and authority; methods of decision making and conflict resolution; standards of moral, ethical, and spiritual principles; safeguarding of human rights and responsibilities; and benefiting from the indispensable insights provided by science. All these and other important issues of community life in the Bahá'í Faith take place within the parameters of the "Bahá'í Covenant," which is one of its most distinguishing features. In the words of 'Abdu'l-Bahá:

> As to the most great characteristic of the revelation of Bahá'u'lláh—a specific teaching not given by any of the Prophets of the past—it is the ordination and appointment of the Center of the Covenant ['Abdu'l-Bahá]. By this appointment and provision He [Bahá'u'lláh] has safeguarded and protected the religion of God against differences and schisms, making it impossible for any one to create a new sect or faction of belief. To insure unity and agreement He has entered into a Covenant with all the people of the world including the Interpreter and Explainer of His teachings so that no one may interpret or explain the religion of God according to his own view or opinion and thus create a sect founded upon his individual understanding of the divine words.[8]

The Covenant is the highest expression of a mature relationship between humanity and the Manifestation of God. After having independently searched for spiritual truth and reached a level of intellectual and spiritual certitude, in a condition of total freedom and autonomy, the individual then commits to live a life within the parameters of the teachings and ordinances of Bahá'u'lláh with certitude and a faith based on conscious knowledge and deepened insight. Here, there is no room for blind acceptance, superstitious belief, or logically unsound concepts. In the context of the Bahá'í Covenant, science and religion are reconciled; power and authority are exercised in the spirit of service, humility, and selflessness; and the members of the community are given the power to express their views in both consultative forums and through truly democratic electoral occasions. The history of the Bahá'í Faith thus far clearly demonstrates the highly beneficial and unifying powers of the Covenant, safeguarding the community from the occasional selfish and shortsighted actions of those individuals who may be tempted to violate its principles. The significance of the Covenant becomes clearer as we address several issues that are particularly relevant to the ultimate goal of the Bahá'í Faith—creating a global progressive civilization of peace.

THE PROCESS OF TRANSITION

Throughout this book I have referred to the issue of individual and collective development on many occasions and have described some of the main features of this extremely important process. Here, I revisit those concepts with special attention to the dynamics of social evolution. Human individuals and societies alike are subject to the laws of growth characteristic of all biological and social living organisms. No living entity is exempt from the laws of growth. Life and growth are mutually interdependent: life creates growth and growth maintains life. While the principles of interdependency of life and growth are clearly observable in each individual life, the operation of similar principles in sociological living entities such as the family; economic, educational, religious, and political institutions; and society as a whole, are not fully appreciated or understood.

Human development, both at individual and group levels, takes place on the axis of consciousness in response to at least four major influences—the physical environment into which we are born; the type of the family and society in which we are reared; the scientific and artistic education we receive and later pursue; and the spiritual principles and religious teachings to which we are exposed and eventually adopt or reject. Of these four categories, the first two are totally outside our control. We cannot choose the type of environment or the family into which we are born. However, with respect to the latter two categories—our scientific and artistic pursuits, and our spiritual and religious orientation—we have increasingly higher levels of autonomy as we leave our childhood and adolescence behind and also as we become parents and teachers in our own unique manner. This autonomy is most precious and allows us to discover our singular individual capacities, to increase our depth of understanding, to shape our character according to universal spiritual principles, and in the process to transform ourselves and our world.

The sacred writings of the Bahá'í Faith place great emphasis on the study of arts and sciences, and on the independent search for spiritual truth. The ultimate objective is for each human individual and for the society as a whole to develop and to fulfil their inherent potentials to the fullest extent possible. There are similarities between the process of development of human societies and their social institutions, and the maturation of human individuals traversing the three main stages of childhood, adolescence, and adulthood. These stages are not merely indicators of the age and duration of a specific entity such as an individual, an institution, or a society. They also denote the nature of the collective worldview, according to which a given society formulates its perspectives on the nature of reality, human nature, and the primary purpose of life, and establishes its patterns of relationships, governance, economy, and ethics—in short, all aspects of the life of society. Our worldviews are indicators of the level of maturation of our consciousness.

Thus, a society functioning according to the first level of its collective development tends to be primarily concerned with the survival needs of its population. Individuals in such a society expend most of their time and energy in subsistence activities. These societies are usually organized like a traditional family with one person, most frequently a male, as the ultimate leader of the group. Consequently, power is concentrated in one or a few individuals, who tend to administer their society according to authoritarian and dictatorial practices. Conformity is demanded of all citizens, and innovation and free thinking are forcefully discouraged. The worldviews current in these societies are dichotomous. They tend to separate people from each other by gender, race, religion, ethnicity, language, wealth, class, and along other lines of demarcation. All these distinctions are ultimately related to issues of authority and power. Therefore, it is not surprising to note that throughout history in many societies, religion and politics have been very much intertwined.

Politics, in one sense, revolves around the issue of seeking and holding power. Religion, in contrast, provides the necessary legitimacy for the exercise of power. For political leaders to succeed, they require both power and legitimacy; therefore, it is not surprising that we observe the marriage of political power and religious authority in most authoritarian forms of government. Even those authoritarian regimes that reject religion are obliged to find another source of legitimacy, which is usually an ideology such as communism.

The second level of collective maturity corresponds with an adolescent mindset and is preoccupied with issues of identity, competition, separation of church and state, and considerable power-struggle. Prevalent in the West, adversarial multi-party democratic systems, which are now being gradually introduced to the rest of the world, are political indicators of the current level of the collective development of humanity. While the worldview of the first level of collective development is dichotomous, high levels of individualism and competition mark the second stage. These societies are highly individualistic and divided. Nationalism and group identity in their manifold expressions are the hallmarks of the second level of the collective development of every society. These group identities, individualistic attitudes, competitive practices, and conflicted perspectives are also present within and among major religious communities of our world. And it is also not surprising that in many parts of the world religion has lost its role as the ultimate source of moral authority and has been replaced by public opinion, transitory ideologies, and scientific facts and fallacies.

Although the mindsets of the first and second phases of development are distinct, nevertheless, it is a characteristic of human consciousness to operate at several different levels simultaneously. Therefore, it is not surprising that we observe a predominant admixture of both the first and second levels of developmental mindset in every culture. As well, we also observe the presence of a certain degree of the third level, which is a strong indication that humanity, at last, is coming of age and entering its long-anticipated phase of maturity. On 17 November 1912, 'Abdu'l-Bahá's talk at Genealogical Hall in New York City, referred to this fundamental process, stating that all biological and social living entities—plants, animals, humans, societies, arts, sciences, and religions—go through stages of development. Here is a portion of his discourse:

> All created things have their degree, or stage, of maturity. The period of maturity in the life of a tree is the time of its fruit bearing.... The animal attains a stage of full growth and completeness, and in the human kingdom man reaches his maturity when the lights of intelligence have their greatest power and development. From the beginning to the end of his life man passes through certain periods, or stages, each of which is marked by certain conditions peculiar to itself. For instance, during the period of childhood his conditions and requirements are characteristic of that degree of intelligence and capacity. After a time he enters the period of youth, in which his former conditions and needs are superseded by new requirements applicable to the advance in his degree....At last he passes out of the period of youth and enters the stage, or station, of maturity, which necessitates another transformation and corresponding advance in his sphere of life activity....Similarly, there are periods and stages in the life of the aggregate world of humanity, which at one time was passing through its degree of childhood, at another its time of youth but now has entered its long presaged period of maturity, the evidences of which are everywhere visible and apparent. Therefore, the requirements and conditions of former periods have changed and merged into exigencies which distinctly characterize the present age of the world of mankind....From every standpoint the world of humanity is undergoing a reformation. The laws of former governments and civilizations are in process of revision; scientific ideas and theories are developing and advancing to meet a new range of phenomena; invention and discovery are penetrating hitherto unknown fields, revealing new wonders and hidden secrets of the material universe.

In the same discourse, 'Abdu'l-Bahá, further elaborates on this theme and addresses the sensitive issue of transformation in the domain of religion:

> This is the cycle of maturity and reformation in religion as well. Dogmatic imitations of ancestral beliefs are passing. They have been the axis around which religion revolved but now are no longer fruitful; on the contrary, in this day they have become the cause of human degradation and hindrance. Bigotry and dogmatic adherence to ancient beliefs have become the central and fundamental source of animosity among men, the obstacle to human progress, the cause of warfare and strife, the destroyer of peace, composure and welfare in the world. Consider conditions in the Balkans today [1912]: fathers, mothers, children in grief and lamentation, the foundations of life

overturned, cities laid waste and fertile lands made desolate by the ravages of war. These conditions are the outcome of hostility and hatred between nations and peoples of religion who imitate and adhere to the forms and violate the spirit and reality of the divine teachings....

While this is true and apparent, it is, likewise, evident that the Lord of mankind has bestowed infinite bounties upon the world in this century of maturity and consummation. The ocean of divine mercy is surging, the vernal showers are descending, the Sun of Reality is shining gloriously. Heavenly teachings applicable to the advancement in human conditions have been revealed in this merciful age. This reformation and renewal of the fundamental reality of religion constitute the true and outworking spirit of modernism, the unmistakable light of the world, the manifest effulgence of the Word of God, the divine remedy for all human ailment and the bounty of eternal life to all mankind.[9]

The third level of collective development of human societies revolves around the all-important issue of unity. The unity-based worldview addresses all basic human needs: biological, psychosocial, and spiritual. History does not provide us with an example of a well-established advanced civilization functioning at the third level of collective development. Such a civilization will be integrative in all its operations; based on the universal principles of peace; and characterized by ongoing progress in the context of diversity and creativity within the parameters of unity, justice, and moral rectitude. In such a civilization, science and religion are equally integrated into the life of the society. Technological advances, economic resources, and political powers are all put at the service of peace. And the industries of war are, once and for all, made superfluous.

Through the process of spiritual development, human beings begin to demonstrate those qualities and capacities that we most admire, both in ourselves and in each other. Among these qualities are love, truth, justice, service, and attraction to beauty and refinement. To develop these qualities, both as individuals and societies, we need to spiritualize our lives, a process that takes us beyond a life according to the dictates of our instinctual forces and self-centred objectives. We could give other names to this third phase of human development. However, the fact remains that the entire drama of human evolution is that of moving away from the limited, concrete constrictions of matter to the unlimited, equally real, yet abstract domains of consciousness and spirit. The singularly unique aspect of humanness is that the seemingly irreconcilable realities of matter and consciousness come together to create an integrated whole—the human reality. Here sight, hearing, touch, smell, and taste—the body's sensors of the environment—are integrated with imagination, thought, comprehension, and memory, which are human psychological powers.[10] Here, the duality of the body and soul are translated into the integrated unity of the living person. In the following statement 'Abdu'l-Bahá describes the nature and dynamics of the relationship of the body and soul in the context of unity:

> [T]he various organs and members, the parts and elements, that constitute the body of man, though at variance, are yet all connected one with the other by that all-unifying agency known as the human soul, that causeth them to function in perfect harmony and with absolute regularity, thus making the continuation of life possible. The human body, however, is utterly unconscious of that all-unifying agency, and yet acteth with regularity and dischargeth its functions according to its will.[11]

Elsewhere, 'Abdu'l-Bahá elaborates on these themes and points to one of the fundamental reasons for the appearance of Bahá'u'lláh and other earlier Manifestations of God. After recounting the many years of suffering, sacrifice, imprisonment, torture, displacement, and injustices that characterized Bahá'u'lláh's life, he explains that Bahá'u'lláh

> bore these ordeals, suffered these calamities and difficulties in order that a manifestation of selflessness and service might become apparent in the world of humanity; that the Most Great Peace should become a reality; that human souls might appear as the angels of heaven; that heavenly miracles would be wrought among men; that human faith should be strengthened and perfected; that the precious, priceless bestowal of God, the human mind, might be developed to its fullest capacity in the temple of the body; and man become the reflection and likeness of God, even as it hath been revealed in the Bible: "We shall create man in Our own image."[12]

While in London in 1911, 'Abdu'l-Bahá, elaborated on this theme by drawing a parallel between the relationship of the body and the soul, and the material and spiritual civilizations:

> Bahá'u'lláh taught that hearts must receive the Bounty of the Holy Spirit, so that Spiritual civilization may be established. For material civilization is not adequate for the needs of mankind and cannot be the cause of its happiness. Material civilization is like the body and spiritual civilization is like the soul. Body without soul cannot live.[13]

This all-encompassing web of relationships between the material and spiritual, body and soul, life and growth, material civilization and spiritual civilization, diversity and unity, and change and transformation are all aspects of the unity-based worldview that characterizes the coming of age of humanity and the dynamics of its collective maturation.

While the central objectives of biological and psychosocial phases of human development are survival, domination, pleasure seeking, and personal advantage, the spiritual phase of development is characterized by the consciousness of the oneness of the human race and by wholesome growth and transformation. In this phase, the individual and the society, together, embark upon a coordinated process of making life safer and more comfortable, equitable, fruitful, beautiful, joyful, creative, meaningful, and peaceful. In other words, the utopian, seemingly unrealistic hopes and dreams of past generations become realistic objectives during the third phase—the spiritual phase—of human collective development.

Achievement of this monumental objective requires a fundamental shift in our thinking. This shift of consciousness is already upon us, but we are responding to it by doing everything in our powers to ignore, discredit, and downgrade its revolutionary and far-reaching implications. We resist this new paradigm of reality because it goes squarely against our views and experiences of our individual and collective lives during the childhood and adolescent phases of our collective development. This shift is nothing less than the gradual realization of our fundamental *unity.* Unity is the watchword and the main characteristic of the mature phase—the spiritual phase—of human collective development.

THE EMERGING SPIRITUAL CIVILIZATION

Civilization is the outcome of human creative powers, and its nature is determined by people's understanding of such fundamental issues as the nature of human reality, the purpose of human life, and the process of human development. These are both scientific and spiritual issues, and can only be adequately understood through insights derived from both science and religion. From a Bahá'í perspective, science and religion are neither contrary nor separable. 'Abdu'l-Bahá, states that the "[d]ivine religions enjoin upon and encourage all the faithful to adopt such principles as will conduce to continuous improvements, and to acquire from other peoples sciences and arts."[14] In the same book 'Abdu'l-Bahá writes that

> religion is the light of the world, and the progress, achievement, and
> happiness of man result from obedience to the laws set down in the

holy Books. Briefly, it is demonstrable that in this life, both outwardly and inwardly the mightiest of structures, the most solidly established, the most enduring, standing guard over the world, assuring both the spiritual and the material perfections of mankind, and protecting the happiness and the civilization of society—is religion.[15]

With respect to the relationship of science and religion, he says:

God has endowed man with intelligence and reason whereby he is required to determine the verity of questions and propositions. If religious beliefs and opinions are found contrary to the standards of science they are mere superstitions and imaginations; for the antithesis of knowledge is ignorance, and the child of ignorance is superstition. Unquestionably there must be agreement between true religion and science. If a question be found contrary to reason, faith and belief in it are impossible and there is no outcome but wavering and vacillation.[16]

Once again, the all-important issue of unity—in this case, unity of science and religion—comes to the forefront. Within the framework of harmony of science and religion, the Bahá'í community endeavors to establish an enlightened and progressive state of unity, based on the principle of justice. Bahá'u'lláh states that "the purpose of justice is the appearance of unity"[17] among people. Based on the primacy of the issue of justice, the administrative structure proposed by Bahá'u'lláh for the emerging New World Order calls for the establishment of Houses of Justice at local, national, and international levels (see chapter ten for a fuller discussion of these institutions). At the present time in Bahá'í administration, the local and national Houses of Justice are respectively called local and national Spiritual Assemblies. The international administrative body of the Bahá'í Faith is called the Universal House of Justice, which was first elected in 1963. Since then, international conventions attended by the members of all national Spiritual Assemblies have been held every five years for consultation on the worldwide affairs of the Bahá'í Community and the election of the Universal House of Justice for a five-year term. Local and national Spiritual Assemblies are elected by adult voters in their community in a similar manner annually.

Bahá'í elections are totally free from such practices as nominations, electioneering, and partisan politics. The electorate, in an atmosphere of prayerful contemplation and through secret ballot, vote for those individuals who they feel are imbued with the qualities of service, humility, and detachment and who possess well-trained minds and mature experience. The membership of these elected institutions of the

Bahá'í Faith at all three levels of Bahá'í administration is, at the present time, set at nine members each.

As there is no clergy in the Bahá'í Faith, and as every individual is solely responsible for his/her own spiritual progress and well-being, no one person has any spiritual authority over others. The authority in the Bahá'í Faith lies with the institutions of the religion and is not vested in the members of these institutions or any other individuals. The fundamental responsibility of the members of these institutions is to make the best decisions on matters before them within the framework of the spiritual principles of the Bahá'í Faith and the relevant available scientific facts. To arrive at a unity of thought and resolve about each and every matter before them, Bahá'í individuals and institutions have the benefit of a unique instrument: the Bahá'í method of consultation, which is discussed in chapter nine.

The Bahá'í Writings view justice as a spiritual state with personal, interpersonal, social, political, and legal expressions. At the personal level, justice refers to the processes of independent, objective search for truth and freedom from prejudice. Bahá'u'lláh states:

> The best beloved of all things in My sight is Justice....By its aid thou shalt see with thine own eyes and not through the eyes of others, and shalt know of thine own knowledge and not through the knowledge of thy neighbour.[18]

> The essence of all that We have revealed for thee is Justice, is for man to free himself from idle fancy and imitation, discern with the eye of oneness His glorious handiwork, and look into all things with a searching eye.[19]

The interpersonal, social, and political expressions of justice revolve around the issue of unity, which is considered the ultimate purpose of justice. A truly just relationship, be it between individuals or groups, is by its very nature unifying because justice in human interpersonal and social relationships is only possible when equality of rights and opportunities are established and clear levels of responsibility are identified. Within the parameters of this type of equality, all individuals have the opportunity and freedom to shape the nature and direction of their lives and to benefit from the reciprocal benefits of cooperation, mutuality, and interconnectedness that are inherent in truly equal, just relationships. The social expression of justice is with respect to issues of reward and punishment. The following statement from Bahá'u'lláh addresses some of the issues related to social justice:

We cherish the hope that the light of justice may shine upon the world and sanctify it from tyranny. If the rulers and kings of the earth, the symbols of the power of God, exalted be His glory, arise and resolve to dedicate themselves to whatever will promote the highest interests of the whole humanity, the reign of justice will assuredly be established amongst the children of men, and the effulgence of its light will envelop the whole earth....The structure of world stability and order hath been reared upon, and will continue to be sustained by, the twin pillars of reward and punishment....There is no force on the earth that can equal in its conquering power the force of justice and wisdom.[20]

The local and national Spiritual Assemblies, which as they mature will become respectively local and national Houses of Justice, fulfill their social and spiritual mandate by fostering communities that are socially unified and just; intellectually searching and progressive; morally upright and transparent; and spiritually enlightened and universal. A fundamental factor in the achievement of these objectives is the complete avoidance of all divisive and conflict-ridden political activities. As responsible citizens of their respective communities, Bahá'ís are obedient to their governments; shun all partisan political activities; under no circumstances engage in disorderly or violent conduct; and scrupulously follow the laws of their societies. And when faced with injustice, either by individuals, groups, or by the institutions of their own government, they seek justice through peaceful legal means by appealing to the highest authorities and institutions in their respective national communities, as well as to pertinent international agencies and institutions. Bahá'u'lláh states that it "is incumbent upon every man, in this Day, to hold fast unto whatsoever will promote the interests, and exalt the station, of all nations and just governments."[21] Elsewhere, He emphasizes that "[i]n this day, it is incumbent and obligatory upon all to adhere to that which is conducive to the progress and elevation of the just government and people."[22] Finally, 'Abdu'l-Bahá's counsel to Bahá'ís in this regard is that

each and every one is required to show obedience, submission and loyalty towards his own government. Today no state in the world is in a condition of peace or tranquility, for security and trust have vanished from among the people. Both the governed and the governors are alike in danger...the Bahá'ís are the well-wishers of the government, obedient to its laws and bearing love towards all peoples.[23]

The combination of spiritual, moral, and ethical discipline; consciousness of the oneness of humanity; avoidance of partisan politics; and total dedication to creating conditions of equality, justice, and diversity that characterizes the life of the Bahá'í community and its institutions is responsible for the remarkable degree of unity that exists among Bahá'í communities around the globe. These are all aspects of the Covenant uniting all Bahá'í individuals and institutions. Furthermore, Bahá'ís, both individually and in their work together, use Bahá'í consultation for reaching decisions and resolving whatever disagreements and conflicts that may arise among them. Consultation is the focus of the next chapter.

Aside from the methods of decision-making and conflict resolution, the all-pervasive issues of economics and prosperity are also of considerable practical significance. The state of the economy and the nature of distribution of wealth in a given society is a reflection of its level of economic development, standards of justice and equality, the character and quality of its civilization, and its moral and ethical principles. These issues are briefly addressed next with a few references to the relevant Bahá'í teachings.

PROSPERITY AND SPIRITUALITY

Economic issues occupy a prominent place on the agenda of governments and people alike in every society and are closely related to issues of survival, equality, justice, and unity. Governments rise and fall according to their economic success and failure. Much of the talent and resources of society are dedicated to economic issues and performance. However, despite all this attention and effort, economic crises of the world are on the increase. While communism has already demonstrated its complete inability to create a prosperous, progressive, and equitable economy, capitalism also has begun to demonstrate its main flaws. The gap between the poor and the rich is widening, and alarming signs of deep-rooted discontent on the part of the majority of the people are discernible in every nation despite of the fact the world as a whole is richer and more prosperous than ever. More ominous, the very moral fabric of human societies is weakening at an alarming rate, and this development is closely related to the economic practices, even in the most developed societies. Economist Joseph Schumpeter (1883–1950) argued that "[c]apitalism creates a critical frame of mind which, after having destroyed the moral authority of so many other institutions, in the end turns against its own."[24] This astute observation and ominous prediction seems to be remarkably accurate in the context of very serious economic crises that the major economies of the world have experienced and continue to experience since the autumn of 2008.

From a Bahá'í perspective, one of main the reasons for many of the negative issues related to the current economic inequity and injustice is the absence of a spiritual dimension in the world economic systems. The Bahá'í Faith calls for a spiritual solution to the economic woes of humanity. Bahá'u'lláh explains that there is a direct relationship between wealth and the level of maturity of humanity, and therefore with those moral, ethical, and spiritual codes of conduct that characterize mature humanity:

> Man should know his own self and recognize that which leadeth unto loftiness or lowliness, glory or abasement, wealth or poverty. Having attained the stage of fulfillment and reached his maturity, man standeth in need of wealth, and such wealth as he acquireth through crafts or professions is commendable and praiseworthy in the estimation of men of wisdom, and especially in the eyes of servants who dedicate themselves to the education of the world and to the edification of its peoples.[25]

The dynamics and characteristics of the *spiritual economy* are elaborated by 'Abdu'l-Bahá. He writes:

> Wealth is praiseworthy in the highest degree, if it is acquired by an individual's own efforts and the grace of God, in commerce, agriculture, art and industry, and if it be expended for philanthropic purpose....Wealth is most commendable, provided the entire population is wealthy. If, however, a few have inordinate riches while the rest are impoverished, and no fruit or benefit accrues from that wealth, then it is only a liability to its possessor. If, on the other hand, it is expended for the promotion of knowledge, the founding of elementary and other schools, the encouragement of art and industry, the training of orphans and the poor—in brief, if it is dedicated to the welfare of society—its possessor will stand out before God and man as the most excellent of all who live on earth.[26]

These statements clearly demonstrate that in the Bahá'í Faith prosperity and spirituality are not contradictory. Rather, the fundamental objective of the teachings of the Bahá'í Faith is to create and promote a spiritual economy: progressive, prosperous, and productive. A *progressive* economy is characterized by the equality of opportunity for all, by justice in every sphere of life, by freedom to develop our God-given talents, by a spirit of service, and by the all-important standards of universality and unity in diversity.

A *prosperous* economy requires that every individual be engaged in productive useful work and that this work be performed in the spirit of service. From a Bahá'í perspective, "work done in the spirit of service is the highest form of worship."[27] The correlative requisite here is that there must be opportunities available for everyone to work. Thus the individual and the society are mutually interdependent with respect to the wealth and welfare of the society. The standards of productivity in a spiritual economy are determined by the degree of their contribution to the welfare and betterment of all humanity, rather than by the level of income achieved.

A *productive*, spiritually oriented economic system produces generosity, not greed; moderation, not extremes of wealth and poverty; interconnectedness, not indifference to the poverty and suffering of others; and a creative, not destructive approach to the society and the environment alike. The products of a spiritual economy are universal compulsory education, high standards of health care, adequate shelter and means of support for all, and security and peace in every part of the globe. Such an economy must be based on the pillars of scientific and technological development; just and equitable distribution of the material resources of the planet; and ethical and transparent conduct of the managers of human wealth. A spiritual economy is not based on production of instruments of destruction and war.

The challenge before humanity regarding economic issues, as with all other elemental life issues, is primarily a spiritual challenge, and its remedy lies in a fundamental change of perspective, attitude, and ethics of wealth. These are aspects of a dynamic spiritual transformation that forms the core and the purpose of religion.

POWER, AUTHORITY, AND LEADERSHIP

The concept of power presented here refers to the ability to produce an effect and have control over our actions and domains of responsibility. Authority refers to the source of validation and influence, usually of a moral and/or intellectual nature, in human affairs. In history, political power has traditionally been in the hands of kings and emperors and, in recent times, also presidents and prime ministers. Similarly, authority has been assumed by religious leaders and, most recently, by those possessing specialized knowledge and information, such as scientists and professionals. History also shows that in many societies the possessors of power or authority, often after a period of conflict and competition, have come together and created a common front in order to maintain their respective positions of advantage over the masses of humanity. Thus we encounter kings and emperors who, with the help of religious leaders, proclaim themselves as demigods, God's shadow on earth, the defender of the faith, and many other such appellations. These titles all indicate the close relationship and interdependence of possessors of power and authority, an alliance that has resulted in numerous episodes of horrific abuse on the part of the leaders of both society and religion.

However, Bahá'u'lláh abolished the institution of priesthood, replacing it with a fully democratic system of elected Houses of Justice at local, national, and global levels for the administration of the affairs of the worldwide Bahá'í community. Also, Bahá'u'lláh, as the Emissary of God to humanity for its age of maturation, declared that power has been taken away from the kings of the world and placed in the hands of people. While a prisoner [of conscience] (1863–1892) of two major empires—Persia and Ottoman—Bahá'u'lláh proclaimed that from "two ranks amongst men power hath been seized: kings and ecclesiastics."[28] The weakening of the reins of power and authority of government and religious leaders respectively and the rise of democracies since He uttered this weighty statement are notable examples of this remarkable transition. Addressing the kings of the earth (in letters revealed during September and October of 1867), He admonished and warned them in a clear and emphatic manner:

> Lay not aside the fear of God, O kings of the earth, and beware that ye transgress not the bounds which the Almighty hath fixed....Be vigilant, that ye may not do injustice to anyone, be it to the extent of a grain of mustard seed. Tread ye the path of justice, for this, verily, is the straight path. Compose your differences, and reduce your armaments, that the burden of your expenditures may be lightened, and that your minds and hearts may be tranquillized. Heal the dissensions that divide you, and ye will no longer be in need of any armaments except what the protection of your cities and territories demandeth. Fear ye God, and take heed not to outstrip the bounds of moderation, and be numbered among the extravagant....Know ye that the poor are the trust of God in your midst. Watch that ye betray not His trust....If ye pay no heed unto the counsels....We have revealed in this Tablet, Divine chastisement shall assail you from every direction, and the sentence of His justice shall be pronounced against you.[29]

Since the revelation of these strong and unequivocal counsels—published as *The Summons of the Lord of Hosts*—both government and religious leaders have committed, and continue to commit, innumerable acts of violence and injustice that have brought untold misery to humanity.[30] It is in light of this dismal record that Bahá'u'lláh's approach to issues of violence and peace assume their significance. On the occasion of the public announcement of His mission to the world on 21 April 1863 in Baghdad, Bahá'u'lláh annulled the rule of the sword and inaugurated the era of peace dreamt of and hoped for by all peoples of the world. All religions have peace as one of their stated objectives. However, the followers of these religions have all failed in this regard and have not been able to create a truly equal, just, united, and peaceful world. To the contrary, the history of the major religions of world is marred by innumerable episodes of conflict and violence both within and between their respective communities. It is in this light that the annulment of the rule of the sword by Bahá'u'lláh marks a momentous and unique event in the spiritual history of humanity. "Know thou that We have annulled the rule of the sword," Bahá'u'lláh asserts, "and substituted for it the power born of the utterance of men. Say: O people! Sow not the seeds of discord among men, and refrain from contending with your neighbor...."[31]

Every Manifestation of God is the inaugurator of a new historical era and creator of a new civilization. Thus we encounter, for example, the Buddhist, Christian, Hindu, Islamic, Jewish, and Zoroastrian civilizations in different regions and ages. All these civilizations are based on the foundational teachings of the founders of these major religions. Likewise, Bahá'u'lláh, the Manifestation of God for this age, has brought to humanity teachings and ordinances that are directly applicable to the needs of humanity in an emerging global society. These teachings revolve around the fundamental principle of Oneness—oneness of God, oneness of religion, and oneness of humanity.

Bahá'u'lláh asserts that the fundamental purpose of His divine mission is to create a civilization of peace characterized by justice, equality, and true democracy, free from oppression, prejudice, conflict, and authoritarianism. The civilization of peace is spiritual, democratic, and universal. A unique aspect of this spiritual civilization is the fact that it is free from the potential abuses of the ecclesiastical establishment. Thus, Bahá'u'lláh counsels:

> O people of Bahá [Bahá'ís]! Subdue the citadels of men's hearts with the swords of wisdom and of utterance. They that dispute, as

prompted by their desires, are indeed wrapped in a palpable veil. Say: The sword of wisdom is hotter than summer heat, and sharper than blades of steel, if ye do but understand.[32]

And again,

It followeth, therefore, that rendering assistance unto God, in this day, doth not and shall never consist in contending or disputing with any soul; nay rather, what is preferable in the sight of God is that the cities of men's hearts, which are ruled by the hosts of self and passion, should be subdued by the sword of utterance, of wisdom and of understanding. Thus, whoso seeketh to assist God must, before all else, conquer, with the sword of inner meaning and explanation, the city of his own heart and guard it from the remembrance of all save God, and only then set out to subdue the cities of the hearts of others.[33]

This absolute rejection of conflict, strife, and violence by the Bahá'í Faith and their substitution with harmony, cooperation, and peace is apparent in all of the teachings and practices of the religion. Shoghi Effendi describes some of the main principles of the Bahá'í approach to the administration of human affairs:

Let us also bear in mind that the keynote of the Cause of God is not dictatorial authority but humble fellowship, not arbitrary power, but the spirit of frank and loving consultation. Nothing short of the spirit of a true Bahá'í can hope to reconcile the principles of mercy and justice, of freedom and submission, of the sanctity of the right of the individual and of self-surrender, of vigilance, discretion, and prudence on the one hand, and fellowship, candour, and courage on the other.[34]

NOTES ON LEADERSHIP

From the above it is apparent that the Bahá'í approach to leadership is quite distinct from both the authoritarian and adversarial modes of leadership current in our world. The Universal House of Justice, in their 19 May 1994 letter to a National Spiritual Assembly, outlines the fundamentals of the Bahá'í approach to leadership and the role of the individuals and the institutions of the Bahá'í Faith in this process:

…the importance of the Bahá'í administration is its value in serving as a facilitator of the emergence and maintenance of community life in a wholly new mode, and in catering to the requirements of the spiritual relationships which flow from love and unity among the friends. This touches upon a distinguishing characteristic of Bahá'í life which such spiritual relationships foster, namely, the spirit of servitude to God, expressed in service to the Cause, to the friends and to humanity as a whole. The attitude of the individual as a servant, an attitude pre-eminently exemplified in the life and person of 'Abdu'l-Bahá, is a dynamic that permeates the activities of the Faith; it acquires collective, transformative force in the normal functioning of a community. In this regard, the institutions of the Faith stand as channels for the promotion of this salient characteristic. It is in this framework that the concepts of rulership and leadership, authority and power are properly understood and actualized.[35]

Shoghi Effendi, has written extensively about the nature of Bahá'í administration and its approach to leadership and governance, which merits extensive and in-depth treatment beyond the scope and objectives of this book. In the *World Order of Bahá'u'lláh*, written in 1934, he points out:

> The Bahá'í Commonwealth of the future, of which this vast Administrative Order is the sole framework, is, both in theory and practice, not only unique in the entire history of political institutions, but can find no parallel in the annals of any of the world's recognized religious systems. No form of democratic government; no system of autocracy or of dictatorship, whether monarchical or republican; no intermediary scheme of a purely aristocratic order; nor even any of the recognized types of theocracy, whether it be the Hebrew Commonwealth, or the various Christian ecclesiastical organizations, or the Imamate or the Caliphate in Islam—none of these can be identified or be said to conform with the Administrative Order which the master-hand of its perfect Architect has fashioned. This new-born Administrative Order incorporates within its structure certain elements which are to be found in each of the three recognized forms of secular government, without being in any sense a mere replica of any one of them, and without introducing within its machinery any of the objectionable features which they inherently possess. It blends and harmonizes, as no government fashioned by mortal hands has as yet accomplished, the salutary truths which each of these systems undoubtedly contains without vitiating the integrity of those God-given verities on which it is ultimately founded.[36]

The above two statements explain that the Bahá'í approach to leadership is integrative in nature, unity-based in approach, and consultative in practice. I have developed the following diagram to depict some of the main components of various forms of leadership based on these concepts within the framework of the worldview models presented earlier in chapter one.

This brief discussion of issues of covenant, leadership, and authority provides a broad framework within which we can envision the type of future society that Bahá'u'lláh calls upon us to create.

	Authoritarian Leadership	Adversarial Leadership	Unity-Based Leadership
Human Nature	Bad/sinful	Selfish/Greedy	Noble/ Spiritual
Worldview	World is Dangerous	World is a Jungle	World is One
Mindset	Dichotomous	Individualistic	Integrative
Mode of Leadership	Control and Force	Power Struggle	Consultation
Main Goal of Leadership	To Dominate and Control	To Win and Get Ahead	To Unite and Create
Institutional Structure	Power-Based (Hierarchical)	Conflict-Based (Adversarial)	Unity-Based (Organic)
Methodology	Problem-denying	Problem-solving	Unity-building

Diagram 8.1. Leadership models.
(Adapted from *Leadership for Peace Program*
by Roshan Danesh and H.B. Danesh)

SUMMARY

Civilization is the expression of human social life. There are two kinds of civilization—material and spiritual. Material civilization refers to scientific, technological, and economic developments, while spiritual civilization constitutes those moral, ethical, and spiritual principles that determine the manner in which the material civilization is utilized. In the contemporary world, material civilization has made remarkable progress, while spiritual civilization is lagging behind. This dissymmetry has resulted in truly destructive abuse of scientific discoveries, technological innovations, and economic developments. The inordinate dedication of human scientific and technological capacities to the development of instruments of war is one example of this abuse, and the inhuman and shameful extremes of wealth and poverty is yet another example. The extremely dangerous disregard for the environment is another. The Bahá'í concept of the future of human society is that of a true integration of material and spiritual civilizations, the like of which no human society has ever witnessed. On 14 April 1912 in New York, 'Abdu'l-Bahá, who had been recently freed from almost a half-century of imprisonment and exile (on the account of his spiritual teachings) by two powerful empires—Persian and Ottoman—stated:

> Since my arrival in this country I find that material civilization has progressed greatly, that commerce has attained the utmost degree of expansion; arts, agriculture and all details of material civilization have reached the highest stage of perfection, but spiritual civilization has been left behind. Material civilization is like unto the lamp, while spiritual civilization is the light in that lamp. If the material and spiritual civilization become united, then we will have the light and the lamp together, and the outcome will be perfect. For material civilization is like unto a beautiful body, and spiritual civilization is like unto the spirit of life. If that wondrous spirit of life enters this beautiful body, the body will become a channel for the distribution and development of the perfections of humanity.[37]

Later in the same year, on 20 October 1912 in Paris, 'Abdu'l-Bahá again emphasized the importance of the integration of material and spiritual civilizations:

> In these days the East is in need of material progress and the West is in want of a spiritual idea. It would be well for the West to turn to the East for illumination, and to give in exchange its scientific knowledge. There must be this interchange of gifts. The East and the West must unite to give to each other what is lacking. This union will bring about a true civilization, where the spiritual is expressed and carried out in the material.[38]

This integration of material and spiritual civilization is essential for creating a civilization of peace, which is the ultimate objective of the Bahá'í Faith.

CHAPTER NINE

UNITY-BASED DECISION-MAKING AND CONFLICT RESOLUTION

The heaven of divine wisdom is illumined with the two luminaries of consultation and compassion. Take ye counsel together in all matters, inasmuch as consultation is the lamp of guidance which leadeth the way, and is the bestower of understanding.[1]

—Bahá'u'lláh

In this Cause consultation is of vital importance, but spiritual conference and not the mere voicing of personal views is intended. In France I was present at a session of the senate, but the experience was not impressive. Parliamentary procedure should have for its object the attainment of the light of truth upon questions presented and not furnish a battleground for opposition and self-opinion. Antagonism and contradiction are unfortunate and always destructive to truth. In the parliamentary meeting mentioned, altercation and useless quibbling were frequent; the result, mostly confusion and turmoil; even in one instance a physical encounter took place between two members. It was not consultation but comedy.[2]

—'Abdu'l-Bahá

Consultation must have for its object the investigation of truth.[3]

—'Abdu'l-Bahá

No sensible decision can be made any longer without taking into account not only the world as it is, but the world as it will be.[4]

—Isaac Asimov

New Era, New Decisions

In 1991, the year when Leningrad was again renamed as St. Petersburg, I was invited to give a plenary presentation and hold a training workshop on the theme of consultation for all the participants at an international conference on modern trends in education. In preparation, I reviewed the conceptual foundations of the major decision-making and conflict resolution practices, including those of the Bahá'í method of consultation. This exercise proved most rewarding. As I delved into the reasons why we human beings—even with all our intellectual capacities, rational faculties, wealth of experience, and abundance of evidence—have so much difficulty making decisions that are positive both for ourselves and for all others concerned, I realized that the fundamental challenge was with regard to our worldviews. Stated differently, the fundamental reason that human decisions are so often fraught with conflict and our conflict resolution efforts usually produce new conflicts lies in the fact that we consider conflict as a necessary and unavoidable aspect of human life. However, my research pointed to a diametrically opposite conclusion, namely, that unity, not conflict, is the primary law of life and its operating principle. Thereafter, my son Roshan and I together developed Conflict-Free Conflict Resolution, the concept of unity-based and conflict-free decision-making and conflict resolution that has been referred to earlier (chapters four and six) and will be further considered here.[5] This chapter is based on my original presentation in St. Petersburg and our subsequent work. The first part of the chapter is a general discussion of decision-making, followed by a review of the concepts, processes, and skills of Bahá'í consultation as a unity-based decision-making and conflict-resolution concept and practice.

Decision-Making: Processes and Components

Decision-making is a complex human activity, and conflict resolution is one form, albeit an extremely important form, of decision-making. We make decisions by ourselves (solitary decision-making) or in interaction with others (group decision-making). Solitary decision-making is the outcome of the interface among the main human capacities of knowledge, love, and will. When we are faced with a dilemma and must make a decision, we inevitably use the powers of our mind. We begin to think about the issue before us; we examine our feelings about it; we consider the moral and ethical principles that we hold to be important; and we reflect on the intensity of our motivation to deal with the issue at hand. In this process, by using our powers to know, love, and will, we eventually reach a decision and embark on a plan of action. This is a complex process. Not infrequently, we experience an inner conflict among our thoughts, feelings, and desires, and we find it very difficult to make a decision, especially if our thoughts and feelings go contrary to our moral and ethical principles. Therefore, to make a good decision we need to create a state of *inner unity.*

The same dynamics are operational in the course of group decision-making and conflict resolution activities. Here again, an interface between the powers of the mind—to know, love, and will—takes place. However, group decision-making is a more complex and differentiated process because the individuals involved have their own unique and often diverse thoughts, feelings, objectives, and ethical standards and principles. These diverse issues and processes confront the decision-making group with many layers of interests, objectives, and inclinations, making the task of reaching a unified decision quite complex. Therefore, the immediate task of a decision-making group is to create a state of *interpersonal* and *group unity.*

The scope of group decision-making is immense. Such human activities as conflict resolution, negotiation, mediation, compromise, litigation, war, and peace are all variations and outcomes of decisions made by human beings. As stated, decision-making and conflict resolution depend on our powers of knowledge, love, and will along with our moral and ethical principles that together determine the nature and quality of any and all human decisions. As these powers mature, so too do our decision-making and problem-solving abilities. This point becomes clearer when we review the developmental stages of decision-making and conflict resolution. However, we first need to discuss the main components of a decision: *perspective, principle,* and *purpose.*

Perspective

Every decision is made from a particular *perspective* based on our worldview and our understanding of the meaning and purpose of life. Our individual perspectives on life are often founded on certain principles shared by a community of people. However, each individual tends to relate to these principles in a unique manner. In addition, because sufficient communication does not usually take place between people, not infrequently, under similar circumstances, different individuals and groups make remarkably different decisions about the same issues.

A few examples help to clarify this point. Two young couples living in the same apartment building are each expecting the birth of their second child. The day after normal uncomplicated deliveries, one husband asks his wife for forgiveness and goes back to work because of job pressures. The other husband, who has a similar job with a similar company and is under similar pressures, asks for a leave of absence and stays with his family. Here, the circumstances are alike, but the perspectives on the relative importance of employment and family are quite different. Another example: three companies have similar financial problems and must cut costs. One company decides to lay off some employees. Another company consults with their employees, and together they reach an equitable and realistic solution to the company's financial problems. The third company chooses to increase pressure on their employees by asking them to increase productivity. The circumstances are basically the same for all three companies, but their respective perspectives on both profits and the employee–employer relationship differ dramatically. Yet, a third example: a now militarily more powerful nation decides to attack another country with which the nation had previously signed a peace treaty when it was in a weaker condition. In this example, the aggressive nation makes two completely opposite decisions: first peace, when it was in a weaker military condition, then war, after it became militarily more powerful. Neither the perspective on power of the leaders of this nation nor its role in international affairs altered. The two opposite decisions were made according to the principle of a particular perspective—that *might is right*. However, their perspective on war and peace changed according to their changing status regarding power and might.

PRINCIPLES

The second component of a decision refers to those *principles* according to which perspectives are formed and decisions are made. Principles are moral and ethical in nature and are usually shared by a group or a community of people. Until the advent of the modern era, the main source of principles that shaped people's perspectives on life and "right and wrong" was religion. However, religion has been losing much of its authority in many parts of the world; consequently, in the contemporary world we witness profound confusion in this respect. Many people insist on invoking personal principles, which they modify as they deem necessary. Others argue that the main principles governing life are those of self-preservation, self-gratification, and self-promotion. Still others cling to limited outmoded perspectives such as supremacy of one's race, gender, nationality, or creed. It is partly due to this confusing state that most models of conflict resolution are based on the principle that *conflict is unavoidable.*

In today's world, *principles* are invoked by individuals, organizations, or nations to justify their worldviews—their *perspectives* on themselves and others, on life and its purpose, and on the nature and purpose of human relationships. As such, the "*principle*" component of a decision refers to that essential truth upon which other truths are based. Here, we are dealing with a decision's moral and ethical components. A decision, therefore, cannot be made solely on the basis of what we alone consider to be of primary importance, i.e., our personal preferences and wishes. A decision must also have moral legitimacy and universal applicability. In other words, our decisions have to be made not only because we agree with them but also because they are right. Therefore, in all decision-making and conflict resolution activities there is a need for a set of universal principles that, on the one hand, takes into consideration the enormously important fact of the diversity of people and, on the other hand, allows for a range of creative solutions to various human conflicts while safeguarding the fundamental unity among all stakeholders, both direct and indirect. In the three examples above, we are dealing not only with differing perspectives but also with contrasting principles. Clearly, many of the decisions by individuals, companies, institutions, or nations in the above examples do not take into consideration those universal principles that will safeguard the rights of all affected, directly or indirectly, by these decisions.

Purpose

Finally, there is the third component of a decision: its *purpose*. The purpose of a decision is intertwined with its perspective and principle. The purpose refers to the end-result that we desire to obtain and that we constantly keep in mind when engaged in a decision-making process. The purpose component of a decision, however, is highly personal and is usually not shared with others. This is particularly the case if the personal and private purpose(s) of those engaged in a given deliberation are at variance with both the perspective(s) and the underlying principle(s) that have been openly expressed by that person or by others involved in the process. In other words, people who are engaged in decision-making and conflict resolution quite frequently have hidden agendas that they try to hide behind more acceptable perspectives based on lofty principles they articulate but do not truly espouse. This fundamental discordance among the perspective, principle, and purpose components of most conflict resolution and decision-making activities leads many to conclude that conflict is unavoidable. The implications of this conclusion, which I believe is erroneous, are monumental. As we will see, the unity-based decision-making and conflict resolution approaches clearly show that human conflicts are primarily expressions of certain stages of our development. In other words, as we enter the era of our collective adulthood with a more informed and universal consciousness and worldview, we will notice a dramatic, substantive decrease both in the frequency and intensity of human conflicts.

In the three examples cited above, the ultimate purpose of the individuals involved dramatically affects their decisions. For example, the main purpose of the husband who chooses to return to work the day after his child's birth may not be the pressure of work, but rather his unwillingness to be troubled by the demands of a newly born child and a wife who clearly needs help. However, the same person may change his mind if his wife became very angry and created considerable discomfort for him. For this man, the overriding purpose of his decisions may be personal comfort, and whatever perspectives and principles he offers are all to satisfy this underlying personal agenda. His actions, therefore, are insincere, opportunistic, devoid of integrity, and in the long run do more harm to him than good. The same dynamics apply to the other examples discussed above.

DEVELOPMENTAL STAGES OF DECISION-MAKING

The human decision-making faculty is primarily a conscious, deliberate process shaped by the nature of our worldview and the specific circumstances of each situation. Because worldviews are subject to change and development, so too are our decision-making practices. In other words, our decisions reflect different stages of our individual and group development. Within this framework we can identify four types of decision-making that tend to roughly correspond with the universally recognized stages of infancy/early childhood, late childhood, adolescence, and adulthood (maturity), each with its unique mindset and worldview. These designations are chosen because they are easily identifiable and descriptively all-inclusive. This ease of recognition is due to the fact that we all experience these stages in our own individual and family life and also observe them in our places of work, communities, and decision-making institutions. These stages are all-inclusive because they encompass all aspects of the life of the individual or group in a given situation. They are also universal because they depict the main characteristics of all different human societies in their ongoing march of development and progress.

Therefore, when we say that an individual, institution, or a nation, or by that matter the whole world, is functioning at the third level, which developmentally corresponds with the adolescent stage, the main qualities and characteristics of the third stage—the sense of self and the world; the nature of thoughts, feelings, and behavior; and the perspectives on moral and ethical principles; in short every aspect of the consciousness and the worldview of the entity under consideration—are automatically included. There is, however, a danger in choosing commonly used terminologies because they are open to oversimplification, misunderstanding, and judgmental abuse. Extreme care must be taken not to place a value judgment on the identification of various stages of development. Each stage of development is appropriate and essential for the wholesome growth of peoples and societies. However, when the process of human growth stagnates because of lack of opportunity, the nature of education we receive, unforeseen calamities, unjust circumstances, etc., an unhealthy, unnatural state develops, primarily marked by a high level of conflict, both individually and collectively. For purposes of clarity, I have incorporated the hierarchy of decision-making practices and their correspondence with our individual and collective stages of development in Table 9.1.

LEVEL I

The nature and dynamics of decision-making and conflict resolution at this level correspond with the nature of consciousness and worldview as observed in the earliest stages of individual and social development. In this stage the organism (individual, institution, or society) has not yet made a clear distinction between itself and the world. In fact, the individual and the group view themselves to *be* the world, and their

Decision-Making	Perspective (Worldview)	Principles (Operating)	Purpose (Ultimate)	Stage of Development	Nature of Conflict Resolution
Level 1	World is Me	Self-Interest	Self-Preservation (Instinctual)	Infancy / Early Childhood	Self-centered (S Mode)
Level 2	World is Dangerous	Might is Right (Domination)	Self/Group Preservation (Instinctual & Intentional)	Late Childhood	Authoritarian (A Mode)
Level 3	World is a Jungle	Survival of the Fittest	To Win	Adolescence	Power-Struggle (P Mode)
Level 4	World is One	Truth & Justice	Unity & Peace	Adulthood	Consultative (C Mode)

Table 9.1. A developmental model of conflict resolution (Modified from a version by Danesh and Danesh).[6]

perspectives are very vague and totally self-centered. Likewise, the *operating principles* in such early stages of development are biologically based and autonomic. They are not yet formulated intellectually and have the quality of total self-absorption. A young child, a group in its first stage of development, and humanity in its early phases of biological evolution are all in a condition of profound vulnerability, and, therefore, of necessity they function according to the principles of self-preservation and self-interest. The primary *purpose* at this level of functioning is to safeguard the very survival of the organism, be it an infant, an institution in its early stages of development, a newly formed clan, or a nation not yet evolved beyond its early formative years, or the human species as a whole during its early phase of evolution. At this level the organism functions according to the *principles* based on the basic instincts of self-preservation with survival as its ultimate *purpose.*

Level 2

Decision-making and conflict resolution at this level are characterized by our awareness that we are dependent on others and that the world is an unsafe and unequal arena of power. The worldview of the organism—individual, group, or collective—functioning at this level is based on the *perspective* that the world is a dangerous place and that because of the unequal distribution of power among various members of the group, the rules of domination and submission are operative. Therefore, the *operating principle* here is that power is the most precious commodity in human relationships. Because of these dynamics, the authoritarian modes of decision-making and conflict resolution are common at this level. Here the *ultimate purpose* of those involved in the decision-making and conflict resolution is to create a state of "guaranteed security." The elusive goal of guaranteed security renders this stage very dangerous because, on the one hand, it gives an apparent (but not real) justification for the abuse of power by authoritarian and tyrannical leaders, and, on the other hand, it causes hopeless and passive resignation or unquestioned submission on the part of the masses.

Level 3

At this level, which corresponds with the adolescent stage, decisions are made according to the *principles* of the survival of the fittest and in the context of the *perspective* that the world is a jungle and that power struggle and competition are not only unavoidable but also desirable and necessary for the ultimate *purpose* of winning and acquiring either power or pleasure, ideally both. Adolescent consciousness revolves around issues of individuality, uniqueness, and identity. Therefore, individuals and societies functioning according to the mindset of this stage are highly individualistic, self-centered, and concerned with establishing a unique identity for themselves and being "winners" in all their relationships. Levels 2 and 3 together correspond with the psychosocial phase of human individual and social evolution, with power-seeking and power-struggle as their main characteristics.

LEVEL 4

Decision-making and conflict resolution practices of level 4 belong to the stage of humanity's coming of age and our collective functioning according to the *principles* of truth, justice, and unity. At this level, the group or individual's *perspective* is that the world is one and that unity in diversity is the ultimate state towards which the world now is driven. The *operating principles* of level 4 revolve around the issues of truth and justice and how can we search for the best solutions to the challenges before us, while maintaining our fundamental unity and also achieving our *ultimate purpose* of creating a state of peace. These principles and perspectives are not yet universally accepted, and much controversy and misunderstanding surround them. However, the processes of development and maturation are essential for both maintenance and continuation of life and inevitably take place in all living entities, be they individual human beings, social institutions, or societies and nations. Level 4 corresponds with the spiritual phase of human evolution and gives appropriate attention to the biological, psychological, social, as well as ethical aspects of decision-making and conflict resolution.

From the preceding discussion it should be clear that in our world today the first three methods of decision-making and conflict resolution are all present. However, the predominant methods belong to levels 2 and 3, the authoritarian and power-struggle/adversarial modes respectively. These methods of decision-making and conflict resolution are, to an unhealthy degree, highly individualistic, aggressive, power-based, and focused on winning and domination. They tend to use force in pursuit of their objectives, even though history clearly shows that "the harvest of force is turmoil and the ruin of the social order."[7] The Authoritarian (A Mode) and Power-Struggle (P Mode) methods of decision-making and conflict resolution ignore other fundamental qualities of human nature, such as our enormous capacity for love, cooperation, other-directedness, and our ongoing quest for meaning, for doing that which is right, and our ever-present need for togetherness and unity.

It is interesting to note that the first set of qualities (individualism, aggression, power-seeking, winning, and domination) is frequently described as masculine and the second set (love, cooperation, other-directedness, and quest for togetherness and unity) as feminine in character. This demarcation along gender lines should not come as a surprise. Historically, over the long period of human evolution, we observe a clear differentiation between the areas of decision-making assigned to men and women. Men generally took upon themselves, and at times were assigned, the task of making decisions that often involved conflict. Such tasks as securing the safety of oneself and others, obtaining food, and gaining control and maintaining order in a given territory (family, clan, tribe, city, nation, the world) are all tasks with major potential for conflict and power-struggle. This potential for conflict is at its maximum during the first three stages of our individual and collective growth and development when self-interest, power, and force play primary roles in determining the nature of human relationships. Consequently, in the course of history the decision makers and leaders of human societies have relied heavily on the use of force and have attempted to resolve conflicts according to the authoritarian (A Mode) and power-struggle (P Mode) methods of decision-making in pursuit of their self-centered (S Mode) interests.

While until now men have, and largely still are, engaged in conflict-ridden modes of decision making, women in most societies have historically engaged in making decisions on how to care for and guide the next generation; how to bring comfort and solace to the hungry, the sick, and the needy; and how to bring a certain degree of comfort and beauty to an otherwise often uncomfortable and ugly life. Consequently, women have developed unique decision-making and conflict resolution abilities, which, instead of primarily relying on power, competition, and force, use the qualities of compassion, cooperation, and reconciliation. In their monumental tasks as mothers, teachers, and caregivers, throughout history and in all cultures, women have learned to make decisions that are less prone to create conflict. However, because the world has been and still is predominantly power-oriented, the value of women's contributions to our decision-making and conflict resolution practices is not justly or adequately appreciated and promoted.

As we enter our collective age of adulthood and embark upon a phase of our collective evolution when spiritual matters assume primary importance, we are beginning to realize that authoritarian and power-struggle types of decision-making and conflict resolution have to be abandoned. What will replace them is a totally new approach to these issues. Already, a number of insightful individuals have put forward new approaches for conflict resolution that are clearly cognizant of the shortcomings of the past approaches. These new approaches are usually known under general umbrella of Alternative Dispute Resolution (ADR) and include such practices as arbitration, negotiation, and mediation.[8] As these approaches are well known and widely practiced, I will not attempt to discuss them here. Rather, I will present Consultation (C Mode) as a body of theory and practice for decision-making and conflict resolution, which, I posit, is most in accord with the characteristics and needs of humanity in its age of adulthood and maturity.

However, before we embark on a presentation of consultation, a word about the most elemental level of decision-making—Self-Centered (S Mode) method of conflict-resolution and decision-making—is in order. Because of its selfish approach to resolving conflicts, S Mode is usually either avoided or else, when it is employed, much effort is made by the decision-makers to conceal it behind convoluted explanations. However, not infrequently, we encounter those who proclaim with pride that they are selfish and are proud of it. Therefore, it is not surprising that while the S Mode of conflict resolution is relatively common, thoughtful people everywhere are increasingly appreciating the perils inherent in this approach to resolution of conflicts.

GROUP DYNAMICS OF DECISION-MAKING

Group dynamics of decision-making are complex, and those that revolve around issues of leadership, power-struggle, suggestibility, and identity merit special attention. The nature of group dynamics is closely related to the nature of worldview, the main objectives, and the norms and value systems of the group. In other words the *perspective, principle,* and *purpose* of the group and its members will determine, to a very significant degree, the nature of the group dynamics.

In the authoritarian framework (A Mode), group members almost immediately look for a leader. In these groups, not infrequently, a leader is already appointed or nominated and then summarily ratified by the group. Furthermore, often the aims and the purposes of the group have also been predetermined, and group members are prepared and/or expected to approve them with little or no objection. These dynamics are further accentuated by the fact that in these types of groups the individual members tend to regress and to behave more like children or adolescents. Consequently, the group members become more suggestible, prone to manipulation, and fearful of self-expression. Many devastating and startling examples of authoritarian group dynamics are found in history, the most notorious of recent examples being the behavior of the masses of people in the 20th century toward charismatic political and religious leaders in all parts of the globe. Clearly, in these types of groups the members act like children, and the leader determines the nature and focus of the group decision-making process.

However, in non-authoritarian settings where the decision-making group is not restricted and its operation is not fixed by predetermined objectives, two distinctive processes are observable. If the group's purpose is focused on an individual or a specific group accomplishment to the exclusion of other individuals and groups, then a fierce struggle for power and control ensues. The rivalry for leadership becomes intense, and frequently the group is divided into competing "interest subgroups" and "power blocks." If the competition is very strong, the group may even self-destruct and dissolve. Otherwise, a leader with the support of the majority eventually emerges. However, those in the minority continue their own agenda, and the decision-making (and conflict-resolution) process becomes the arena of power struggle, factionalism, and conflict. Such groups tend to waste an enormous percentage of their resources on these rivalries and conflicts, and consequently accomplish relatively little.

Another version of this process occurs when one group sets itself up in competition with another group. Here, the arena of power-struggle and aggressive pursuit of self-interests has been broadened from a focus on competing individuals to a focus on competing groups. In this scenario, although the competing groups may be internally somewhat harmonious, nevertheless, the overall outcome and dynamics are similarly wasteful and uncreative. These group dynamics clearly correspond to the adolescent phase of our collective growth and decision-making (P Mode)—hence their ubiquitous prevalence in our world today. The multiparty adversarial political democracies are examples of this type of group process.

However, as humanity comes of age, a new type of group dynamics begins to evolve. Therefore, it should not be surprising that we do not yet fully understand their dynamics or trust their effectiveness or even consider them desirable. As stated before, central to these dynamics are issues of unity, truth, justice, and service. However, in our world today there is considerable fear of unity, lest it result in uniformity/conformity. Likewise, there is a fear that cooperation will remove the tension of conflict considered necessary for creativity and progress. There is also concern that the process of search for truth may result in the negation of the principles of unfettered freedom of expression and conviction. There are still other objections such as the deeply rooted pseudoscientific view that greed, aggression, selfishness, power-seeking, and unrestrained pursuit of liberties and pleasures are true states of human nature in its more evolved expressions. Based on these perspectives it is argued that any attempt to alter these conditions and replace them with their opposites—generosity, compassion, universality, cooperation, and self-discipline—is psychologically unhealthy and realistically impractical.

The reasons for holding these sentiments are understandable. They are, on the one hand, in accordance with the present views of the majority of materialistically oriented scientists and the general public, and on the other hand, in harmony with our present level of collective maturity—adolescence. These views are also self-serving. They justify all our selfish and divisive acts. They remove any true sense of responsibility and guilt for the terrible consequences of our destructive ways of life. They lighten the urgency of the need for us to mature. After all, the process of maturation is painful and arduous. It demands discipline, postponement of gratification, and sacrifice of our self-centered pursuits. However, notwithstanding all the vested interest in these views on human nature, they are false. Two distinct but interrelated processes assist us to put aside our misgivings about our next stage of development and begin to approach the administration of our personal and collective affairs along parameters of maturity. They are (1) the imperatives of growth inherent in every living organism and society, and (2) the increasing emergence of insights and conclusions showing that peacefulness and cooperation are indeed true characteristics of human nature, particularly in its period of maturity.[9]

Societies and institutions formed on the principles of truth, unity, service, and justice would eliminate the evils of authoritarianism and excesses of power struggle, aggression, competition, and pernicious individualism common in our world today. In these new societies and institutions, the unique capacities and contributions of each person are fully acknowledged, appreciated, integrated, and synthesized into a new creative whole that is greater than the sum of its constituent parts. This new creative wholeness will produce results we can only partly anticipate at this early stage of its development. In my considered view, consultation (C Mode)[10] will not just be the main approach to decision-making and conflict resolution in these more evolved group entities; the use of consultation will also facilitate the process of development and maturation of these same entities.

Thus far, I have attempted to demonstrate that human activities of decision-making and conflict resolution throughout the ages have gone through an evolutionary process. Within the framework of biological, psychological, social, and spiritual phases of human evolution and individual developmental stages of infancy, childhood, adolescence, and adulthood, four models of decision-making and conflict resolution were identified: Self-Centered Model (S Mode), Authoritarian Model (A Mode), Power-Struggle/Adversarial Model (P Mode), and the Consultative/Integrative Model (C Mode). I also described the individual and group dynamics operant in each of these models. Another issue that merits attention in any group decision-making process is with regard to the dynamics of human communication.

COMMUNICATION AND DECISION-MAKING

Not infrequently, human communications are burdened with conflict, disunity, hurt, and injustice. On many occasions people engaged in relationships find, to their dismay, that the quality of their communication deteriorates despite their considerable desire and effort to facilitate its process and improve its level of excellence. Likewise, many people, despite their best efforts, find it very difficult to master the art of group consultation and to solve problems in a positive, meaningful manner. In fact, many times those engaged in these processes may say or do something that goes squarely against their own best judgment and intentions. There are many reasons and explanations for this phenomenon. However, under all circumstances, the nature and quality of human communications reflect both the degree of insight (self-knowledge) and the nature of the underlying objectives of those engaged in the process. Therefore, it will be useful to review the issue of human communications along the same developmental model as employed in this book.

Viewed from a developmental perspective, we can identify four types of communications: playful, industrious, competitive, and creative. These four types of communication roughly correspond to the developmental stages of infancy and early childhood, late childhood, adolescence, and adulthood. At any given time, all four types of communication can be found among the adult population of any given society, but the predominant mode of communication in that same society typically corresponds with its level of collective growth. Thus a society in its phase of collective adolescence will primarily communicate in a highly competitive, individualistic, adversarial, and erratic manner. However, because human conditions are flexible, malleable, and changing, in the same group we also observe episodes of communication in the other three modes. Also, it should be noted that all four types of communication have a legitimate and valuable place within group decision-making. A brief elaboration will make this point clearer.

Playful communication is based on the fantasies, hopes, and aspirations of those involved. It allows the participants to project themselves into the future, to use the power of their imagination, and to dream of conditions in which ideal communication could take place and problems could be solved as though by magic. This type of communication, also called "brainstorming," is very helpful, especially during the beginning stages of any consultative process. It forms the basis for more complex and specific discussion later on during consultation. It is, therefore, useful to include in our consultative process a period in which participants are able to express their hopes, aspirations, and fantasies without fear of being judged unrealistic, superficial, utopian, or silly.

The second type of communication is focused on the quality of being *industrious*. We observe this kind of communication among individuals who are engaged in concrete specific tasks such as building a home, creating a new company, or rebuilding a society following a disaster or revolution. Participants in these processes are willing to work hard, and their main form of communication is in the context of involvement in the same shared enterprise. Here, the participants know more about one another's skills and capacities, rather than their thoughts and feelings. This type of communication is particularly useful when in the course of the consultative process the members are engaged in fact-finding and research on the issue(s) before them. Here, the experience, expertise, and knowledge of each person become highly valuable.

The third type of communication has *competition* as its main quality and takes place in the context of the interface of the thoughts, sentiments, and wills of the participants. Every human being has unique thoughts and feelings, which he/she wishes to communicate to others. The manner in which this communication takes place determines the nature of the communication. Thus, when several willful individuals in the consultative process begin to share their views with force and authority, not infrequently, a situation of comparison and competition develops. This happens because ideas have to be compared and weighed against other ideas and evaluated in light of the facts of the situation and the respective *perspectives* of all members of the group. Inevitably, some ideas will be rejected, others will require modification, and still others will be received with enthusiasm and approval. These conditions put high demands on our sense of *who* we are and *how* we wish to be perceived. Naturally, we all want to have the best ideas and be perceived as being very intelligent, capable, insightful, etc., by others. Therefore, it should not be surprising if a certain degree of comparison, competition, and clash of ideas take place in the course of even the most refined group decision-making deliberations. However, as we will see later, Bahá'í consultation, by virtue of introducing to the decision-making process the principles and practices of unity-based modes of communication, helps the participants elevate their deliberations to a much higher level of operation. Thus, the same types of communication, which in other modes of decision-making and conflict resolution become obstacles to the process, in consultation become vehicles through which the decision-making process is both enriched and facilitated.

The fourth type of communication is *creative* and corresponds with a yet higher degree of maturity akin to what we observe in our more refined types of personal and group development. Maturity calls for both self-assurance and selflessness. In a mature stage, information and knowledge are used with insight and wisdom. The capacity for patience, perseverance, and contemplation is considerable. Humility and genuine respect and regard for others are ever present, as is the willingness to consider views of others with the same degree of attention and care as one's own views. Mature communication, by virtue of its truthfulness, inclusiveness, and universality is both unifying and edifying in its effects. This is obviously the acme of human communications and cannot easily be mastered by all the participants in decision-making or even be employed by the same person under all circumstances.

With this review of the components of a 'decision' and different levels of the 'decision-making' process in mind, I will now attempt to describe some of the main elements of Bahá'í consultation within this framework. The main hypothesis here is that as human individuals and societies go through different stages of development, they experience different types of challenges and conflicts and approach the tasks of decision-making and conflict resolution in qualitatively distinctive manners. It will be shown that our decision-making and conflict resolution practices correspond with our individual and collective stages of our worldview development: The higher the level of human development, the lesser the degree of conflict and its destructive consequences. Because humanity is now approaching its collective stage of adulthood, it needs totally new perspectives and approaches to its interpersonal, intergroup, international, and global deliberations. In my considered view, Bahá'í consultation offers a particularly potent and effective tool for human decision-making that is commensurate with the needs and opportunities of humanity at this monumental time of change and transformation.

BAHÁ'Í CONSULTATION
FROM CONFLICT AND COMPROMISE TO UNITY AND JUSTICE

Consultation as a method of decision-making and conflict resolution was introduced in the writings of the Bahá'í Faith in the latter part of the nineteenth century. As a contemporary world religion, the Bahá'í Faith is particularly concerned about the manner in which human society is organized and governed. From a Bahá'í perspective, humanity is now poised to move to its next phase of collective maturity, characterized by a global civilization of peace based on the principles of equality, justice, and unity in the context of diversity. To achieve these challenging objectives requires two simultaneous developments. As individuals, we need to develop perspectives, qualities, and abilities commensurate with the coming of age of humanity and era of peace. Simultaneously, we have to create social, academic, religious, and governmental institutions capable of functioning within the parameters of a civilization of peace based on the principles of truth and truthfulness, equality and justice, unity and diversity, and compassion and service. Among the most important tools to achieve these objectives is *consultation*.

Consultation has been practiced in Bahá'í communities around the globe as early as the beginning decades of the twentieth century.[11] Naturally, this practice started at a rather basic level, and even today, after more than a century of implementation of consultation by Bahá'í individuals and institutions in all parts of the world and by people in all walks of life, it is evident that there is still much to be learned about this seemingly simple but, in fact, extremely complex and sophisticated approach to decision-making, conflict resolution, and community-building aimed at creating a civilization of peace.

Bahá'í consultation is a unity-based method of human deliberation. Its primary goals are to find equitable, just, and constructive solutions to the question and conflict at hand, while maintaining the unity of all individuals and/or groups who, directly or indirectly, are involved in and affected by the decision. As such, consultation is a process of collective search for truth within the framework of unity, with scrupulous attention to the administration of justice and the observance of its principles in an atmosphere of equality, compassion, purity of intent, and freedom from prejudice. Bahá'í consultation is the process of the application of spiritual principles to the all-important tasks of human deliberations—decision-making, conflict resolution, community-building, and peace creation. The spiritual principles of love and unity, truth and truthfulness, and service and justice are the essential requisites for consultation. In their absence, conflict and dissension, deceit and intrigue, and self-interest and injustice will characterize the decision-making process, and attempts at resolution of differences result in the introduction of new and usually more destructive conflicts. Thus a vicious cycle is created, and the spiraling movement toward the destructive outcome of conflict—violence—is accelerated.

CONCEPTUAL FRAMEWORK OF CONSULTATION

Bahá'í consultation, as an established conceptual and practical approach to conflict resolution, is almost totally unknown in the current literature of this field. However, as will be seen, Bahá'í consultation, both with regard to its conceptual foundations and practical application, is particularly suited to the contemporary challenges of an emerging global society. The strength of the concept of consultation lies in its comprehensive framework, integrative approach, and developmental relevance. Consultation is a very effective vehicle for access to justice in conditions of unity and truth seeking. Truth by its very nature is both simple and elegant, and our access to it is relative, not absolute. No one individual or group could, in reality, claim to understand the whole truth about anything. Our knowledge of truth is always partial. The potency of the consultative process is due to fact that it encourages and assists the participants to search together for the facts, to establish the "truth" of the situation to the best of their collective abilities, and to find just solutions to the issues before them. The decisions reached through the consultative process must be at once logical, ethical, educational, and practical.

The following statements from the Bahá'í Writings about consultation address some of the main issues discussed above. The first two statements, by Bahá'u'lláh, describe the significance of consultation, its essential functions, and its relationship with some other fundamental aspects of human maturation processes and relationships:

> ...no man can attain his true station except through his justice. No power can exist except through unity. No welfare and no well-being can be attained except through consultation.

> Consultation bestoweth great awareness and transmuteth conjecture into certitude. It is a shining light which, in the dark world, leadeth the way and guideth. For everything there is and will continue to

be a station of perfection and maturity. The maturity of the gift of understanding is made manifest through consultation.[12]

The following four statements from the writings of 'Abdu'l-Bahá describe the qualities required by those engaged in the consultation, as well as the dynamics of the consultative process itself:

The prime requisites for them that take counsel together are purity of motive, radiance of spirit, detachment from all else save God,... humility and lowliness...patience and long suffering in difficulties and servitude.

The members thereof must take counsel together in such wise that no occasion for ill-feeling or discord may arise. This can be attained when every member expresseth with absolute freedom his own opinion and setteth forth his argument. Should any one oppose, he must on no account feel hurt for not until matters are fully discussed can the right way be revealed. The shining spark of truth cometh forth only after the clash of differing opinions. If after discussion, a decision be carried unanimously well and good; but if,...differences of opinion arise, a majority of voice must prevail.

The first condition is love and harmony amongst the members of the assembly (the consultative body). They must be wholly free from estrangement....They must in every matter search out the truth and not insist upon their opinions, for stubbornness and persistence in one's views will lead ultimately to discord and wrangling and the truth will remain hidden. The honoured members must with all freedom express their own thoughts, and it is in no wise permissible for one to belittle the thought of another....

Consultation must have for its object the investigation of truth...true consultation is a spiritual conference in the attitude and atmosphere of love....Members must love each other in the spirit of fellowship in order that good results may be forthcoming. Love and fellowship are the foundation.[13]

The above statements make it clear that the most demanding aspect of consultation is with respect to our worldviews, attitudes, and perspectives, and the necessity of making sure that they are in harmony with those called for by consultation.[14] Consultation is only possible in the context of a universal worldview, a selfless attitude, and a unity-based perspective. It demands freedom from estrangement and disunity, and requires love and fellowship in the midst of differences of views, expectations, and patterns of behavior. Consultation invites us not to take offence and not to offend when we are opposed. It demands that individuals—men and women, young and old, rich and poor, highly educated and those less so, and those in the position of authority and those who are not—participate in all forms of decision-making and conflict resolution on an equal basis. It calls on those engaged in consultation to replace reliance on power and competition with a new set of principles and approaches commensurate with the coming of age of humanity. Among these are the ability to endow the decision-making body with a strength based on truth, unity, and cooperation in the context of diversity of views and differences of approach. These and other qualities and conditions of consultation all require emotional maturity and spiritual enlightenment. They demand that we abandon the modes of behavior characteristic of our collective childhood and adolescence. Herein lies the main reason for the challenging nature of the seemingly simple art of consultation.

The main objective of consultation is to reach just decisions, based on verified facts—truths—in the context of unity. Unity, truth, and justice are the three pillars of consultation. Truth is one and unity is oneness. As such, truth and unity are totally interrelated. One is not achieved without the other. Furthermore, unity and truth are not accomplished unless the participants in the consultative process treat each other with complete equality and respect, and together endeavor to make just decisions that will safeguard the human rights of all affected by those decisions, either directly or indirectly. The issue of just decisions is extremely important because justice is a prerequisite of unity. Consultation offers a new paradigm that corresponds with the coming of age of humanity. This new paradigm affirms that human nature, once nurtured and directed by the civilizing forces of science and religion, can be peaceful not aggressive, generous not greedy, cooperative not competitive, loving not uncaring, creative not destructive, and universal not self-centered. What in the past has been, and still is, viewed as unalterable human nature, when considered from the perspectives of this new paradigm, is understood to be as yet another stage in the process of humanity's on-going development.

The creative expressions of human nature, of course, are evident in not only the life of the individual but also the society through creation of civilization. As we enter this new era in human evolution, a new order, world-embracing in its scope, equitable and just in its approach, and unifying and peaceful in its effects, is gradually but surely emerging. Consultation is an indispensable component of this specific vision of the new world order. Among other fundamental components of this new world order are new perspectives on the issues of power, authority, democracy, and global politics, formulated and practiced in the framework of freedom, justice, unity, and peace. Consultation is the essential mode of decision-making and conflict resolution in these processes.

Requisites of Consultation

Consultation employs the human capacities to know, love, and will in order to search for truth, to create ever higher levels of unity, and to reach just decisions in the spirit of service. In the consultative process, all participants must have equal rights and opportunities so that they can together reach a final decision in the context of unity and cooperate in its implementation. These requisites indicate that consultation is most effective in the context of a worldview corresponding to the age of maturity of humanity and the era of spiritualization of human life. Such a worldview affirms the fundamental nobility of human nature and the purposefulness of human life. It empowers those holding this worldview to replace the inordinate quest for power and pleasure—the main objectives of life during earlier stages of our development—with striving to grow in a wholesome and healthy manner: physically, emotionally, intellectually, and spiritually. A mature worldview reconciles such seemingly irreconcilable realities as personal interest and group interest, unity and diversity, freedom and discipline, and science and religion. It also challenges us to understand and use power and authority in a new light. (See chapter eight.)

In authoritarian and totalitarian systems, usually one person or a group of individuals assumes both power and authority. In these systems decisions are made under duress, and force is always used to achieve the desired objectives. The adversarial democratic systems create a legitimated arena of power-struggle and power-seeking. Authority is enshrined in the rule of law, the democratic practices of election, and governance by majority decree. In these systems, authority and power are more differentiated and distributed, and necessary checks and balances are created to ensure that the leaders do not abuse their power and authority. However, because of the inordinate and unhealthy power-struggle and individualism inherent in these systems, quite frequently the boundaries between power and authority are obscured, and considerable liberties, not infrequently unlawful, are taken by those in positions of leadership and authority. Decision-making in adversarial systems operates according to the practices of winning and losing, often creating a considerable degree of conflict and disparity among the population.

Consultation, by its dependence on the principles of truth, unity, and justice, does not allow this kind of abuse of power and authority. Instead, consultation brings people together and gives them both the responsibility and empowerment to find the best solution(s) to the issues before them. In other words, in the consultative process the authority to decide belongs to the consultative group, not to any individual within or outside the group. The consultative group's authority remains legitimate only as long as it makes decisions that are within the framework of the overriding principles of truth, unity, and justice. In the Bahá'í model of governance, the democratically elected institutions of the Bahá'í Faith have the authority to make decisions. However, the power to implement these decisions lies with the individual community members. Both the institutions and their constituents are bound by the same principles and work together through the instrumentality of consultation regularly, at least nineteen times a year.[15]

INDIVIDUAL AND GROUP DYNAMICS IN CONSULTATION

Consultation places considerable demands on those engaged in the process, calling as it does for a high degree of emotional, intellectual, ethical, and spiritual maturity. The participants in the consultative process are required to approach consultation like true scientists. They must put aside all preconceived notions. They must free themselves from their personal preferences and prejudices. They must search for truth rather than insist on their own ideas. They must accept the outcome even if it seems contrary to their own ideas and interests. They must be humble, pure of heart, dispassionate, respectful, patient with the process, and not easily hurt or discouraged.

The participants in the consultative process are also called upon to display a very high degree of intellectual courage. Their objective is to search for truth. Their approach, therefore, must be methodical, well reasoned, and adequately researched. They must freely and unhesitatingly express their considered views without fear of hurting others. In like manner they should be intellectually honest and accept refutation of their own views and validity of the views of others with magnanimity and radiance of spirit. Like true scientists they should not be afraid of the "clash of differing opinions"[16] and never lose sight of their primary objective: *to search for truth in a condition of unity for the purpose of reaching a just and equitable decision or resolution to the issue at hand.*

Those engaged in consultation not only must function at a high level of maturity and within the parameters of scientific method in its broadest definition but also must possess a high degree of love, care, and genuine interest for all other members of the consultative process. This is probably the most challenging aspect of consultation. To love everyone with a high degree of sincerity and ease is difficult under the best of circumstances. However, to love others who may have very different perspectives on some of the most important issues of life is particularly difficult. Due to this fact, consultation demands unconditional love, and unconditional love is only possible in the context of what I have termed *"selfless unity."* By "selfless," I mean the capacity to engage in the consultative process with objectivity, humility, and open-mindedness. By "unity" is meant that the members of the consultative group are unique parts of a whole (the consultative group and those affected by its decisions) and that the welfare of one is dependent on the welfare of all. To achieve the quality of selfless unity, we need to achieve transcendence and see others through the eye of our Creator, not through a faultfinding critical eye. This does not mean that we do not judge for ourselves, but rather it means that we judge ideas and actions, not people. This is, at once, an intellectual, emotional, and spiritual undertaking.

Finally, the will of each participant in the consultative process is greatly tasked. We all know that it is not easy to discard long-held and cherished ideas or to fully accept and participate in the implementation of a decision if it has gone contrary to our views and wishes. In the consultative process our personal freedom is best achieved in the context of unity in diversity rather than competitive individualism. As individuals we still have the freedom to ask for reconsideration of issues—another scientific investigation, so to speak. But the manner in which we exercise this freedom is crucial. At all times and under all circumstances, it should be remembered that preservation of the integrity of consultative principles is essential to the success of the process. Therefore, consultation and compromise do not mix. The participants need to ensure that the principles are not ignored and that expediency is not introduced into the consultative process. At the same time, it is essential not to allow ourselves to become obstinate and stubborn obstacles to the consultative process. Consultation calls for humility, selflessness, and sacrifice.

MAIN FEATURES OF CONSULTATION

The main features of consultation can be summarized under five areas of focus.

THE MAIN PREREQUISITE FOR CONSULTATION IS UNITY

The unity paradigm is the framework within which consultation operates. Obviously, the participants in the consultative process do not come together having already developed a unified view about the issue(s) before them. In fact, they may have many diverse perspectives, some totally at odds with one another. The ultimate aim of consultation is to achieve and maintain *unity of thought, sentiment, and approach* among the participants. However, for this objective to be achieved, the participants need to come together with a *unity of purpose* to share with one another their own *unique perspectives* in the framework of the *universal principles* of truth, unity, justice, and service. In effect, the main prerequisite of consultation is the agreement and harmony among the members of the consultative process about the central role of *unity* regarding both the process and the purpose of consultation.

THE MAIN OBJECTIVE OF CONSULTATION IS TO REACH JUST DECISIONS BASED ON THE FACTS (TRUTHS) ABOUT THE ISSUE(S) UNDER CONSIDERATION

Truth, in the context of consultation, refers to those objective and verified facts that make it possible for the group to find the best possible solution(s) to the issue at hand. As such, we are dealing with relative, not absolute, truth. It is, furthermore, clear that the consultative group will not always make the right decision and occasionally needs to reconsider its decisions in light of new facts and information. Unity and justice are two important yardsticks that the participants in the consultative process can use to measure the degree of "truth" of their decisions. To the degree a decision increases the unity of all involved and reaches just decisions based on all available facts, to that same degree the decision accords with the principle of truth. Unity, justice, and truth are interdependent. Therefore, it follows that those engaged in the consultative process should always search for just solutions that would safeguard the rights of both the affected individuals and the decision-making group and that would promote ever higher levels of unity among all. This is only possible when a decision is not only just but also perceived to be just.

THE MAIN TOOLS OF CONSULTATION ARE FRANKNESS AND OPENNESS

Nothing destroys the effectiveness of the consultative process as does lack of candor and openness. Hidden agendas are totally contrary to the spirit of consultation, as are backroom politicking and intrigue. Consultation calls for integrity of character and courage of conviction. It also calls for full trust and respect for our fellow human beings. When these qualities are all present, then there will be no fear of frankness in consultation. When we are certain about our purity of motive and fully respect the equality of the members of the consultative group, then we are able to open our hearts and minds to express what needs to be said without fear of hurting others or becoming the object of their anger and rejection. However, under all circumstances we need to follow the principles of love, care, humility, compassion, and moderation in expressing our views. Justice requires that we treat others as we expect to be treated by them. Frankness is a difficult art. It could easily deteriorate into verbal abuse and injury. It is easily prone to exaggeration and, not infrequently, is perceived to be an act of hostility and arrogance. Consequently, it is essential that frankness take place in the context of mature forms of communication described earlier. Also, the consultative body must put in place the necessary guidelines, reminders, and procedures that would not allow for either discouraging expression of frank and open views and sentiments, or encouraging extreme and deleterious inputs in the guise of frankness. The duty for ensuring a united, frank, yet loving consultation is the responsibility of both every individual and the consulting group as a whole.

THE MAIN PERSONAL CHALLENGES IN CONSULTATION ARE OBJECTIVITY AND DETACHMENT

All ideas, once expressed in the course of consultation, become the property of the consulting group and not of the individual(s) who initially expressed the idea. This concept has profoundly freeing properties. How often in decision-making and conflict resolution groups we observe individuals who either pitifully defend a half-formed or ill-conceived idea they have expressed, or else who are viciously attacked by others for the shortcomings of their views. Under these circumstances a battleground of *perspectives* is created, and opportunities for making the best decisions are lost. However, consultation brings a totally unexpected dimension to the decision-making process. It assumes group possession of all ideas expressed and thus frees all members to agree, disagree, and change their views about the ideas before them without any need for self-defense or attack by others. In the consultative process, it is not at all unusual for members to disagree with their own initially expressed views and vote against them. This freedom is a very precious aspect of the consultative process. However, to achieve this freedom, the members must make conscious efforts to act objectively, to become detached from their expressed views, and to approach the consultative process with humility and mutual respect.

IN CONSULTATION IT IS BETTER TO BE WRONG AND UNITED THAN RIGHT AND DISUNITED

Here, we come full circle again to the all-important issue of unity. Earlier, it was stated that truth is one and unity is oneness. Without unity, mistrust and suspicion are introduced in human relationships, and, consequently, all possibilities for finding the truth about any thing are lost. Therefore, unity assumes primacy in the consultation process, because without unity we lose our access to truth. In light of this fact, in consultation it is better to be wrong and united than right and disunited. As long as we maintain and nurture our unity, our opportunities for finding the truth and making the best decisions are open to us. However, as soon as we become disunited, we lose all those opportunities to access the truth and make creative, just decisions.

STAGES OF CONSULTATION

Altogether, there are seven stages in decision-making and conflict-resolution activities according to Consultative Model (C Mode).

STAGE 1: UNITY OF PURPOSE

First and foremost, a unity of purpose must exist among those engaged in consultation. This unity is required, both with respect to the *principles* and *purpose* of consultation. As consultation progresses, other areas of agreement will develop, and eventually a decision, preferably unanimous but otherwise by majority vote, will be made.

STAGE 2: PERSONAL PREPARATION

Because of the challenging nature of consultation, all individuals involved in the consultative process will greatly benefit by constantly reminding themselves, both before and during consultation, about the essential requirements for their approach to this very important and sacred task. They will recall that in consultation they succeed only when they approach their task with objectivity, detachment, freedom from prejudice, active search for truth, cooperation, humility, mutual respect, compassion, and constant attention to the all-important principles of unity, truth, and justice. In this process of personal preparation, prayers, meditation, reflection, or a combination of such and other contemplative exercises are very helpful.

In addition to these attitudinal preparations, all individuals involved in consultation also have the duty to familiarize themselves with the facts of the issues before them and to become informed of the principles involved. The issue of principles refers to those scientific, legal, and spiritual matters that need to be considered so that the decisions reached by the group are reasonable, fact-based, ethical, compassionate, and fair. These are among the main prerequisites for reaching a just and unifying decision.

STAGE 3: GROUP PREPARATION

A period of time for group preparation is set aside at the beginning and, as the need arises, at different intervals in the course of consultation. The purpose of this preparation is to create a group ambience conducive to intrapersonal and interpersonal conditions characterized by love, respect, trust, cooperation, encouragement, and humble fellowship. The participants will remind themselves that they are engaged in consultation in order to find, together, the best answer(s) to the question(s) and problem(s) before them. They will recall that their objective is to make just decisions while maintaining and increasing the level of their unity. They also need to remember that power-struggle, domination, and control are not conducive to the consultative process. The objective is not win/win but, rather, to find the truth, to create justice, and to maintain unity. The manner in which the preparation period is arranged varies according to the characteristics and orientation of the group and its members. The group may choose a long period of silent meditation, reflection, or shared prayers. The participants may decide to listen to music or participate in other activities conducive to the overall objectives of the preparation component of consultation. Bahá'ís, whose community has practiced the art of consultation for more than a century, usually use prayers, chanting, music, and readings from Bahá'í Writings for this purpose.

In addition to these preparations, the consultative group also must identify the main scientific and spiritual principles applicable to each agenda item before them. The group needs to ensure that all members agree on both the significance and applicability of these principles to the case before them. Through this careful approach, the consultation process is facilitated, and confusion and misunderstanding are avoided. Furthermore, identification of principles makes it much easier for those involved to remain objective and free from their preconceived notions, which may be poorly or even erroneously formulated. The scientific principles refer to expert views—medical, legal, technical, etc.—which are necessary for setting the parameters for approaching the issues before the decision-making body. Spiritual principles are more complex and difficult to determine. However, as a rule, spiritual principles, in their very nature, applicability, and effect are universal, truth-based, unifying, and just. The very process of attention to these matters and their presence in the consultative process help both the group and its members not only make better decisions but also further refine their decision-making skills.

STAGE 4: PROCESS

All individuals engaged in the consultative process are required to freely share their ideas, thoughts, sentiments, hopes, and despairs with frankness, moderation, and care. They are urged to receive with total respect, attentiveness, and sensitivity the inputs of each person who contributes to the consultative process. If someone chooses to be silent, the group respects this decision; however, through encouraging words and attitude, all individuals involved would endeavor to facilitate the expression of views by everyone. In this respect, more vocal and forceful individuals have a special responsibility to be particularly sensitive to the hesitation that many people may have under these circumstances, particularly, when the participants come from many different backgrounds and socioeconomic or educational strata of society. Also, men, in general, and assertive men, in particular, must assume major responsibility for facilitating the expression of views by women.

By not allowing themselves to have ulterior motives, neither will consultants introduce self-serving private hidden agendas to the consultative process, nor will the consultative body allow any of its members to do so. The sole objective must be to deal with the issue(s) with objectivity, frankness, knowledge of facts, and detachment. Under no circumstances should personal desires and preferences be allowed to take precedence over the fundamental objectives of the consultative process: to search for truth in a condition of unity in order to reach just decisions.

Although, for ease of process, the consultative group is encouraged to elect or appoint (depending on the nature and permanence of the group) a chairperson and a secretary, it should nevertheless be remembered that these individuals have no special privileges or station in the group. The duty of the chairperson is to serve the group and facilitate the process of consultation. Under no circumstances should this person be seen as the leader or be allowed to assume such a position. Likewise, the responsibility of the secretary is to record the decisions of the consultative group faithfully and accurately; convey them, in the same manner, to those who must receive the results of their deliberations and to those who are affected by it; and ensure proper implementation of decisions.

STAGE 5: DECISIONS

The consultative group should aim at reaching unanimous decisions. Otherwise, a majority vote has the same status as a unanimous decision. It should be remembered that a decision is not a composite of opinions, thoughts, and feelings expressed by different members. Rather, the final decision is a new entity emerging from the unencumbered interchange of thoughts, feelings, and wills in a unified atmosphere of consultation. As such, the final decision is greater than the sum of all the views expressed. Due to this fact all individuals involved in the consultative process should be prepared to sacrifice their individual opinions in their unified search for the best solution to the issue before them. As there is no minority/majority separation in the unified framework of consultation, all members, without exception, will unhesitatingly accept the final unanimous or majority decision and actively participate in its implementation.

STAGE 6: IMPLEMENTATION

The consultative process is incomplete without the implementation of the decisions reached in a united and harmonious manner. No decision, however lofty and honorable, has value unless it is put into action and bears its fruits of justice and unity. To achieve these ends, all involved must participate, either directly or indirectly, in its implementation and offer unconditional support to those who are given the task of carrying out the decision. If in the course of implementing a decision it becomes evident that a new course of action is needed, the consultative group must be willing and available to reconsider the matter. The objective here is not to have winners and losers; rather, the main purpose is to reach a just, unifying decision that best serves the interests and welfare of all involved.

STAGE 7: EVALUATION

Consultation is scientific in its method. It functions according to certain established protocols and guidelines. It is, therefore, essential to make a thorough, objective evaluation of the efficacy of the process. The consultative body and its members owe it to themselves and those affected by their decision to know, objectively and scientifically, the final outcome and impact of their decisions. For this reason, the results of the implementation of the decisions reached through consultation must be subject to thorough evaluation based on regular, well-designed internal and external evaluation and research. This evaluation is necessary, so that we can learn from experience and gradually add to our reservoir of knowledge of the dynamics and skills of the consultative process. For ease of reference, some of the main points about consultation that we need to always remember are provided in Appendix III.

SUMMARY

Bahá'í consultation is a unity-based concept and method of decision-making and conflict resolution. Decisions made in the context of a unity paradigm not only create conditions of justice and freedom but also prevent the pernicious effects of abuse of power and authority, as well as conflict and discord that so frequently characterize our current approaches to decision-making and conflict resolution in all segments of human society. Both unity and justice are achieved when objective truths constitute the foundations upon which decisions are made and conflicts are resolved. The dynamic relationship between unity, truth, and justice has a creative and evolving quality. These three conditions are totally interdependent, and none of them can truly exist in the absence of the other two. Furthermore, unity, truth, and justice have both educative and curative properties. Those engaged in consultation soon discover that this exercise helps them to further mature as individuals with respect to their own intellectual, emotional, relational, moral, and spiritual faculties, bringing them a considerable measure of assurance and inner and interpersonal harmony. Also, those who have systematically employed consultation gradually discover that the consultative process helps them to simultaneously create a culture of peace, a culture of healing, and a culture of excellence in their families, places of work, and institutions in their communities.

CHAPTER TEN

THE BAHÁ'Í COMMUNITY

CREATING A CIVILIZATION OF PEACE

If the learned and worldly-wise men of this age were to allow mankind to inhale the fragrance of fellowship and love, every understanding heart would apprehend the meaning of true liberty, and discover the secret of undisturbed peace and absolute composure.[1]

—Bahá'u'lláh

During the last six thousand years nations have hated one another, it is now time to stop. War must cease. Let us be united and love one another and await the result. We know the effects of war are bad. So let us try, as an experiment, peace, and if the results of peace are bad, then we can choose if it would be better to go back to the old state of war! Let us in any case make the experiment. If we see that unity brings Light we shall continue it. For six thousand years we have been walking on the left-hand path; let us walk on the right-hand path now. We have passed many centuries in darkness, let us advance towards the light.[2]

—'Abdu'l-Bahá

…His [Bahá'u'lláh's] mission is to proclaim that the ages of the infancy and of the childhood of the human race are past, that the convulsions associated with the present stage of its adolescence are slowly and painfully preparing it to attain the stage of manhood, and are heralding the approach of that Age of Ages when swords will be beaten into plowshares, when the Kingdom promised by Jesus Christ will have been established, and the peace of the planet definitely and permanently ensured.[3]

—Shoghi Effendi

The Great Peace towards which people of good will throughout the centuries have inclined their hearts, of which seers and poets for countless generations have expressed their vision, and for which from age to age the sacred scriptures of mankind have constantly held the promise, is now at long last within the reach of the nations….It is the next stage in the evolution of this planet….[4]

—The Universal House of Justice

We, the peoples of the United Nations, determined to save succeeding generations from the scourge of war, which twice in our lifetime has brought untold sorrow to mankind, and to reaffirm faith in fundamental human rights, in the dignity and worth of the human person, in the equal rights of men and women and of nations large and small….And for these ends to practice tolerance and live together in peace with one another as good neighbors…have resolved to combine our efforts to accomplish these aims.[5]

—Preamble, Charter of the United Nations

THE BAHÁ'Í PEACE PROGRAM[*]

The establishment of world peace has been one of the cardinal objectives of the Bahá'í Faith since its inception. The Bahá'í peace program is a complex, evolving process. At this early phase in its development, we can identify at least two distinctive components, with additional ones emerging as humanity draws ever nearer to the goal of world peace. The first and extremely important component is with respect to the Bahá'í concept of peace. The second and equally important is with regard to the worldwide Bahá'í Community as a prototype of a peaceful global community.

UNIQUE ASPECTS OF THE BAHÁ'Í CONCEPT OF PEACE

The Bahá'í sacred writings regarding peace are numerous and varied in content. They deal with the moral and spiritual foundations of peace, identify its prerequisites, outline its social components, and prescribe the necessary social and political structures for a future civilization of peace.

SPIRITUAL FOUNDATIONS OF PEACE

One of the most striking aspects of the Bahá'í concept of peace is that it places the issue of peace at the very core of the purpose of creation, of human life, and of religion. As such, peace is not an option but a fundamental requisite that will eventually characterize all aspects of human life. Furthermore, peace is not viewed solely as a social and political state. Rather, peace is a moral and spiritual state with interpersonal, social, and global expressions. Bahá'u'lláh states:

> The first, the fundamental purpose underlying creation hath ever been, and will continue to be, none other than the appearance of trustworthiness, and godliness, of sincerity and goodwill amongst mankind, for these qualities are the cause of peace, security and tranquility. Blessed are those who possess such virtues.[6]

---

[*] In 1986 I wrote a piece on the Bahá'í Peace Program for the *World Encyclopedia of Peace,* published by Pergamon Books. This segment is a further elaboration of the points covered in that article and my other published works on this topic, including *The Violence-Free Society: A Gift for Our Children, Unity: The Creative Foundation of Peace, Peace Moves,* and other titles included in the bibliography of this book.

'Abdu'l-Bahá further elaborates on this remarkable theme:

Today the most pressing of all tasks is the purification of character, the reforming of morals, the rectification of conduct....The reason for God's having made Himself manifest [through appearance of the Manifestations of God]...is none other than the training of all men's souls and the refining of the characters of all on earth—so that blessed individuals, who have freed themselves from the murk of the animal world, shall rise up with those qualities which are the adornings of the reality of man. The purpose is...that those who thirst for blood should forsake their savagery, and those who are barbed of claw should turn gentle and forbearing, and those who love war should seek instead for true conciliation; it is that the brutal, their talons razor-sharp, should enjoy the benefits of lasting peace....[7]

The above statements suggest that peace first takes place in the domain of the spirit—the realm of human consciousness. The human mind and heart need to be illumined with qualities of truth and trustworthiness, love and goodness, and refinement and purity, so that our thoughts and sentiments are transformed and our wills are employed to create unity and peace. These are elements of worldview transformation from conflict-based to unity-based perspectives.

The process of maturation of the human mind is only possible through search for truth in the context of reason, objectivity, and freedom from all preconceived notions and expectations. This process is at once spiritual and scientific, and is the surest way of attaining unity of thought with regard to perplexing and often conflicting challenges that we face as individual and community members. 'Abdu'l-Bahá states that "truth or reality must be investigated; for reality is one, and by investigating it all will find love and unity."[8] Elsewhere, in a letter to an individual from a Christian background, 'Abdu'l-Bahá explains this process in a language familiar to its recipient and states that the ultimate outcome—the fruit—of progressive divine revelation is none other than *universal peace:*

O thou who art carried away by the love of God! The Sun of Truth [Bahá'u'lláh] hath risen above the horizon of this world and cast down its beams of guidance. Eternal grace is never interrupted, and a fruit of that everlasting grace is universal peace. Rest thou assured that in this era of the spirit, the Kingdom of Peace will raise up its tabernacle on the summits of the world, and the commandments of the Prince of Peace will so dominate the arteries and nerves of every people as to draw into His sheltering shade all the nations on earth. From springs of love and truth and unity will the true Shepherd give His sheep to drink.[9]

This juxtaposition of issues of love, truth, and unity is of singular importance because they are among the most crucial requisites of peace. In an exhortation, 'Abdu'l-Bahá states that our "affections and loving-kindness…must be bountifully and universally extended to all mankind. Regarding this," He emphasizes, "restrictions and limitations are in no wise permitted."[10] In other words, there is no excuse for us to withhold love from anyone, to avoid truth under any conditions, and to not pursue unity in any circumstance. Love, truth, and unity must always be pursued and applied under all conditions. They are hallmarks of humanness and essential requisites of peace.

Another fundamental and essential requirement for peace is justice. In fact, the issue of justice with regard to peace is so fundamental that, as we discussed in chapter four, the entire structure of the administrative order of the Bahá'í Faith is raised on the foundation of justice. 'Abdu'l-Bahá explains the interconnection of issues of justice, peace, and divine revelation at this crucial time in human history when the ancient hopes of humanity for peace can at last become a reality:

> This century* is the century of the oneness of the world of humanity, the century of justice; this century is the century of universal peace, the century of the dawn of the sun of reality; this century is the century of the establishment of the kingdom of God upon this earth; therefore let us grasp every means to promote the federation of the world, that we may become the recipients of the divine outpourings.[11]

Issues of unity and concord are easily subject to misunderstanding and misapplication, the most calamitous of which is to consider unity to mean uniformity in the context of limited unities such as nationalism or to interpret justice to signify that all should be recompensed the same, regardless of their personal efforts and merits. The following statement of Bahá'u'lláh, uttered towards the end of the 19th century, clearly foresees and warns of disastrous attempts at creating limited unities and negating individual rights and responsibilities—two conditions that characterize some of the most important developments of the 20th century, including the rise of fascism and communism:

> Such exhortations to union and concord as are inscribed in the Books of the Prophets by the Pen of the Most High bear reference unto specific matters; not a union that would lead to disunity or a concord which would create discord. This is the station where measures are set unto everything, a station where every deserving soul shall be given his due.[12]

---

* "Century" here denotes an unspecified duration of time.

STRATEGIES FOR CREATING PEACE

As one studies the teachings of the Bahá'í Faith regarding peace and related issues such as conflict, violence, harmony, and unity, it becomes evident that peace is considered to be the ultimate fruit of a profound transformation in human individual and social life. This transformation is spiritual in nature, universal in its scope, and all-encompassing in its domain. It begins in the realm of thought and language, significantly alters our attitudes and relationships, and dramatically changes our behavior and actions—all within an inclusive global framework.

THOUGHTS AND LANGUAGE OF PEACE

Thoughts have lasting and profound power. That is why dictators fear academics, artists, and learned segments of their society, those who possess the power of new thoughts, ideas, and insights, and who are empowered with the power of the word. Thoughts express and shape our understanding of the nature of reality, convey our sentiments and beliefs to others, and form the framework for our relationships and social interactions. And of all thoughts, the most consequential are those regarding our understanding of the question, *Who and why are we?* Because thoughts are expressed through the medium of language, human utterance assumes signal importance and power in human affairs. It is through the process of sharing ideas and using language as a tool of communication that minds are changed, sentiments are aroused, decisions are made, and actions are sanctioned.

Of all categories of language, the language of divine Revelation is the most penetrating and influential. The language of Revelation—the Word of God—is the most authentic and elemental expression of truth and reality, and that is why it so dramatically influences human thoughts, emotions, sentiments, and capacities. History clearly demonstrates that the language of Revelation as enunciated by such figures as Zoroaster, Moses, Krishna, Buddha, Christ, Muhammad, the Báb,[13] and Bahá'u'lláh has shaped the dynamics of human individual and collective life since the dawn of recorded history and will continue to do so in our modern, scientific era. We observe with mixed feelings of awe and despair how humanity has always understood and interpreted the language of Revelation both positively and negatively, and how this understanding has impacted the lives of the multitudes throughout history. It is in this context that the uniqueness of the teachings of the

Bahá'í Faith regarding peace becomes particularly evident. Bahá'u'lláh states:

> Dissension and Strife have always been, and shall remain, rejected by God....The purpose underlying this most mighty Revelation is none other than the rehabilitation of the world and its nations; that perchance the power of utterance may prevail over the power of arms, and the world's affairs be administered through the potency of love.[14]

Elsewhere, He describes the power of the word, how easily it could be used or abused, and how it could be used for nurturing of human understanding and dignity:

> No man of wisdom can demonstrate his knowledge save by means of words....Every word is endowed with a spirit, therefore the speaker or expounder should carefully deliver his words at the appropriate time and place, for the impression which each word maketh is clearly evident and perceptible....One word may be likened unto fire, another unto light, and the influence which both exert is manifest in the world. Therefore an enlightened man of wisdom should primarily speak with words as mild as milk, that the children of men may be nurtured and edified thereby and may attain the ultimate goal of human existence which is the station of true understanding and nobility....[15]

PEACE-BASED ATTITUDES AND RELATIONSHIPS

Along with peace-oriented transformation in the realms of human thought and language, Bahá'u'lláh also, in no uncertain terms, points to the absolute necessity that our thoughts as well as our words, attitudes, and deeds must all be harmonized and focused on the idea and cause of peace. We may classify the teachings of the Bahá'í Faith regarding transformation to peace under three broad categories: rejection of all forms of violence, prescription of peace-creating attitudes and practices, and delineation of the foundations of a civilization of peace. Bahá'u'lláh, addressing all humanity summarizes His teachings with regard to the issue of peace:

> O ye that dwell on earth! The distinguishing feature that marketh the pre-eminent character of this Supreme Revelation consisteth in that We have, on the one hand, blotted out from the pages of God's holy Book whatsoever hath been the cause of strife, of malice and mischief

amongst the children of men, and have, on the other, laid down the essential prerequisites of concord, of understanding, of complete and enduring unity.[16]

Furthermore, He identifies a very specific segment of the society—the learned and the worldly wise of this age—as being fundamentally responsible for the absence of true liberty, composure, and peace in the world of humanity:

> If the learned and worldly-wise men of this age were to allow mankind to inhale the fragrance of fellowship and love, every understanding heart would apprehend the meaning of true liberty, and discover the secret of undisturbed peace and absolute composure.[17]

'Abdu'l-Bahá, in a talk delivered in Pittsburgh on 7 May 1912, explained that world peace is not merely a material, social, and political state. Rather, peace by its very nature is a spiritual phenomenon and an outcome of spiritual transformation:

> The Most Great Peace cannot be assured through racial force and effort; it cannot be established by patriotic devotion and sacrifice; for nations differ widely and local patriotism has limitations. Furthermore, it is evident that political power and diplomatic ability are not conducive to universal agreement, for the interests of governments are varied and selfish; nor will international harmony and reconciliation be an outcome of human opinions concentrated upon it, for opinions are faulty and intrinsically diverse. Universal peace is an impossibility through human and material agencies; it must be through spiritual power. There is need of a universal impelling force which will establish the oneness of humanity and destroy the foundations of war and strife. None other than the divine power can do this.[18]

Figure 10.1 is just a sampling of the teachings of the Bahá'í Faith regarding peace summarized under three categories: rejection of violence, peace-creating attitudes and relationships, and the requirements for founding a civilization of peace.

Rejection of all forms of violence	Peace-creating attitudes and relationships	Foundations of a civilization of peace
• Abolition of the "law of holy war"[19] • Annulment of "the rule of the sword"[20] • Rejection of "dissension and strife"[21] • Abolition of all forms of prejudice[22] • Prohibition of slavery, both chattel slavery and industrial slavery[23] • Abolishment of the institution of priesthood[24] • Many other references to rejection of conflict, strife, disunity, violence and war are made in the voluminous Writings of the Bahá'í Faith • Condemnation of cruelty to animals[25] • Condemnation of backbiting and calumny[26]	• *Central theme:* Consciousness of the oneness of humanity • *Operating principle:* Unity in diversity • Justice as a requisite for peace • Equality of rights between men and women • Racial harmony • Human rights • Harmony of science and religion • Independent investigation of reality and search for truth • Truthfulness and trustworthiness • Earth is one country and mankind its citizens • Religion must be the cause of love and unity • Equality of rights and prerogatives for all humankind	• Establishment of a world commonwealth • Establishment of Houses of Justice at local, national, and international levels • Harmony of science and religion • Setting of world peace as one of the main objectives • Auxiliary international language • Establishment of a world legislature • Establishment of a world executive backed by an international force • Establishment of a world tribunal • Establishment of a world currency • Universal compulsory education[27] • "Readjustment and equalization of the economic standards of mankind"[28]

Figure 10.1. Elements of the Bahá'í Peace Program.

THE BAHÁ'Í COMMUNITY

A PROTOTYPE OF A PEACE-BASED GLOBAL CULTURE

Traditionally, community is defined as an integrated, cohesive, and homogenous social entity where the interests of individual and group coincide.[29] As such, throughout history and in all parts of the world there have been and still are many such communities that give their members a sense of identity, belonging, and exclusivity. However, in the modern world with its ease of travel, high level of mobility, and increasingly heterogeneous composition, many communities have lost their cohesion and solidarity. Human relationships in many of these communities are tenuous and transitory. These modern communities are more a collection of individuals with their personal, diverse, and often conflicting interests, than a unified body of individuals whose personal and group interests coincide. It is in this context that the worldwide Bahá'í community assumes its significance in our painfully divided, suspicious, and uncertain world.[30]

According to the latest available statistics, the Bahá'í Community, with its more than five million adherents, is established in some 190 independent countries and 46 significant territories and islands. There are 182 National/Regional Spiritual Assemblies that are elected annually at their respective national conventions. Bahá'ís reside in 127,381 towns, cities, and villages around the globe, some with one or a few Bahá'ís and others with thousands. Every year, Bahá'ís in sufficiently large communities (at least nine or more adults 21 years or older) elect their respective local spiritual assemblies. In 2001, some 11,740 local spiritual assemblies were elected. This broadly and thinly spread community is a highly divers and united community of people comprising many languages, races, and ethnicities. The same survey showed that the Bahá'í literature is translated into 802 languages, and some 2,112 different tribes, races, and ethnic groups are represented in the Bahá'í community. Figure 10.2 provides further details about these statistics.[31] Figure 10.3 provides a glimpse of the growth of the Bahá'í Community.

The statistics for the spiritual assemblies are of particular importance. Both national and local spiritual assemblies[32]—the future national and local Houses of Justice—are fundamental components of the Bahá'í Community and its Administrative Order and are essential for ending strife and creating unity and peace. 'Abdu'l-Bahá states that "Spiritual

National Spiritual Assemblies	
Africa	46
Americas	43
Asia	39
Australasia	17
Europe	37
World Total	**182**

Local Spiritual Assemblies	
Africa	3,808
Americas	3,152
Asia	2,948
Australasia	856
Europe	976
World Total	**11,740**

Countries where the Bahá'í Faith is established: independent countries

Africa	53
Americas	35
Asia	44
Australasia	14
Europe	44
World Total	**190**

Countries where the Bahá'í Faith is established: dependent territories/ overseas departments

Africa	5
Americas	17
Asia	3
Australasia	13
Europe	8
World Total	**46**

Localities where Bahá'ís reside

Africa	30,003
Americas	24,502
Asia	59,821
Australasia	6,746
Europe	6,309
World Total	**127,381**

Indigenous tribes, races, and ethnic groups

Africa	1,250
Americas	340
Asia	250
Australasia	250
Europe	22
World Total	**2,112**

Languages into which Bahá'í literature is translated

Africa	266
Americas	172
Asia	174
Australasia	110
Europe	80
World Total	**802**

Bahá'í Publishing Trusts

Africa	7
Americas	3
Asia	9
Australasia	2
Europe	12
World Total	**33**

Figure 10.2. Bahá'í World Statistics 2001.

Notes: Information about national spiritual assemblies and publishing trusts is as of April 2001, as are the statistics on the countries and territories where the Bahá'í Faith is established. The statistics for local spiritual assemblies and localities come primarily from the 2000 Annual Statistical Reports from national spiritual assemblies, which contain information as of 2 May 2000. The figures for indigenous tribes, races, and ethnic groups, and for languages into which Bahá'í literature is translated, were last updated in 1986.

	1968	± 1986	2001
National Spiritual Assemblies	81	165	182
Local Spiritual Assemblies	6,840	18,232	11,740
Countries the Bahá'í Faith is established: independent countries		187	190
Countries the Bahá'í Faith is established: dependent territories/ overseas departments		45	46
Localities where Bahá'ís reside	31,572	>116,000	127,381
Indigenous tribes, races, and ethnic groups	1,179	>2,100	2,112
Languages into which Bahá'í literature is translated	417	800	802
Bahá'í Publishing Trusts	9	26	33

Figure 10.3. A comparative table of growth of the Bahá'í Community.

Note: The decrease in the number of local spiritual assemblies in 2001 was due to a change in the election schedule that took effect in 1997. The numbers for local spiritual assemblies after 1997 reflect those assemblies formed each year on the 21st of April, which is the day for election of all local spiritual assemblies around the globe. (Source: Bahá'í World Centre Department of Statistics)

Assemblies are collectively the most effective of all instruments for establishing unity and harmony." [33] He further counsels:

> Organize ye Spiritual Assemblies; lay ye the foundation of union and concord in this world; destroy ye the fabric of strife and war from the face of the earth; construct ye the temple of harmony and agreement; enkindle ye the light of the realm of the oneness of humanity; open ye your eyes; gaze and behold ye the other world! The kingdom of peace, salvation, uprightness and reconciliation is founded in the invisible world, and it will by degrees become manifest and apparent through the power of the Word of God![34]

As stated before, there is a direct positive relationship between issues of peace, unity, and justice. Peace is only possible when conditions of unity (in the context of diversity) and justice are present in the world at both local and global levels. Justice, unity, and peace have always been at the core of human quest. However, humanity in its long journey to maturity has not yet been able to establish standards of true and all-inclusive justice that would strengthen its unity, protect its diversity, and hasten the era of global peace. Speaking of the state of justice in this time in history, Bahá'u'lláh says:

> In these days the tabernacle of justice hath fallen in the clutches of tyranny and oppression...it behoveth every ruler to weigh his own being every day in the balance of equity and justice and then to judge between men and counsel them to do that which would direct their steps to the path of wisdom and understanding. This is the cornerstone of statesmanship and the essence thereof. From these words every enlightened man of wisdom will readily perceive that which will foster such aims as the welfare, security and protection of mankind and the safety of human lives.[35]

It is in the context of humanity's age-old quest and need for justice and the current ascendancy of injustice in the world that the cardinal importance of election and operation of Houses of Justice at local, national, and global levels—which is now an established aspect of the Bahá'í community life—becomes clearly evident. Creation of justice is within the power of human beings, and for Bahá'ís it is a sacred personal, social, and spiritual responsibility. 'Abdu'l-Bahá states that "[s]ome things are subject to the free will of man, such as justice, equity, tyranny and injustice,"[36] a statement that is a reminder to tens of thousands of Bahá'ís around the globe who each year are elected as members of their respective local and national spiritual assemblies and suddenly find themselves honored and responsible for the truly challenging task of learning the ways of justice and its implementation in the context of unity and peace.

The above is an incomplete surface sketch of the profile of the Baháʼí community, in general, and its administrative order, in particular. The Baháʼí Community is a new kind of community, at once local and global, united and diverse, multi-ethnic and integrated, rich and poor, highly educated and becoming literate, isolated and cosmopolitan. The unity of the members of the Baháʼí community is based on a shared faith, a world-embracing vision, and a common set of clear objectives. Baháʼís have full trust and faith that human life is the outcome of the creative Will of God (in the context of its evolutionary process); that all which is created by God is good; that the covenant between God and humanity is eternal; that God fulfills the covenant with humanity through the progressive appearance of divine Manifestations (Messengers, Prophets); that Baháʼuʼlláh is the latest, but not the last, Mouthpiece of God to humanity for this age; that Baháʼuʼlláh is the fulfillment of expectations of the appearance of the Universal Messenger from God as foretold in all major religions; and that by accepting Baháʼuʼlláh as the Manifestation of God, they have made a fundamental covenant to live their lives according to certain inviolable principles.

Among these principles are the oneness of humanity, the fundamental unity of all religions, the harmony of science and religion, the equality of women and men, the primacy of the law of unity in diversity, rejection of all forms of prejudice, and the essential necessity of applying universal moral and spiritual principles to all areas of human life—personal, interpersonal, institutional, social, and global. It is in this context that Baháʼís, together and in collaboration with all other individuals and groups around the world, endeavor to create local communities with universal and global perspectives with the ultimate aim of creating a global, progressive, sustainable, equitable, free, inclusive, and highly diverse and complex civilization of peace. This focused attention on the positive issues of justice, unity, and peace does not mean that Baháʼís ignore the reality of human suffering and problems or are indifferent towards them. The fact is that we are all subject to those problems and tests (see chapter three) and need to deal with them in a realistic, methodical, and thoughtful manner.

The Baháʼí Community is still in its infancy. Many of its members are new converts from a wide range of backgrounds—various religions, no religion at all; highly educated scientists, top-caliber professionals, extremely poor and disadvantaged people; individuals reared in authoritarian families and communities and those reared in free and competitive environments. Some Bahá'ís are children of the families who have been members of the Bahá'í Faith since its early decades, and a good number of them can recite tales of heroic acts of service, sacrifice, oppression, and persecution that they or their parents, grandparents, or other family members have suffered to help to create this new experiment in community-building.

Bahá'ís are highly mobile. A significant number of them travel and reside in countries far from their native lands. Many of them adopt these new lands as their home. Quite frequently, they marry across racial, ethnic, and religious lines. Their children are thus individuals with multiple integrated identities. A significant number of children of Bahá'í families are reared to see themselves both as citizens of their respective countries and as citizens of the world. These young generations of children and youth readily realize that the world belongs to them and they belong to the world. Many of these young people are further expanding the diversity and universality of the Bahá'í community through the choice of their places of residence, the marriages they establish, the types of education and work they pursue, the ethnic populations and races they dedicate their services to, and the manner in which they try to serve the cause of unity, justice, and peace.

This highly diverse, complex, and evolving global community of many local and national communities—a community of communities— faces the same challenges as their fellow compatriots encounter. They are concerned about the proper education of their children and guidance of their youth, healthy development of their marriages and families, strengthening of their economic status, safety and excellence in their schools and neighborhoods, enrichment of the community life through promotion of arts and culture, protection of the environment, and participation in the life of their society. In their efforts to address these and other challenges of individual and community life, Bahá'ís apply the latest scientific knowledge concomitantly with the relevant spiritual principles. It is this last issue—spiritual principles—that is the most consequential in all human affairs. Spiritual principles are not merely a set of moral and ethical edicts to be followed as given and obligatory. Rather, spiritual principles refer to those fundamental essential relationships that emanate from the inmost realities of things. Central to these principles is the principle of the oneness of humanity, which is simultaneously a scientific and spiritual verity. A life lived according to this overriding principle is conducive to all other fundamental spiritual principles such as unity in diversity, justice, equality, and sustainable and inclusive peace.

Application of these spiritual principles to various aspects of life and to our decisions has salutary effects on all concerned. It decreases our natural tendency for self-centeredness, heightens our consciousness of others, gives us courage to aim high and do good, and provides us with a profound sense of security emerging from realization of our belonging. Spiritual principles also help us to understand science in its most creative, life-enhancing qualities, making the abuse of science totally unacceptable. Within the parameters of spiritual principles, abuses of science such as making technologies of war, violence, and destruction cannot take place. Likewise, use of remarkable tools such as the Internet, television, and radio for pornography, online theft and crime, promotion of hatred and prejudice, and encouragement of immoral and destructive lifestyles becomes a rare aberrance, rather than commonplace, as happens now. In other words, transformation of the technologies of war and conflict-based worldviews to those of peace requires systematic, thorough application of the spiritual principles to science and technology on the part of scientists, policy-makers, entrepreneurs, and political and civic leadership at a regional, national, and global scale.

Within the parameters of the Bahá'í community, the institutions (such as the elected local and national spiritual assemblies and their committees, and the appointed boards of counselors and their auxiliary members), as well as individuals (in the context of their families, social relationships, scientific studies, professional activities and occupations), make valiant effort to consider spiritual principles in reaching and implementing their decisions. This is a demanding task that requires acquisition of a habitual pattern of employing spiritual principles, which is relentlessly and forcefully discouraged and ridiculed in our materialistic world. It takes courage to bring the spiritual dimension to our interpersonal and public life. But it is necessary if we are to free ourselves from the strong clutches of the seductive and destructive self-centered, cold-hearted materialism of the prevailing dominant cultures of the world.

How the Bahá'í Community Came to Be

With this brief review of some of the main characteristics of the Bahá'í Community, we may well ask how is it that such an inclusive, united, diverse, spiritually minded, scientifically oriented, and forward-looking global community based on the principles of world peace could emerge and evolve from a cultural and historical context marked by hatred, violence, prejudice, superstition, and insularity. The answer to this question requires an in-depth, multilayered, and transdisciplinary study, which is both beyond the scope of this book and the expertise of a single author. Here, I will briefly focus on two main issues—spiritual awakening and worldview transformation.

Spiritual awakening refers to that mystic and undeniable influence of divine Revelation and the creative Word of God on the human soul, transforming every aspect of human individual and group life. It enlightens the human mind with fundamental spiritual truths, transforms human sentiments by means of universal love and the power of unity, and employs the formidable power of human will in the service of justice and peace. The phenomenon of spiritual awakening is observed throughout history in response to all revealed religions of the world. It is, therefore, not surprising that peoples of all orientations, faiths, and backgrounds have and continue to become Bahá'ís through this process of spiritual awakening. Bahá'ís come from all types of background: agnostic, atheist, Buddhist, Christian, communist, Jewish, Hindu, Muslim, Zoroastrian, aboriginal religions, and many other belief-systems and faiths. Every one of these individuals makes a covenant of faith with Bahá'u'lláh as the Manifestation of God for this age and dedicates himself/herself to a life of action within the framework of Bahá'í teachings. This process of religious conversion and affiliation takes place in the context of Bahá'u'lláh's command that every individual must investigate the truth independently within a rational and logical framework and according to the mysterious promptings of his or her spirit.

The process of worldview transformation is the intellectual, attitudinal, and behavioral expression of spiritual awakening—a new consciousness. The newly spiritualized soul looks at the world with a new eye and a new comprehension of reality, of human nature, of purpose of life, and of human relationships. In order to demonstrate the manner in which the members of the Bahá'í community, ever since its beginnings in the mid-19th century, have been assisted in their processes of spiritual reawakening and worldview transformation, I have chosen several statements from the vast body of Bahá'í sacred writings that are pertinent to this theme. These statements are presented here with little or no commentary.

Bahá'u'lláh thus counsels:

O people of God! Do not busy yourselves in your own concerns; let your thoughts be fixed upon that which will rehabilitate the fortunes of mankind and sanctify the hearts and souls of men. This can best be achieved through pure and holy deeds, through a virtuous life and a goodly behaviour....It is incumbent upon every man, in this Day, to hold fast unto whatsoever will promote the interests, and exalt the station, of all nations and just governments....'Consort with the followers of all religions in a spirit of friendliness and fellowship.' Whatsoever hath led the children of men to shun one another, and hath caused dissensions and divisions amongst them, hath, through the revelation of these words, been nullified and abolished. From the heaven of God's Will, and for the purpose of ennobling the world of being and of elevating the minds and souls of men, hath been sent down that which is the most effective instrument for the education of the whole human race....'It is not his to boast who loveth his country, but it is his who loveth the world.'[37]

The counsels of Bahá'u'lláh, however, were not limited to Bahá'ís. He, as the Manifestation of God, addressed all humanity and many of the most powerful political and religious leaders of His time. Among them were "emperors, kings and princes, chancellors and ministers, the Pope himself, priests, monks and philosophers, the exponents of learning, parliamentarians and deputies, the rich ones of the earth, the followers of all religions" as well as "the people of Bahá."[38] Shoghi Effendi explains that in these tablets all recipients "are brought within the purview of the Author of these Messages, and receive, each according to their merits, the counsels and admonitions they deserve."[39] Bahá'u'lláh gives an uncompromising indictment of the conditions of human society and holds its leaders—especially political and religious leaders—primarily responsible for its devastating state. In these messages that cover a wide range of issues, He addresses the issue of peace and points out the fact that He—through His teachings and example—has "bestowed the gift of peace and tranquility" and beseeches "God to assist the kings of the earth to establish peace on earth."[40]

In these messages issued between 1867 and 1870, Bahá'u'lláh condemns most of the rulers He addressed for their injustice and greed. However, in His letter to Queen Victoria He congratulated her for abolishing the slave trade and for allowing democratic government to flourish. He, further in that same letter, counseled the elected members of the parliaments in all lands:

O ye the elected representatives of the people in every land! Take ye counsel together, and let your concern be only for that which profiteth mankind and bettereth the condition thereof, if ye be of them that scan heedfully. Regard the world as the human body which, though at its creation whole and perfect, hath been afflicted, through various causes, with grave disorders and maladies. Not for one day did it gain ease, nay its sickness waxed more severe, as it fell under the treatment of ignorant physicians, who gave full rein to their personal desires and have erred grievously. And if, at one time, through the care of an able physician, a member of that body was healed, the rest remained afflicted as before....[41]

'Abdu'l-Bahá, as the Centre of the Covenant of the Bahá'í Faith, followed the same pattern established by His father—Bahá'u'lláh. He, lovingly and patiently, focused on the development of the newly emerging and greatly expanding Bahá'í Community as a model of unified, universal, diverse, and peaceful culture and, at the same time, presented the same principles to His vast audiences in Asia, North America, Europe, and parts of Africa. The objectives were the same: spiritual awakening and worldview transformation, both aimed at creating an ever-advancing, spiritually enlightened, and scientifically advanced civilization of peace. On the eve of his departure from Paris for Alexandria on June 12, 1913, he gave the following admonitory farewell to the Bahá'ís and the general population of England and France:

"Work," he said unceasingly, "for the day of Universal Peace. Strive always that you may be united. Kindness and love in the path of service must be your means. I bid a loving farewell to the people of France and England. I am very much pleased with them. I counsel them that they may day by day strengthen the bond of love and amity to this end,—that they may become the sympathetic embodiment of one nation.—That they may extend themselves to a Universal Brotherhood to guard and protect the interests and rights of all the nations of the East,—that they may unfurl the Divine Banner of justice,—that they may treat each nation as a family composed of the individual children of God and may know that before the sight of God the rights of all are equal. For all of us are the children of one Father. God is at peace with all his children; why should they engage in strife and warfare among themselves? God is showering down kindness; why should the inhabitants of this world exchange unkindness and cruelty?"[42]

In numerous letters, messages, books, and public talks, 'Abdu'l-Bahá unceasingly counseled and guided the members of the Bahá'í Community on how to become the architects of peace. Here is one example:

O ye dear friends! The world is engaged in war and struggle, and mankind is in the utmost conflict and danger. The darkness of unfaithfulness has enshrouded the earth and the illumination of faithfulness has become concealed. All nations and tribes of the world have sharpened their claws and are warring and fighting with each other. The edifice of man is shattered. Thousands of families are wandering disconsolate. Thousands of souls are besmeared with dust and blood in the arena of battle and struggle every year, and the tent of happiness and life is overthrown. The prominent men become commanders and boast of bloodshed, and glory in destruction.... Then, O ye friends of God! To the orphans be ye kind fathers, and to the unfortunate a refuge and shelter. To the poor be a treasure of wealth, and to the sick a remedy and healing. Be a helper of every oppressed one, the protector of every destitute one, be ye ever mindful to serve any soul of mankind. Attach no importance to self-seeking, rejection, arrogance, oppression and enmity. Heed them not. Deal in the contrary way. Be kind in truth, not only in appearance and outwardly. Every soul of the friends of God must concentrate his mind on this, that he may manifest the mercy of God and the bounty of the Forgiving One. He must do good to every soul whom he encounters, and render benefit to him, becoming the cause of improving the morals and correcting the thoughts so that the light of guidance may shine forth and the bounty of His Holiness the Merciful One may encompass. Love is light in whatsoever house it may shine and enmity is darkness in whatsoever abode it dwell. O friends of God! Strive ye so that this darkness may be utterly dispelled and the Hidden Mystery may be revealed and the realities of things made evident and manifest.[43]

'Abdu'l-Bahá dedicated much of His time to bring harmony and understanding among all religions. He explained that the "Heavenly Books, the Bible, the Qur'án, and the other Holy Writings have been given by God as guides into the paths of Divine virtue, love, justice and peace. Therefore I say unto you that ye should strive to follow the counsels of these Blessed Books, and so order your lives that ye may, following the examples set before you, become yourselves the saints of the Most High!"[44]

After the death of 'Abdu'l-Bahá in 1921, Shoghi Effendi—the Guardian of the Bahá'í Faith (1921–1957)—further advanced this process through (a) his systematic program of the development of the Bahá'í Community and its essential institutions; (b) his penetrating and uniquely insightful analyses of the historical, political, and social developments of the 19th and 20th centuries and their significance for the future of the Bahá'í Faith and the world; and (c) his patient and tireless guidance of individual Bahá'ís on their path of moral and spiritual growth in an increasingly immoral, materialistic, and violent world. During his 36-year guardianship of the Bahá'í Faith, Shoghi Effendi composed many books, epistles, letters, and telegraphic messages, all of which had direct or indirect relevance to the overall Bahá'í peace program. Here is just one example from his work. In his message of November 28, 1931, addressed to the "Fellow-believers in the Faith of Bahá'u'lláh," while outlining some of the characteristics and goals of the World Order of Bahá'u'lláh, he wrote:

> Let there be no mistake. The principle of the Oneness of Mankind— the pivot round which all the teachings of Bahá'u'lláh revolve—is no mere outburst of ignorant emotionalism or an expression of vague and pious hope. Its appeal is not to be merely identified with a reawakening of the spirit of brotherhood and good-will among men, nor does it aim solely at the fostering of harmonious cöoperation among individual peoples and nations. Its implications are deeper, its claims greater than any which the Prophets of old were allowed to advance. Its message is applicable not only to the individual, but concerns itself primarily with the nature of those essential relationships that must bind all the states and nations as members of one human family. It does not constitute merely the enunciation of an ideal, but stands inseparably associated with an institution adequate to embody its truth, demonstrate its validity, and perpetuate its influence. It implies an organic change in the structure of present-day society, a change such as the world has not yet experienced. It constitutes a challenge, at once bold and universal, to outworn shibboleths of national creeds—creeds that have had their day and which must, in the ordinary course of events as shaped and controlled by Providence, give way to a new gospel, fundamentally different from, and infinitely superior to, what the world has already conceived. It calls for no less than the reconstruction and the demilitarization of the whole civilized world—a world organically unified in all the essential aspects of its life, its political machinery, its spiritual aspiration, its trade and finance, its script and language, and yet infinite in the diversity of the national characteristics of its federated units.
>
> It represents the consummation of human evolution—an evolution that has had its earliest beginnings in the birth of family life, its subsequent development in the achievement of tribal solidarity, leading in turn to the constitution of the city-state, and expanding later into the institution of independent and sovereign nations. The principle of the Oneness of Mankind, as proclaimed by Bahá'u'lláh, carries with it no more and no less than a solemn assertion that attainment to this final stage in this stupendous evolution is not only

necessary but inevitable, that its realization is fast approaching, and that nothing short of a power that is born of God can succeed in establishing it.[45]

Since 1963, with the election of the first Universal House of Justice, the worldwide Bahá'í Community has witnessed a dramatic acceleration in the degree of its diversity and spread around the globe, and the march of the community towards its peace-based objective continues in the same manner and according to the same principles established at the very inception of the religion in the mid-19th century. In their October 1985 weighty and hope-inspiring statement—*The Promise of World Peace*—addressed to the peoples of the world, the Universal House Justice once again reiterated the fundamental and profound commitment of the Bahá'í Faith and its worldwide community to the cause of peace, within an all-inclusive unity in the context of diversity as its fundamental characteristic:

> The experience of the Bahá'í community may be seen as an example of this enlarging unity. It is a community of some three to four million people drawn from many nations, cultures, classes and creeds, engaged in a wide range of activities serving the spiritual, social and economic needs of the peoples of many lands. It is a single social organism, representative of the diversity of the human family, conducting its affairs through a system of commonly accepted consultative principles, and cherishing equally all the great outpourings of divine guidance in human history. Its existence is yet another convincing proof of the practicality of its Founder's vision of a united world, another evidence that humanity can live as one global society, equal to whatever challenges its coming of age may entail. If the Bahá'í experience can contribute in whatever measure to reinforcing hope in the unity of the human race, we are happy to offer it as a model for study.[46]

Aside from the twin processes of spiritual awakening and worldview transformation that are essential for creating peace, we are also in need of an effective modality that can help both to decrease and prevent conflict and violence and that will deal with them effectively and in a manner conducive to justice, unity, and peace if they occur. The objective is to ensure that human differences do not deteriorate into intractable conflicts and violent conditions. The previous chapter discussed one such modality—Bahá'í consultation—which is an ideal modality for creating a civilization of peace. The remaining part of this chapter is a brief portrait of a small Bahá'í Community that starkly demonstrates both the promise and challenge of creating a civilization of peace.

THE BAHÁ'Í COMMUNITY OF KATA

A PORTRAIT

In 1961, shortly after I graduated from medical school, a few friends and I decided to visit the Bahá'í Community of Kata, a small settlement in the tribal territories surrounded by three provinces of Fars, Isfahan, and Khuzistan (see Figure 10.4, map of Iran). We decided on this visit because since the 1955–1956 attacks on the Bahá'ís of Iran (see "A Perilous Revolution" in chapter four) some five years earlier, there had been little or no contact with the Bahá'ís of Kata, and we wanted to check how they were managing under very difficult circumstances. Previously, my friends and I had made a good number of such social and economic visits to various rural communities in several provinces in Iran.

Considering the particular circumstances and needs of the poor, remote places we often visited, we usually organized a team with at least four areas of sufficient expertise and preparedness: medical, educational, community development, and logistics. Thus, our teams had at least four, usually more members. On this occasion there were six of us. One person was given the education portfolio with the responsibility of preparing and bringing sufficient packages of educational materials and textbooks for all children and those adults who were participating in literacy classes. The same person, with the help of another team member would also consult with the parents and teachers about the educational needs of children and adults once we were in Kata. Two persons dealing with community development were assigned the responsibility to research the Boyer Ahmad tribal society, in general, and the Bahá'í Community of Kata, in particular. This task proved to be both difficult and revealing. We, for example, learned that the only road to Kata was a logging road, which ended some 100 kilometers before reaching Kata. The rest of the road was even more primitive. We also, by chance, met one of the most notorious leaders of the Boyer Ahmad tribe who had just been released from jail after five-years' imprisonment on the charge of murder. His home was the settlement next to Kata and when he learned of our intention to visit Kata, he expressly and threateningly stated to us that he was not particularly happy about our visiting "his territory." As far as the Bahá'í Community of Kata was concerned, we did not get much more information than what we already knew some five years earlier. I had the medical portfolio, and in preparation I purchased and gathered as much medical supplies as I

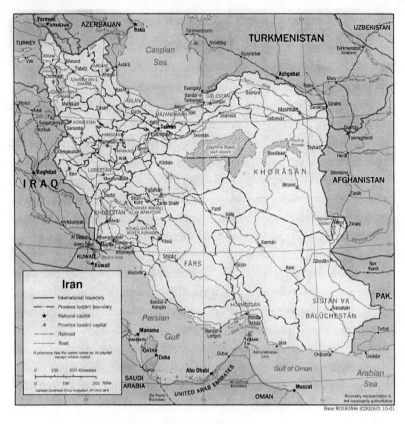

Figure 10.4. Map of Iran and its 28 Provinces.
(Source: Central Intelligence Agency, http://www.lib.utexas.edu/maps/iran.html)

could because we all knew that the medical condition of the entire tribe was extremely poor and their needs very great. Those that were given the logistical tasks had to find a suitable car with a driver who would be willing to undertake such a journey with its inherent dangers. They also had to look after all food and other supplies, as we were going to a region seldom traveled with no hotels, no easily accessible gas stations, nor other such travel facilities. In many respects it was the most difficult and consequential part of our preparation.

From our interviews with several individuals, both from Boyer Ahmad and Isfahan, who were familiar with the history of the Bahá'í Faith among the Boyer-Ahmad [Buyr-Ahamd] tribespeople, we learned that in the early 1930s during a new wave of persecution against the Bahá'ís in several parts of the province of Isfahan, a certain Akhund Abdu'llah and his daughter who were the target of hostile mobs escaped their village in the middle of night and headed on foot towards the mountainous region of the Dena or Dinar. The Dena mountain range lies within the Zagros Mountains of west-southwestern Iran and is situated on the boundary of the now newly constituted provinces of Isfahan, Kohkilooyeh Va Boyer Ahmad, and Chahar Mahal Va Bakhtiyari. After a long and arduous foot journey, they eventually arrived in the Kata settlement. Here, they were received with hospitality, as is the norm in this part of the world, and were welcomed to settle among them.

This father and daughter were learned individuals, and some of the tribespeople were attracted to them and established close friendships, in the process learning of their background, their flight from their home village, and the reason for it. Gradually, as the occasion allowed, Akhund Abdu'llah informed some of the more interested individuals about the Bahá'í Faith and its teachings. In the process, several Boyer Ahmadies joined the Bahá'í Faith and gradually a significant number of others did so too. When we visited Boyer Ahmad, we were informed that at that time (1961) Bahá'ís were located in 12 geographically close, small and large villages, a few with the majority being members of the Bahá'í Faith. Kata was the largest and most established of these communities and at that time had some 300 Bahá'ís and 30 or so Muslims, some of whom were married to Bahá'ís.

At the time of our visit in 1961, Kata and several other Bahá'í Communities in Boyer Ahmad had elaborate and highly developed institutions and social organizations. Among these was the unique institution of the Spiritual Assembly. In the 1930s, soon after several families and individuals in Kata became Bahá'ís, they, under the guidance of Akhund Abdu'llah, elected the first Spiritual Assembly of the Bahá'ís of Kata, a democratically elected institution composed of nine members—first men only and later both men and women—that was dramatically different from the tribal structure of governance, which was a mixture of self-appointed regional chieftains and a federal government appointee who had a certain degree of authority over the tribal chiefs. These individuals were all men who approached their tasks within the parameters of a power-based, authoritarian worldview and in a highly suspicious, fearful, conflicted, and violent manner.

However, the Bahá'ís approached the task of the organization and governance of their community in a dramatically different manner. Every year, on the 21st of April, which is the election day in all Bahá'í communities around the globe, the Bahá'ís of Kata would gather together, and after a period of reflection, prayer, and reading of the Bahá'í sacred writings, each member of the community 21 years or older would cast a secret ballot for nine individuals—men or women, 21 years or older—who he or she believes are most suited to be the members of the spiritual assembly. The nine individuals who receive the highest number of votes become members of the assembly. They work on a voluntary basis and ensure the proper discharge of the responsibilities of the spiritual assembly—unity and the welfare of the community, development and protection of the family, proper education and guidance of children and youth, officiating new marriages, care of the sick, assistance to the poor, protection of the disadvantaged members, comfort of the grieving, organization of the 19-day Bahá'í Feasts (for community consultation and consolidation), holding of special events for Bahá'í holy days and celebrations, philanthropic services to the larger community, continuing efforts to familiarize others with the teachings of the Bahá'í Faith, and welcoming new individuals to the community.

We learned that for the first few years the Spiritual Assembly of the Bahá'ís of Kata was highly dependent on Akhund Abdu'llah, who was the only literate person in the community. However, when he died, the assembly took upon itself to hire the only other literate person in the region primarily for two purposes: (a) to read the holy writings of the Bahá'í Faith for them, so that they would know what to do as an Assembly and also as individual believers; and, (b) to act as an assistant to the secretary of the Assembly who had the responsibility to record the decisions of the Assembly, conduct correspondence with the National Spiritual Assembly of the Bahá'ís of Iran, and handle communication with government officials and others, if and when required. Among the things they learned was that it was the responsibility of the parents and the Assembly to ensure that all children—boys and girls—should be educated in reading, writing, arts and sciences, and ethical and spiritual matters. The Assembly, therefore, hired the services of the same person—who happened to be the only Muslim cleric in the region—to start a rudimentary school for the children and some of the adults who wished to be literate. Thus, in 1961 we found that their school was well established and that all Bahá'ís who were 30 years or younger and some older individuals had at least the equivalent of six years of schooling. This was dramatically different from the rest of the tribe whose population was mostly illiterate and the women, with a few exceptions, were all illiterate.

A further distinguishing feature of the Kata Bahá'í Community was with respect to the role of women in the administration of the affairs of the community. In the 1930s when spiritual assemblies were being elected in many cities and villages across Iran, the membership on these assemblies was limited to men. This was because of the enormous restrictions placed upon women in this predominantly Islamic culture, which did not provide the opportunity and freedom for women, including Bahá'í women, to pursue their education and to participate in the administration of their respective communities with men on an equal basis. To remedy the situation, the National Spiritual Assembly of the Bahá'ís of Iran started a nationwide program for the development and education of women, which, in a period of about two decades, greatly improved the social and educational conditions of women in the community. By our 1961 visit to Kata, women had for several years already been elected as members of their spiritual assembly. Such a development was an anathema to the thinking and traditions of the Boyer Ahmadies, to the extent that many of them believed that such activities on the part of women would bring the wrath of God against the whole community. However, as we will see later, it was not the wrath of God, but rather the anger and fanaticism of the Muslim majority that brought much grief to this and many other communities across Iran.

Another issue that set the Bahá'ís of Kata apart from their fellow tribespeople was with respect to the manner in which they used guns. In the tribe guns were used for personal security, in self-defense, for attacks on other communities, for hunting, and as a symbol of one's virility and prowess. As such, guns were both aspects of people's sense of self and identity, as well as the tools for safety and security. However, Bahá'ís, following the teachings of their religion decided that they would use guns only when they hunted. Otherwise, they did not carry guns, did not engage in violent interpersonal fights, and did not participate in raids on outsiders. The fact that Bahá'ís did not carry guns at all times, as all others in the tribe did, baffled their fellow tribespeople. They did not know how was it possible for anyone, either alone or along with family members, not to carry a gun in such a dangerous and unpredictable world populated by untrustworthy and suspicious *others*. To make sense of such an unusual act—not carrying a gun at all times—a notion gradually developed among this superstitious and illiterate population that *Bahá'ís did not carry guns because they possessed special powers that rendered them invincible to guns.* Several stories and myths begun to circulate in the population to the effect that on various occasions when someone had fired a gun at a Bahá'í, the bullet instead of killing or injuring its intended target, had instead ricocheted and injured the attacker himself. Kata Bahá'ís, with their ironic sense of humor, told us: "We let them believe the stories, because it was the best protection we had!"

In response to the community-building aspects of the Bahá'í Faith such as the emphasis on systematic and comprehensive education of children, the primacy accorded to the institutions of marriage and family, the central role of the spiritual assembly in the administration of the community, and other related considerations, the Bahá'ís of Kata and a few other communities in Boyer Ahmad decided to abandon their nomadic lifestyle and settle in one geographic region. This decision required considerable courage, unity, and cooperation on their part because by changing their nomadic way of life, Bahá'ís had to face two new types of challenge—social and environmental. In social terms, they were abandoning their ancient ways of social and community life, thus separating themselves from their extended families, friends, and compatriots. In environmental terms, they had to learn how to deal with harsher and colder climates, rather than leaving Kata during the colder months and returning when it was warmer and more hospitable. However, settle they did, and in so doing they dramatically advanced the quality and strength of their personal, interpersonal, and community life.

During the course of our six-day stay in Kata, we first held a consultation with the spiritual assembly, which provided us with a thorough review of the situation in their community and its challenges and opportunities. They welcomed our plans with regard to the educational, medical, and community development services that we could render. The education team had thorough consultation about the operation of the Kata School and their adult literacy program. The school welcomed the gifts of books and classroom materials and liked the idea of establishing a community library with the books they had collected both as individuals and as a community, plus those that we offered. During a community meeting, they consulted on the name of the library and decided to call it the "Akhund Abdu'llah Library" in the honor of the first Bahá'í pioneer and his daughter to their region.

The community development team consulted with the Assembly and its "Feasts and Holy-Days" and "Marriage and Family Development" Committees. They wanted to know how to make their 19-Day Feasts more productive, how to conduct the consultative portion of the Feast, how to include children and youth in the organization and conduct of the Feast, and how to educate their community members about the importance and procedures of voting for the Spiritual Assembly and the use of Bahá'í consultation for personal, interpersonal, and community decisions and resolution of conflicts. In the depth and scope of their questions and comments they were truly remarkable. Likewise, their questions about gender equality, prevention of family violence, preparation of young men and women for marriage, consolidation of the foundations of the family, and a proper approach to parenting were both insightful and to the point.

The medical team meanwhile had its challenges. Soon it became evident that practically everyone in the village needed some kind of medical attention. In addition, many individuals in the neighboring communities quickly learned about the presence of a doctor in the region and asked to be seen. In the course of six days, I saw close to 500 individuals, dispensed enormous amounts of medication we had brought, and offered first-aid and disease prevention lessons to several individuals in the community who had some training as nurses and medical assistants. Among my patients were men and women, children and adults, Muslims and Bahá'ís, and rich and poor. One of the patients happened to be the mother of the leader who had just been released from prison. She had pneumonia and with the help of antibiotics made a "miraculous" recovery from a disease that because of its high rate of mortality—when untreated—is simply called "The Disease" by the tribespeople. The leader subsequently became a good friend of the Bahá'ís.

One memorable event happened when I was woken up from a rather restless sleep—because of the presence of many uninvited bugs and ticks—in the middle of the night by our host. He said there were two persons who wanted to see the doctor on an urgent matter. A young man and young woman, both in their late teens, were waiting for me. They introduced themselves. He was a shepherd and a Bahá'í. She had household responsibilities in her family. She was a Muslim. Every day, the shepherd took his cattle to one of the slopes surrounding Kata to graze. On many days the young woman was sent to another slope to gather wood for the oven. While he tended his cattle and she gathered wood, they would communicate by singing love songs. In the process they had fallen in love. However, for them to get married they had to obtain the approval of their respective parents, which is mandatory for all Bahá'ís who wish to marry and a traditional custom for the young people in the Boyer Ahmad culture. While the young man had received approval from his parents, the young woman had not had much success with her parents. However, they informed me, that on the previous day the girl's mother had been among my patients, and she had told her daughter that if the doctor approved of this marriage, she would then give her consent. I asked her parents to come to visit me the following day. They did, and the young couple then married—I hope happily ever after!

Our trip to Kata had to be cut short because of the sudden change of weather, which indicated the early arrival of autumn rains in the plains and snow at the higher altitudes. We had to cross the Dena before the snow came. Otherwise, we would have to stay for several months. We left the following morning and, despite car trouble, were able to traverse the Dena just before the first snow of the season.

I never had the opportunity to return to Kata itself. But three years later I made a visit to a village in Isfahan, where a *Jin Geer*—a traditional healer—from the Boyer Ahmad was conducting a healing ceremony. This was of a great interest for me, both as a physician and a psychiatrist in training. Later, I published a paper entitled, "In Search of a Violence-Free Community"[47] about my visit to Kata and another paper, "Growth and Psychotherapy,"[48] reporting on the approach and perspective used by the Jin Geer to help his patients, often with surprising effective results.

My first and only visit to Kata took place almost half a century ago. The most deeply felt and sustaining impressions that have remained with me about that unique region are with regard to its remarkably hospitable, intelligent, and beautiful people. The larger tribal community was living life as their ancestors had done for centuries. The small Bahá'í communities were demonstrating the remarkable capacity of the Boyer Ahmadies to embrace changes of monumental nature in their worldviews, attitudes, and relationships. While these two communities were quite different in their respective perspectives on the purpose and processes of human individual and social life, nevertheless, both groups related to each other along certain parameters of civility and mutual understanding that made it possible for them to live together, intermarry, continue business and commerce relationships, and join together in times of joy and sorrow.

However, from the information now available about that part of Iran, it is evident that life in that tribal region of Iran has changed dramatically in both economic and social terms. The region is now divided into two provinces: Kohkilooyeh Va Boyer Ahmad and

Chahar Mahal Va Bakhtiyari. In March 1974, Kohkilooyeh Va Boyer Ahmad was accorded the status of a province. Kata is located in the Kohkilooyeh Va Boyer Ahmad Province. This province, with an area of 15,563 square kilometers, is located in central southwestern Iran. Yasooj is the provincial capital. In 2005, this province had a population of 696,000 with 40% of the population living in urban areas and 60% in rural areas. The province has three universities. The official website of the province[49] provides information about its economic, educational, and political activities, all of which are described within the framework of the overall objectives of the Islamic Republic of Iran. It is in the same context that we learn of grievous persecution of the Bahá'ís of Boyer Ahmad since the start of the Islamic Revolution in 1979. In this process the Bahá'ís of Kata and Boyer Ahmad have been subjected to much cruelty, injustice, and persecution. The following are a few representative examples. In "Update on the Situation of the Bahá'ís in Iran and Arab Countries," we come across this brief, but sobering report:

> And in October 2004, six Bahá'í homes in the village of Katá in the Buyír-Ahmad region were confiscated by the authorities—solely on the basis of the owners' membership in the Bahá'í Faith. Bahá'ís in this village have previously endured shootings, mob attacks, and the burning of their properties; since the early days of the Islamic Revolution they have been subjected to pressure intended to force their conversion to Islam.[50]

And after further search we come across a confidential memorandum from the Ministry of Science, Research and Technology of the Islamic Republic of Iran issued by the Central Protection Office of Region 5 to the provinces of Fars, Bushehr, Kahkilooyeh and Boyer Ahmad. Here is the full text of the memorandum:

> To the Honourable Directors of all the Centres,
>
> Greetings,
>
> With respect, according to the ruling of the Cultural Revolutionary Council and the instructions of the Ministry of Information and the Head Protection Office of the Central Organization of Payám-i-Núr University, Bahá'ís cannot enrol in universities and higher education centres. Therefore, such cases if encountered should be reported, their enrolment should be strictly avoided, and if they are already enrolled they should be expelled.
>
> Confirmation comes from God alone.

[Signature]
Central Protection Office of Payám-i-Núr University
Protection Officer of Payám-i-Núr University, region 5

[Signature]
(Provinces of Fárs, Búshihr, KahKílúyih and Buyr-Ahmad)

[Stamp][51]

And, finally our search shows that the active process of persecution of the Bahá'ís of Boyer Ahmad continues to this very date:

> On 23 November 2008, three Baha'is of Yasuj…were tried and sentenced by the first branch of the Islamic Revolutionary Court in that city. The charges against these individuals were "propaganda against the Islamic Republic regime and to the benefit of groups opposing the regime" and "formation and organization of groups and activities intended to disrupt the nation's security." These three individuals were each sentenced to four-years in prison, of which 2 years is suspended. All three are married and have children.…The reason for the arrests and charges against three individuals is that early this year, Mrs.…, who is an elementary school teacher, offered classes on morality, basic education, drawing and theater arts to children of ages 5 to 7 years (pre-school). These children were all from the poor village of Mehryan, located on the outskirt of Yasuj, in Kohgiluyeh and Boyer-Ahmad Province. The classes were completely free of charge. At the beginning of this humanitarian effort, Mrs. (another Baha'i) and her husband,…provided a room in their home in the same village in which to hold these classes. Despite knowing that the organizers were Baha'is, a large number of villagers eagerly brought their children to these classes. It is estimated that about 70 children from this village participated in these sessions.…[52]

These developments bring to mind the following statement of Bahá'u'lláh that applies to the conditions of the world today, as it did more than one and a half centuries ago when it was first uttered:

> Justice is, in this day, bewailing its plight, and Equity groaneth beneath the yoke of oppression. The thick clouds of tyranny have darkened the face of the earth, and enveloped its peoples.[53]

However, Bahá'u'lláh follows His observation of the lamentable conditions of injustice, inequity, oppression, and tyranny in the world by offering counsels to the leaders, sovereigns, and kings of the world and calling upon them to establish the foundations of political peace, as an essential step for creating a world-embracing and ever-advancing civilization of peace:

We pray God…and cherish the hope that He may graciously assist the manifestations of affluence and power and the daysprings of sovereignty and glory, the kings of the earth…to establish the Lesser Peace.[54] This, indeed, is the greatest means for insuring the tranquility of the nations. It is incumbent upon the Sovereigns of the world—may God assist them—unitedly to hold fast unto this Peace, which is the chief instrument for the protection of all mankind. It is Our hope that they will arise to achieve what will be conducive to the well-being of man. It is their duty to convene an all-inclusive assembly, which either they themselves or their ministers will attend, and to enforce whatever measures are required to establish unity and concord amongst men. They must put away the weapons of war, and turn to the instruments of universal reconstruction. Should one king rise up against another, all the other kings must arise to deter him. Arms and armaments will, then, be no more needed beyond that which is necessary to insure the internal security of their respective countries. If they attain unto this all-surpassing blessing, the people of each nation will pursue, with tranquility and contentment, their own occupations, and the groanings and lamentations of most men would be silenced.…It would be preferable and more fitting that the highly honored kings themselves should attend such an assembly, and proclaim their edicts. Any king who will arise and carry out this task, he verily will, in the sight of God, become the cynosure of all kings. Happy is he, and great is his blessedness![55]

SUMMARY

The following statement by Shoghi Effendi is a concise rendition of the Bahá'í perspective in the emerging global civilization of peace:

Unification of the whole of mankind is the hall-mark of the stage which human society is now approaching. Unity of family, of tribe, of city-state, and nation have been successively attempted and fully established. World unity is the goal towards which a harassed humanity is striving. Nation-building has come to an end. The anarchy inherent in state sovereignty is moving towards a climax. A world, growing to maturity, must abandon this fetish, recognize the oneness and wholeness of human relationships, and establish once [and] for all the machinery that can best incarnate this fundamental principle of its life.…

The unity of the human race, as envisaged by Bahá'u'lláh, implies the establishment of a world commonwealth in which all nations, races, creeds and classes are closely and permanently united, and in which the autonomy of its state members and the personal freedom and initiative of the individuals that compose them are definitely and completely safeguarded. This commonwealth must, as far as we can visualize it, consist of a world legislature, whose members will, as the trustees of the whole of mankind, ultimately control the entire resources of all the component nations, and will enact such laws as shall be required to regulate the life, satisfy the needs and adjust the relationships of all races and peoples. A world executive, backed by an international Force, will carry out the decisions arrived at, and apply the laws enacted by, this world legislature, and will safeguard the organic unity of the whole commonwealth. A world tribunal will adjudicate and deliver its compulsory and final verdict in all and any disputes that may arise between the various elements constituting this universal system.

A mechanism of world inter-communication will be devised, embracing the whole planet, freed from national hindrances and restrictions, and functioning with marvellous swiftness and perfect regularity. A world metropolis will act as the nerve center of a world civilization, the focus towards which the unifying forces of life will converge and from which its energizing influences will radiate. A world language will either be invented or chosen from among the existing languages and will be taught in the schools of all the federated nations as an auxiliary to their mother tongue. A world script, a world literature, a uniform and universal system of currency, of weights and measures, will simplify and facilitate intercourse and understanding among the nations and races of mankind. In such a world society, science and religion, the two most potent forces in human life, will be reconciled, will cöoperate, and will harmoniously develop. The press will, under such a system, while giving full scope to the expression of the diversified views and convictions of mankind, cease to be mischievously manipulated by vested interests, whether private or public, and will be liberated from the influence of contending governments and peoples. The economic resources of the world will be organized, its sources of raw materials will be tapped and fully utilized, its markets will be cöordinated and developed, and the distribution of its products will be equitably regulated.

National rivalries, hatreds, and intrigues will cease, and racial animosity and prejudice will be replaced by racial amity, understanding and cöoperation. The causes of religious strife will be permanently removed, economic barriers and restrictions will be completely abolished, and the inordinate distinction between classes will be obliterated. Destitution on the one hand, and gross accumulation of ownership on the other, will disappear. The enormous energy dissipated and wasted on war, whether economic or political, will be consecrated to such ends as will extend the range of human inventions and technical development, to the increase of the productivity of mankind, to the extermination of disease, to the extension of scientific research, to the raising of the standard of physical health, to the sharpening and refinement of the human brain, to the exploitation of the unused and unsuspected resources of the planet, to the prolongation of human life, and to the furtherance of any other agency that can stimulate the intellectual, the moral, and spiritual life of the entire human race....[56]

AFTERWORD

They whose sight is keen, whose ears are retentive, whose hearts are enlightened, and whose breasts are dilated, recognize both truth and falsehood, and distinguish the one from the other.[1]

—Baháʾuʾlláh

We live at a time and in a world when insincerity, dishonesty, and hypocrisy are commonplace; when the foundations of belief and faith are shaken; when attachment to a materialistic way of life is almost universally prized and pursued; and when the anthems of compassion, care, and love are silenced by cries of self-interest, self-protection, and fear and hatred of 'others'. It is in this context that I decided to write this book and invite readers to investigate, objectively and fairly, the cause of religion in a new light and seriously consider the Baháʾí perspectives on the fundamental challenges of our time.

It is my conviction that many people sincerely and with noble and pure motivation are seeking answers to the manifold ills of our world. I am also certain that a large number of adherents of various religions, as well as many thoughtful individuals who have for whatever reasons chosen to reject religion, are nevertheless genuinely looking for a more coherent understanding of the universal and ubiquitous presence of religion throughout history and its undeniable place in human life and impact on human behavior. As well, it is increasingly evident to those who are not seduced by the prevailing materialistic way of life—with its extremes of wealth and poverty, its cold indifference to the suffering of the less privileged and downtrodden masses, and its misguided and destructive doctrine of the 'survival of the fittest'—that materialism, like a cancerous malady, will eventually destroy the very civilization it has labored to create. And finally, I think many people agree that neither science and technology nor faith and religiosity, alone or together, will be able to correct the ills of an afflicted humanity, unless and until we tread the path of unity in the valley of diversity on the steed of love, guided by the light of the consciousness of the oneness of humanity.

The four groups I have identified here are inspired by one of the weightiest Writings of Baháʾuʾlláh in which He likens Himself to the "Nightingale of Paradise" singing on the branches of the divine "Tree of Eternity," addressing four categories of peoples of the world concerning this renewal of the Covenant of God with humanity. The four groups are: "the sincere ones," "the believers in the Divine Unity," "the severed ones," and "the lovers."[2] These four categories constitute most of humanity, are inclusive in their scope, and harmonious in their ultimate objective—to improve the conditions of the world for ourselves and for all people. When qualities of sincerity, unity, universality, and love characterize all our personal and social endeavors, then the path to a sustained and all-inclusive peace—inner, interpersonal, familial, intergroup, international, and global—is paved, and humanity's long-cherished hope for it begins to be realized. Peace is not utopia; it is the finest fruit of human earthly life. Peace-building is not the work of the faint at heart and the fearful; it requires resolve and courage far superior to any other human endeavor. Peace is the hallmark of humanity's coming of age and the outward expression of our spiritual transformation. This is the main message of this book and its main invitation to you.

I am aware that the language and the style of the book is neither classically scientific—in its current restricted definition—nor in the style of traditional religious writing with primary reliance on belief, faith, and personal experience. I have chosen to address various issues covered in the book in an integrated language according to both scientific and spiritual principles, as I understand them. In the book I invited my readers to re-evaluate their already established worldviews in the light of the 'unity paradigm'; to consider religion in the unique framework of the concept of Progressive Revelation; to re-examine their understanding of themselves and their life goals according to certain universal spiritual and scientific principles; to take a new look at the institutions of marriage and family and the reasons for their dismal current situation and historic shortcomings; to reflect on the nature of society, leadership, and governance in the context of unity and peace; and to consider how they can become active agents of transformation and change in their own lives, communities, and the world as a whole. These are lofty far-reaching objectives, and I am therefore aware that many topics have been less than fully addressed and that there are many other issues that need to be studied besides those dealt with here. As such, this book is a work in progress.

This is, ultimately, the most important and most consequential undertaking for every person—to discover, what, if any, is the call of God to us in our lifetime:

> Now is the moment in which to cleanse thyself with the waters of detachment that have flowed out from the Supreme Pen, and to

ponder, wholly for the sake of God, those things which, time and again, have been sent down or manifested, and then to strive, as much as lieth in thee, to quench, through the power of wisdom and the force of thy utterance, the fire of enmity and hatred which smouldereth in the hearts of the peoples of the world. The Divine Messengers have been sent down, and their Books were revealed, for the purpose of promoting the knowledge of God, and of furthering unity and fellowship amongst men. But now behold, how they have made the Law of God a cause and pretext for perversity and hatred. How pitiful, how regrettable, that most men are cleaving fast to, and have busied themselves with, the things they possess, and are unaware of, and shut out as by a veil from, the things God possesseth![3]

—Bahá'u'lláh

To be continued...

APPENDIX I

The following is the summary statement on the history and teachings of the Bahá'í Faith written in 1947 by Shoghi Effendi, the Guardian of the Bahá'í Faith, as a submission to the Special UN Committee on Palestine. For an update of the current statistics on the Bahá'í Faith, its more detailed history, and up-to-date information about its worldwide community, please refer to <http://info.bahai.org/>.

THE FAITH OF BAHÁ'U'LLÁH: A WORLD RELIGION

The Faith established by Bahá'u'lláh was born in Persia about the middle of the nineteenth century and has, as a result of the successive banishments of its Founder, culminating in His exile to the Turkish penal colony of 'Akka, and His subsequent death and burial in its vicinity, fixed its permanent spiritual center in the Holy Land, and is now in the process of laying the foundations of its world administrative center in the city of Haifa.

Alike in the claims unequivocally asserted by its Author and the general character of the growth of the Bahá'í community in every continent of the globe, it can be regarded in no other light than a world religion, destined to evolve in the course of time into a world-embracing commonwealth, whose advent must signalize the Golden Age of mankind, the age in which the unity of the human race will have been unassailably established, its maturity attained, and its glorious destiny unfolded through the birth and efflorescence of a world-encompassing civilization.

RESTATEMENT OF ETERNAL VERITIES

Though sprung from Shiah Islam, and regarded, in the early stages of its development, by the followers of both the Muslim and Christian Faiths, as an obscure sect, an Asiatic cult or an offshoot of the Muhammadan religion, this Faith is now increasingly demonstrating its right to be recognized, not as one more religious system superimposed on the conflicting creeds which for so many generations have divided mankind and darkened its fortunes, but rather as a restatement of the eternal verities underlying all the religions of the past, as a unifying force instilling into the adherents of these religions a new spiritual vigor, infusing them with a new hope and love for mankind, firing them with a new vision of the fundamental unity of their religious doctrines, and unfolding to their eyes the glorious destiny that awaits the human race.

The fundamental principle enunciated by Bahá'u'lláh, the followers of His Faith firmly believe, is that religious truth is not absolute but relative, that Divine Revelation is a continuous and progressive process, that all the great religions of the world are divine in origin, that their basic principles are in complete harmony, that their aims and purposes are one and the same, that their teachings are but facets of one truth, that their functions are complementary, that they differ only in the non-essential aspects of their doctrines, and that their missions represent successive stages in the spiritual evolution of human society.

To Reconcile Conflicting Creeds

The aim of Bahá'u'lláh, the Prophet of this new and great age which humanity has entered upon—He whose advent fulfils the prophecies of the Old and New Testaments as well as those of the Qu'ran regarding the coming of the Promised One in the end of time, on the Day of Judgment—is not to destroy but to fulfill the Revelations of the past, to reconcile rather than accentuate the divergencies of the conflicting creeds which disrupt present-day society.

His purpose, far from belittling the station of the Prophets gone before Him or of whittling down their teachings, is to restate the basic truths which these teachings enshrine in a manner that would conform to the needs, and be in consonance with the capacity, and be applicable to the problems, the ills and perplexities, of the age in which we live. His mission is to proclaim that the ages of the infancy and of the childhood of the human race are past, that the convulsions associated with the present stage of its adolescence are slowly and painfully preparing it to attain the stage of manhood, and are heralding the approach of that Age of Ages when swords will be beaten into plowshares, when the Kingdom promised by Jesus Christ will have been established, and the peace of the planet definitely and permanently ensured. Nor does Bahá'u'lláh claim finality for His own Revelation, but rather stipulates that a fuller measure of the truth He has been commissioned by the Almighty to vouchsafe to humanity, at so critical a juncture in its fortunes, must needs be disclosed at future stages in the constant and limitless evolution of mankind.

Oneness of the Human Race

The Bahá'í Faith upholds the unity of God, recognizes the unity of His Prophets, and inculcates the principle of the oneness and wholeness of the entire human race. It proclaims the necessity and the inevitability of the unification of mankind, asserts that it is gradually approaching, and claims that nothing short of the transmuting spirit of God, working through His chosen Mouthpiece in this day, can ultimately succeed in bringing it about. It, moreover, enjoins upon its followers the primary duty of an unfettered search after truth, condemns all manner of prejudice and superstition, declares the purpose of religion to be the promotion of amity and concord, proclaims its essential harmony with science, and recognizes it as the foremost agency for the pacification and the orderly progress of human society. It unequivocally maintains the principle of equal rights, opportunities and privileges for men and women, insists on compulsory education, eliminates extremes of poverty and wealth, abolishes the institution of priesthood, prohibits slavery, asceticism, mendicancy and monasticism, prescribes monogamy, discourages divorce, emphasizes the necessity of strict obedience to one's government, exalts any work performed in the spirit of service to the level of worship, urges either the creation or the selection of an auxiliary international language, and delineates the outlines of those institutions that must establish and perpetuate the general peace of mankind.

The Herald

The Bahá'í Faith revolves around three central Figures, the first of whom was a youth, a native of Shiraz, named Mírzá 'Alí-Muhammad, known as the Báb (Gate), Who in May, 1844, at the age of twenty-five, advanced the claim of being the Herald Who, according to the sacred Scriptures of previous Dispensations, must needs announce and prepare the way for the advent of One greater than Himself, Whose mission would be according to those same Scriptures, to inaugurate an era of righteousness and peace, an era that would be hailed as the consummation of all previous Dispensations, and initiate a new cycle in the religious history of mankind. Swift and severe persecution, launched by the organized forces of Church and State in His native land, precipitated successively His arrest, His exile to the mountains of Azarbaijan, His imprisonment in the fortresses of Máh-Kú and Chihríq, and His execution, in July, 1850, by a firing squad in the public square of Tabriz. No less than twenty thousand of his followers were put to death with such barbarous cruelty as to evoke the warm sympathy and the unqualified admiration of a number of Western writers, diplomats, travelers and scholars, some of whom were witnesses of these abominable outrages, and were moved to record them in their books and diaries.

BAHÁ'U'LLÁH

Mírzá Husayn-'Alí, surnamed Bahá'u'lláh (the Glory of God), a native of Mazindaran, Whose advent the Báb had foretold, was assailed by those same forces of ignorance and fanaticism, was imprisoned in Tihrán, was banished, in 1852, from His native land to Baghdad, and thence to Constantinople and Adrianople, and finally to the prison city of 'Akka, where He remained incarcerated for no less than twenty-four years, and in whose neighborhood He passed away in 1892. In the course of His banishment, and particularly in Adrianople and 'Akka, He formulated the laws and ordinances of His Dispensation, expounded, in over a hundred volumes, the principles of His Faith, proclaimed His Message to the kings and rulers of both the East and the West, both Christian and Muslim, addressed the Pope, the Caliph of Islam, the Chief Magistrates of the Republics of the American continent, the entire Christian sacerdotal order, the leaders of Shi'a and Sunni Islam, and the high priests of the Zoroastrian religion. In these writings He proclaimed His Revelation, summoned those whom He addressed to heed His call and espouse His Faith, warned them of the consequences of their refusal, and denounced, in some cases, their arrogance and tyranny.

'ABDU'L-BAHÁ

His eldest son, 'Abbas Effendi, known as 'Abdu'l-Bahá (the Servant of Bahá), appointed by Him as His lawful successor and the authorized interpreter of His teachings, Who since early childhood had been closely associated with His Father, and shared His exile and tribulations, remained a prisoner until 1908, when, as a result of the Young Turk Revolution, He was released from His confinement. Establishing His residence in Haifa, He embarked soon after on His three-year journey to Egypt, Europe and North America, in the course of which He expounded before vast audiences, the teachings of His Father and predicted the approach of that catastrophe that was soon to befall mankind. He returned to His home on the eve of the first World War, in the course of which He was exposed to constant danger, until the liberation of Palestine by the forces under the command of General Allenby, who extended the utmost consideration to Him and to the small band of His fellow-exiles in 'Akka and Haifa. In 1921 He passed away, and was buried in a vault in the mausoleum erected on Mount Carmel, at the express instruction of Bahá'u'lláh, for the remains of the Báb, which had previously been transferred from Tabríz to the Holy Land after having been preserved and concealed for no less than sixty years.

ADMINISTRATIVE ORDER

The passing of 'Abdu'l-Bahá marked the termination of the first and Heroic Age of the Bahá'í Faith and signalized the opening of the Formative Age destined to witness the gradual emergence of its Administrative Order, whose establishment had been foretold by the Báb, whose laws were revealed by Bahá'u'lláh, whose outlines were delineated by 'Abdu'l-Bahá in His Will and Testament, and whose foundations are now being laid by the national and local councils which are elected by the professed adherents of the Faith, and which are paving the way for the constitution of the World Council, to be designated as the Universal House of Justice, which, in conjunction with me, as its appointed Head and the authorized interpreter of the Bahá'í teachings, must coordinate and direct the affairs of the Bahá'í community, and whose seat will be permanently established in the Holy Land, in close proximity to its world spiritual center, the resting-places of its Founders.

The Administrative Order of the Faith of Bahá'u'lláh, which is destined to evolve into the Bahá'í World Commonwealth, and has already survived the assaults launched against its institutions by such formidable foes as the kings of the Qajar dynasty, the Caliphs of Islam, the ecclesiastical leaders of Egypt, and the Nazi regime in Germany, has already extended its ramifications to every continent of the globe, stretching from Iceland to the extremity of Chile, has been established in no less than eighty-eight countries of the world, has gathered within its pale representatives of no less than thirty-one races, numbers among its supporters Christians of various denominations, Muslims of both Sunni and Shiah sects, Jews, Hindus, Sikhs, Zoroastrians and Buddhists. It has published and disseminated, through its appointed agencies, Bahá'í literature in forty-eight languages; has already consolidated its structure through the incorporation of five National Assemblies and seventy-seven local Assemblies, in lands as far apart as South America, India and the Antipodes—incorporations that legally empower its elected representatives to hold property as trustees of the Bahá'í community. It disposes of international, national and local endowments, estimated at several million pounds, and spread over every continent of the globe, enjoys in several countries the privilege of official recognition by the civil authorities, enabling it to secure exemption from taxation for its endowments and to solemnize Bahá'í marriage, and numbers among its stately edifices, two temples, the one erected in Russian Turkistan and the other on the shore of Lake Michigan at Wilmette, on the outskirts of Chicago.

This Administrative Order, unlike the systems evolved after the death of the Founders of the various religions, is divine in origin, rests securely on the laws, the precepts, the ordinances and institutions which the Founder of the Faith has Himself specifically laid down and unequivocally established, and functions in strict accordance with the interpretations of the authorized Interpreters of its holy scriptures. Though fiercely assailed, ever since its inception, it has, by virtue of its character, unique in the annals of the world's religious history, succeeded in maintaining the unity of the diversified and far-flung body of its supporters, and enabled them to launch, unitedly and systematically, enterprises in both Hemispheres, designed to extend its limits and consolidate its administrative institutions. The Faith which this order serves, safeguards and promotes, is, it should be noted in this connection, essentially supernatural, supranational, entirely non-political, non-partisan, and diametrically opposed to any policy or school of thought that seeks to exalt any particular race, class or nation. It is free from any form of ecclesiasticism, has neither priesthood nor rituals, and is supported exclusively by voluntary contributions made by its avowed adherents. Though loyal to their respective governments, though imbued with the love of their own country, and anxious to promote, at all times, its best interests, the followers of the Bahá'í Faith, nevertheless, viewing mankind as one entity, and profoundly attached to its vital interests, will not hesitate to subordinate every particular interest, be it personal, regional or national, to the over-riding interests of the generality of mankind, knowing full well that in a world of interdependent peoples and nations the advantage of the part is best to be reached by the advantage of the whole, and that no lasting result can be achieved by any of the component parts if the general interests of the entity itself are neglected.

Nor should the fact be overlooked that the Faith has already asserted and demonstrated its independent religious character, has been emancipated from the fetters of orthodoxy in certain Islamic countries, has obtained in one of them an unsolicited testimony to its independent religious status, and succeeded in winning the allegiance of royalty to its cause.

TRIBUTES BY LEADERS

"It is like a wide embrace," is Queen Marie of Rumania's own tribute, "gathering together all those who have searched for words of hope. It accepts all great Prophets gone before, ' it destroys no other creeds and leaves all doors open.... The Bahá'í teaching brings peace to the soul and hope to the heart. To those in search of assurance, the words of the Father are as a fountain in the desert after long wandering.... It is a wondrous message that Bahá'u'lláh and His son 'Abdu'l-Bahá have given us. They have not set it up aggressively, knowing that the germ of eternal truth which lies at its core cannot but take root and spread.... It is Christ's Message taken up anew, in the same words almost, but adapted to the thousand years and more difference that lies between the year one and today.... If ever the name of Bahá'u'lláh or 'Abdu'l-Bahá comes to your attention, do not put their writings from you. Search out their books, and let their glorious, peace-bringing, love-creating words and lessons sink into your hearts as they have into mine."

"The teachings of the Babis," wrote Leo Tolstoy, "...have a great future before them.... I therefore sympathize with Babism with all my heart, inasmuch as it teaches people brotherhood and equality and sacrifice of material life for service to God.... The teachings of the Babis which come to us out of Islam have through Bahá'u'lláh's teachings been gradually developed, and now present us with the highest and purest form of religious teaching."

"Take these principles to the diplomats," is the late President Masaryk's advice, "to the universities and colleges and other schools, and also write about them. It is the people who will bring the universal peace." "The Bahá'í teaching," is President Eduard Benes' testimony, "is one of the great instruments for the final victory of the spirit and of humanity.... The Bahá'í Cause is one of the great moral and social forces in all the world today. I am more convinced than ever, with the increasing moral and political crises in the world, we must have greater international coordination. Such a movement as the Bahá'í Cause which paves the way for universal organization of peace is necessary."

"If there has been any Prophet in recent times," asserts the Rev. T. K. Cheyne in his 'The Reconciliation of Races and Religions', "it is to Bahá'u'lláh that we must go. Character is the final judge. Bahá'u'lláh was a man of the highest class-that of Prophets." "It is possible indeed," declares Viscount Samuel of Carmel, "to pick out points of fundamental agreement among all creeds. That is the essential purpose of the Bahá'í religion, the foundation and growth of which is one of the most striking movements that have proceeded from the East in recent generations."

"Palestine," is Professor Norman Bentwich's written testimony, "may indeed be now regarded as the land not of three but of four faiths, because the Bahá'í creed, which has its center of faith and pilgrimage in 'Akka and Haifa, is attaining to the character of a world religion. So far as its influence goes in the land, it is a factor making for international and inter-religious understanding."

And, finally, is the judgment passed by no less outstanding a figure than the late Master of Balliol, Professor Benjamin Jowett: "The Babi movement may not impossibly turn out to have the promise of the future." Professor Lewis Campbell, an eminent pupil of Dr. Jowett, has confirmed this statement by quoting him as saying: "This Bahá'í Movement is the greatest light that has come into the world since the time of Jesus Christ. You must watch it and never let it out of your sight. It is too great and too near for this generation to comprehend. The future alone can reveal its import."

Shoghi Effendi,
1947 Summary Statement to the
Special UN Committee on Palestine[1]

APPENDIX II

A SUMMARY OF THE TEACHINGS OF THE BAHÁ'Í FAITH

'Abdu'l-Bahá, after "a tragic life spent almost wholly in exile and imprisonment,"¹ embarked on a historic journey to Western Europe, the United States of America, and Canada. He was then almost seventy. During this journey he gave many talks about the main teachings of the Bahá'í Faith aimed at creating a sustainable, progressive, and universal civilization of peace. In God Passes By, *his grandson Shoghi Effendi provides the following summary of these teachings:*

It was in the course of these epoch-making journeys and before large and representative audiences, at times exceeding a thousand people, that 'Abdu'l-Bahá expounded, with brilliant simplicity, with persuasiveness and force, and for the first time in His ministry, those basic and distinguishing principles of His Father's Faith, which together with the laws and ordinances revealed in *The Kitáb-i-Aqdas* [The Most Holy Book] constitute the bed-rock of God's latest Revelation to mankind. The independent search after truth, unfettered by superstition or tradition; the oneness of the entire human race, the pivotal principle and fundamental doctrine of the Faith; the basic unity of all religions; the condemnation of all forms of prejudice, whether religious, racial, class or national; the harmony which must exist between religion and science; the equality of men and women, the two wings on which the bird of humankind is able to soar; the introduction of compulsory education; the adoption of a universal auxiliary language; the abolition of the extremes of wealth and poverty; the institution of a world tribunal for the adjudication of disputes between nations; the exaltation of work, performed in the spirit of service, to the rank of worship; the glorification of justice as the ruling principle in human society, and of religion as a bulwark for the protection of all peoples and nations; and the establishment of a permanent and universal peace as the supreme goal of all mankind—these stand out as the essential elements of that Divine polity which He proclaimed to leaders of public thought as well as to the masses at large in the course of these missionary journeys. The exposition of these vitalizing truths of the Faith of Bahá'u'lláh, which He characterized as the "spirit of the age" He supplemented with grave and reiterated warnings of an impending conflagration which, if the statesmen of the world should fail to avert, would set ablaze the entire continent of Europe. He, moreover, predicted, in the course of these travels, the radical changes which would take place in that continent, foreshadowed the movement of the decentralization of political power which would inevitably be set in motion, alluded to the troubles that would overtake Turkey, anticipated the persecution of the Jews on the European continent, and categorically asserted that the "banner of the unity of mankind would be hoisted, that the tabernacle of universal peace would be raised and the world become another world."[2]

Appendix III

Bahá'í Consultation

Points to Remember

1. Unity is the prerequisite condition for the success of consultation.
2. Unity is possible only if diversity (i.e., the uniqueness and equality of all individuals and their ideas) is safeguarded, respected, nurtured, and appreciated.
3. The purpose of consultation is to reach fact-based just decision(s) on the issue at hand.
4. Truth is relative, not absolute, i.e., truth is relative depending on our level of understanding and knowledge of a given issue, at a given time and circumstance.
5. Unity and truth are totally interrelated. Truth is one and unity is oneness.
6. Every individual has the capacity to make a unique contribution to consultation. Through the consultative process we together look at the issue at hand, each from a different perspective. The outcome of consultation under ideal circumstances is often both enlightening and unifying.
7. Individuals involved in the consultative process do not represent a block, a group, a party, a race, a gender, a religion, or a nation—in short, a constituency. The participants contribute to the consultation by drawing upon their own conscience, knowledge, experience, and inspiration.
8. Guiding principles of the consultative process are the overriding spiritual principles of truth, unity, justice, and service.
9. Those who are engaged in consultation need to constantly remind themselves that the consultative process is fundamentally a spiritual undertaking. As such, it requires that we approach this sacred task in a condition of humility, prayerfulness, selflessness, universality, cooperation, love, and dedication to the cause of justice and unity.

10. Although unanimity is by far the preferred outcome of reaching a decision, the majority vote has, nevertheless, the same weight as far as the legitimacy of the decision is concerned.

11. In consultation there is no opposition (minority) group. Once a decision is made by a majority vote, all must unhesitatingly accept the decision and make it unanimous.

12. There is no abstention in consultation. An abstention is regarded as a negative vote.

13. Once a decision is reached, even if by a majority vote, all must wholeheartedly participate in its implementation.

14. The sanctity of the right of the individual must always be safeguarded in the consultative process. Therefore, every individual has the right to ask the consultative group to reconsider its decision. If the person still feels dissatisfied, that individual has the right to ask that the matter be put before a higher authority for review and decision. However, under all circumstances, the unity of the consultative group must be safeguarded. This is possible when all members respect one another and are open to reconsideration of the issue before them. The decision for reconsideration also requires a unanimous or majority agreement.

15. In consultation it is better to be wrong and united than right and disunited. If in a consultative process unity cannot be reached, then it is preferable to postpone a decision until unity is restored.

And on a Personal Basis, Remember

16. The prime requisites for those who consult together are pure motives, mature detachment, humility, and patience.

17. The best way to have a consultation without ill-feeling and discord is for all participants to express with absolute freedom their own opinions and put forward their arguments.

18. If one opposes another's opinion, that individual should, on no account, feel hurt, because not until the matter is fully discussed will the right way be found.

19. The clash of differing opinions creates the "shining spark of truth."

20. Participants in consultation must always be loving, courteous, dignified, caring, and moderate.

21. One's objective in consultation is search for the truth and not insistence on personal opinion.

22. Stubbornness and persistence in one's views will ultimately lead to discord and wrangling.

23. For Baháʼís (who use consultation as the main vehicle for their personal, interpersonal, and administrative decisions) turning to God, reminding themselves of the spiritual, moral, and ethical principles that should operate in the life of humanity, and seeking guidance and inspiration from the Writings of the Baháʼí Faith are essential aspects of the consultative process.[1]

Appendix IV

Recommended Bahá'í Reading List

Selected Writings of Bahá'u'lláh

The Kitáb-i-Aqdas (The Most Holy Book)
Bahá'u'lláh's charter for a new world civilization, written in Arabic in 1873. First authorized English translation in 1993

The Kitáb-i-Íqán (The Book of Certitude)
Bahá'u'lláh's teachings on the subject of progressive revelation

The Hidden Words of Bahá'u'lláh
A compilation of moral aphorisms and brief verses that distill the spiritual guidance contained in all past divine revelations

The Seven Valleys and the Four Valleys
Two mystical writings on the stages in the spiritual growth of the soul

Tablets of Bahá'u'lláh
A collection of some of Bahá'u'lláh's writings after the *Kitáb-i-Aqdas*

Epistle to the Son of the Wolf
One of Bahá'u'lláh's last writings, this is essentially Bahá'u'lláh's anthology of His own teachings

Gleanings from the Writings of Bahá'u'lláh
A collection of Bahá'u'lláh's sacred writings translated and compiled by Shoghi Effendi—the Guardian of the Bahá'í Faith—covering many fundamental subjects about human spiritual progress

Prayers and Meditations

A large collection of prayers and meditations revealed by Bahá'u'lláh

SELECTED WRITINGS OF THE BÁB

Selections from the Writings of the Báb

This is the first compilation of the Báb's writings to be translated into English

SELECTED WRITINGS OF 'ABDU'L-BAHÁ

Paris Talks: Addresses Given by 'Abdu'l-Bahá in Paris in 1911–1912

This book contains addresses given to a wide variety of audiences explaining the basic teachings of the Bahá'í Faith

The Secret of Divine Civilization

This book, addressed to the rulers and people of Persia in 1875, explains the fundamental causes of the fall and rise of civilization, elucidates the spiritual foundations of true civilization, and is as relevant to the conditions of the world as it was in 19th century

The Promulgation of Universal Peace

Talks delivered during His 1912 visit to the United States and Canada by 'Abdu'l-Bahá in churches, universities, public forums, private homes, etc. on the fundamental teachings of the Bahá'í Faith, its message of unity and its focus on peace

Selections from the Writings of 'Abdu'l-Baha

A collection of important passages from the writings of 'Abdu'l-Bahá on a wide range of topics pertaining to spiritual, social, and intellectual aspects of life in our rapidly changing world

Some Answered Questions

A collection of "table talks" in which 'Abdu'l-Bahá answered a number of posed questions on a wide range of philosophical, religious, and social questions, including the relationship of the Bahá'í teachings to the Bible and evolution

SELECTED WRITINGS OF SHOGHI EFFENDI

God Passes By
A detailed history of the first century of the Bahá'í Faith

The Promised Day is Come
A commentary on Bahá'u'lláh's letters to the kings and rulers of the world

The World Order of Bahá'u'lláh: Selected Letters
An exposition of the relationship between the Bahá'í community and the process of social evolution under the dispensation of Bahá'u'lláh, outlined in a series of letters to the Bahá'ís of the West between 1929 and 1936

The Advent of Divine Justice
This book outlines the role of America in the establishment of permanent global peace—The Most Great Peace—and identifies three prerequisite spiritual principles that must be internalized by all members of the community for its successful fulfillment: moral rectitude, absolute chastity, and complete freedom from prejudice

COLLECTIONS FROM THE BAHÁ'Í WRITINGS

Bahá'í Prayers
Prayers from Bahá'u'lláh, the Báb, and 'Abdu'l-Bahá, arranged by subject

The Divine Art of Living
Bahá'í teachings on various aspects of living a spiritual life

Unto Him Shall We Return
Bahá'í teachings on the purpose of life,, death, and life after death

The Power of Unity

Bahá'í teachings on the application of the spiritual principle of unity in general and to race unity in particular

Peace: More Than an End to War

Bahá'í teachings about the establishment of universal world peace and the prerequisites for its accomplishment

Bahá'í History

God Passes By

The history of the first century of the Bahá'í Faith (1844–1944) written by its appointed Guardian, Shoghi Effendi

The Dawn-Breakers (Nabíl's Narrative)

The history of the dramatic and extraordinary first 20 years of the Bahá'í Faith written by an observer of many of the events described

Bahá'u'lláh: King of Glory
The Báb: The Herald of the Day of Days
'Abdu'l-Bahá: The Centre of the Covenant of Bahá'u'lláh

Trilogy on the lives of the central figures of the Bahá'í Faith by Hasan Balyuzi

Introductory Works

There are many introductory books on the Bahá'í Faith. The following is a suggested list for readers of diverse interests:

Bahá'u'lláh

Bahá'í International Community, Office of Public Information, 1991
A brief statement detailing Bahá'u'lláh's life and work, and issues on the occasion of the centenary of His passing

The Bahá'ís

A magazine format overview of the Bahá'í Faith covering the basics of Bahá'í beliefs and history. Available on the World Wide Web at <http://oneworld.wa.com/bahai/magazine/cover.html>.

Bahá'u'lláh and the New Era

John Esslemont
Bahá'í Publishing Trust (United Kingdom), 318 pp.

The best-known introductory book, translated into 30 languages, and in continuous print since 1923. Written by a distinguished early British Bahá'í, this book presents a thorough outline of the history, principal figures, spiritual and social teachings, and administrative organization of the Bahá'í Faith. An especially interesting section examines the relationship of Bahá'u'lláh to the expectations and prophecies, such as the Second Coming of the Kingdom of God in Christianity, that are to be found in all faiths.

The Bahá'í Faith: The Emerging Global Religion

William S. Hatcher and J. Douglas Martin
Harper & Row, 248 pp.

As the publishers describe it, "Here is the first definitive introduction—sure to become a standard reference work—of the history, teaching, administrative structure and community life of the Bahá'í Faith, the youngest and one of the fastest growing of the world's independent religions." Martin, an historian, and Hatcher, a professor of mathematics and logic, have produced a survey of the Bahá'í Faith especially strong in its examination of the turbulent early history of the Faith and its relationship to Islam. The authors stress the pivotal concept of the Bahá'í Faith: the oneness of the human race and an emerging global order. As well, they examine a wide range of Bahá'í teachings, such as the oneness and progressive character of religion, the unity of science and religion, the equality of woman and man, economic justice, the spiritual foundation of life, the institutions of the Bahá'í Faith, and disciplines for daily living.

I Shall Come Again

Hushidar Motlagh

Global Perspective, ~500 pp.

Briefly, this book, the first in a (projected) 5-volume series, goes into great detail about biblical prophecies—especially time prophecies— and their fulfillment by the Bahá'í Faith and contains numerous citations— many of them quoting Christian scholars and authorities

The Imperishable Dominion

Udo Schaefer

George Ronald Publisher, 320 pp.

An analysis of modern thought since the 1700s showing how it has contributed to society's current crises, and presenting the Bahá'í answers to today's dilemmas

Preparing for a Bahá'í/Christian Dialogue: Understanding Biblical Evidence

Michael Sours

Oneworld Publications, Ltd.

A multi-volume study program designed to help Bahá'ís familiarize themselves with the Bible and Christian theology; well written and not cumbersome; among the features one finds practical advice on how to study the Bible; methods of interpreting the Bible; answers to the most common Christian questions concerning proofs and progressive revelation; and answers to Christian questions about Bahá'í teachings, the Bible, and Christ

To a Seeker

Nathan Rutstein

George Ronald Publisher, 121pp.

The need for spiritual development as a pathway to happiness is frequently overlooked. The author describes how the Bahá'í Faith can show us the way to that elusive happiness; a dramatic vision of the future, and the steps now being taken by Bahá'ís to attain it, is offered to the seeker who searches for a "new day"

SELECT BAHÁ'Í BIBLIOGRAPHY

'Abdu'l-Bahá. *Foundations of World Unity.* Wilmette, Ill.: Bahá'í Publishing Trust, 1968.

——. *Paris Talks: Addresses Given by 'Abdu'l-Bahá in Paris in 1911–1912.* 11th ed. London: Bahá'í Publishing Trust, 1979.

——. *The Promulgation of Universal Peace.* 2d ed. Wilmette, Ill.: Bahá'í Publishing Trust, 1982.

——. *The Secret of Divine Civilization.* Wilmette, Ill.: Bahá'í Publishing Trust, 1990.

——. *Selections from the Writings of 'Abdu'l-Bahá.* Haifa: Bahá'í World Centre, 1978.

——. *Some Answered Questions.* Wilmette, Ill.: Bahá'í Publishing Trust, 1981.

——. *Tablets of the Divine Plan.* Rev. ed. Wilmette, Ill.: Bahá'í Publishing Trust, 1977.

——. *A Traveller's Narrative Written to Illustrate the Episode of the Bab.* Trans. Edward Granville Browne. 2 vols. Cambridge: Cambridge University Press, 1891.

——. *Will and Testament of 'Abdu'l-Bahá.* Wilmette, Ill.: Bahá'í Publishing Committee, 1944.

Báb, The. *Selections from the Writings of the Báb.* Wilmette, Ill.: Bahá'í Publishing Trust, 1976.

Bahá'í Prayers. Wilmette, Ill.: Bahá'í Publishing Trust, 1985.

Bahá'í World Faith. 2d ed. Wilmette, Ill.: Bahá'í Publishing Trust, 1976.

Bahá'u'lláh. *Epistle to the Son of the Wolf.* Trans. Shoghi Effendi. New ed. Wilmette, Ill.: Bahá'í Publishing Trust, 1988.

——. *Gleanings from the Writings of Bahá'u'lláh.* Comp. and trans. Shoghi Effendi. 2d rev. ed. Wilmette, Ill.: Bahá'í Publishing Trust, 1976.

——. *The Hidden Words of Bahá'u'lláh.* Trans. by Shoghi Effendi with the assistance of some English friends. Rev. ed. Wilmette, Ill.: Bahá'í Publishing Trust, 1979.

——. *Kitáb-i-Aqdas, the Most Holy Book.* Haifa: Bahá'í World Centre, 1992.

——. *The Kitáb-i-Íqán, the Book of Certitude.* Trans. Shoghi Effendi. 2d ed. Wilmette, Ill.: Bahá'í Publishing Trust, 1974.

——. *Prayers and Meditations by Bahá'u'lláh.* Trans. Shoghi Effendi. Wilmette, Ill.: Bahá'í Publishing Trust, 1979.

——. *The Proclamation of Bahá'u'lláh to the Kings and Leaders of the World.* Haifa: Bahá'í World Centre, 1972.

——. *The Seven Valleys and the Four Valleys.* 3d rev. ed. Wilmette, Ill.: Bahá'í Publishing Trust, 1978.

Bahá'u'lláh. *Tablets of Bahá'u'lláh Revealed After the Kitáb-i-Aqdas.* Haifa: Bahá'í World Centre, 1978.

Shoghi Effendi. *The Advent of Divine Justice.* Wilmette, Ill.: Bahá'í Publishing Trust, 1984.

——. *Bahá'í Administration.* Wilmette, Ill.: Bahá'í Publishing Trust, 1974.

——. *God Passes By.* Wilmette, Ill.: Bahá'í Publishing Trust, 1974.

——. *The World Order of Bahá'u'lláh: Selected Letters.* 2d rev. ed. Wilmette, Ill.: Bahá'í Publishing Trust, 1974.

Universal House of Justice. *The Constitution of the Universal House of Justice.* Haifa: Bahá'í World Centre, 1972.

——. *The Promise of World Peace.* Haifa: Bahá'í World Centre, 1985. George Ronald Publisher, 121pp.

INTRODUCTORY WORKS

Many general introductory books have been written about the Bahá'í Faith. Among the better known ones are:

Bausani, Alessandro. *Religion in Iran: From Zoroaster to Bahá'u'lláh.* New York: Bibliotheca Persica Press, 2000. Trans. by J. M. Marchesi. Distributed as vol. 11 of the *Studies in the Bábí and Bahá'í Religions* Series.

Collins, William P. *Bibliography of English-Language Works on the Bábí and Bahá'í Faith 1844–1985.* Oxford: George Ronald, 1990. The most comprehensive bibliography of English-language publications.

Derkse, René. *What is the Bahá'í Faith?* Oxford: George Ronald, 1987. Specially written for young people.

Esslemont, J.E. *Bahá'u'lláh and the New Era, An Introduction to the Bahá'í Faith.* Wilmette, Ill.: Bahá'í Publishing Trust, 1980.

Ferraby, John. *All Things Made New: A Comprehensive Outline of the Bahá'í Faith.* 2d rev. ed. London: Bahá'í Publishing Trust, 1987.

Hatcher, William S., and J.Douglas Martin. *The Bahá'í Faith: The Emerging Global Religion.* Wilmette, Ill: Bahá'í Publishing Trust, 2003.

Huddleston, John. *The Earth Is But One Country.* 3d ed. London: Bahá'í Publishing Trust, 1988.

Momen, Wendy. *A Basic Bahá'í Dictionary.* Oxford: George Ronald, 1989.

Ruhe, David S. *Door of Hope: A Century of the Bahá'í Faith in the Holy Land.* Oxford: George Ronald, 1983.

Smith, Peter. *Bahá'í Religion.* Oxford: George Ronald, 1988.

The Bahá'í World. Haifa: Bahá'í World Centre. An annual survey on Bahá'í activities around the world.

How to Obtain Bahá'í Books
(including electronic versions)

1. Visit your public library.
2. Visit Amazon and other such Internet book outlets.
3. Contact your local Bahá'í community. Many local communities have a local phone number listed under "Bahá'í Faith," or "Bahá'í Community." If a local listing is not available, you can call 1-800-22UNITE in the United States.
4. Many of the books by Bahá'u'lláh, 'Abdu'l-Bahá, and Shoghi Effendi (as well as some others) are available at:

   a. Bahá'í Reference Library <http://reference.bahai.org/en/t/b/> provides access to some of the most important original literature on the Bahá'í Faith;

   b. The Bahá'ís <http://www.bahai.org/> provides important basic information on the Bahá'í Faith and its worldwide community;

ENDNOTES

INTRODUCTION

1. Richard Dawkins, *The God Delusion*, pp. 179–90.
2. Paul Bloom, a professor of psychology and linguistics at Yale, in his article "Is God an Accident?" states: "But the universal themes of religion are not learned. They emerge as accidental by-products of our mental system. They are part of human nature." <www.theatlantic.com/doc/200512/god-accident>, accessed 9 March 2009.

CHAPTER ONE

1. 'Abdu'l-Bahá, *'Abdu'l-Bahá in London*, p. 19.
2. Albert Einstein, <http://www.quotationspage.com/quote/1388.html#email>, accessed 9 March 2009.
3. Imam Ali (599–661 Christian Era; 24 BH–40 AH Islamic Era), son-in-law of Prophet Muhammad, as quoted by 'Abdu'l-Bahá, *Paris Talks*, p. 131.
4. Albert Einstein, (1948) <http://www.spaceandmotion.com/Theology-Albert-Einstein.htm>, accessed 9 March 2009.
5. Albert Einstein refers to the relationship between the *mysterious* and *science*: "The most beautiful thing we can experience is the mysterious. It is the source of all true art and science." <http://www.quotationspage.com/quote/1388.html#email>, accessed January 2008.
6. 'Abdu'l-Bahá, who is the Centre of the Covenant of the Bahá'í Faith, referred to by Bahá'u'lláh as the "Mystery of God" and "Master" among many other appellations, is a unique figure in the annals of religion. Here is a brief account about 'Abdu'l-Bahá on the occasion of His death:

   > On November 29, 1921, ten thousand people—Jews, Christians, and Muslims from all persuasions and denominations—gathered on Mount Carmel in the Holy Land to mourn the passing of One who was eulogized as the essence of "Virtue and Wisdom, of Knowledge and Generosity." On that occasion, 'Abdu'l-Bahá—Bahá'u'lláh's Son and chosen successor—was described by a Jewish leader as a "living example of self-sacrifice," by a Christian orator as One who led humanity to the "Way of Truth," and by a prominent Muslim leader as a "pillar of peace" and the embodiment of "glory and greatness." His funeral, according to a Western observer, brought together a great throng "sorrowing for His death, but rejoicing also for His life."

   > Throughout the Occident and the Orient, 'Abdu'l-Bahá was known as an ambassador of peace, a champion of justice, and the leading exponent of a new Faith. Through a series of epoch-making travels across North America and Europe, 'Abdu'l-Bahá —by word and example—proclaimed with persuasiveness and force the essential principles of His Father's religion. Affirming that *"Love*

is the most great law" that is the foundation of *"true civilization,"* and that the *"supreme need of humanity is cooperation and reciprocity"* among all its peoples, 'Abdu'l-Bahá reached out to leaders and the meek alike, to every soul who crossed His path. (Source: <http://info.bahai.org/abdulbaha-center-of-covenant.html>, accessed 9 March 2009. For more details about the life of 'Abdu'l-Bahá, see *God Passes By* by Shoghi Effendi and *'Abdu'l-Bahá: The Centre of the Covenant of Bahá'u'lláh* by Hasan Balyuzi.)

7. 'Abdu'l-Bahá, *Some Answered Questions,* p. 157.

8. 'Abdu'l-Bahá, *Paris Talks,* p. 131.

9. Johan Galtung and Carl. G. Jacobsen, *Searching for Peace: The Road to TRANSCEND,* p. vii.

10. Brian Muldoon, *The Heart of Conflict,* p. 9.

11. H. B. Danesh and R. P. Danesh, "Has Cconflict Rresolution Ggrown Up? Toward a New Model of Decision-making and Conflict Resolution," pp. 59–76.

12. Ibid., pp. 59–76.

13. See, for example, Plato's *Republic* <http://www.constitution.org/pla/republic. htm>, accessed 9 March 2009.

14. For a detailed account of the life and writings of Sigmund Freud, see <http:// www.freudfile.org/>, accessed 9 March 2009.

15. For a detailed account of the life and writings of Carl Jung, see <http://www. cgjungpage.org/>, accessed 9 March 2009.

16. H.B. Danesh, *The Psychology of Spirituality.*

17. Mawlānā Jalāl-ad-Dīn Muhammad Rūmī, also known as Mawlānā Jalāl-ad-Dīn Muhammad Balkhi, but known to the English-speaking world simply as Rumi, (September 30, 1207–December 17, 1273), was a 13th-century Persian (Tādjīk) poet, Islamic jurist, and theologian. <http://en.wikipedia.org/wiki/Jalal_ad-Din_ Muhammad_Balkhi-Rumi#Philosophical_outlook>, accessed 9 March 2009.

18. For more details on the concept of worldview, see: Sara Clarke-Habibi, "Transforming Worldviews: The Case of Education for Peace in Bosnia-Herzegovinia"; H.B. Danesh, "Breaking the Cycle of Violence: Education for Peace," "Towards an Integrative Theory of Peace Education," "Education for Peace: The Pedagogy of Civilization," and "Creating a Culture of Healing in Multiethnic Communities: An Integrative Approach to Prevention and Amelioration of Violence-induced Conditions"; H.B. Danesh and Sara Clarke-Habibi, *Education for Peace Curriculum Manual;* and H. B. Danesh and R. P. Danesh, "Has Conflict Resolution Grown Up? Toward a New Model of Decision Making and Conflict Resolution."

19. This table is based on my work on the concept of worldview that has been addressed in the articles and book chapters outlined in note 29.

20. Thomas Kuhn, *The Structure of Scientific Revolution,* p. 91.

21. Bahá'u'lláh, *The Book of Certitude.*

22. A concise review and critical analysis of these concepts are presented in *Theories of Developmental Psychology* by Patricia H. Miller.

CHAPTER TWO

1. Bahá'u'lláh, *Gleanings from the Writings of Bahá'u'lláh*, p. 215.

2. 'Abdu'l-Bahá, *Paris Talks*, p. 130.

3. Shoghi Effendi, *The Advent of Divine Justice*, p. 47.

4. Richard Dawkins, *The God Delusion*, p. 188.

5. Sam Harris, <http://mindprod.com/religion/rquote.html#HARRIS>, accessed 9 March 2009.

6. Carl Jung, <http://www.wisdomquotes.com/000881.html>, accessed 9 March 2009.

7. It should be noted that the Bahá'í Chair in Development Studies was formed in 1989 at DAVV Indore University in India, and the Bahá'í Chair for World Peace was formed at the University of Maryland in 1993. However, the endowed Chair at the Hebrew University in Jerusalem is the first of its kind devoted to Bahá'í Studies at any university.

8. *The Christian Science Monitor* in a 1998 article, "Top 10 Organized Religions in the World," provides a further example, listing the largest organized religions: Christianity 1.9 billion, Islam 1.1 billion, Hinduism 781 million, Buddhism 324 million, Sikhism 25 million, Judaism 14 million, the Bahá'í Faith 6.1 million, Confucianism 5.3 million, Jainism 4.9 million, and Shinto 2.8 million <http://en.wikipedia.org/wiki/Major_religious_groups>, accessed 9 March 2009. Another site <http://www.adherents.com/Religions_By_Adherents.html>, accessed 9 March 2009, gives somewhat larger numbers for these religions and adds several other smaller religious groups. It also gives an estimate of 1.1 billion for those who are secular/nonreligious/agnostic/and atheist.

9. One of the unique features of the Bahá'í Faith is the institution of the Covenant, which was established by Bahá'u'lláh in the Most Holy Book. Bahá'u'lláh's Covenant guarantees both unity of understanding of His Faith's fundamental doctrines and safeguards its unity. The Bahá'í Covenant is designed, unlike any religious system of the past, to preserve the unity of all humanity through the organic workings of a social order based on spiritual principles. The Bahá'í Faith is thus the first religion in history that has survived its critical first century and a half with its unity firmly established. 'Abdu'l-Bahá was appointed by Bahá'u'lláh as the Centre of His Covenant. For more details, see: Shoghi Effendi, *God Passes By* and <http://info.bahai.org/covenant-of-bahaullah.html>, accessed 9 March 2009.

10. 'Abdu'l-Bahá, *Bahá'í World Faith*, pp. 228–29.

11. It should be noted that all the dates of birth and death of these Founders of religions, with the exception of those given for Bahá'u'lláh, are estimates and not universally accepted.

12. Bahá'u'lláh, *The Book of Certitude*, pp. 153–54.

13. Bahá'u'lláh, *Gleanings from the Writings of Bahá'u'lláh*, p. 87.

14. 'Abdu'l-Bahá, *Foundations of World Unity*, pp. 8–9.

15. Shoghí Effendí Rabbání (March 1, 1897–November 4, 1957), known as Shoghi Effendi, was the appointed Guardian (head) of the Bahá'í Faith from 1921 until his death in 1957. After the death of 'Abdu'l-Bahá in 1921, the leadership of the Bahá'í community entered a new phase, evolving from that of a single individual to an administrative order with executive and legislative branches, the head of

each respectively being the Guardianship and the Universal House of Justice. As the Guardian, Shoghi Effendi held the explicit authority to interpret the writings of the three central figures of the religion and define the sphere of legislative authority. Future hereditary Guardians were permitted in the Bahá'í scripture by appointment from one to the next. However, Shoghi Effendi who died in 1957 did not appoint another Guardian, as the prerequisites for such an appointment as outlined by 'Abdu'l-Bahá were not present. The Universal House of Justice, the only institution authorized to adjudicate on situations not covered in scripture, later announced that it could not legislate to make possible the appointment of a successor to Shoghi Effendi. Thus Shoghi Effendi is the first and last Guardian of the Bahá'í Faith.

16. Shoghi Effendi, *The World Order of Bahá'u'lláh*, p. 202.

17. Ibid., p. 163.

18. Bahá'u'lláh, *Gleanings from the Writings of Bahá'u'lláh*, p. 215.

19. Ibid., p. 286.

20. Ibid., p. 288.

21. 'Abdu'l-Bahá as quoted by Shoghi Effendi, *The World Order of Bahá'u'lláh*, p. 36.

22. 'Abdu'l-Bahá, *Selections from the Writings of 'Abdu'l-Bahá*, p. 28.

23. Shoghi Effendi, *The World Order of Bahá'u'lláh*, p. 203.

24. 'Abdu'l-Bahá, *Bahá'í World Faith*, p. 247.

25. For a brief review of the concept of humanism, see: Encyclopedia Britannica <http://www.britannica.com/eb/article-9106290/humanism>, accessed 9 March 2009; and Wikipedia <http://en.wikipedia.org/wiki/Humanism>, accessed 9 March 2009. "Scientific Humanism and the Humanist Manifestos" that appears on the website <http://www.religioustolerance.org/humanism.htm>, accessed 9 March 2009, provides the following summary: "Secular Humanism is a non-theistically based philosophy which promotes humanity as the measure of all things. It had its roots in the rationalism of the 18th Century and the free thought movement of the 19th Century."

26. For a brief review of the concept of scientism, see: Wikipedia <http://en.wikipedia.org/wiki/Scientism>, accessed 18 March 2009. Martin Ryder of the University of Colorado at Denver <http://carbon.cudenver.edu/~mryder/scientism_este.html>, accessed 18 March 2009, provides the following definition: "Scientism is a philosophical position that exalts the methods of the natural sciences above all other modes of human inquiry. Scientism embraces only empiricism and reason to explain phenomena of any dimension, whether physical, social, cultural, or psychological. Drawing from the general empiricism of The Enlightenment, scientism is most closely associated with the positivism of August Comte (1798–1857) who held an extreme view of empiricism, insisting that true knowledge of the world arises only from perceptual experience. Comte criticized ungrounded speculations about phenomena that cannot be directly encountered by proper observation, analysis and experiment. Such a doctrinaire stance associated with science leads to an abuse of reason that transforms a rational philosophy of science into an irrational dogma (Hayek, 1952). It is this ideological dimension that we associate with the term *scientism*. Today the term is used with pejorative intent to dismiss substantive arguments that appeal to scientific authority in contexts

where science might not apply. This over commitment to science can be seen in epistemological distortions and abuse of public policy...."

27. For views on capitalism, see: The European Enlightenment Glossary <http://www.wsu.edu/~dee/GLOSSARY/CAPITAL.HTM> and Encyclopaedia Britannica <http://www.britannica.com/eb/article-9020150/capitalism> accessed 9 March 2009.

28. For definitions of materialism, see: The Dictionary of Philosophy of Mind <http://philosophy.uwaterloo.ca/MindDict/materialism.html>, accessed 9 March 2009:

> Materialism is a general view about what actually exists. Put bluntly, the view is just this: Everything that actually exists is material, or physical. Many philosophers and scientists now use the terms 'material' and 'physical' interchangeably (for a version of physicalism distinct from materialism, see physicalism). Characterized in this way, as a doctrine about what exists, materialism is an *ontological*, or a *metaphysical*, view; it is not just an epistemological view about how we know or just a semantic view about the meaning of terms....

29. "A new religious movement or NRM is a term used to refer to a religious faith, or an ethical, spiritual or philosophical movement of recent origin that is not part of an established denomination, church, or religious body. The term NRM comprises a wide range of movements which range from loose affiliations based on novel approaches to spirituality or religion to communitarian enterprises that demand a considerable amount of group conformity and a social identity that separates its adherents from mainstream society. Its use isn't universally accepted among the groups to which it is applied." Source: <http://en.wikipedia.org/wiki/New_religious_movement >, accessed 9 March 2009.

30. Bahá'u'lláh, *The Book of Certitude*, p. 192.

31. Bahá'u'lláh, *Gleanings from the Writings of Bahá'u'lláh*, pp. 63–68.

32. 'Abdu'l-Bahá, *Foundations of World Unity*, pp. 64–65.

33. 'Abdu'l-Bahá, *Some Answered Questions*, p. 218.

34. 'Abdu'l-Bahá, *Paris Talks*, p. 154.

35. Bahá'u'lláh, *The Kitáb-i-Aqdas (The Most Holy Book)*, p. 19.

36. Ibid., p. 19.

37. Ibid., p. 20.

38. Bahá'u'lláh, *The Hidden Words*, number 5 of part 1 (Arabic).

39. Bahá'u'lláh, *Tablets of Bahá'u'lláh*, p. 93.

40. Bahá'u'lláh, *Epistle to the Son of the Wolf*, p. 27.

41. Bahá'u'lláh, *Tablets of Bahá'u'lláh*, p. 125.

42. Ibid., p. 251.

43. Bahá'u'lláh, *Tablets of Bahá'u'lláh*, p. 222.

44. Bahá'u'lláh, *Gleanings from the Writings of Bahá'u'lláh*, p. 250.

45. Bahá'u'lláh, *Tablets of Bahá'u'lláh*, p. 120.

46. Ibid., p. 73.

47. Ibid., p. 75.

48. 'Abdu'l-Bahá, *Foundations of World Unity*, pp. 55–56.

49. Bahá'u'lláh, *The Kitáb-i-Aqdas (The Most Holy Book)*, p. 62.

50. Bahá'u'lláh, *Tablets of Bahá'u'lláh*, p. 196.

51. Bahá'u'lláh *The Kitáb-i-Aqdas (The Most Holy Book)*, p. 70.

52. Bahá'u'lláh, *Epistle to the Son of the Wolf*, p. 24.

53. Bahá'u'lláh, *Tablets of Bahá'u'lláh*, p. 155.
54. Bahá'u'lláh, *Proclamation of Bahá'u'lláh*, p. 61.
55. Ibid., p. 77.
56. 'Abdu'l-Bahá, *Selections from the Writings of 'Abdu'l-Bahá*, p. 125.
57. 'Abdu'l-Bahá, *The Promulgation of Universal Peace*, p. 53.
58. 'Abdu'l-Bahá, *The Secret of Divine Civilization*, p. 40.
59. Shoghi Effendi, as quoted in *A Compilation on Bahá'í Education*, p. 52.
60. Shoghi Effendi, *The World Order of Bahá'u'lláh*, pp. xi–xii.

CHAPTER THREE

1. From *The World Parliament of Religion*, volume 2, 13th day, under "Criticism and Discussion of Missionary Methods," p. 1122. At the Columbian Exposition of 1893 at Chicago.
2. Leo Tolstoy, from a communication dated 1908 quoted in *The Bahá'í World: 1954–1963*, p. 818.
3. Dowager Queen Marie of Romania, *Toronto Daily Star*, (Canada), May 4, 1926.
4. Herbert Adams Gibbons, excerpt from personal letter dated May 18, 1934. <http://bahai-library.com/books/appreciations.html>, accessed 10 March 2009.
5. Vincenc Lesný, quoted in *The Bahá'í World: 1954–1963*, p. 822.
6. Euard Benes, quoted in *The Bahá'í World: 1954–1963*, p. 823.
7. Z.T.Ing, from an interview in San Jose, Nicaragua, 1942, reproduced in *The Bahá'í World: 1954–1963*, p. 827.
8. Chikao Fujisawa, member of the Secretariat of the League of Nations, Chair of International Politics, Kyushu Imperial University, Japan. This statement is from an address in Tokyo in 1932 and is quoted in *The Bahá'í World: 1954–1963*, p. 828.
9. David Starr Jordan, quoted in *The Bahá'í World: 1954–1963*, p. 822.
10. Helen Keller, from a personal letter written to an American Bahá'í after Keller's having read the Braille edition of *Bahá'u'lláh and the New Era* by J.E. Esslemont, quoted in *The Bahá'í World: 1954–1963*, p. 821.
11. Summarized from *The Jews of Islam* by Bernard Lewis, pp. 181–83. Also see *Weathering the Storm*, accessed 18 March 2009, about Jews in present-day Iran.
12. Daryush Jahanian, *The History of Zoroastrians After Arab Invasion*, European Centre for Zoroastrian Studies <http://www.gatha.org/english/articles/000258.html>, accessed 18 March 2009.
13. *The Bahá'í Question: Cultural Cleansing in Iran*, <http://question.bahai.org>, accessed 18 March 2009.
14. For details of persecution of Bahá'ís, refer to <http://www.bahai.org/dir/worldwide/persecution>, accessed 18 March 2009.
15. For more information on the ongoing persecution of Bahá'ís in Iran, see <http://en.wikipedia.org/wiki/Persecution_of_Bahá'ís>, and *Closed Doors: Iran's Campaign to Deny Higher Education to Bahá'ís*, <http://denial.bahai.org/>, accessed 18 March 2009.
16. Interested readers can find a helpful summary of these beliefs at <http://en.wikipedia.org/wiki/End_times >, accessed 18 March 2009.

17. For more information about Yazd, see <http://www.mideasttravelling.net/iran/
    yazd/yazd_history.htm> and <http://www.northill.demon.co.uk/relstud/yazd.
    htm>, accessed 18 March 2009.

18. For information about Avesta and other scriptures of the Zoroastrian Faith, refer
    to <http://www.avesta.org/>, accessed 18 March 2009.

19. Columbia Encyclopedia <http://www.bartleby.com/65/ha/Hafiz.html>, accessed
    18 March 2009, provides this summary about Hafiz:

    > (häfz') (KEY) [Arab.,=one who has memorized the Qur'an], 1319–1389?,
    > Persian lyric poet, b. Shiraz. His original name was Shams al-Din Muhammad.
    > He acquired the surname from having memorized the Qur'an at an early age. A
    > teacher of the Qur'an who associated with mystics, his lyrical poetry is acclaimed
    > as the finest ever written in Persian. his lyrics are always vehement, especially his
    > amatory verses, his drinking songs, and his invective. Muslim critics interpret his
    > passionate lines as allegorical, while critics in the West incline to construe them
    > literally. Hafiz enlivened the conventional imagery of the *ghazal,* a form of love
    > poetry in rhyming couplets, comparable to the sonnet. His poetry, in *ghazal* and
    > in the other poetic forms of *qasida* (long rhyming poem), *mathnawi* (couplets),
    > and *rubaiyyat* (quatrains), survives in his *Divan* or *Diwan,* a collection that
    > prompted numerous commentaries. His *Diwan* was so popular that it is used
    > for bibliomancy: predictions are made from randomly selected verses. Goethe's
    > *Westöstlicher Diwan* (1819) was inspired by Hafiz. Hafiz is buried in a splendid
    > tomb near Shiraz, Iran.

20. Columbia Encyclopedia <http://www.bartleby.com/65/ru/Rumi-Jal.html>,
    accessed 18 March 2009, provided this summary about Rumi:

    > (jäläl' d-dn' r'm) (KEY), 1207–73, great Islamic Persian sage and poet mystic, b.
    > in Balkh. His father, a scholar, was invited by the Seljuk sultan of Rum to settle
    > in Iconium (now Konya), Turkey. His apprenticeship as a Sufi mystic was guided
    > by the mysterious Shams ad-Din Tabrizi (d. 1247), who was considered one of
    > the spiritual masters of Rumi's age. His major work is the *Mathnawi,* a vast 6 vol.
    > work of spiritual teaching and Sufi lore in the form of stories and lyric poetry
    > of extraordinary quality. The *Mathnawi* is one of the enduring treasures of the
    > Persian-speaking world, known and memorized by most. It is popularly called
    > "the Qur'an in Persian." The singing of the *Mathnawi* has become an art form in
    > itself. Rumi also founded the Mawlawiyya (Mevlevi) Sufi order, who use dancing
    > and music as part of their spiritual method, and who are known in the West as
    > Whirling Dervishes. Rumi's influence spread to Persian-speakers in Afghanistan
    > and central Asia, and beyond, to Turkey and India. His tomb in Konya is a place
    > of pilgrimage, and the Mawlawiyya order is still centered in Konya.

21. Columbia Encyclopedia <http://www.bartleby.com/65/sa/Sadi.html>, accessed
    18 March 2009, provided this summary about Saadi:

    > Sadi or Saadi (both: säd) (KEY), Persian poet, 1184–1291. b. Shiraz. Orphaned
    > at an early age, Sadi studied in Baghdad, where he met Suhrawardi, a major Sufi
    > figure. Having to flee Baghdad because of the Mongol threat, he went on a long
    > journey that took him to central Asia and India, then to Yemen and Ethiopia
    > through Mecca. Sadi was captured by the Franks in Syria and worked at hard
    > labor until ransomed. He proceeded to N Africa and Anatolia, before returning
    > to his native Shiraz in 1256. His *Bustan* [fruit garden], an ethical-didactic text,
    > was composed in *mathnawi* (rhyming couplets). Even more popular is his
    > *Gulistan* [Garden of Roses], written in rhyming prose. Sadi is also the author

of many *qasidas* (long panegyrics) in Persian and Arabic, of mystic *ghazal* (love poems), and of satiric poetry. His tomb in Shiraz is a shrine.

22. H.B. Danesh, *The Psychology of Spirituality.*

23. For a review of the life and work of Sigmund Freud, refer to < http://www. freudfile.org/>, accessed 18 March 2009.

24. Sigmund Freud, *New Introductory Lessons on Psychoanalysis,* < http://www.freudfile. org/quotes.html>, accessed 18 March 2009.

25. Source: <http://www.angelfire.com/or/sociologyshop/marxrel.html>, accessed 18 March 2009.

26. Charles Darwin, *The Autobiography of Charles Darwin (1809–1882),* with original omissions restored, edited with appendix and notes by his grand-daughter Nora Barlow (1958). These quotations are taken from the website Fredrik Bendz, <http://www.update.uu.se/~fbendz/library/cd_relig.htm>, accessed 18 March 2009.

27. Darwin, *The Autobiography of Charles Darwin* (with an introduction by Brian Regal), p. 295.

28. See, for example, R. Stark, "Psychopathology and Religious Commitment," pp. 165–76 and T. Pilarzyk, "Conversion and Alternation Processes in the Youth Culture," pp. 51–72.

29. See, for example, M. Singer, "Coming out of the Cults"; J.T.Richardson and B. Kilbourne, "Classical and Contemporary Applications of Brainwashing Models"; and D. Anthony, "Religious Movements and Brainwashing Litigation."

30. See, for example, T. Solomon, "Programming and Deprogramming the Moonies" and T. Pilarzyk, "Conversion and Alternation Processes in the Youth Culture."

31. For more recent research on religious conversion, see J.T. Richardson, "The Active Versus Passive Convert" and "Studies of Conversion"; J. Lofland and R. Stark, "Becoming a World-Saver"; and Lewis R. Ranbo, *Understanding Religious Conversion.*

32. Bahá'u'lláh, *The Hidden Words,* no. 5, part 2 (Persian).

33. For information about the beginnings of the Bahá'í Faith and The Báb, see <http://www.bahai.org/dir/thebab>, < http://en.wikipedia.org/wiki/Báb> and < http://www.bahai.org/>, accessed 18 March 2009.

34. Friedrich Nietzsche, *The Gay Science* [aka *Joyous Wisdom*](1882, 1887), para. 125; pp.181–82.

35. For more information, see <http://www.bahai.com/thebahais/pg17b.htm>, accessed 18 March 2009.

36. Bahá'u'lláh, quoted in H. M. Balyuzi, *Edward Granville Browne and the Bahá'í Faith,* pp. 56–57.

37. Bahá'u'lláh, *The Book of Certitude,* pp. 192–93.

CHAPTER FOUR

1. Bahá'u'lláh, *Gleanings from the Writings of Bahá'u'lláh,* p. 65.

2. 'Abdu'l-Bahá, *The Promulgation of Universal Peace,* p. 187.

3. Richard Dawkins, *River Out of Eden,* ch. 4, quoted in *The New Penguin Dictionary of Modern Quotations.*

4. 'Abdu'l-Bahá, as quoted in H.M. Balyuzi, *Edward Granville Browne and the Baháí Faith,* pp. 56–57.

5. My research on issues of peace, conflict resolution, and spiritual psychology addresses the concept of unity in its varied expressions. See especially H.B. Danesh, "Towards an Integrative Theory of Peace Education," "Breaking the Cycle of Violence: Education for Peace," *The Psychology of Spirituality, Peace Moves,* "Education for Peace: The Pedagogy of Civilization," and "Creating a Culture of Healing in Multiethnic Communities: An Integrative Approach to Prevention and Amelioration of Violence-induced Conditions."

6. Baháʼu'lláh, *Gems of Divine Mysteries,* pp. 41–42.

7. H.B. Danesh, *The Psychology of Spirituality.*

8. H.B. Danesh, *The Mysterious Case of the IWs,* forthcoming.

9. For details of these events, see *The Baháí Question: Cultural Cleansing in Iran,"* and Geoffrey Nash, "The Persecution of the Baháí Community of Iran: Ridván 1979–Ridván 1983," in *The Baháí World (1979–1983),* pp. 249–30.

10. Geoffrey Nash, op.cit., p. 285.

11. For more details of the persecution of Baháʼís in Iran, see William P. Collins and Janet Beavers, "Persecution of the Baháʼís in Iran: A Partial Bibliography of References from Books and Pamphlets, Journals, Newspaper Articles and Official Documents in Some European Languages," in *The Baháí World (1979–1983),* pp. 369–79; and Moojan Momen, "A Chronology of Some of the Persecutions of the Bábís and Baháʼís in Iran: 1844–1978," in *The Baháí World (1979–1983),* pp. 380–92.

12. J. Douglas Martin, "The Case of the Baháí Minority in Iran," in *The Baháí World (1992–1993),* pp. 247–71.

13. Geoffrey Nash, op.cit., p. 256.

14. For information about Falsafi machinations against the Baháí Faith, see: Elizabeth Sanasarian, *Religious Minorities in Iran,* pp. 52–53, and *Khatirat va Mubarizat-i Hojjatolislam Mohammad Taqi Falsafi* [The Memories and Campaigns of Hojjatol-Islam Mohammad Taqi Falsafi].

15. For more information about Islam, see: Ira Lapidus, *A History of Islamic Societies,* p. 47; P.M. Holt, Bernard Lewis, Ann Katherine, and Swynford Lambton, *Cambridge History of Islam,* pp.70–72; Sayyid Mohammad Hosayn Tabatabaei, *Shi'ite Islam,* pp. 50–57 and 192; "al-Hussein ibn 'Ali." <http://en.wikipedia.org/wiki/Husayn_ibn_Ali>, accessed 2 April 2009; and Moojan Momen, *An Introduction to Shi'i Islam: The History and Doctrines of Twelver Shi'ism.*

16. For detailed information about the persecution of Baháʼís in Iran, see "The Ramadan Riots of 1955," *A Faith Denied: The Persecution of the Baháís of Iran,* prepared by Iran Human Rights, pp. 7–10. <http://www.scribd.com/doc/322153/bahai-report?query2=taslimi%20nsa%20iran>, accessed 18 March 2009.

17. See, for example, Edward O. Wilson, *On Human Nature;* Richard Dawkins, *The God Delusion;* and Stephen Jay Gould, *The Structure of Evolutionary Theory.*

18. For more details on formulations offered by the evolutionary psychology, see: D.M. Buss, ed., *The Handbook of Evolutionary Psychology;* Deborah Keleman, "Are Children 'Intuitive Theists'?"; M.A. Preissler and P. Bloom, "Two-year-olds Appreciate the Dual Nature of Pictures"; Paul Bloom, "Is God an Accident?";

Paul Bloom, *Descartes' Baby: How the Science of Child Development Explains What Makes Us Human;* and Richard Dawkins, *The God Delusion.*

19. Paul Bloom, <http://www.yale.edu/psychology/FacInfo/Bloom.html>, accessed 18 March 2009.

20. 'Abdu'l-Bahá, *Paris Talks,* pp. 96–97.

21. Bahá'u'lláh, *Bahá'í World Faith,* pp. 121–22.

22. 'Abdu'l-Bahá, *Bahá'í World Faith,* p. 242.

23. 'Abdu'l-Bahá, *Selections from the Writings of 'Abdu'l-Bahá,* pp. 52–53.

24. There are many schools of psychology. Among the most influential of these schools that started at the end of the 19th and the beginning of the 20th century are behaviorism, the psychoanalytic school of Freud, functionalism, humanistic/Gestalt, and cognitivism.

25. For an analysis of this process, see Bruno Bettelheim, (1984), *Freud and Man's Soul.*

26. For a brief review of Freud's views on religion, refer to <http://psychology.about.com/od/sigmundfreud/p/freud_religion.htm>. These three quotations are from this site accessed 18 March 2009.

27. For a review of the views of Leda Cosmides, and John Tooby, refer to <http://www.wilderdom.com/personality/L7-1EvolutionaryPsychology.html> (1997), accessed 18 March 2009.

28. Richard Dawkins, *The God Delusion,* p. 179.

29. Ibid., p. 188.

30. 'Abdu'l-Bahá, *Selections from the Writings of 'Abdu'l-Bahá,* p. 108.

31. Shoghi Effendi, *God Passes By,* p. 281.

32. Albert Einstein, *Out of My Later Years,* p. 26.

33. Shoghi Effendi, *The Promised Day is Come,* pp. 112–14.

34. 'Abdu'l-Bahá, *Bahá'í World Faith,* p. 331.

35. Bahá'u'lláh, *Kitáb-i-Íqán (The Book of Certitude),* p. 241.

36. 'Abdu'l-Bahá, *Bahá'í World Faith: Selected Writings of Bahá'u'lláh and 'Abdu'l-Bahá,* p. 368.

37. 'Abdu'l-Bahá, *Bahá'í Prayers: A Selection of Prayers Revealed by Bahá'u'lláh, the Báb, and 'Abdu'l-Bahá,* pp. 115–16.

38. Ibid., Bahá'u'lláh, p. 173.

39. Ibid., 'Abdu'l-Bahá, p. 333.

40. Ibid., 'Abdu'l-Bahá, p. 4.

41. Ibid., Bahá'u'lláh, p. 238.

42. Ibid., 'Abdu'l-Bahá, p. 239.

43. 'Abdu'l-Bahá, *Tablets of 'Abdu'l-Bahá,* vol.1, p. 180.

44. 'Abdu'l-Bahá, *The Promulgation of Universal Peace,* pp. 246–47.

45. The Báb, *Selections from the Writings of the Báb,* p. 78.

46. 'Abdu'l-Bahá, *Bahá'í World Faith,* pp. 377–78.

47. 'Abdu'l-Bahá, *Paris Talks,* pp. 176–77.

48. 'Abdu'l-Bahá, quoted in *Divine Art of Living: Selections from the Writings of Bahá'u'lláh and 'Abdu'l-Bahá,* pp. 86–87.

49. For research and analytical reviews on fear of death and denial of death and their impact on life, see Charles Darwin, *The Expression of the Emotions in Man and Animals;* Sigmund Freud, "Thoughts for the Times on War and Death"; Ernest

Becker, *The Denial of Death;* V. Florian and M. Mikulincer, "Fear of Death and the Judgment of Social Transgressions: A Multidimensional Test of Terror"; T. Pyszczynski, J. Greenberg, and S. Solomon, "A Dual Process Model of Defense Against Conscious and Unconscious Death-related Thoughts: An Extension of Terror Management Theory"; J.L.Goldenberg et al., "Fleeing the Body: A Terror Management Perspective on the Problem of Human Corporeality"; J.L.Goldenberg et al., "I Am Not an Animal: Mortality, Salience, Disgust, and the Denial of Human Creatureliness"; M. Mikulincer, V. Florian, and G. Hirschberger, "The Existential Function of Close Relationships: Introducing Death into the Science of Love"; Camilla Zimmermann and Gary Rodin, "The Denial of Death Thesis: Sociological Critique and Implications for Palliative Care"; H.B. Danesh, *The Psychology of Spirituality;* and E. Fromm, *Escape from Freedom.*

50. Richard Dawkins, *The God Delusion,* p. 357.

51. 'Abdu'l-Bahá, *Bahá'í World Faith,* pp. 265–66.

52. Bahá'u'lláh, *Gleanings from the Writings of Bahá'u'lláh,* pp. 155–56.

53. 'Abdu'l-Bahá, *Selections from the Writings of 'Abdu'l-Bahá,* pp. 170–71.

54. For a discourse on this theme, see H.B. Danesh, *The Psychology of Spirituality,* pp. 161–66.

55. 'Abdu'l-Bahá, *The Secret of Divine Civilization,* p. 98.

56. The exact statement from which the summary points are drawn is: "Believe thou in God, and keep thine eyes fixed upon the exalted Kingdom; be thou enamoured of the Abhá Beauty; stand thou firm in the Covenant; yearn thou to ascend into the Heaven of the Universal Light. Be thou severed from this world, and reborn through the sweet scents of holiness that blow from the realm of the All-Highest. Be thou a summoner to love, and be thou kind to all the human race. Love thou the children of men and share in their sorrows. Be thou of those who foster peace. Offer thy friendship, be worthy of trust. Be thou a balm to every sore, be thou a medicine for every ill. Bind thou the souls together. Recite thou the verses of guidance. Be engaged in the worship of thy Lord, and rise up to lead the people aright. Loose thy tongue and teach, and let thy face be bright with the fire of God's love. Rest thou not for a moment, seek thou to draw no easeful breath. Thus mayest thou become a sign and symbol of God's love, and a banner of His grace" ('Abdu'l-Bahá, *Selections from the Writings of 'Abdu'l-Bahá,* pp. 26–27).

Chapter Five

1. Bahá'u'lláh, *Bahá'í Prayers: A Selection of Prayers Revealed by Bahá'u'lláh, The Báb, and 'Abdu'l-Bahá,* p. 118.

2. 'Abdu'l-Bahá, *Selections from the Writings of 'Abdu'l-Bahá,* p. 120.

3. Socrates, <http://www.wisdomquotes.com/001337.html>, Wisdom Quotes, compiled by Jone Johnson Lewis, accessed 19 March 2009.

4. Khalil Gibran, source: <http://www.quotationspage.com/quote/33236.html>, accessed 19 March 2009.

5. 'Abdu'l-Bahá, *Paris Talks,* p. 179.

6. The following list is a sampling of the large body of research about the role of love in human development: J. Bowlby, *Child Care and the Growth of Love and*

Attachment and Loss; L. Casler, "Maternal Deprivation. A Critical Review of the Literature"; H.F. Harlow, "The Nature of Love"; R.E. Helfer and C.H. Kempe, eds., *The Battered Child;* A.Montagu, *Touching: The Human Significance of the Skin,* "Mutilated Humanity," and *The Direction of Human Development;* National Institute of Child Health and Human Development, *Perspectives on Human Deprivation: Biological, Psychological, and Sociological;* James W. Prescott, "The Origins of Human Love and Violence"; R.A. Spitz, *The First Year of Life;* and Brian Vandenberg, "Levinas and the Ethical Context of Human Development."

7.   Rumi, *The Essential Rumi,* p. 10.

8.   Christopher Marlowe, *Hero and Leander,* quoted in William Shakespeare, *As You Like It,* Act 3, Scene 5. Web source: <http://www.nosweatshakespeare.com/quotes/shakespeare-love-quotes.htm>, accessed 19 March 2009.

9.   William Shakespeare, *Troilus & Cressida,* Act 3, Scene 2. Web source: <http://www.nosweatshakespeare.com/quotes/shakespeare-love-quotes.htm>, accessed 19 March 2009.

10. Source: <http://www.quoteworld.org/category/love/author/albert-einstein>, accessed 19 March 2009.

11. Sigmund Freud, <http://www.quoteworld.org/category/love/author/sigmund-freud>, accessed 19 March 2009.

12. Sigmund Freud, <http://www.answers.com/topic/quote-4?author=Freud,%20Sigmund&s2=Sigmund%20Freud>, accessed 19 March 2009.

13. Martin Luther King, Jr., <http://www.quotesdaddy.com/quote/546353/sigmund-freud/those-who-love-fairy-tales-do-not-like-it-when-people>, accessed 19 March 2009.

14. Confucius, <http://www.brainyquote.com/quotes/authors/c/confucius.html>, accessed 19 March 2009.

15. 'Abdu'l-Bahá, *Paris Talks,* pp. 35–37.

16. 'Abdu'l-Bahá, *Bahá'í World Faith,* p. 218.

17. An accurate informational and a pictorial presentation of Yazd can be seen at <http://en.wikipedia.org/wiki/Yazd>, accessed 19 March 2009.

18. Jerome H. Barkow, Leda Cosmides, and John Tooby, eds., *The Adapted Mind: Evolutionary Psychology and the Generation of Culture.*

19. 'Abdu'l-Bahá, *Bahá'í Scriptures, Selections from the Utterances of Bahá'u'lláh and 'Abdu'l-Bahá,* p. 50. This quotation was accessed from the website http://www.bahai-education.org/ocean/download.htm, accessed 15 April 2009.

20. 'Abdu'l-Bahá, *Tablets of Abdul-Baha Abbas,* p. 474.

21. For more specific teachings of the Bahá'í Faith about marriage and the family, refer to *Compilation of Compilations,* Family Life section, pp. 385–416.

22. 'Abdu'l-Bahá, *Tablets of Abdul-Baha Abbas,* p. 609.

23. 'Abdu'l-Bahá, *Bahá'í World Faith,* p. 372.

24. 'Abdu'l-Bahá, *Bahá'í World Faith,* pp. 372–73.

25. 'Abdu'l-Bahá, *Selections from the Writings of 'Abdu'l-Bahá,* p. 120.

26. Ibid., p. 302.

27. 'Abdu'l-Bahá, *The Promulgation of Universal Peace,* pp. 174–75.

28. Shoghi Effendi, quoted in *Lights of Guidance: The Bahá'í Reference File,* p. 369.

CHAPTER SIX

1. Bahá'u'lláh, *The Kitáb-i-Aqdas (The Most Holy Book)*, pp. 139–40.

2. 'Abdu'l-Bahá, *Bahá'í World Faith*, p. 290.

3. Ibid., pp. 329–30.

4. <http://www.wisdomquotes.com/001733.html>, accessed 19 March 2009.

5. For detailed information of the life and teaching of Mahatma Gandhi, see <http://www.mkgandhi.org/>, accessed 19 March 2009.

6. Landegg International University (formerly Landegg Academy) was a small private university in Switzerland that was closed in 2004 due to financial problems. During to its short life, the university had some 100 graduates (MA and BA) who continued their higher studies in universities in North America, Europe, and elsewhere.

7. For detailed information about the Education for Peace Institute, refer to <http://www.efpinternational.org>, accessed 19 March 2009.

8. H.B. Danesh and Sara Clarke-Habibi, *Education for Peace Curriculum Manual*, p. 193–230.

9. For a review of the main concepts and methodologies of the Education for Peace program, see H.B. Danesh and Sara Clarke-Habibi, *Education for Peace Curriculum Manual.*

10. For a review of the concepts and methodologies of Conflict-Free Conflict Resolution, see H.B. Danesh and R.P. Danesh, "Has Conflict Resolution Grown Up? Toward a New Model of Decision-Making and Conflict Resolution," "A Consultative Conflict-Resolution Model: Beyond Alternative Dispute-resolution," and "Conflict-free Conflict Resolution (CFCR): Process and Methodology."

11. Epictetus, The Internet Encyclopedia of Philosophy, <http://www.iep.utm.edu/e/epictetu.htm>, accessed 19 March 2009.

12. This talk later was published as a small book: H.B. Danesh, *The Violence-Free Family: Building Block of a Civilization of Peace.*

13. For various views on this issue see, among others, the following: Véronique Munoz-Dardé, "Is the Family to be Abolished Then?"; Germaine Greer, *The Female Eunuch;* <http://en.wikipedia.org/wiki/Criticisms_of_the_institution_of_marriage>, accessed 19 March 2009; *The Russian Effort To Abolish Marriage* by A Woman Resident in Russia. This article first appeared in the *Atlantic Monthly* in July 1926, volume 138, no. 1; pp. 108–14.<http://www.ejfi.org/Civilization/Civilization-4.htm>, accessed 19 March 2009.

14. 'Abdu'l-Bahá, quoted in J. E. Esslemont, *Bahá'u'lláh and the New Era,* p. 149.

15. This analogy is based on a statement of 'Abdu'l-Bahá in *Selections from the Writings of 'Abdu'l-Bahá,* p. 302.

16. For details, see <http://www.excellence-earlychildhood.ca/documents/AhnerLambANGxp.pdf>, accessed 19 March 2009.

17. For additional research on the impact of daycare on the children see, among others: L. Alnert and M.E. Lamb, "Child Care and its Impact on Young Children (2–5)," <http://www.child-encyclopedia.com/Pages/PDF/Ahnert-LambANGxp.pdf>, accessed 19 March 2009; Jeree H. Pawl, "Impact of Day Care on Parents and Family"; Jack Weitzman, "The Impact of Home Daycare on the Biological Children of Providers: Case Examples of Unintended Consequences"; Daycare:

How Is It Influencing the Teens of the Future? <http://www.earthskids.com/impactofdaycare.aspx>, accessed 19 March 2009; Daycare, Wikipedia, <http://en.wikipedia.org/wiki/Day_care>, accessed 19 March 2009; and <http://www.nichd.nih.gov/new/releases/child_care.cfm>, accessed 19 March 2009.

18. UNICEF, Progress for Children: A World Fit for Children Statistical Review, <http://www.unicef.org/progressforchildren/2007n6/files/Progress_for_Children_-_No._6.pdf>, accessed 2 April 2009.

19. The Vanier Institute of the Family website, <www.vifamily.ca>, accessed 19 March 2009.

20. American Academy of Family Physicians, <http://www.aafp.org/x6799.xml>, accessed 19 March 2009.

21. According to constitutional law scholar, Janet L. Dolgin in "The Constitution As Family Arbiter: A Moral in the Mess?"

22. David K. Jordan, *Traditional Chinese Family and Lineage*, <http://weber.ucsd.edu/~dkjordan/chin/hbfamilism-u.html>, accessed 19 March 2009.

23. The quotation's original author is unknown; cited by Gloria Steinem in the September 1981 issue of *Ms.* magazine. As quoted in *American Quotations*, p. 227.

24. 'Abdu'l-Bahá, *The Promulgation of Universal Peace*, p. 157.

25. For an elaboration of the uses and abuses of power and love in human relationships, see H. B. Danesh, *Unity: The Creative Foundation of Peace*.

26. Ibid., pp. 47–56.

27. H.B. Danesh, *The Violence-Free Family: Building Block of a Peaceful Civilization*. In *The Violence-Free Family* I discuss the concept of "indulgence-based family," which concept I have since further developed and renamed as the "identity-based family."

28. 'Abdu'l-Bahá, *The Promulgation of Universal Peace*, p. 168.

29. Rose-Marie Ambert, *Cohabitation and Marriage: How Are They Related?* On the Vanier Institute of the Family website, <http://www.vifamily.ca/library/cft/cohabitation.html>, accessed 19 March 2009.

30. Z. Wu, *Cohabitation: An Alternative Form of Family Living*.

31. Rose-Marie Ambert, *Cohabitation and Marriage: How Are They Related?* On the Vanier Institute of the Family website, <http://www.vifamily.ca/library/cft/cohabitation.html>, accessed 19 March 2009.

32. The Vanier Institute of the Family website, <www.vifamily.ca>, accessed 19 March 2009.

33. Rose-Marie Ambert, *Cohabitation and Marriage: How Are They Related?* On the Vanier Institute of the Family website, <http://www.vifamily.ca/library/cft/cohabitation.html>, accessed 19 March 2009.

34. The concept of culture of healing was developed by the author (H.B. Danesh) in the course of the implementation of the EFP Program in Bosnia and Herzegovina, and many of its elements have been identified, which are the subject of the article "Creating a Culture of Healing in Multiethnic Communities: An Integrative Approach to Prevention and Amelioration of Violence-induced Conditions" published in the *Journal of Community Psychology*. For a preliminary description of the concept of culture of healing, refer to <www.efpinternational.org>, accessed 19 March 2009.

35. For a more detailed description of the unity-based family, see H.B. Danesh, *The Violence-Free Family: Building Block of a Peaceful Civilization* and *Unity: The Creative Foundation of Peace.*

36. Bahá'u'lláh, *Gleanings from the Writings of Bahá'u'lláh*, p. 250.

CHAPTER SEVEN

1. Bahá'u'lláh, *Gleanings from the Writings of Bahá'u'lláh*, p. 259.

2. 'Abdu'l-Bahá, *The Promulgation of Universal Peace*, p. 133.

3. John Dewey, <http://www.wisdomquotes.com/cat_education.html>, accessed 19 March 2009.

4. Confucius, <http://www.light-a-fire.net/quotations/authors/confucius/>, accessed 19 March 2009.

5. Bertrand Russell, <http://www.lhup.edu/~dsimanek/eduquote.htm>, accessed 19 March 2009.

6. 'Abdu'l-Bahá, *Foundations of World Unity*, p. 22.

7. 'Abdu'l-Bahá, *'Abdu'l-Baha in London*, p. 51.

8. April 21–May 2 corresponds with the Festival of Ridván, a twelve-day period of commemoration of the public declaration of Bahá'u'lláh as the Manifestation of God for this age. The declaration took place in the garden of Ridván on the banks of Tigris River. These twelve days are the most joyous of Bahá'í holy days.

9. UNICEF, <http://www.unicef.org/protection/index_bigpicture.html>, accessed 19 March 2009.

10. John Dewey, < http://www.wisdomquotes.com/cat_education.html>, accessed 19 March 2009.

11. Bahá'u'lláh, *The Kitáb-i-Aqdas (The Most Holy Book)*, p. 41.

12. 'Abdu'l-Bahá, *Some Answered Questions*, p. 7.

13. Bahá'u'lláh, *Tablets of Bahá'u'lláh*, p. 34.

14. Ibid., p. 34.

15. The exact statement of Bahá'u'lláh is: "It is not for him to pride himself who loveth his own country, but rather for him who loveth the whole world. The earth is but one country, and mankind its citizens" (Bahá'u'lláh, *Gleanings from the Writings of Bahá'u'lláh*, p. 250).

16. 'Abdu'l-Bahá, *'Abdu'l-Bahá in London*, p. 124.

17. Ibid., p. 34.

18. 'Abdu'l-Bahá, *Bahá'í Prayers*, p. 28.

19. Ibid., pp. 29–30.

20. Ibid., p. 254.

21. 'Abdu'l-Bahá, *The Secret of Divine Civilization*, pp. 109–10.

22. Bahá'u'lláh, *Gleanings from the Writings of Bahá'u'lláh*, p. 79.

23. Ibid., p. 213.

24. 'Abdu'l-Bahá, *Bahá'í World Faith*, p. 248.

25. 'Abdu'l-Bahá, *The Promulgation of Universal Peace*, p. 411.

26. For an account of the life of Fadil Yazdi, see volume 7 of 'Azizu'llah Sulaymani, *Masabih-i Hidayat* (Lamps of Guidance).

27. For information on the life and writings of Ishraq-Khavari, see: <http://library.bahai.org/sc/ishraq5.html>, <http://www.h-net.org/~bahai/index/diglib/Ishraq-Khavari.htm, http://www.jstor.org/pss/194982 > and volume 9 of 'Azizu'lláh Sulaymani, *Masabih-i Hidayat* (Lamps of Guidance), <http://www.h-net.org/~bahai/areprint/authors/sulayman/sulaymani.htm>, accessed 19 March 2009.

28. Anonymous. <http://quotations.about.com/od/teachersday/a/teacherquotes2.htm>, accessed 19 March 2009.

29. As stated in the "Purpose" section of the Association for Bahá'í Studies: http://www.ncf.ca/ip/community.associations/bahai/abs/abs.txt, accessed 19 March 2009.

30. Bahá'u'lláh, *The Hidden Words of Bahá'u'lláh*, pp. 3–4.

31. 'Abdu'l-Bahá, *Some Answered Questions*, p. 158.

32. 'Abdu'l-Bahá, *Foundations of World Unity*, p. 23.

33. Bahá'u'lláh, *Gleanings from the Writings of Bahá'u'lláh*, p. 250.

34. Wikipedia, <http://en.wikipedia.org/wiki/Spiritual_Assembly>, accessed 19 March 2009.

35. 'Abdu'l-Bahá, *Selections from the Writings of 'Abdu'l-Bahá*, pp. 114–15.

36. Ibid., pp. 295–96.

37. Bahá'u'lláh, *Bahá'í Prayers*, p. 4.

38. Bahá'u'lláh, *Gleanings from the Writings of Bahá'u'lláh*, p. 213.

39. *Compilation on Scholarship*. p. 28.

40. Peter Gay, *The Enlightenment: An Interpretation, The Science of Freedom*, p. 563.

41. Ibid., p. 567.

42. Ibid., p. 567.

43. Ibid., p. 567.

44. 'Abdu'l-Bahá, *Paris Talks*, p. 152.

45. Jerome R. Ravetz, *Scientific Knowledge and its Social Problems*.

46. Shigeru Nakayama, "The Future of Research—A Call for a 'Service Science'."

47. Robert N. Bellah, "The Ethical Aims of Social Inquiry."

48. H.B. Danesh and Sara Clarke-Habibi, *Education for Peace Curriculum Manual*, p.164.

49. For information about Conflict-Free Conflict Resolution (CFCR) and Education for Peace (EFP), please visit: <www.efpinternational.org>. Also, see the bibliography for a list of publications on these issues.

50. See Chapter 6, endnote 9.

51. Salih, Foco, "The Political-Economic and Social Status of Bosnia and Herzegovina."

52. H.B. Danesh, "The Education for Peace Integrative Curriculum: Concepts, Contents, and Efficacy."

53. Geoffrey Hodgetts, et al., "Post-traumatic Stress Disorder among Family Physicians in Bosnia and Herzegovina."

54. For information about the Education for Peace Program, see the following volumes in the Education for Peace Series: H.B. Danesh, *Peace Moves*, vol. 3; H.B. Danesh and Sara Clarke-Habibi, *Education for Peace Curriculum Manual: A Conceptual and Practical Guide*, vol. 1; H.B. Danesh and Sara Clarke-Habibi, *Education for Peace Curriculum Manual: A Conceptual and Practical Guide*, vol. 10, bk. 1; H.B. Danesh and Sara Clarke-Habibi, *Education for Peace Curriculum Manual: A*

Conceptual and Practical Guide, vol. 11, bk. 2; and H.B. Danesh, *The Mysterious Case of the IWs, A Book on Death for Children,* vol. 7 (forthcoming). As well, the following selected articles are recommended: Sara Clarke-Habibi, "Transforming Worldviews: The Case of Education for Peace in Bosnia and Herzegovina"; H.B. Danesh, "Breaking the Cycle of Violence: Education for Peace," "Towards an Integrative Theory of Peace Education," "Education for Peace: The Pedagogy of Civilization," "Unity-Based Peace Education," "The Education for Peace Integrative Curriculum: Concepts, Contents, and Efficacy," and "Creating a Culture of Healing in Multiethnic Communities: An Integrative Approach to Prevention and Amelioration of Violence-Induced Conditions."

55. For more comments and evaluation reports on EFP, please refer to: <www.efpinternational.org>, accessed 19 March 2009.

56. Mahatma Gandhi, <http://www.light-a-fire.net/quotations/authors/mahatma-gandhi/>, accessed 19 March 2009.

57. 'Abdu'l-Bahá, *The Promulgation of Universal Peace,* p. 31.

CHAPTER EIGHT

1. Bahá'u'lláh, *Gleanings from the Writings of Bahá'u'lláh,* p. 288.

2. 'Abdu'l-Bahá, *Selections from the Writings of 'Abdu'l-Bahá,* p. 285.

3. Friedrich Nietzsche, <http://thinkexist.com/quotation/the_world_is_beautiful-but_has_a_disease_called/174687.html>, accessed 19 March 2009.

4. Anton Chekhov, <http://www.enotes.com/famous-quotes/humankind-has-understood-history-as-a-series-of> accessed on 6 June 2008.

5. Charlie Chaplin, <http://www.brainyquote.com/quotes/quotes/c/charliecha398024.html>, accessed 19 March 2009.

6. Mark Twain, <http://www.quotecosmos.com/quotes/12908/view>, accessed 19 March 2009.

7. In August 2006, after some 14 years of absence (living in Europe), I attended the 30th annual conference of the Association for Bahá'í Studies-North America. I was one of the founders of this association, and for the first 16 years of its existence I spent considerable time and energy ensuring its healthy and rigorous development. As such, the Association for Bahá'í Studies is very dear to my heart, and I consider its ongoing development to be of vital importance. In this 30th annual conference I spoke briefly about issues of vision, courage, and sacrifice as they pertain to all human endeavors, including leadership. This is a considerably abbreviated version of that presentation.

8. 'Abdu'l-Bahá, *Bahá'í World Faith,* p. 248.

9. 'Abdu'l-Bahá, *The Promulgation of Universal Peace,* pp. 438–40.

10. 'Abdu'l-Bahá, *Some Answered Questions,* p. 210.

11. 'Abdu'l-Bahá, *Bahá'í World Faith,* p. 340.

12. 'Abdu'l-Bahá, *Bahá'í World Faith,* pp. 223–24.

13. 'Abdu'l-Bahá, *'Abdu'l-Bahá in London,* p. 29.

14. 'Abdu'l-Bahá, *The Secret of Divine Civilization,* p. 99.

15. Ibid., pp. 71–72.

16. 'Abdu'l-Bahá, *Bahá'í World Faith,* p. 240.

17. Bahá'u'lláh, *Tablets of Bahá'u'lláh*, p. 67.
18. Bahá'u'lláh, *The Hidden Words*, number 2 of part 1 (Arabic).
19. Bahá'u'lláh, *Tablets of Bahá'u'lláh*, p. 157.
20. Bahá'u'lláh, *Gleanings from the Writings of Bahá'u'lláh*, pp. 218–19.
21. Bahá'u'lláh, *Tablets of Bahá'u'lláh*, p. 86.
22. Bahá'u'lláh, *Bahá'í World Faith*, p. 174.
23. 'Abdu'l-Bahá, *Selections from the Writings of 'Abdu'l-Bahá*, p. 293.
24. As quoted by Michael Gerson in his article in the Friday, February 20, 2009 (section A23) issue of *The Washington Post*.
25. Bahá'u'lláh, *Tablets of Bahá'u'lláh*, pp. 34–35.
26. 'Abdu'l-Bahá, *The Secret of Divine Civilization*, pp. 24–25.
27. 'Abdu'l-Bahá, *'Abdu'l-Bahá on Divine Philosophy*, as quoted in *The Compilation of Compilations*, volume 2, p. 376.
28. Bahá'u'lláh, as quoted by Shoghi Effendi, *God Passes By*, p. 230.
29. Bahá'u'lláh, *Gleanings from the Writings of Bahá'u'lláh*, pp. 250–52.
30. A collection of the tablets of Bahá'u'lláh, founder of the Bahá'í Faith, *The Summons of the Lord of Hosts* was written to the kings and rulers of the world during his exile in Adrianople and in the early years of his exile to the fortress town of 'Akká in 1868. Bahá'u'lláh claimed to be the Promised One of all religions and all ages and summoned the leaders of East and West to recognize him as the promised one. *The Summons of the Lord of Hosts* is the printing of five distinct tablets of this material. <http://en.wikipedia.org/wiki/Summons_of_the_Lord_of_Hosts>, accessed 19 March 2009.
31. Bahá'u'lláh, *Gleanings from the Writings of Bahá'u'lláh*, p. 303.
32. Bahá'u'lláh, *The Summons of the Lord of the Hosts*, p. 78.
33. Ibid., p. 109.
34. Shoghi Effendi, *Principles of Bahá'í Administration*, p. 44.
35. Universal House of Justice, *Unlocking the Power of Action: A Compilation*, p. 65.
36. Shoghi Effendi, *The World Order of Bahá'u'lláh*, pp. 152–53.
37. 'Abdu'l-Bahá, *The Promulgation of Universal Peace*, p. 11.
38. 'Abdu'l-Bahá, *Paris Talks*, pp. 21–22.

CHAPTER NINE

1. Bahá'u'lláh, *Tablets of Bahá'u'lláh*, p. 126.
2. 'Abdu'l-Bahá, *The Promulgation of Universal Peace*, p. 72.
3. Ibid., p. 72.
4. Isaac Asimov <http://www.quoteworld.org/quotes/646>, accessed 19 March 2009.
5. For a review of the theory and practice of Conflict-Free Conflict Resolution, refer to the articles identified in Chapter Six, endnote 9 above.
6. This table is a slightly modified version of the table included in Danesh and Danesh, "Has Conflict Resolution Program Grown Up? Toward a Developmental Model of Decision Making and Conflict Resolution," p. 72.
7. 'Abdu'l-Bahá, *Selections from the Writings of 'Abdu'l-Bahá*, p. 115.

8. For a sampling of many resources on mediation and conflict resolution, see: Robert A. Baruch Bush and Joseph P. Folger, *The Promise of Mediation: Responding to Conflict through Empowerment and Recognition;* Bruce D. Bonta, "Conflict Resolution Among Peaceful Societies: The Culture of Peacefulness," and Cris M. Currie, "Opinion Wanted: A Theoretical Construct for Mediation Practice."

9. For more details about the creative role of cooperation in the development and evolution of humanity, see, for example, Richard Leakey and Roger Lewin, *Origins Reconsidered.*

10. In our work we have applied the designation of C Mode to both Consultation and Conflict-Free Conflict Resolution (CFCR). The conceptual framework and practical methods employed by CFCR are largely derived from those of Consultation and in the final analysis CFCR should be viewed as an offshoot of Consultation.

11. Shoghi Effendi in *God Passes By* (first published in 1944) provides the following summary of the history of expansion of the Bahá'í Faith during its first century. Consultation was the main mode of decision-making and administration of the Bahá'í community affairs in these countries. Since 1944, the Bahá'í Faith has expanded dramatically and now is established in some 180 countries of the world:

> The light of the Faith which during the nine years of the Bábí Dispensation had irradiated Persia, and been reflected on the adjoining territory of Iraq; which in the course of Bahá'u'lláh's thirty-nine-year ministry had shed its splendor upon India, Egypt, Turkey, the Caucasus, Turkistan, the Sudan, Palestine, Syria, Lebanon and Burma, and which had subsequently, through the impulse of a divinely-instituted Covenant, traveled to the United States of America, Canada, France, Great Britain, Germany, Austria, Russia, Italy, Holland, Hungary, Switzerland, Arabia, Tunisia, China, Japan, the Hawaiian Islands, South Africa, Brazil and Australia, was now to be carried to, and illuminate, ere the termination of the first Bahá'í century, no less than thirty-four independent nations, as well as several dependencies situated in the American, the Asiatic and African continents, in the Persian Gulf, and in the Atlantic and the Pacific oceans. In Norway, in Sweden, in Denmark, in Belgium, in Finland, in Ireland, in Poland, in Czechoslovakia, in Rumania, in Yugoslavia, in Bulgaria, in Albania, in Afghanistan, in Abyssinia, in New Zealand and in nineteen Latin American Republics ensigns of the Revelation of Bahá'u'lláh have been raised since 'Abdu'l-Bahá's passing, and the structural basis of the Administrative Order of His Faith, in many of them, already established. In several dependencies, moreover, in both the East and the West, including Alaska, Iceland, Jamaica, Porto Rico [sic], the island of Solano in the Philippines, Java, Tasmania, the islands of Bahrayn and of Tahiti, Baluchistan, South Rhodesia and the Belgian Congo, the bearers of the new born Gospel have established their residence, and are bending every effort to lay an impregnable basis for its institutions. (p. 259)

12. Bahá'u'lláh, *Bahá'í Consultation: A Compilation,* p. 4.

13. 'Abdu'l-Bahá, *Bahá'í Consultation: A Compilation,* pp. 5–7.

14. For a review of the relationship between "worldview" and "consultation," see Hossain B. Danesh and Roshan Danesh, "Bahá'í Consultation: Worldview or Process?"

15. The Bahá'í calendar comprises 19 months of 19 days each. The remaining few days are allotted as days of celebration prior to the last month, which is the Month of Fast for Bahá'ís. During this month, adults refrain from eating and drinking from sunrise to sunset. The Bahá'í New Year starts on the first day of Spring (21st of March). On the first day of every Bahá'í month, in every Bahá'í Community, all over the globe, Bahá'ís gather together in the Bahá'í Feast, which is a consultative occasion between the members of the community and their elected institutions—Local and National Spiritual Assemblies and the Universal House of Justice.

16. 'Abdu'l-Bahá, *Selections from the Writings of 'Abdu'l-Bahá*, p. 87.

CHAPTER TEN

1. Bahá'u'lláh, *Gleanings from the Writings of Bahá'u'lláh*, p. 260.

2. 'Abdu'l-Bahá, *'Abdu'l-Bahá in London*, pp. 61–62. This quotation is from a talk by 'Abdu'l-Bahá, September, 1911, in London, England.

3. Shoghi Effendi, *The Promised Day is Come*, p. v.

4. The Universal House of Justice, *The Promise of World Peace*, p. 1. This document can be accessed at the Bahá'í Reference Library: <http://reference.bahai.org/en/t/uhj/PWP/download.html>, accessed 19 March 2009.

5. <http://www.un.org/aboutun/charter/>, accessed 19 March 2009.

6. Bahá'u'lláh, *The Compilation of Compilations*, vol. 2, p. 328.

7. 'Abdu'l-Bahá, *Selections from the Writings of 'Abdu'l-Bahá*, pp. 10–11.

8. 'Abdu'l-Bahá, *The Promulgation of Universal Peace*, p. 127.

9. 'Abdu'l-Bahá, *Selections from the Writings of 'Abdu'l-Bahá*, p. 246.

10. 'Abdu'l-Bahá, *Bahá'í World Faith*, p. 445.

11. 'Abdu'l-Bahá, quoted in *Divine Philosophy*, as requoted in *The Compilation of Compilations*, p. 172.

12. Bahá'u'lláh, *Tablets of Bahá'u'lláh*, p. 167.

13. The Báb is one of two Manifestations of God in the Bahá'í Dispensation. For a brief reference to the Báb, see Appendix 1 in this book. For the dramatic story of life and teachings of the Báb, see Nabil Zarandi, *The Dawn-Breakers: Nabil's Narrative of the Early Days of the Bahá'í Revelation*.

14. Bahá'u'lláh, *The Compilation of Compilations*, vol. 2, no. 1032, p. 5.

15. Bahá'u'lláh, *Tablets of Bahá'u'lláh*, p. 168.

16. Ibid., p. 93.

17. Ibid., p. 162.

18. 'Abdu'l-Bahá, *The Promulgation of Universal Peace*, p. 109.

19. Bahá'u'lláh, *Tablets of Bahá'u'lláh*, p. 21.

20. Bahá'u'lláh, *The Summons of the Lord of the Hosts*, p. 78.

21. 'Abdu'l-Bahá, *Bahá'í World Faith*, p. 144.

22. 'Abdu'l-Bahá, *The Promulgation of Universal Peace*, p. 318.

23. J.E. Esslemont, *Bahá'u'lláh and the New Era: An Introduction to the Bahá'í Faith*, pp. 144–46.

24. Bahá'u'lláh, *The Kitáb-i-Aqdas (The Most Holy Book)*, p. 14.

25. Ibid.

26. Ibid.

27. Except for the second point, all the other above points are enumerated by Shoghi Effendi in *The World Order of Bahá'u'lláh*, pp. 202–4.

28. 'Abdu'l-Bahá *The Promulgation of Universal Peace*, p. 108.

29. F. Tönnies, *Community and Society.*

30. For an in-depth look at the concept of the community, see: Ann Boyles "World Watch," pp. 197–219.

31. Issued by the Department of Statistics, Bahá'í World Centre, in August 2001, <http://bahai-library.com/?file=bolhuis_bahai_statistics_2001>, accessed April 17, 2009.

32. Bahá'u'lláh, *The Kitáb-i-Aqdas (The Most Holy Book)*, p. 189 (Notes Section). Local and Secondary Houses of Justice are, for the present, known as Local Spiritual Assemblies and National Spiritual Assemblies. Shoghi Effendi has indicated that this is a "temporary appellation," which,

> as the position and aims of the Bahá'í Faith is better understood and more fully recognized, will gradually be superseded by the permanent and more appropriate designation of House of Justice. Not only will the present-day Spiritual Assemblies be styled differently in future, but they will be enabled also to add to their present functions those powers, duties, and prerogatives necessitated by the recognition of the Faith of Bahá'u'lláh, not merely as one of the recognized religious systems of the world, but as the State Religion of an independent and Sovereign Power.

33. 'Abdu'l-Bahá, *Selections from the Writings of 'Abdu'l-Bahá*, pp. 83–84.

34. 'Abdu'l-Bahá, *Bahá'í World Faith*, p. 408.

35. Bahá'u'lláh, *Tablets of Bahá'u'lláh*, pp. 166–67.

36. 'Abdu'l-Bahá, *Some Answered Questions*, p. 248.

37. Bahá'u'lláh, *Tablets of Bahá'u'lláh*, pp. 87–88.

38. Shoghi Effendi, quoted by the Universal House of Justice in the introduction to *Summons of the Lord of Hosts* (Tablets of Bahá'u'lláh), p. 4.

39. Ibid., p. 4.

40. Ibid., p. 43.

41. Ibid., pp. 45–46.

42. 'Abdu'l-Bahá, *'Abdu'l-Bahá in London*, pp. 121–23.

43. 'Abdu'l-Bahá, *Bahá'í World Faith*, pp. 215–17.

44. 'Abdu'l-Bahá, *Paris Talks*, pp. 61–62.

45. Shoghi Effendi, *The World Order of Bahá'u'lláh*, pp. 42–43.

46. Universal House of Justice, *The Promise of World Peace*, pp. 13–14. Can be accessed at <http://reference.bahai.org/en/t/uhj/PWP/>, accessed 19 March 2009.

47. H.B. Danesh, "In Search of a Violence-Free Society."

48. Hossain B. Danesh, " 'Growth' and Psychotherapy."

49. The official website of Kohkiluyeh Va Boyer Ahmad: <http://www.ostan-kb.ir/home-fa.html>, accessed 19 March 2009.

50. Update on the Situation of the Bahá'ís in Iran and Arab Countries (2003–2004): <http://info.bahai.org/pdf/iran_update2003-04.pdf>, accessed 19 March 2009.

51. <http://info.bahai.org/pdf/payame_noor_univ_memo_english.pdf>, accessed 19 March 2009.

52. For more information about this matter, see <http://www.iranpresswatch.org/2008/12/update-on-three-baha%E2%80%99is-in-yasuj/>, accessed 19 March 2009.

53. Bahá'u'lláh, *Tablets of Bahá'u'lláh,* p. 84.

54. In the Bahá'í sacred writings, "Lesser Peace" refers to political peace as described in the text of this quotation. "The Most Great Peace" refers to an all-inclusive peace based on all aspects of human life including political, social, and religious peace.

55. Bahá'u'lláh, *Epistle to the Son of the Wolf,* pp. 30–31.

56. Shoghi Effendi, *The World Order of Bahá'u'lláh,* pp. 202–4.

AFTERWORD

1. Bahá'u'lláh, *Epistle to The Son of the Wolf,* p. 4. This Epistle is the last book written by Bahá'u'lláh before His death on May 29, 1892. The book was addressed to a prominent Shiah cleric in Isfahan—Sheikh Muhammad Taqqiy-i-Najafi—who along with his father committed barbarous cruelties upon many Bahá'ís. Bahá'u'lláh called the father and the son, respectively the Wolf and the Son of the Wolf. The Epistle was translated from Persian into English by Shoghi Effendi and first published in 1941.

2. For the full text, see Bahá'u'lláh, *Bahá'í Prayers: A Selection of Prayers Revealed by Bahá'u'lláh, The Báb, and 'Abdu'l-Bahá,* pp. 307–11.

3. Bahá'u'lláh, *Epistle to the Son of the Wolf,* pp. 5–6.

APPENDIX ONE

1. For an update of the current statistics on the Bahá'í Faith, its more detailed history, and up-to-date information about its worldwide community refer, to <http://info.bahai.org/>, accessed 19 March 2009.

APPENDIX TWO

1. Shoghi Effendi, *God Passes By,* p. 278.

2. Ibid., pp. 281–82.

APPENDIX THREE

1. The Points to Remember are drawn from the publication *Bahá'í Consultation: A Compilation.*

BIBLIOGRAPHY

'Abdu'l-Bahá. *'Abdu'l-Bahá in London*. London: Bahá'í Publishing Trust, 1983.

———. *Bahá'í Scriptures, Selections from the Utterances of Bahá'u'lláh and 'Abdu'l-Bahá*. Edited by Horace Holley. Nc: Brentano's, 1928. 50. This quotation was accessed from the website "Ocean" at: <http://www.bahai-education.org/ocean/>, accessed 15 April 2009.

———. *Foundations of World Unity*. Wilmette, Illinois: Bahá'í Publishing Trust, 1968.

———. *Paris Talks*. 10th ed. London: Bahá'í Publishing Trust, 1961.

———. *The Promulgation of Universal Peace*. Wilmette, Illinois: Bahá'í Publishing Trust, 1982.

———. *Selections from the Writings of 'Abdu'l-Bahá*. Haifa: Bahá'í World Centre, 1978.

———. *The Secret of Divine Civilization*. Wilmette, Illinois: Bahá'í Publishing Trust, 1990.

———. *Some Answered Questions*. Wilmette, Illinois: Bahá'í Publishing Trust, 1987.

———. *Tablets of 'Abdu'l-Bahá Abbas*. Trans. Edward G. Browne. Vols. 2 and 3. New York: Bahá'í Publishing Committee, 1940.

Ahnert L. Lamb ME. Child care and its impact on young children (2-5). In: Tremblay RE, Barr RG. Peters RDeV, eds. Encyclopedia on Early Childhood Development (online). Montreal Quebec: Centre of Excellence for Early Childhood Development; 2004:1-6 at: <http://www.child-encyclopedia.com/Pages/PDF/Ahnert-LambANGxp.pdf>, accessed 17 April 2009.

Anthony, D. "Religious Movements and Brainwashing Litigation." In *In Gods We Trust*. Ed. T. Robbins and D. Anthony. 2nd ed. New Brunswick, N.J.: Transaction, 1990. 295–344.

The Báb. *Selections from the Writings of the Báb*. Haifa: Bahá'í World Centre, 1982.

Bahá'í Consultation: A Compilation. Thornhill, Ontario: The Bahá'í Community of Canada, 1980.

Bahá'í Prayers: A Selection of Prayers Revealed by Bahá'u'lláh, the Báb, and 'Abdu'l-Bahá. Wilmette, IL: Bahá'í Publishing Trust, 2002.

Bahá'í Question: Cultural Cleansing in Iran, The. New York: Bahá'í International Community, 2005. <http://question.bahai.org>. Accessed 6 March 2009.

Bahá'í World, The. 1954–1963. The Universal House of Justice, Haifa: 1970.

Bahá'í World, The. 1979–1983. Haifa: Bahá'í World Centre, 1986.

Bahá'í World, The. 1992–1993. Haifa: Bahá'í World Centre, 1993.

Bahá'í World Faith. Rev. ed., Wilmette, IL: Bahá'í Publishing Trust, 1976.

Bahá'u'lláh. *The Book of Certitude*. Trans. Shoghi Effendi. Rev. ed. Wilmette, Illinois: Bahá'í Publishing Trust, 1974.

———. *Epistle to the Son of the Wolf*. Wilmette, Illinois: Bahá'í Publishing Committee, 1988. Translated from Persian into English by Shoghi Effendi and first published in 1941.

———. *Gems of Divine Mysteries*. Haifa: Bahá'í World Centre, 2002.

Bahá'u'lláh. *Gleanings from the Writings of Bahá'u'lláh*. Trans. and comp. Shoghi Effendi. 5th ed. Wilmette, Illinois: Bahá'í Publishing Trust, 1971.

———. *The Hidden Words*. Trans. Shoghi Effendi. Wilmette, Illinois: Bahá'í Publishing Trust, 1992.

———. *The Kitáb-i-Aqdas (The Most Holy Book)*. Haifa: Bahá'í World Centre, 1992.

———. *Proclamation of Bahá'u'lláh*. Wilmette, IL: Bahá'í Publishing Trust, 1978.

———. *The Summons of the Lord of the Hosts*. Haifa: Bahá'í World Centre, 2002.

———. *Tablets of Bahá'u'lláh*. Haifa: Bahá'í World Centre, 1978.

Balyuzi, H.M. *'Abdu'l-Bahá: The Centre of the Covenant of Bahá'u'lláh*. Oxford: George Ronald, 2001.

———. *Edward Granville Browne and the Bahá'í Faith*. London: George Ronald, 1970.

Baruch Bush, Robert A., and Joseph P. Folger. *The Promise of Mediation: Responding to Conflict through Empowerment and Recognition*. San Francisco: Jossey-Bass, 1994.

Barkow, Jerome H., Leda Cosmides, and John Tooby, eds. *The Adapted Mind: Evolutionary Psychology and the Generation of Culture*. New York: Oxford University Press, 1995.

Becker, Ernest. *The Denial of Death*. New York: Simon & Schuster, 1973.

Bellah, Robert N. "The Ethical Aims of Social Inquiry." *Teachers College Record* 83(1981): 1–18.

Bettelheim, Bruno. *Freud and Man's Soul*. New York: Vintage Books, 1984.

Bloom, Paul. *Descartes' Baby: How the Science of Child Development Explains What Makes Us Human*. New York: Basic Books, 2004.

———. "Is God an Accident?" <http://www.theatlantic.com/doc/200512/god-accident>. Accessed 9 March 2009.

Bonta, Bruce D. "Conflict Resolution Among Peaceful Societies: The Culture of Peacefulness." *Journal of Peace Research* 3.4 (1996): 403–20.

Bowlby, J. *Attachment and Loss*. Vols. 1 & 2. New York: Basic Books, 1969/1973.

———. *Child Care and the Growth of Love*. Baltimore: Pelican/Penguin, 1953.

Boyles, Ann. "World Watch." *The Bahá'í World*. 1996–1997. Haifa: Bahá'í World Centre, pp. 197–219.

Buss, D. M., ed. *The Handbook of Evolutionary Psychology*. Hoboken, NJ: Wiley, 2005.

Casler, L. "Maternal Deprivation. A Critical Review of the Literature." *Monograph of Society for Research in Child Development* 26.2(1961): 1–64.

Clarke-Habibi, Sara. "Transforming Worldviews: The Case of Education for Peace in Bosnia-Herzegovina" *Journal of Transformative Education* 3.1 (2005): 33–56.

Compilation on Bahá'í Education. Comp. Research Department of the Universal House of Justice. Haifa: Bahá'í World Centre, 1976. Revised 1990.

Compilation of Compilations. Comp. Research Department of the Universal House of Justice. Vol. 2, Mona Vale: Bahá'í Publications Australia, 1991.

Compilation on Scholarship. Comp. Research Department of the Universal House of Justice. Haifa: Bahá'í World Centre, 1995.

Currie, Cris M. "Opinion Wanted: A Theoretical Construct for Mediation Practice." *Dispute Resolution Journal* 53(1998): 70–75.

Danesh, H. B. "Breaking the Cycle of Violence: Education for Peace." *African Civil Society Organization and Development: Re-evaluation for the 21st Century.* New York: United Nations, September 2002.

———. "Creating a Culture of Healing in Multiethnic Communities: An Integrative Approach to Prevention and Amelioration of Violence-induced Conditions." *Journal of Community Psychology* 36.6 (9 July 2008): 814–32.

———. "The Education for Peace Integrative Curriculum: Concepts, Contents, and Efficacy." *Journal of Peace Education* 5. 2 (September 2008): 157–73.

———. "Education for Peace: The Pedagogy of Civilization." In Zvi Beckerman and Claire McGlynn, eds. *Addressing Ethnic Conflict through Peace Education: International Perspective.* New York: Palgrave Macmillan, 2007.

———. "'Growth' and Psychotherapy." *The Chicago Medical School Quarterly* 28.3 (1969): 75–86.

———. "In Search of a Violence-Free Society." *Mental Health and Society* 5 (1978): 63–71.

———. *The Mysterious Case of the IWs.* Forthcoming.

———. *Peace Moves.* Switzerland, Canada, Bosnia and Herzegovina: EFP-International Press, 2004.

———. *The Psychology of Spirituality.* Switzerland: Landegg Academy Press, 1997.

———. "Unity-Based Peace Education." *Encyclopedia of Peace Education.* Ed. Monisha Bajaj. Charlotte, NC: Information Age Publishing, nd.147–56.

———. *Unity: The Creative Foundation of Peace.* Ottawa: Bahá'í Studies Publications and Toronto: Fitzhenry-Whiteside, 1986.

———. *The Violence-Free Family: Building Block of a Civilization of Peace.* Ottawa: Bahá'í Studies Publications, 1995.

———. *The Violence-Free Society: A Gift for Our Children.* Ottawa: Bahá'í Studies Publications, 1979.

———. "Towards an Integrative Theory of Peace Education." *Journal of Peace Education* 3.1 (March 2006): 55–78.

Danesh, H.B., and Sara Clarke-Habibi. *Education for Peace Curriculum Manual.* Switzerland: EFP-International Press, 2007.

Danesh, Hossain B., and Roshan Danesh. "Bahá'í Consultation: Worldview or Process?" In *Healing the Body Politic.* Ed. Charles Lerche. Oxford: George Ronald, 2004. 47–83.

———. "Conflict-free Conflict Resolution (CFCR): Process and Methodology." *Peace and Conflict Studies* 11.2(2004): 55–84.

———. "A Consultative Conflict Resolution Model: Beyond Alternative Dispute-resolution." *International Journal of Peace Studies* 7.2(2002b): 17–33.

———. "Has Conflict Resolution Grown Up? Toward a New Model of Decision Making and Conflict Resolution." *International Journal of Peace Studies* 7.1(2002a): 59–76.

Darwin, Charles. *The Autobiography of Charles Darwin (1809–1882).* With original omissions restored. Edited with Appendix and Notes by his grand-daughter Nora Barlow (1958). These quotations are taken from the website Fredrik Bendz, <http://www.update.uu.se/~fbendz/library/cd_relig.htm>. Accessed Aug. 2008.

Darwin, Charles. *The Autobiography of Charles Darwin* (with an introduction by Brian Regal), New York: Barnes & Noble, 2005, p. 295.

——. *The Expression of the Emotions in Man and Animals.* 3rd ed. New York: Harper Collins, 1872/1998.

Dawkins, Richard. *The God Delusion.* New York: Houghton Mifflin, 2006.

Divine Art of Living: Selections from the Writings of Bahá'u'lláh and 'Abdu'l-Bahá. New ed. Comp. Mable Hyde Paine. Revised by Ann Marie Scheffer. Willmette: Bahá'í Publishing Trust, 1986, pp. 86–87.

Dolgin, Janet L. "The Constitution As Family Arbiter: A Moral in the Mess?" *Columbia Law Review* 102 (March 4, 2002): 337–401.

Einstein, Albert. *Out of My Later Years.* New York: Philosophical Library, 1950.

Esslemont, J.E. *Bahá'u'lláh and the New Era.* 5th rev. ed. Wilmette, Ill.: Bahá'í Publishing Trust, 1987.

Florian, V. and M. Mikulincer. "Fear of Death and the Judgment of Social Transgressions: A Multidimensional Test of Terror." *Journal of Personality and Social Psychology* 73.2(1997): 369–80.

Foco, Salih. "The Political-Economic and Social Status of Bosnia and Herzegovina." *South-East Europe Review for Labour and Social Affairs* (2/2001): 37–54.

Freud, Sigmund. *New Introductory Lessons on Psychoanalysis—Complete Works.* Nc: Ivan Smith, 2000.

——. *New Introductory Lessons on Psychoanalysis,* <http://www.freudfile.org/quotes.html>. Accessed 15 April 2009.

——. "Thoughts for the Times on War and Death." In *The Standard Edition of the Complete Psychological Works of Sigmund Freud.* Vol. 4. London: Hogarth Press, 1953.

Fromm, E. *Escape from Freedom.* New York: Holt, Rinehart and Winston, 1941.

Galtung, Johan, and Carl. G. Jacobsen. *Searching for Peace: The Road to TRANSCEND.* London: Pluto Press, 2000.

Gay, Peter. *The Enlightenment: An Interpretation, The Science of Freedom.* New York: W.W. Norton, 1969.

Goldenberg, J.L., T. Pyszczynski, J. Greenberg, and S. Solomon. "Fleeing the Body: A Terror Management Perspective on the Problem of Human Corporeality." *Personality and Social Psychology Review* 4.3(2000): 200–218.

Goldenberg, J.L. et al. "I am not an animal: Mortality salience, disgust, and the denial of human creatureliness." *Journal of Experimental Psychology* 130.3 (2001): 427–35.

Gould, Stephen Jay. *The Structure of Evolutionary Theory.* Cambridge: Harvard University Press, 2002.

Greer, Germaine. *The Female Eunuch.* New York: McGraw-Hill, 1971.

Harlow, H. F. "The Nature of Love." *American Psychologist* 13: (1958): 673–85.

Hatcher, William S., and J. Douglas Martin. *The Bahá'í Faith: The Emerging Global Religion.* New Edition. Wilmette, IL: Bahá'í Publishing, 2002.

Helfer, R. E., and C.H. Kempe, eds. *The Battered Child.* Chicago: University of Chicago Press, 1968.

Hodgetts, Geoffrey et al. "Post-traumatic Stress Disorder among Family Physicians in Bosnia and Herzegovina." *Family Practice* 20.4 (2003): 489–91.

Holt, P. M., Bernard Lewis, Ann Katherine, and Swynford Lambton. Cambridge: *Cambridge History of Islam*. Cambridge University Press, 1970. 70–72.

Jahanian, Daryush. *The History of Zoroastrians After Arab Invasion*. Brussels: European Centre for Zoroastrian Studies, 2007. <http://www.gatha.org/english/articles/000258.html>. Accessed 6 March 2009.

Keleman, Deborah. "Are Children 'Intuitive Theists'?" *Psychological Science* 15.5 (2004): 295–301.

Khatirat va Mubarizat-i Hojjatolislam Mohammad Taqi Falsafi [The Memories and Campaigns of Hojjatol-Islam Mohammad Taqi Falsafi]. Ali Davani, ed. The Center for Islamic Revolution Documents, 2003. Translated in Iran Human Rights Documentation Center, 2007.

Kuhn, Thomas. *The Structure of Scientific Revolution*. Chicago: University of Chicago Press, 1962.

Lapidus, Ira. *A History of Islamic Societies*. 2nd ed. Cambridge: Cambridge University Press, 2002.

Lewis, Bernard. *The Jews of Islam*. Princeton: Princeton University Press, 1984.

Leakey, Richard, and Roger Lewin. *Origins Reconsidered*. New York: Doubleday, 1992.

Lights of Guidance: The Bahá'í Reference File. 2nd ed. Comp. Helen Hornby. New Delhi: Bahá'í Publishing Trust, 1988. 369.

Lofland, J., and R. Stark. "Becoming a World-Saver," *American Sociological Review* 30(1965): 863–74.

Mikulincer, M., V. Florian, and G. Hirschberger. "The Existential Function of Close Relationships: Introducing Death into the Science of Love." *Personality and Social Psychology Review* 7.1(2003): 20–40.

Miller, Patricia H. *Theories of Developmental Psychology*. 3rd ed. New York: W. H. Freeman and Company Worth Publishers, 1999.

Momen, Moojan. *An Introduction to Shi'i Islam: The History and Doctrines of Twelver Shi'ism*. New Haven: Yale University Press, 1987.

Montagu, Ashley. *Touching: The Human Significance of the Skin*. New York: Columbia University Press, 1971.

Montagu, M. F. Ashley. *The Direction of Human Development*. New York: Harper & Brothers, 1955.

Muldoon, Brian. *The Heart of Conflict*. New York: Perigree, 1996.

Nakayama, Shigeru. "The Future of Research—A Call for a 'Service Science'." *Fundamenta Scientiae* 2.1(1981): 85–97.

The New Penguin Dictionary of Modern Quotation. London: Penguin Books, 2000.

Nietzsche, Friedrich. *The Gay Science* [aka *Joyous Wisdom*](1882, 1887). Walter Kaufmann ed. New York: Vintage, 1974.

NICHD/NIH, *Perspectives on Human Deprivation: Biological, Psychological, and Sociological*. National Institute of Child Health and Human Development. Washington: DHEW, 1968.

Pawl, Jeree H. "Impact of Day Care on Parents and Family." *Peadiatrics* 91.1 (January 1993) 222–24.

Pilarzyk, T. "Conversion and Alternation Processes in the Youth Culture." In *The Brainwashing/Deprogramming Controversy*. Ed. D. G. Bromley and J. T. Richardson. Lewiston, NY: Mellen, 1983. 51–72.

Prescott, James W. "The Origins of Human Love and Violence." *Pre- and Perinatal Psychology Journal* 10.3 (Spring 1996): 143–88.

Preissler, M. A., and P. Bloom. "Two-year-olds Appreciate the Dual Nature of Pictures." *Psychological Science* 18 (2007): 1–2.

Pyszczynski, T., J. Greenberg, and S. Solomon. "A Dual Process Model of Defense Against Conscious Extension of Terror Management Theory." *Psychology Review* 106.4(1999): 835–45.

Ranbo, Lewis R. *Understanding Religious Conversion.* New Haven: Yale University Press, 1993.

Ravetz, Jerome R. *Scientific Knowledge and its Social Problems.* Oxford: Oxford University Press, 1971.

Richardson, J. T. "The Active Versus Passive Convert." *Journal for the Scientific Study of Religion* 24(1985): 163–79.

———."Studies of Conversion." In *The Sacred in a Secular Age.* Ed. P. Hammond. Berkeley: University of California Press, 1985. 104–21.

Richardson, J.T., and B. Kilbourne. "Classical and Contemporary Applications of Brainwashing Models." In *The Brainwashing/Deprogramming Controversy.* Ed. D. G. Bromley and J. T. Richardson. Lewiston, NY: Mellen, 1983. 29–45.

Rumi. *The Essential Rumi.* Trans. Coleman Barks with John Moyne. San Francisco: Harper, 1995.

Sanasarian, Eliz. *Religious Minorities in Iran.* Cambridge: Cambridge University Press, 2000.

Shoghi Effendi. *Advent of Divine Justice.* First pocket-size ed. Wilmette, Ill.: Bahá'í Publishing Trust, 1990.

———. *God Passes By.* Rev.ed. Wilmette, Ill.: Bahá'í Publishing Trust, 1974.

———. *Principles of Bahá'í Administration.* London: Bahá'í Publishing Trust, 1976.

———. *The Promised Day is Come.* Wilmette, Ill.: Bahá'í Publishing Trust, 1941.

———. *The World Order of Bahá'u'lláh.* Wilmette, Ill.: Bahá'í Publishing Trust, 1974.

Singer, M. "Coming out of the Cults." *Psychology Today* 12(Jan. 1979): 72–82.

Solomon, T. "Programming and Deprogramming the Moonies." In *The Brainwashing/ Deprogramming Controversy.* Ed. D. G. Bromley and J. T. Richardson. Lewiston: Mellen, 1983. 163–82.

Spitz, R. A. *The First Year of Life.* New York: International University Press, 1965.

Stark, R. "Psychopathology and Religious Commitment." *Review of Religious Research* 12(1965): 165–76.

Sulaymani, 'Azizu'llah. *Masabih-i Hidayat* (Lamps of Guidance). Biographical accounts of 99 prominent Bahá'ís. Volumes 1–10. Tehran: Bahá'í Publishing Trust, 129 BE/ 1973. Digitally republished, East Lansing, MI: H-Bahai, 2006. <http:// www.h-net.org/~bahai/areprint/authors/sulayman/sulaymani.htm>. Accessed 19 March 2009.

Tabatabaei, Sayyid Mohammad Hosayn. *Shi'ite Islam.* Trans. Seyyed Hossein Nasr. Nc: Suny Press, 1979.

Tönnies, F. *Community and Society.* Trans. and ed. C. P. Loomis. East Lansing: Michigan State University Press, 1975.

Unlocking the Power of Action: A Compilation. Research Department of the Universal House of Justice. Haifa: Bahá'í World Centre, 1994.

Universal House of Justice. *The Promise of World Peace*. Haifa: Bahá'í World Centre, 1985. Web access Bahá'í Reference Library: http://reference.bahai.org/en/t/uhj/PWP/download.html. Accessed 6 March 2009.

Vandenberg, Brian. "Levinas and the Ethical Context of Human Development." *Human Development* 42(1999): 31–44.

Vanier Institute of the Family website. <http://www.vifamily.ca>. Accessed 6 March 2009.

Wilson, Edward O. *On Human Nature*. Cambridge: Harvard University Press, 1978.

World Parliament of Religion. Volume 2, 13th Day. Under Criticism and Discussion of Missionary Methods, page 1122. At the Columbian Exposition of 1893, held at Chicago. Edited by the Rev. John Henry Barrows, D.D. Chicago: The Parliament Publishing Company, 1893.

Wu, Z. *Cohabitation: An Alternative Form of Family Living*. Toronto: Oxford University Press, 2000.

Zimmermann, Camilla, and Rodin, Gary. "The Denial of Death Thesis: Sociological Critique and Implications for Palliative Care." *Palliative Medicine* 18. 2(2004): 121–28.

INDEX

ABOUT THE AUTHOR

Dr. H. B. Danesh is the founder and president of the International Education for Peace Institute and has taught on issues of peace education, conflict resolution, and adult and family psychiatry at various universities in Austria, Canada, Switzerland, and the United States. Dr. Danesh was elected to the nine-member National Spiritual Assembly of the Bahá'ís of Canada for nineteen consecutive years and for more than ten of these years served either as its executive secretary or chairperson. He is one of the founding members of the Association for Bahá'í Studies and the Bahá'í International Health Agency. He has conducted research and published on issues of peace education, leadership studies, the causes and prevention of violence, unity-based conflict resolution, and the psychology of spirituality. He is the creator of the Education for Peace Program and the main author of its eleven-volume curriculum. He is the author of a number of books, including *The Violence-Free Society: A Gift for Our Children, Unity: The Creative Foundation of Peace, The Violence-Free Family: Building Block of a Peaceful Civilization, Peace Moves,* and *Education for Peace Curriculum Manual: A Conceptual and Practical Guide.* His book *Psychology of Spirituality: From Divided Self to Integrated Self* has been translated and published into Arabic, Chinese, Persian, and Spanish.

LaVergne, TN USA
12 October 2010
200406LV00002B/2/P